teach
yourself

arabic
jack smart
and frances altorfer

D1078579

For over sixty years, more than
40 million people have learnt over
750 subjects the **teach yourself**
way, with impressive results.

be where you want to be
with **teach yourself**

For UK order enquiries: please contact Bookpoint Ltd, 130 Milton Park, Abingdon, Oxon OX14 4SB. Telephone: +44 (0) 1235 827720. Fax: +44 (0) 1235 400454. Lines are open 09.00–18.00, Monday to Saturday, with a 24-hour message answering service. Details about our titles and how to order are available at www.teachyourself.co.uk

For USA order enquiries: please contact McGraw-Hill Customer Services, PO Box 545, Blacklick, OH 43004-0545, USA. Telephone: 1-800-722-4726. Fax: 1-614-755-5645.

For Canada order enquiries: please contact McGraw-Hill Ryerson Ltd, 300 Water St, Whitby, Ontario L1N 9B6, Canada. Telephone: 905 430 5000. Fax: 905 430 5020.

Long renowned as the authoritative source for self-guided learning – with more than 40 million copies sold worldwide – the **teach yourself** series includes over 300 titles in the fields of languages, crafts, hobbies, business, computing and education.

British Library Cataloguing in Publication Data: a catalogue record for this title is available from the British Library.

Library of Congress Catalog Card Number: on file.

First published in UK 2001 by Hodder Education, 338 Euston Road, London, NW1 3BH.

First published in US 2001 by Contemporary Books, a Division of the McGraw-Hill Companies, 1 Prudential Plaza, 130 East Randolph Street, Chicago, IL 60601 USA.

This edition published 2003.

The **teach yourself** name is a registered trade mark of Hodder Headline.

Copyright © 2001, 2003 Jack Smart and Frances Altorfer

In UK: All rights reserved. Apart from any permitted use under UK copyright law, no part of this publication may be reproduced or transmitted in any form or by any means, electronic or mechanical, including photocopy, recording, or any information, storage and retrieval system, without permission in writing from the publisher or under licence from the Copyright Licensing Agency Limited. Further details of such licences (for reprographic reproduction) may be obtained from the Copyright Licensing Agency Limited, of 90 Tottenham Court Road, London W1T 4LP.

In US: All rights reserved. Except as permitted under the United States Copyright Act of 1976, no part of this publication may be reproduced or distributed in any form or by any means, or stored in a database or retrieval system, without the prior written permission of Contemporary Books.

Typeset by g-and-w PUBLISHING, Oxfordshire, UK.
Printed in Great Britain for Hodder Education, a division of Hodder Headline, 338 Euston Road, London NW1 3BH, by Cox & Wyman Ltd, Reading, Berkshire.

Hodder Headline's policy is to use papers that are natural, renewable and recyclable products and made from wood grown in sustainable forests. The logging and manufacturing processes are expected to conform to the environmental regulations of the country of origin.

Impression number   10 9 8 7
Year   2010 2009 2008 2007 2006 2005

CONTENTS

Introduction & How to use this course _____ 1

Arabic script and pronunciation guide _____ 8

1 فلنبدأ **fal-nábda'** *Let's get started!* _____ 24
Greeting people, making short descriptive phrases,
definites and indefinites

2 التفاصيل الشخصية **at-tafaaSíil ash-shakhSíyyah**
Personal details _____ 40
Meeting people, saying where you are from, simple
sentences with *is/are*, saying *there is/there are*,
numbers 1–10

3 كيف تصف نفسك **kayfa taSif nafs-ak**
How you describe yourself _____ 54
Saying your nationality, saying which languages you
speak, talking about more than one object, some places
around town, what your profession is

4 هذا وذلك **háadhaa wa-dháalik** *This and that* ____ 68
Telling the time, asking about opening times, days of the
week, numbers 11–20, making phrases and sentences
with *this, that, those*

5 بيتنا بيتكم **báyt-naa báyt-kum**
Our house is your house _____ 90
Talking about your family, saying who things belong to,
describing things, numbers 21–100

6 أين وسط المدينة؟ **áyna wásaT al-madíinah?** ____102
Where is the town centre?
Giving simple directions, talking about more places
around town and their location, saying what belongs
to whom

7 | ماذا فعلت؟ **máadhaa fa:ált?** *What did you do?* ___**117**
Talking about things which happened in the past, means
of transport, Arabic verbs, saying *me, him, them,* etc.

8 | كان يا ما كان **kaana yaa maa kaan**
Once upon a time _____**135**
Saying *was/were, is/are not*; describing something,
saying *became*, a new type of *is/are* sentence, saying
you *had done* something

9 | أكثر من واحد **akthar min waaHid**
More than one _____**158**
Looking for a job in the paper, looking for a flat or a
house, talking about more than one person or thing,
saying *these/those*, talking about two people or things

10 | ماذا تعمل؟ **maadhaa ta:mal?** *What do you do?* ___**179**
Saying what you do every day, talking about your
interests, saying what you like or dislike, saying what
you will do in the future; more about *not*

11 | الأعياد الإسلامية **al-a:yaad al-islaamiyyah**
Islamic Festivals _____**202**
The main Islamic Festivals, special greetings for festival
days, the Islamic calendar; asking questions, saying *to
have*

12 | صفحة المرأة **SafHat al-mar'ah** *Woman's page* ___**222**
Talking about nationalities

13 | الخليج العربي **al-khaliij al-:arabi**
The Arabian Gulf _____**231**
More about describing places, saying *who, which, that,*
etc., passive verbs

14 | السمع والطاعة **as-sam: wa T-Taa:ah**
Hearing is obeying (The Arabian Nights) _____**249**
Following a recipe, telling people to do something,
addressing people or attracting their attention, duals and
masculine plurals in possessive constructions

15 | العرب في هوليوود al-:arab fii huuliiwuud
The Arabs in Hollywood _____ 265
Making comparisons, saying how things are done,
shopping

16 | صفحة الرياضة SafHat ar-riyaaDah
Sports page _____ 282
Sports and leisure activities, talking about colours,
describing how or when you have done something

17 | إن شاء الله in shaa' Al-laah *If God wills* _____ 296
Talking about what you hope to do, making suggestions

18 | من كل بلد خبر min kull balad khabar
News from every country _____ 311
Talking about *each, every, all* and *some*. Using irregular
nouns and adjectives

Key to the exercises _____ 329
Listening transcripts _____ 355
Glossary of language terms _____ 357
Verb tables _____ 361
Arabic–English vocabulary _____ 383
English–Arabic vocabulary _____ 397
Grammar index _____ 410

ACKNOWLEDGEMENTS

We would like to thank, first of all, H.H. Dr. Sheikh Sultan bin Muhammad al-Qasimi, Ruler of Sharjah, for his great generosity to us while we were collecting material for this book. Thanks also to Brian Pridham, Mike Pinder, Sharjah Television, Bob Coles and Ruth Butler at the Institute for Arab and Islamic Studies at Exeter University, and Frances Taylor, for helping us with realia and materials.

We are most grateful to Western Union for permission to use material.

Thanks are also due to Dorothea and Fred Altorfer, who had to make do with a part-time daughter for far too long, and to Lynne and Brent Noble, and Denise Mountford, for their generous help.

We are particularly grateful to our editors at Hodder and Stoughton, Sue Hart and Rebecca Green, for their endless patience and understanding during the preparation of this book.

We would also like to thank Mr Jim Doran for his helpful comments on the first edition.

INTRODUCTION

Welcome to *Teach Yourself Arabic!*

The aims of the course

If you are an adult learner with no previous knowledge of Arabic and studying on your own, then this is the course for you. Perhaps you are taking up Arabic again after a break, or perhaps you are intending to learn with the support of a class. Again, you will find this course very well suited to your purposes.

The language you will learn is based on the kind of material seen in Arabic newspapers and magazines, or heard on radio and television news broadcasts. The main emphasis is on understanding Arabic, but we also aim to give you an idea of how the language works, so that you can create sentences of your own.

If you are working on your own, the audio recordings will be all the more important, as they will provide you with the essential opportunity to listen to Arabic and to speak it within a controlled framework. You should therefore try to get a copy of the audio recordings if you haven't already done so.

The structure of the course

This course contains:

- **a guide to Arabic script and pronunciation**
- **18 course units**
- **a reference section**
- **an optional audio cassette or CD**

How to use the course

All the important information that you need for the basic structures of Arabic are given in the first ten units. The following eight units introduce more advanced but essential structures, through texts and dialogues

Statement of aims

At the beginning of each unit is a summary of what you can expect to learn by the end of the unit.

Presentation of new language

This is in the form of dialogues or texts introducing the new language, which are also recorded. These are followed by questions and phrase-matching exercises to help you check your comprehension. The answers to these and a translation of the texts are in the *Key* at the end of the book. New words are given in the order in which they appear, and they are followed where necessary by *Notes* (**al-mulaaHaDHáat** الملاحظات) which explain how the language works. The language is presented in manageable chunks, building carefully on what you have learned in earlier units. Throughout the course the texts and vocabulary are given both in Arabic script and in transliteration, that is, in English letters. Try to rely less on the transliteration as you progress through the units.

Key Phrases (ta:biiráat ra'iisíyyah تعبيرات رئيسية)

To sum up what you have learned in the texts or dialogues, the Key Phrases section will provide a valuable reference. These contain the main language elements of the unit, and will help you when you come to the exercises.

Structures (taraakíib al-lughah تراكيب اللغة)

In this section the forms of the language are explained and illustrated. Main grammatical concepts have often been grouped together for ease of reference, and they gradually build up to provide you with all the structures you need to read and write Arabic.

Cultural tips (ma:luumáat thaqaafíyyah معلومات ثقافية)

These highlight some of the social and cultural aspects of life in the Arab world.

Word Shapes (awzáan al-kalimáat أوزان الكلمات)

This section will help you familiarise yourself with the way Arabic words are formed.

Practice (tamriináat تمرينات)

The **tamriináat** provide a variety of activities so that you can start using the new words and structures. Practice is graded so that activities which require mainly recognition come first. As you grow in confidence in manipulating language forms, you will be encouraged to write and speak the language yourself. The answers can be found at the end of the book, in the *Key*. Transcripts of listening comprehension exercises follow the *Key*.

Reference

The reference section contains a *Glossary of Grammar Terms*, a *Grammar Summary* of the main structures of the Arabic language, and a set of *Verb Tables*, so that every verb you come across in the book can be matched in the tables to a verb which works in the same way. There are also reference sections on *Arabic Numerals* and *Plurals*.

Selected *Arabic–English* and *English–Arabic* glossaries are provided so that you can look up words alphabetically, and finally a *Grammar Index* will enable you to look up specific points.

Study tips

Remember that the first step in learning a language is listening and understanding. Concentrate initially on that, and then work on your writing skills, using the information in the units and, if possible, by listening to native speakers.

In using a course such as this, it is important to pace yourself, with a view to consolidating what you have learned before moving on.

Due to the nature of the language, the units are of varying length and complexity. There is no need to attempt to absorb a whole unit in one sitting.

Our suggestion is that you concentrate on the texts first, with reference to the transcripts and the audio if you have it. This includes mastering the vocabulary as far as possible. The translations are there to help you if you get stuck. You should then look at the *Structures* section and make sure you understand how the language is working. Finally work through the exercises. These are based on the constructions explained in the unit and will help you consolidate what you have learned. Try to do each exercise before checking your work in the *Key*.

What kind of Arabic will I learn?

The Arabic taught in this book is the standard written language of more than 150 million inhabitants of the Arab states, ranging from Morocco in the West, to Iraq in the East. In addition to this large number of native speakers, it is used by Muslims all over the world as a language of religion. There are millions of Muslims in Pakistan, Afghanistan and, further east, Malaysia and Indonesia. If you are a Muslim, you have to read the Koran and pray in Arabic. Translations – as in, for example, the European versions of the Bible – are only used for reference or as an aid to understanding the Arabic. All the commentaries on the Holy Text, and other subsidiary literature on practices, interpretation and rules for daily life are written in and have to be read in Arabic. In addition, it is a matter of pride for Muslims to regard Arabic as a prestige language.

In modern everyday life in the Arab countries, so-called vernacular or dialect Arabic has supplanted Standard Arabic for spoken communication, but all these dialects derive from the parent root. The result of this is that, if you have a grounding in Standard Arabic, it will be easier to learn the modern local dialects which are based on it. Standard Arabic is also the *lingua franca* of the Arab world and can be understood anywhere in conversation with educated speakers.

Written Arabic has existed for about twelve centuries without major change. Its literature is vast and a key to understanding the development of world history. While Europe entered the Dark Ages after the fall of the Roman Empire, Arabic carried the torch of classical learning. Much that we know today in the realms of chemistry, medicine, astronomy and other branches of scientific endeavour would have been lost, were it not for the achievements of Arab scholars and translators.

Nowadays, due to oil resources and the influence this brings, the importance of many Arab states in political and economic terms cannot be overestimated. The oil in much of the Arab world has had very powerful influences on the West, which is dependent on the Middle East for its supplies of the substance which largely drives their economies.

So, whether your interests are historical, cultural, religious or economic, there is a lot to be gained from learning Arabic.

To help you, we have tried to present the modern language in its most easily accessible form. As you will be learning, Arabic script differs from European scripts in that it does not explicitly write the short vowels. The traditional language of the Holy Koran and classical literature used special endings on words which consisted mainly of vowels. With a few exceptions, these are not now written and have been largely ignored in this book. The form of Arabic taught in this book is based on its modern form, i.e. that used in the press, fiction and similar written material, usually referred to as Modern Standard Arabic. As a spoken language, it survives in formal TV and radio broadcasts, political speeches, and so on. Many examples of these are included in the units.

If you go through this book carefully, you should achieve a level of proficiency which will enable you to read newspapers and listen to radio and TV broadcasts. A little further study will introduce you to the world of Arabic literature, for instance the novels of the Egyptian writer Naguib Mahfouz, a winner of the Nobel Prize for Literature.

Finally, many people are put off learning Arabic because of the apparently difficult script. In fact, this is one of the easiest and most rewarding aspects of learning Arabic. The Arabic alphabet consists of only 29 letters, and its spelling is 95 per cent phonetic and therefore largely self-explanatory – something that could never be said for English. Once you have mastered the basic forms of the letters, you will never have to ask yourself the (equivalent) question of "How many *p*'s are there in *apartment?*" and the like.

Hints for further study

This book covers all the main structures of Arabic and a reasonable amount of vocabulary.

If you want to dig deeper, you will first need a pair of dictionaries. The use of these has been discussed in the *Review Unit*.

- Arabic–English: Hans Wehr *A Dictionary of Modern Written Arabic* (edited by J. Milton Cowan) is an essential tool.
- English–Arabic: the best available is Munir Ba'albaki *Al-Mawrid, A Modern English–Arabic Dictionary*. This very comprehensive work was designed for use by native Arabic speakers and so, to select the correct word for a given context, some cross-referencing with Wehr may be necessary.

These two dictionaries are the best for the serious student, but there are others available.

There is a multitude of Arabic grammars on the market, of widely differing merits

- David Cowan, *Modern Literary Arabic* provides a concise look at the structures of written Arabic at a slightly deeper level than this book.
- John Mace, *Arabic Verbs and Essential Grammar*, published in the *Teach Yourself* series, is an extremely useful reference work which provides easy access to all the verb types and a summary of Arabic grammar.

Spoken Arabic varies widely from country to country, and you should choose from the wide selection of material available according to which country you intend to visit. Very roughly the Arabic dialects divide into the following groups: North Africa from Morocco to Libya; Egypt and the Sudan; Lebanon Jordan and

Syria; Iraq and the Arabian peninsula.

The Arabic of the last of these groups is probably the nearest to the written Arabic you have learned in this book, and is covered by the present writers' *Teach Yourself Gulf Arabic* in the same series.

Good luck! We hope you will enjoy learning Arabic!

ARABIC SCRIPT AND PRONUNCIATION GUIDE

1 Basic characteristics

The Arabic script looks difficult because it is so different from what we are used to. In fact, it is easy to master, and, with one or two easily definable exceptions, all sounds are written as they are pronounced. There are no combinations of vowels (*dipthongs*) which result in a totally different sound, such as, for example, the English words *plough*, *dough*, *through*, *enough*.

Some important facts about the Arabic script:

- Arabic is written from *right* to *left*. As a result of this, what we would regard as the back cover of a book, magazine or newspaper is in fact the front cover of an Arabic publication.
- Arabic script is always *joined*, or *cursive*, like English handwriting. There is no equivalent of the English text you are now reading, where all the letters have separate forms with spaces between them. An exception to this is in crossword puzzles.
- There are no capital letters.
- The joining strokes between letters, called *ligatures*, have the effect of slightly altering the shape of the letters on either side. As a result, Arabic letters have varying forms, depending on whether they come at the beginning, middle, or end of a word.
- A few letters do not join to the *following* letter, but all Arabic letters join to the preceding one.
- The three short vowels, **a**, **i** or **u**, as opposed to the long vowels **aa**, **uu** and **ii**, are not shown in the script. For example, the word **bank** (borrowed from English), is written **b-n-k**. This is not so much of a problem as you might think, since the number of shapes or forms which Arabic words take is limited. There is a system (not normally used in Modern Arabic) to show the short

vowels, which is explained below. As almost all Modern Arabic is written without the short vowels, we have generally not included them in the Arabic script in this course, although the transliteration (pronunciation guide) given for all the Arabic vocabulary and structures will show you what they are. However, we have included the short vowels in the Arabic script in some places where it is especially helpful.

2 The alphabet

Because Arabic is a cursive language, we have given the *initial*, *medial* and *final* forms of each letter, used depending on where they occur in the word. A separate form has also been included, since some letters do not join to the one after them. If you look at the letters carefully you will see that there are really only two shapes, although four forms of the non-joining letters have been given.

The Arabic alphabet is given below in its traditional order. Letters which do not join to the following one are marked with an asterisk (*).

The term *final* in the table should be interpreted as meaning final after a joining letter. If the preceding letter is a non-joiner, the separate form will be used. If you look closely, you can see that final and separate letters are usually elongated in form, or have a 'flourish' after them.

In most cases, the initial form of the letter can be regarded as the basic or nucleus form. For example, if you look at **baa'** (the second letter in the following list), you will see that its basic (initial) form is a small left-facing hook with a single dot below it. The medial form is more or less the same, with a ligature coming in from the right (remember Arabic reads from right to left). The final form is the same as the medial, with a little flourish to the left, at the end of the word, and the separate form is the same as the initial, but again with the flourish to the left. Study the letters bearing these features in mind, as many of them follow the same principle. Fuller descriptions and other hints on deciphering will be given in the units.

Here are the four shapes of **baa'** in enlarged type:

ـب	ـبـ	ـب	ب
initial	*medial*	*final*	*separate*

You will see that the nucleus is the hook with a dot under it (the initial form). The medial shape has joining strokes before and after the letter, and the final form has an elongation or flourish.

The Arabic letters

Name	Initial	Medial	Final	Separate	Pronunciation
alif*	ا	ـا	ـا	ا	*see below*
baa'	ـب	ـبـ	ـب	ب	b
taa'	ـت	ـتـ	ـت	ت	t
thaa'	ـث	ـثـ	ـث	ث	th
jiim	ـج	ـجـ	ـج	ج	j
Haa'	ـح	ـحـ	ـح	ح	H
khaa'	ـخ	ـخـ	ـخ	خ	kh
daal*	د	ـد	ـد	د	d
dhaal'	ذ	ـذ	ـذ	ذ	dh
raa'*	ر	ـر	ـر	ر	r
zaay*	ز	ـز	ـز	ز	z
siin	ـس	ـسـ	ـس	س	s
shiin	ـش	ـشـ	ـش	ش	sh
Saad	ـص	ـصـ	ـص	ص	S
Daad	ـض	ـضـ	ـض	ض	D
Taa'	ـط	ـطـ	ـط	ط	T
DHaa'	ـظ	ـظـ	ـظ	ظ	DH

Name	Initial	Medial	Final	Separate	Pronunciation
:ain	ﻋ	ﻌ	ﻊ	ع	:
ghain	ﻏ	ﻐ	ﻎ	غ	gh
faa'	ﻓ	ﻔ	ﻒ	ف	f
qaaf	ﻗ	ﻘ	ﻖ	ق	q
kaaf	ﻛ	ﻜ	ﻚ	ك	k
laam	ﻟ	ﻠ	ﻞ	ل	l
miim	ﻣ	ﻤ	ﻢ	م	m
nuun	ﻧ	ﻨ	ﻦ	ن	n
haa'	ﻫ	ﻬ	ﻪ	ه	h
waaw	و	ﻮ	ﻮ	و	w
yaa'	ﻳ	ﻴ	ﻲ	ي	y

There is one combination consonant **laam-alif**. This must be used
when this series of letters occurs, and it is a non-joiner:

Name	Initial	Medial/Final	Separate
laam-alif	لا	ﻼ	لا

Also note that, in some styles of type and handwriting, when the
letter **miim** comes after **laam**, the small circle of the **miim** is filled
in and looks like a little tag attached to the **laam**, for example:

المكتب **al-máktab** *the desk, office*

The **taa' marbuuTah**, referred to in this book as the 'hidden **-t**', is
the Arabic feminine ending. As it only occurs at the end of words,
it has only two forms: *final* (after joiners) and *separate* (after non-
joiners). It is always preceded by a short **a**-vowel:

Final	Separate
ﺔ	ة

If you look carefully at this letter, you will see that it is a **haa'** with the two dots above of the **taa'** added. It is normally ignored in speech, or rendered as a very weak **h**, but in certain combinations of words it is pronounced as **t**. It has therefore been transcribed as **h** or **t** accordingly.

The **hamzah** is regarded by the Arabs as a supplementary sign, not as letter of the alphabet. Its official pronunciation is a 'glottal stop' (as the *t*'s in the cockney pronunciation of *bottle*), and it has been transliterated by means of an apostrophe ('). It is sometimes omitted in speech, but should be shown in written Arabic, where it occurs either on its own, or written over an **alif**, **waaw** or **yaa'**. In the last case, the two dots under the **yaa'** are omitted. It can also occur written below an **alif**, but this is less common. The actual **hamzah** never joins to anything, but its 'supporting' letters take the form required by their position in the word:

	Initial	Medial	Final	Separate
independent		ﻉ *in all cases*		
over **alif**	أ	ﺎ	ﺎ	أ
under **alif**	إ	*does not occur*		إ
over **waaw**	–	ـﺆ	ـﻮ	ؤ
over **yaa'**	–	ـﺌـ	ـﺊ	ئ

Note that, at the beginning of a word, **hamzah** is always written above or below **alif**.

The writing of the **hamzah** is a frequent source of spelling errors among native speakers, and it is often omitted in print and writing.

In foreign loanwords the letter **p** is usually written as a **baa'** and the letter **v** is written either as **faa'** or with the Persian letter ڤ – a **faa'** with three dots above it instead of one.

Script Exercise 1

In the photograph below, which five well-known international companies are sponsors of this race-course?

3 Vowels

The letters of the Arabic alphabet are all regarded as consonants.

In Arabic writing the short vowels are not usually marked except in children's school textbooks, the Holy Koran and ancient classical poetry.

The long vowels are expressed by the three letters **alif**, **waaw** and **yaa'**. **Alif** almost always expresses the vowel **aa**, but **waaw** and **yaa'** can also be consonantal **w** and **y** (as in English *wish* and *yes*).

The most important factors to consider in Arabic words are firstly the consonants, and secondly the long vowels. It will not make much difference in most cases whether you pronounce a word with **a**, **u** or **i** (short vowels), but it is important to get the long vowels right. See page 18 for more details on vowels.

4 Variations in handwriting

Think of the Arabic script as essentially handwriting (since it is always cursive, no matter how it is produced – by hand or on a computer). Since calligraphy is a highly developed art in the Arab world, there are more variations in the form of the letters than is the case in English.

The most common of these is that two dots above or below a letter are frequently combined into one dash, and three dots (which only occur above) into an inverted *v* like the French circumflex (^). Here is an example showing **taa'** and **thaa'**:

Another common variation is the writing of **siin** (**s**) and **shiin** (**sh**) simply as long lines, ironing out their 'spikes', and often with a small hook below at the beginning:

This occurs frequently in handwriting, signwriting and newspaper and advert headings – in fact everywhere where the original copy has been prepared by a calligrapher rather than typeset.

Above all, Arabic writing is fun. Look at it as an art form!

5 Transliteration

Transliteration means expressing a language which uses a different writing system (like Arabic) in terms of symbols based on the Roman alphabet, usually for teaching purposes. There is no standard way of doing this and we have tried to keep the system used in this book as simple as possible.

The essential feature of a transliteration system is that it has to have a precise equivalent for every sound used in the target language. This differs from conventional spelling, e.g. in English the letter *s* has totally different sounds in the two words *loafs*, and *loaves*. Consider also that the same sound in the former can be spelled *ce*, e.g. *mince*. Transliteration systems have to iron out such discrepancies.

We have adapted the English alphabet, using capital letters to distinguish between Arabic sounds which seem related to speakers of English. For instance, Arabic has two sorts of *t* which we have distinguished in this way: **rattab** means *arranged*, whereas **raTTab** means *moistened*. Consequently you will not find capital letters used as they are conventionally, e.g. in personal and place names. (An exception has, however, been made in the case of **Al-laah** *God, Allah*.)

6 The Arabic sounds

We have divided the pronunciation table into three parts:
- Group 1: Sounds that are more or less as in English.
- Group 2: Sounds which do not occur in English, but are found in other European languages with which you may be familiar.
- Group 3: Sounds which are specific to Arabic.

Note: The letter **alif** has no sound of its own, and is used only to express the long vowel **aa** and as a support for the **hamzah** (see the relevant sections below).

Group 1

b   as in *but*

d   as in *duck*

dh   as in the hard *th* in *this* or *mother*. Do not confuse with the sound **th** (see below), as they convey entirely different meanings in Arabic (**dhawb** *melting*, **thawb** *a garment*).

f   as in *force*

h   as in *hold*, but never omitted in speech as it very often is in English (e.g. *vehement*). An exception is the common feminine ending **-ah**, see above.

j   as in *jar*

k   as in *kick*

l   mostly as in *line*, but sometimes has a duller sound, roughly
         as in English *alter*. This distinction is not meaningful in
         Arabic but depends on the surrounding consonants.

m   as in *mum*

n   as in *nib*

s   as in *sit*, (it is <u>not</u> pronounced *z* as in *things*: see **z** below)

sh   as in *flash*

t   as in *tart*

th   as in *think* (<u>not</u> as in *this*; see **dh** above)

w   as in *wonder*

y   as in *yonder*

z   as in *sneeze*, *bees* (sometimes spelled *s* in English, but in
         Arabic **s** and **z** never interchange; see also **th** and **dh**)

Group 2

r   The Arabic **r** sound does not occur in standard English, but
         is familiar in dialect pronunciation. It is the trilled **r** of
         Scottish *very* (*'verry'*), and common in Italian and Spanish
         (*Parma, Barcelona*).

gh   Near to the *r* of Parisian French. It is actually a more guttural
         scraping sound, and occurs in Dutch, e.g. *negen*. The
         Parisian *r* is near enough as an intermediate measure.

kh   Roughly sound of *ch* in Scottish *loch* and *och aye*. Also
         familiar in German *doch* and (written *j*) in Spanish *José*.

Group 3

These sounds are particular to Arabic. To pronounce them requires
practice and it is best to listen to native speakers if possible.

S,T,   With the exception of **H** (see below), the capitalised
D,   consonants are pronounced in a way similar to their small
DH   letter versions **s**, **t**, **d** and **dh**, except that the tongue is
        depressed into a spoon shape, and the pressure of air from
        the lungs increased. This gives a forceful and hollow sound,
        often referred to as *emphatic*. These sounds have a marked

effect on surrounding vowels, making them sound more hollow. A rough (British) English equivalent is the difference in the *a* as in *Sam* and (with of course silent *p*) *psalm*.

:   We have a muscle in our throat which is never used except in vomiting. Think about that and pretend you are about to be sick. You will find that what is normally called in English gagging is actually a restriction in the deep part of the throat. If you begin to gag, and then immediately relax the muscles in order to release the airstream from the lungs, you will have produced a perfect : (called **:ayn** in Arabic). This sound must be distinguished from the glottal stop **hamzah** as the difference affects the meaning. For instance, **:amal** means work, but **'amal** means hope.

H   Pronounced in exactly the same way as **:ayn**, except that, instead of completely closing the muscles referred to above, they are merely constricted and the air allowed to escape. The only time English speakers come near to a (weakish) **H** is when they breathe on their spectacle lenses before cleaning them. Both **:ayn** and **Haa'** should always be pronounced with the mouth fairly wide open (say '*ah*').

'   The **hamzah** occurs in English between words pronounced deliberately and emphatically (e.g. '*She [pause] is [pause] awful.*'), but is probably more familiar as the Cockney or Glaswegian pronunciation of *t* or *tt* as in *bottle*.

q   is officially pronounced as a 'back of the throat' English *c* or *k*. If you try to imitate the sound of a crow cawing you will not be far away. A rough equivalent is the difference in articulation of the letter *c* in (British) English *cam* and *calm*. *Note:* The symbol **q** has been chosen only for convenience: it has really nothing to do with the English combination *qu*.

Local variations

As with any language spoken over such a wide area, regional pronunciations occur. The versions given above are the officially correct ones, always used in reciting the Holy Koran, but local variants often slip into the pronunciation of politicians, radio and

T.V. announcers etc. The most important of these affect the following letters:

th   Many speakers in the North and West of the Arab world find this sound difficult to pronounce and render it as either **t** or **s**.

j   In Egypt and a few other areas, this is rendered **g** as in *gold*. In Lebanon, parts of Syria and Jordan it sounds like the **j** of French *Jacques* (which is the same as the **s** in English *pleasure*).

dh   Sometimes becomes **d** or **z** (see **th** above).

D   Pronounced identically to **DH** in most of the Eastern Arab world (Iraq, the Gulf and Saudi Arabia).

DH   See **D** above. Additionally, in many urban parts of Egypt, Lebanon, Syria and Jordan it often becomes a sort of emphatic **z**-sound.

q   In informal speech, this is often pronounced as **g** in many parts of the Arab world. In the spoken Arabic of urban areas of Egypt, Lebanon and Syria it is pronounced as a glottal stop (**hamzah**).

Note: the above variants are given to help you avoid confusion when listening to 'live' Arabic in various parts of the Arab world. It is probably better to stick to the more formal values until your ear becomes attuned but if – as is highly recommended – you enlist the help of a native speaker, imitate his or her pronunciation.

🎧 7 Vowels

There are only three common vowels, all of which occur both long and short. These have been transcribed as follows:

a   roughly as in *hat*

aa   an elongated emphatic *a* as in the word *and* as in: *'Did she actually say that?' 'Yes... and she had the cheek to repeat it!'*. In juxtaposition with some of the consonants (mainly the capitalised ones **S**, **D**, **T**, **DH**, but also **q**, **gh** and sometimes **l** and **r** it sounds more like the vowel in the English *palm*.

i	as in *if*
ii	the long equivalent of **i**, as in *seen*, French *livre*
u	as in *put* (never as in *sup*)
uu	as in *food*, French *nous*
aw	roughly as in English *bound*
ay	as in *aye* (often pronounced like **ai** as in *bail* in informal situations)
oo	as in like French *beau* or *home* as pronounced in Scotland – occurs in less formal speech and in some foreign loanwords

8 Writing vowels and other signs

As short vowels are not normally written in Modern Arabic, it is better to become used to recognising Arabic words without them. However, the transliterated Arabic throughout this course will show you which short vowel should be pronounced and the short vowels are also sometimes included on the Arabic script where helpful to understanding the patterns of words.

Note: All these signs are written above or below (as indicated) the consonant which they *follow*. For instance, to express the word **kutiba**, you write the (Arabic) consonant **k** + the vowel sign for **u**, consonant **t** + the sign for **i**, **b** + the sign for **a**, like this:

As all three letters are joining letters, the **k** has the initial form, the **t** the medial form and the **b** the final form.

The long vowels are the same signs, but followed by **alif** for **aa**, **waaw** for **uu** and **yaa'** for **ii**. For example, if the above word had all three vowels long (**kuutiibaa** – an imaginary word, for purposes of illustration only), it would be written like this:

A similar means is used to express the diphthong vowels **aw** and **ay**, except that, as you would expect, the vowel sign preceding the

و or ي is always **a**, for example:

tay   kaw

Zero vowel sign

When a consonant has no vowel after it, this is marked by writing a miniature circle (like a zero) above it; here above the **k**:

maktab

This sign is omitted at the end of words, in this case the **b**.

Doubled consonants

Doubled consonants (written in the transliteration as **bb**, **nn**, **ss**, etc.) are very important in Arabic, as they can change the meanings of words radically. They are only pronounced in English when they span two words, e.g. *'But Tim, my young friend...'* In Arabic, however, they must always be pronounced carefully, wherever they occur, with a slight hesitation between them. **mathal** means *a proverb*, **maththal** means *he acted, represented*.

In Arabic, the consonant is written once only, with the following sign (a little Arabic س **s** without the tail) above it, for example:

maththal

The sign for the vowel following the doubled letter – here an **a** – is written above the doubling sign. As you have already learned, an **i**-vowel is expressed by writing a short oblique stroke under the letter. However, by convention, when a letter already has the doubling sign, the stroke is put under the sign but actually above the letter.

maththil

Other signs

The letter **alif** occasionally appears with a longer, curved stroke above it (similar to a stretched out Spanish *tilde* as in *cañon*). It is then pronounced as a **hamzah** (glottal stop) followed by a long **aa**-vowel. An important word which you will meet often and should take pains to learn to write and pronounce correctly is the Arabic word for the Koran:

$$ اَلْقُرْآن $$

al-qur'aan

Finally a sign used on only a very few (but common) words is a vertical stroke above the preceding letter. This is simply a shorthand way of writing the long **aa**-vowel. Another very important word in Arab culture is *God*, or *Allah*. Here the vertical stroke is written over the doubling sign.

Pronounce this **alláah** with the stress on the second syllable. (It is usually uttered with the 'dark' **l**, i.e. an **l** pronounced with the tongue hollowed at the back of the upper teeth. This gives the **aa** a 'hollow' sound.)

9 Irregular spellings

The letter **yaa'** occurs frequently at the end of words in Arabic. It is usually pronounced **-ii**, but also sometimes **-aa**. In the former case, it is usually written with two dots under it (ي) and in the latter without them (ى), but this rule is not, unfortunately, always adhered to.

$$ بَنَى $$

banaa

Note that in this case, the vowel preceding the **yaa'** is **a**. Words showing this characteristic will be explained as they occur.

The hybrid letter ة, the 'hidden t', is always preceded by **a** (ةـ), see above.

Important note: Both of these spellings can only occur at the end of a word. If any suffix is added to the word, they become ا and ت respectively. (This will be explained fully later in the book.)

10 One-letter words

By convention, Arabic words consisting only of one consonantal letter (and usually a short vowel) are joined to the following word. Thus **wa** (*and*) + **anta** (*you*) is written:

وَأَنْتَ

To make things clearer in transliteration, such words are separated by a hyphen: **wa-anta**.

11 Stress

The rules for stress in Arabic are complex, and it is better to learn from the audio if you have it, or by listening to native speakers.

One simple general rule, however, is that if a word contains a long vowel (**aa**, **uu**, etc.) the stress falls on this; and if there is more than one (long vowel), the stress falls on the one nearest the end of the word, e.g.:

مَكَاتِب **makáatib** but مَكَاتِيب **makaatíib**

The stress will be on the last long syllable before a vowel ending.

To help you, the stressed syllables of words have been marked with an acute accent: **á, áa**, etc. in the first few units so that you become used to where they occur.

12 Case endings

Classical Arabic had a set of three grammatical case endings for nouns and adjectives, but these are nowadays largely ignored in all but very formal speech such as Koranic recitation and ancient poetry.

The only one of these which concerns us is the so-called *indefinite accusative*, because this shows in the script. This is known as the *accusative marker*.

Its form is an **alif** attached to the end of the noun or adjective, technically with two slashes above the preceding consonant: لـ. It is pronounced **-an**, e.g. كتاب **kitáab**, but with accusative marker كتابًا **kitáaban**. In practice, the two slashes before the **alif** are usually omitted:كتابا.

1 أ فلنبدأ fal-nábda'

Let's get started!

In this unit you will learn:

- how to greet people
- how to make short descriptive phrases
- about definites and indefinites

🎧 1 السلام عليكم as-saláamu :aláy-kum *hello*
[lit. Peace be upon you]

In Arabic, it is extremely important to be able to greet people, and to reply when someone greets you. Notice that each greeting has its own particular reply. If you have the recording, listen to these people greeting each other, and see how they respond.

Simple Greetings

السلام عليكم
as-saláamu :aláy-kum

hello [lit. peace be upon you]

وعليكم السلام
wa- :aláy-kum as-saláam

hello (reply) [lit. (and) upon you peace]

Exercise 1

Kamal is visiting an old friend, John, in his hotel in Cairo, and Kamal speaks first. Practise saying each phrase, filling in the gaps. Remember to pronounce the stress on every word where it is shown.

a as-saláamu …, ya John!   السلام ... يا جون!

b wa :aláy-kum …, ya Kamáal!   وعليكم ... يا كمال!

Exercise 2

You are going to dinner with your Arabic-speaking friend Nadia. She welcomes you into her house. What do you say to her?

SabáaH al-kháyr صباح الخير 2 *Good morning*

Suad is about to begin teaching an Arabic course at the university in Cairo. First she greets a new student.

Su:áad	SabáaH al-kháyr.	سعاد صباح الخير.
Táalibah	SabáaH an-núur.	طالبة صباح النور.

Táalibah (pl. Taalibáat) طالبة ، طالبات *female student*

Note

The plurals of nouns and adjectives in Arabic do not follow a logical system, so it is better to learn them along with the singular from the beginning. They are given after the singular noun in the vocabulary, separated by a comma.

In Arabic, there is no word for *good afternoon*, so **masáa' al-kháyr** is used for both late afternoon and evening.

ta:biiráat ra'iisíyyah تعبيرات رئيسية (Key phrases)

How to wish someone good morning, evening:

صباح الخير	*good morning* [lit. morning (of)
SabáaH al-kháyr	the goodness]

صباح النور	*good morning* (reply) [lit.
SabáaH an-núur	morning (of) the light]

مساء الخير
masáa' al-kháyr

good afternoon/good evening
[lit. evening (of) the goodness]

مساء النور
masáa' an-núur

good afternoon/good evening
(reply) [lit. evening (of) the light]

Exercise 3
Fill in the bubbles with the appropriate greetings.

Exercise 4

a It is 11am and you go to the bank for cash. Greet the bank clerk.
b You are in a restaurant one evening and an acquaintance comes up and greets you. What would you say?
c Your partner comes home from work at 7pm. What does he/she say to you?
d You go into a shop in the market. Say hello to the shopkeeper.
e You see your neighbour in the street and she says hello to you. How would you reply?

3 كيف حالك؟ kayfa Háal-ak? *How are you?*

Suad asks one of the students, Michael, how he is:

Su:áad	káyfa Háal-ak?	سعاد كيف حالك؟
Michael	al-Hámdu lil-láah.	مايكل الحمد لله.
Su:áad	áhlan wa-sáhlan.	سعاد أهلا وسهلا.
Michael	áhlan bi-ki. wa ánti,	مايكل أهلا بك.
	káyfa Háal-ik?	وأنت، كيف حالك؟
Su:áad	al-Hámdu lil-láah,	سعاد الحمد لله، بخير.
	bi-kháyr.	

Note the spelling of **ahlan** and **sahlan** with a final **alif**. This is the accusative marker (see Unit 8).

تعبيرات رئيسية ta:biiráat ra'iisíyyah (Key phrases)

كيف حالك؟	**kayfa Háal-ak?**	*how are you?* (to a man)
		[lit. How [is] condition-your?]
كيف حالك؟	**kayfa Háal-ik?**	*how are you?* (to a woman)
الحمد لله **al-Hámdu lil-láah**		*praise [be] to God* (response to above)
أهلا وسهلا **áhlan wa-sáhlan**		*welcome*
أهلا بك **áhlan bi-k**		(reply to a man)
أهلا بك **áhlan bi-ki**		(reply to a woman)
وأنت؟ **wa-ánta/ánti**		*and you?* (sing. masc./fem.)
بخير **bi-khayr**		*well* adj. (lit. in well-being)

> ### al-mulaaHaDHáat (Notes) الملاحظات
>
> ■ **káyfa Háal-ak** If you are speaking to a woman, you must say **káyfa Háal-ik**, although there is no difference in written Arabic. If you are talking a group of people, you must say **káyfa Háal-kum** (كيف حالكم).
>
> ■ **al-Hámdu lil-láah** never changes, and is used in many situations. Even if something unfortunate or unpleasant has happened, the devout Muslim must submit to the will of Allah and praise Him for what He has decreed.
>
> ■ **áhlan bi-k** You must say **áhlan bi-ki** to a woman (same spelling), or **áhlan bi-kum** (أهلا بكم) to a group of people.

Exercise 5

a Mohammad is having a party, and his English friend John arrives. Finish the sentence for Mohammad.

   káyfa ...?   كيف ...؟

b What does John reply?

c Fill in the missing words in the next exchange between Mohammed and John.

   – ... wa sáhlan   ... وسهلا.

   – áhlan ....   أهلا ....

d You meet some Arabic-speaking friends. How do you ask them how they are?

e An Arabic-speaking colleague comes into your office and you greet him. What do you say, and how does he reply?

🎧 4 What do they want?

الأهرام

Exercise 6

Some tourists are spending the day in Cairo. Listen to the recording or read the dialogues below, and try to work out which picture belongs to each dialogue?

a   b   c

Dialogue 1

– táaksi! al-ahráam, min faDl-ak! تاكسي! الأهرام من فضلك!

– ná:am, ya sáyyid-i! نعم يا سيدي!

Dialogue 2

– al-miSbáaH min fáDl-ak. المصباح من فضلك.

– al-kabíir aw aS-Saghíir? الكبير أو الصغير؟

– tafáDDal. تفضل.

– shúkran. شكرا.

Dialogue 3

– shaay wa-sandawíitsh شاي، وسندويتش صغير
 Saghíir min-fáDl-ak. من فضلك.

– shaay bi-súkkar? شاي بسكر؟

– laa shúkran, bidúun súkkar. لا، شكرا، بدون سكر.
 bi-kam háadhaa? بكم هذا؟

– thaláathah junayháat. ثلاثة جنيهات.

Exercise 7
Which dialogue takes place:
a in a café beside the Nile?
b in Khan al-Khalili market?
c in Tahrir Square, in the centre of Cairo?

Exercise 8
Find the words for the following items:
a small
b a tea with sugar
c the lamp
d the pyramids
e a sandwich

ma:luumáat thaqaafíyyah (Cultural tips) معلومات ثقافية

People don't usually use terms like Mr and Mrs. In Egypt and some other northern Arab countries people say **síidi** where we might say *sir*, but in other countries this term is reserved for certain classes of nobility. Its correct formal pronunciation is **sáyyidi**, but this does not show in the Arabic script.

Exercise 9
Which figure from the
Arabian Nights is this?

علاء الدين والمصباح السحري

ta:biiráat ra'iisíyyah (Key phrases) تعبيرات رئيسية

من فضلك min fáDl-ak	*please*
تفضل tafáDDal	*here you are, welcome*
شكرا shúkran	*thank you*

نعم ná:am	*yes*
أو aw	*or*
لا laa	*no*
بـ bi-	*with*
بدون bi-dúun	*without*
بكم هذا؟ bi-kam háadha?	*how much is this?*

تراكيب اللـغة taraakíib al-lúghah (Structures)

1 Definite or indefinite?

It is important in Arabic to be able to distinguish between *definite* words and phrases, and *indefinites*.

Indefinite words have *a* or *an* before them in English. There is no indefinite article, or word for *a* or *an*, in Arabic.

| بيت bayt | *(a) house* |
| سندويتش sandawíitsh | *(a) sandwich* |

There are three types of definite words in English:
a) words which begin with the definite article – *the* house
b) proper nouns – *Mohammed, Cairo, Egypt*
c) pronouns such as *he, I, you*, etc.

The definite article *the* never varies in writing, and is always الـ **al-**. The hyphen shows that, in the Arabic script, **al-** is always attached to the following word.

| البيت al-bayt | *the house* |
| الأهرام al-ahráam | *the pyramids* |

There are two points of pronunciation:
a) If the preceding word ends in a vowel or **-ah**, the **a** of **al-** is omitted in pronunciation, but kept in writing.

Written	Pronounced
باب البيت	**baab al-bayt** *the door of the house*
	after a preceding consonant
في البيت	**fi l-bayt** *in the house*
	after a preceding vowel

b) If the word to which **al-** is attached begins with one of the following consonants, the **l** of the **al-** is omitted in pronunciation and the following letter is doubled.

n	l	DH	T	D	S	sh	s	z	r	dh	d	th	t
ن	ل	ظ	ط	ض	ص	ش	س	ز	ر	ذ	د	ث	ت

You are pronouncing the word properly if you make a small hesitation on the doubled letters.

Written	Pronounced	
	after a consonant	after a vowel
الشمس	ash-shams	sh-shams *the sun*
النور	an-nuur	n-nuur *the light*
السندويتش	as-sandwíitsh	s-sandwíitsh *the sandwich*

Tip: An easy way to remember these letters is to pronounce them all out loud. With the slight exception of **sh**, you will notice that the tip of your tongue is contacting somewhere in the region of your front teeth or the gum above them – where the letter **l** is pronounced, which is why the assimilation occurs. No other Arabic consonants are pronounced in this area.

The Arabs call these the 'sun letters', simply because the word **shams** (شمس) *sun* begins with one of them. The remaining letters

are called the 'moon letters', because **qamar** (قمر) moon does not
begin with an assimilated letter.

Remember: The *written* form remains the same; it is only the
pronunciation which varies. However, to help you, the
assimilations have been represented in the transliteration.

Exercise 10
Listen to the following words on the recording, or study them
carefully:

a الشاي

b الأهرام

c السلام

d السندويتش

e النور

f الكبير

g الصغير

List those which begin with sun letters and those which begin with
moon letters.

2 Nouns and adjectives

Arabic adjectives behave like nouns but:
a) they always follow the noun;
b) they must agree with the noun in definiteness and in gender;
c) additional adjectives are simply added after the first one with no
   punctuation or joining word. If the noun is definite, the
   adjectives must all be definite and have the definite article.

It will be a great help when you are learning Arabic if you can
come to look on nouns and adjectives as being virtually the same
thing. This only happens in slightly archaic English in phrases such
as *'the great and the good', 'the meek shall inherit the earth'*. More
commonly we use the helping word 'one': *'Which dress do you
prefer?', 'The blue one'*.

Arabic grammar will become easier if you mentally add the word '*-one*' to Arabic adjectives, so that you are effectively equating them with nouns. In Arabic the reply to the question above would have been simply '*The blue*'.

بيت صغير **bayt Saghíir**	*a small house = (a) house* *(a) small(-one)*	
الولد الطويل **al-wálad aT-Tawíil**	*the tall boy = the-boy the-tall(-one)*	
بريطانيا العظمى **briiTáanyaa l-:úDHma**	*Great Britain = Britain the-great* *(-one)*	
كتاب كبير جديد **kitáab kabíir jadíid**	*a big new book = (a) book (a) big* *(-one) (a) new(-one)*	
البنت الجميلة الصغيرة **al-bint al-jamíilah** **S-Saghíirah**	*the beautiful young girl = the-girl* *the-beautiful(-one) the-young(-one)*	

بيت، بيوت **bayt, buyúut** house

صغير **Saghíir** young (person), small (thing)

ولد، أولاد **wálad, awláad** boy (pl. also children)

طويل **Tawíil** tall (person), long (thing)

كتاب، كتب **kitáab (kútub)** book

كبير **kabíir** big

جميل (جميلة) **jamíil** (fem. **jamíilah**) beautiful

هرم كبير
háram kabíir
a big pyramid
(a) pyramid (a) big(-one)

هرم صغير
háram Saghíir
a small pyramid
(a) pyramid (a) small(-one)

إلى المركز التجاري
TO THE COMMERCIAL CENTRE
←

Note: Some words end with a final ى (written without the two dots) which is pronounced **-a** (strictly **-aa**, but often shortened). إلى **ila(a)**, *to/ towards* is an example of this.

تمرينات tamriináat (Practice)

Exercise 11
Listen again to the greetings at the beginning of the recording, and repeat the phrases after the speakers. If you don't have the recording, read the dialogues several times until you are sure you are familiar with them.

Exercise 12
Match the following greetings with the appropriate reply.

i	السلام عليكم	a	شكرا
ii	مساء الخير	b	مساء النور
iii	كيف حالك؟	c	أهلا بك
iv	أهلا وسهلا	d	وعليكم السلام
v	تفضل!	e	الحمد لله

Exercise 13

١ الشرق الأوسط

٢ الرباط   ٥ السودان   ٨ الرياض
٣ الجزائر   ٦ الأردن   ٩ المنامة
٤ القاهرة   ٧ السعودية   ١٠ بغداد

Match the Arabic words for the places in the Arab world in the above box with the transliterated words below, and practise saying them. To help you the cities are marked on the map.

a ar-ribáaT   b al-jazáa'ir
c al-qáahirah   d ar-riyáaDH
e al-manáamah   f baghdáad
g ash-shárq al-áwsaT   h as-sa:uudíyyah
i as-suudáan   j al-úrdunn

Now work out the English names for the towns and countries.

Exercise 14

Listen to the recording or read the transliteration, and work out what is being asked for in the café.

a. قهوة من فضلك   **qáhwah min fáDl-ak.**

b. ليمون من فضلك   **laymóon min fáDl-ak.**

c. كوكاكولا صغيرة من فضلك   **kookakóola Saghíirah min fáDl-ak.**

d. أيس كريم بالشوكولاتة من فضلك   **ays kriim bi-sh-shokoláatah min fáDl-ak.**

And where do these people want to be taken?

e السينما من فضلك. **as-síinimaa min fáDl-ak.**

f البنك من فضلك. **al-bank min fáDl-ak.**

Exercise 15
In transliteration, change these words and phrases from indefinite to definite.

a سندويتش **sandawíitsh**

b تلفون **tilifúun**

c بيت **bayt**

d طماطم **TamáaTim**

e سينما **síinima**

f بيرة صغيرة **bíirah Saghíirah**

g برجر كبير **bárgar kabíir**

h راديو جديد **ráadyo jadíid**

Exercise 16
See if you can match the words in Exercise 15 to the drawings below.

1   2   3   4

5   6   7   8

Exercise 17

Choose the correct adjective from the brackets to complete the phrases.

١ – السينما (جديدة، الجديدة) 1 the new cinema

٢ – بنت (صغيرة، الصغيرة) 2 a small girl

٣ – كتاب (جميل، الجميل) 3 a beautiful book

٤ – فيلم (طويل، الطويل) 4 a long film

٥ – البيت الكبير (واسع، الواسع) 5 the big roomy house

أوزان الكلمات awzáan al-kalimáat (Word shapes)

The large majority of Arabic words are built around a three-consonant root. It is conventional to express the first consonant of the root by C^1 – i.e. first consonant – and later consonants as C^2 and C^3. The vowels between are usually stated as they are (**a, i, u, aa, uu, ii** and so on) or, where they are variable, simply by **v**, meaning *vowel*.

The word pattern for this unit is:

$C^1aC^2iiC^3$

The word **kabíir** means *big* (*old* when applied to people). In Arabic, anything to do with the root **k-b-r** will have something to do with *bigness, large size* and so on.

This is a very useful concept, noticed long ago by Arab philologists. Most dictionaries are still arranged according to these three-letter roots.

Here we have the three consonants **k-b-r**. In Arabic they are fleshed out with long and short vowels. You can see that in the word **kabíir**, *big*, the first consonant of the root (**k**) has an **a-** vowel after it and the second consonant (**b**) has a long **ii** after it. This is a very common pattern for adjectives in Arabic.

To help you feel the cadences of the Arabic sounds, an English equivalent (or as near as possible) is given. Such words which are familiar to you will also help with the Arabic stress patterns.

Pattern	Arabic example	Eng. sound-alike
$C^1aC^2iiC^3$	**kabiir** كبير	*marine*

It will help you greatly in learning Arabic if you learn and listen for these patterns.

Here are some more words to show the pattern:

1 صغير **Saghíir**   *young* (person), *small* (thing)

2 طويل **Tawíil**   *tall* (person), *long* (thing)

3 بعيد **ba:íid**   *far, distant*

4 قريب **qaríib**   *near*

5 جديد **jadíid**   *new*

6 قديم **qadíim**   *old* (things)

7 جميل **jamíil**   *beautiful*

8 لطيف **laTíif**   *pleasant, nice*

9 كريم **karíim**   *noble, generous*

10 صحيح **SaHíiH**   *correct, right*

Exercise 18

Write down the roots for the words above in Arabic or transliteration with hyphens between the letters.

Note: For this type of exercise, use the *independent* forms of the letters in the Arabic script.

2 | التفاصيل الشخصية
at-tafaaSíil ash-shakhSíyyah

Personal details

In this unit you will learn how to:
- ask someone's name and give your own name
- say where you are from
- construct simple sentences with *is/are*
- say *there is/there are*
- say the numbers 1–10

1 من أين أنت؟ min áyna ánta? *Where are you from?*

Suad introduces herself to the students, and asks one of them his name and where he is from.

اسمي مايكل   ما اسمك؟

Exercise 1
Listen to the conversation a first time.
a What is the woman's name?
b What is the man's name

Exercise 2

Now listen again to the conversation.
a Where does the man come from?
b Where does the woman come from?

Now read the dialogue.

سعاد حسنا. أنا اسمي سعاد. ما اسمك؟

مايكل أنا اسمي مايكل.

سعاد أهلا وسهلا يا مايكل. من أين أنت؟

مايكل أنا من مانشستر في إنجلترا. وأنت؟

سعاد أنا من الاسكندرية في مصر.

Exercise 3

Find the Arabic for:
a I'm from Manchester.
b And you?

حسنا **Hásanan** (note spelling) *well, right, O.K.*

من **min** *from*

في **fii** *in*

الاسكندرية **al-iskandaríyyah** *Alexandria*

---

2 مصر جميلة miSr jamíilah *Egypt is beautiful*

Suad tells her students a little about Egypt.

Exercise 4

Read or listen to the description and answer the questions.
a What does Suad say about Cairo?
b Where is the Egyptian Museum?
c What does she recommend in the hotel?

مصر جميلة جدا. القاهرة مدينة كبيرة، وهي قديمة جدا.

المتحف المصري في ميدان التحرير قريب من فندق النيل.

هناك مطعم ممتاز في فندق النيل في ميدان التحرير. وطبعا

هناك الأهرام في الجيزة.

مصر **miSr** Egypt

جميلة **jamíilah** beautiful (fem.)

جدا **jíddan** (note spelling) very

القاهرة **al-qáahirah** Cairo

مدينة **madíinah** city

كبيرة **kabíirah** big (fem.)

و **wa** and (joined to next word)

هي **híya** she, it (fem.)

قديمة **qadíimah** old [of things only](fem.)

المتحف المصري **al-mátHaf al-míSri** The Egyptian museum

ميدان التحرير **maydáan at-taHríir** Tahrir Square

قريب من **qaríib min** near

فندق النيل **fúnduq an-níil** Nile Hotel

هناك **hunáaka** there is/are

مطعم **máT:am** restaurant

ممتاز **mumtáaz** excellent

طبعا **Táb:an** naturally, of course

الأهرام **al-ahráam** the pyramids

الجيزة **al-jíizah** Geezah, a district of Cairo [in Egypt the letter ج is pronounced like g in garden]

3 رقم تلفونك كم؟ raqm tilifúun-ak kam?

What's your telephone number?

After the class, some of the students want to arrange to meet up .
They exchange telephone numbers. Look carefully at the Arabic
numbers on page 45 then listen to the audio. Now answer the
questions.

Exercise 5

a What is Zaki's telephone number?
b What is Marie's number?
c What is the Arabic for 'telephone number'?
d How would you say 'My telephone number is...'?

زكي   رقم تلفونك كم يا حامد؟

حامد   رقم تلفوني ٦٣٤٧٢١١. ورقم تلفونك أنت؟

زكي   رقم تلفوني ٦٢١٥٥٠٠. يا ماري، رقم تلفونك كم؟

ماري   رقم تلفوني ٦٢٠٧٥٨٩.

تعبيرات رئيسية ta:biiráat ra'iisíyyah (Key phrases)

In Arabic, verbs and nouns vary in their endings depending on
whether you are speaking to a man, a woman or several people.

Asking people their name and telling them yours

ما اسمك؟   *What is your name?*

maa ísm-ak/ísm-ik (masc./fem.)?

... اسمي ísm-i ...   *My name is ...*

Asking people where they are from and replying

من أين أنت؟   *Where are you from?*

min áyna ánta/ánti (masc./fem.)?

Saying you're from either a town or a country

أنا من الخرطوم   *I am from Khartoum*
ána min al-kharTúum

أنا من لندن ána min lándan   *I am from London*

أنا من السودان   *I am from Sudan*
ána min as-suudáan

أنا من فرنسا ána min faránsa   *I am from France*

أنا من... ána min...   *I am from...*

 مصر **misr**   أمريكا **amríika**   اليابان **al-yaabáan**

 روسيا **rúusiya**   إسكتلندا **iskutlánda**   أستراليا **ustráalya**

The Arabic Numbers 1–10

The numbers are given here in their spoken or colloquial forms. In strictly grammatical Arabic, the use of the numbers is complicated, and so these forms are the ones nearly always used.

There are two main points to remember when writing Arabic numbers:

- The numerals are written from left to right (the opposite direction of the script), for example:

٦٢	٧٣١	٨٥٤	٧٥٩١	٤٠٠٢
62	731	854	7591	4002

- The written forms given here are the standard ones used in most of the Arab world, but some countries (mainly in North Africa) use the same forms as we do (1, 2, 3, 4, etc.), and this tendency seems to be spreading.

We call our numerical system 'Arabic' to distinguish it from Roman, but the forms of the numbers have changed slightly over time. Still, if you use a little imagination – and turn some of them through 90° – you should spot the similarities.

1	2	3	4	5	6	7	8	9	10
١	٢	٣	٤	٥	٦	٧	٨	٩	١٠

These are pronounced (colloquial form) as follows:

wáaHid	١ واحد	**sittah**	٦ ستّة	
ithnáin	٢ اثنين	**sáb:ah**	٧ سبعة	
thaláathah	٣ ثلاثة	**thamáanyah**	٨ ثمانية	
árba:ah	٤ أربعة	**tís:ah**	٩ تسعة	
khámsah	٥ خمسة	**:áshrah**	١٠ عشرة	

zero is **Sifr** صفر.

تراكيب اللغة taraakíib al-lúghah (Structures)

1 How to say *is* and *are* in Arabic

There is no equivalent of the verb *to be* in the present tense in Arabic. Sentences which contain the words *is* or *are* in English are constructed in Arabic by putting together the following:

a) any definite noun with an indefinite noun or adjective

al-bayt kabíir   البيت كبير

the house (is a) big(-one)   *The house is big*

muHámmad mashghúul   محمد مشغول

Muhammad (is a) busy(-person) *Muhammad is busy*

húwa mudíir   هو مدير

He (is a) director   *He is a director*

b) a definite noun or a pronoun with a phrase beginning with a
   preposition:

ána min al-iskandaríyyah   أنا من الاسكندرية

I (am) from Alexandria   *I am from Alexandria*

bayrúut fii lubnáan   بيروت في لبنان

Beirut (is) in Lebanon   *Beirut is in Lebanon*

If a definite noun is put with a definite noun or adjective, a
separating pronoun must be inserted, to make the meaning clear.

muHámmad <u>húwa</u> al-mudíir محمد <u>هو</u> المدير

   Mohammed <u>he</u> (is) the director Mohammed is the director

Here is a summary of how to make definite and indefinite phrases
and sentences in Arabic:

بيت كبير **bayt kabíir**	*a big house*, lit. (a) house (a) big(-one)
البيت الكبير **al-bayt al-kabíir**	*the big house*, lit. the-house the-big(-one)
البيت كبير **al-bayt kabíir**	*the house is big*, lit. the-house (is a) big-one
ناصر هو الرئيس **náaSir húwa r-ra'íis**	*Nasser is the boss*, lit. Nasser he the-boss

2 How to say *there is*, *there are*

This is expressed in modern Arabic by starting the sentence with
هنـاك hunáaka, *there*.

هناك مطعم في الميدان   *there is a restaurant in the*
hunáaka máT:am fi l-maydáan   *square*

هنـاك غرف كثيرة في الفندق   *there are many rooms in the*
hunáaka ghúraf kathíirah   *hotel*
fi l-fúnduq

3 Personal pronouns

Personal pronouns are always definite, i.e. if you say *he* you are
talking about one particular person.

These are the personal pronouns:

أنا **ána** *I*	نحن **náHnu** *we*
أنت **ánta** *you* (masc.)	أنتم **ántum** *you* (masc. pl.)
أنت **ánti** *you* (fem.)	أنتن **antúnna** *you* (fem. pl.)
هو **húwa** *he*	هم **hum** *they* (masc. pl.)
هي **híya** *she*	هن **húnna** *they* (fem. pl.)

Note:

a) The final **alif** of أنا **ana** is there to distinguish it from other
   similarly-spelled words. Pronounce it short, and accent the first
   syllable. (In fact most final **-aa** sounds in informal modern
   Arabic tend to be pronounced short unless they bear the stress.)

b) The male and female forms of *you* are identical in unvowelled
   writing. The context usually makes it clear which is intended.

c) Since all Arabic words are either masculine or feminine, English *it*
   must be translated as *he* or *she*, depending on the gender of the word.

الميدان كبير   *the square is big* (masc.)
al-maydáan kabíir

هو كبير húwa kabíir   *it is big*

السيارة صغيرة   *the car is small* (fem.)
as-sayyáarah Saghíirah

هي صغيرة híya Saghíirah   *it is small*

4 Asking questions in Arabic.

There are several ways to ask questions in Arabic:

a) by using a question word such as *which?*, *what?* or *where?*

ما اسمك؟ **maa ísm-ak?**   *What is your name?*

من أين أنت؟ **min áyna ánta?**   *Where are you from?*
                                     (lit. *from where you?*)

b) if no question word is present, **hal** or **'a** must be placed at the
   beginning of the sentence, acting as a verbal question mark.

هل محمد مشغول؟   *Is Muhammad busy?*
hal muHámmad mashghúul   (?)Muhammad (is a)
                                     busy(-person)

أهو مشغول؟   *Is he busy?*
'a-húwa mashghúul   (?) He (is a) busy
                                     (-person)

There is no precise rule about which to use, except that **a-** is
usually used with personal pronouns. Written question marks are
also used in modern Arabic, in addition to these question words.

Arabic words which consist of only one letter plus a short vowel,
such as أ or و, must not be written alone but attached to the
following word.

Pronunciation

1 al after long vowel

When Arabic prepositions ending with a long vowel, such as **fii**, *in*, are placed before a word beginning with **al-**, *the*, the **a** of **al-** disappears and the vowel of the preposition is pronounced short:

في المدينة   *in the city*

fii al-madíinah ➡ fi l-madíinah

If the word begins with one of the 'sun letters' (see Unit 1) the doubling of the initial consonant still applies.

في السعودية   *in Saudi Arabia*

fi s-sa:uudíyyah

2 Irregular spellings

Some of the most common prepositions (e.g. علي :**álaa**, *on*, إلى **ílaa**, *to/towards*, have an irregular spelling of the final **-aa** vowel which is written as a **yaa'** without the dots. This is also shortened before **al-** (see **fii** above).

أوزان الكلمات awzáan al-kalimáat (Word shapes)

Pattern	Arabic example	Eng. sound-alike
C¹aaC²iC³	**báarid** بارد	*calmish*

This pattern expresses the idea of someone or something doing or carrying out the root meaning. In English for nouns we use the suffix *-er* or a variant (*painter, actor*), and for adjectives we have *-ing*: a *going concern, a stunning performance*. This is another common pattern in adjectives. Again, the root of the word gives an idea of the meaning.

ب–ر–د **b-r-d** the root of the word

يبرد **yábrud** *to be, to become cold* (verb)

بارد **báarid** *cold* (adjective: not used for people)

عادل **:áadil** *just, upright**

لازم **láazim** *necessary*

ناشف **náashif** *dry*

كامل **káamil** *complete, perfect**

نافع: **náafi:** *useful*

صالح **SáaliH** *doing right**

سالم **sáalim** *safe, sound**

*These words are also used for men's names in Arabic.

Exercise 6

Extract the roots from the above words.

تمرينات tamriináat (Practice)

Exercise 7

Change the indefinite noun/adjective phrases below into definite phrases.

e.g. الكتاب الكبير ← كتاب كبير

   kitaab kabiir ➔ **al-kitaab al-kabiir**

سكرتير جديد a

سيارة جميلة b

ولد طويل c

بيت صغير d

مدير مشغول e

Exercise 8

Change the phrases in Exercise 7 into *is/are* sentences.

e.g. الكتاب كبير ← الكتاب الكبير

al-kitaab al-kabiir ← al-kitaab kabiir

Exercise 9

Now substitute a pronoun for the noun in the sentences in Exercise 8.

e.g. هو كبير ← الكتاب كبير

al-kitaab kabiir ← huwa kabiir

Exercise 10

Change the following statements into questions.

٤ الكتاب جديد.	١ أنت من مصر.
٥ يتكلم عربي.	٢ محمد في دبي.
	٣ هي أمريكية.

يتكلم **yatakállam** he speaks

عربي: **árabi** Arab, Arabic

Exercise 11

Change the following questions into statements.

٤ هل محمد هنا؟	١ هل السيارة جديدة؟
٥ أهو مشغول؟	٢ أهي مشغولة؟
	٣ هل الفندق قريب من الأهرام؟

هنا **húna** here

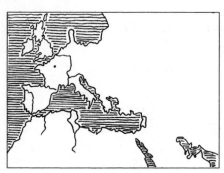

Exercise 12

Where do you think the following people are from? Listen to the recording and repeat what they are saying.

١ أنا من تونس.

٢ أنا من لبنان.

٣ أنا من باريس.

٤ أنا من اسكتلاندا.

٥ أنا من أبو ظبي.

٦ أنا من ايطاليا.

Exercise 13

In the telephone directory, all the UAE airports are listed together. Which of the six airports below would you get if you dialled:

a 245555?

b 448111?

c 757611?

1 Abu Dhabi

2 Dubai

3 Sharjah

4 Ras al Khaimah

5 Fujairah

6 Al Ain

مطارات الإمارات

● مطار أبو ظبي الدولي ٧٥٧٦١١

● مطار دبي الدولي ٢٤٥٥٥٥

● مطار الشارقة الدولي ٥٨١٠٠٠

● مطار رأس الخيمة الدولي ٤٤٨١١١

● مطار الفجيرة الدولي ٢٧٦٢٢٢

● مطار العين الدولي ٨٥٥٥٥٥

Exercise 14

Here is a list of international dialling codes from a United Arab
Emirates telephone directory.

٢٤٩	السودان	٩٦٥	الكويت	٢١٣	الجزائر
٩٦٣	سورية	٩٦١	لبنان	٩٧٣	البحرين
٢١٦	تونس	٢١٨	ليبيا	٢٠	مصر
٩٧١	الإمارات	٢١٢	المغرب	٣٣	فرانسا
المملكة المتحدة ٤٤		٩٦٨	عمان	٩٦٤	العراق
١	أمريكا	٩٧٤	قطر	٣٩	إيطاليا
٩٦٧	اليمن	٩٦٦	السعودية	٩٦٢	الأردن

What is the code for:

a Bahrain?   **d** Qatar?

b Egypt?   **e** Saudi Arabia?

c America?   **f** Italy?

٣ كيف تصف نفسك
kayfa taSif nafs-ak
How you describe yourself

In this unit you will learn:

- how to say your nationality
- how to say which languages you speak
- how to talk about more than one object
- the names of some places around town
- how to talk about professions

🎧 1 أَأَنت سوداني؟ 'a-ánta suudáani? *Are you Sudanese?*

Two of the students in Suad's class are asking each other where they come from.

Exercise 1
Listen to the recording or read the conversation and then answer the questions.

a What nationality is Zaki?

b What town does he come from?

مرحبا. أَأَنت مصري؟	حسام
لا، أنا سوداني من الخرطوم. وأنت؟	زكي
أنا مصري من طنطا.	حسام
أين طنطا؟	زكي
طنطا قريبة من القاهرة.	حسام

من **min** *from*

أين **áyna** *where*

طنطا **TánTaa** *Tanta (a town in Egypt)*

قريب **qariib** *near*

Exercise 2

The students at Suad's class begin to talk about their nationalities.
Listen to the recording, and work out where they all come from.

سعاد   أنا مصرية، وأنت يا مايك؟

مايك   أنا إنجليزي.

كايلي   أنا أسترالية.

يونس   أنا لبناني. أنا من بيروت.

ماري   أنا فرنسية.

a Su'ad

b Mike

c Kylie

d Younis

e Marie

2 هل تتكلم انجليزي؟ hal tatakállam inglíizii?
Do you speak English?

On a flight to Jordan, Julie, an English girl, gets talking to one of
the other passengers. Listen to the first part of the conversation
several times, and answer the questions.

Exercise 3

a Which language does the passenger *not* speak?

b Which language *does* he speak?

راكب   عن إذنك. من أين أنت؟

جولي   أنا من إنجلترا. وأنت؟

راكب   أنا من عمان. أنا أردني.

جولي   هل تتكلم إنجليزي؟

راكب   لا، مع الأسف، لا أتكلم إنجليزي. أتكلم عربي فقط.

راكب   تتكلمين العربية بطلاقة!

جولي   لا قليلة فقط.

عن إذنك :an ídhn-ik *excuse me, by your leave* (to a woman)

إنجلترا ingiltárra (with g as in garden) *England*

عمان :ammáan *Amman*

أردني úrduni *Jordanian*

تتكلم tatakállam *you speak* (to a man)

إنجليزي ingliizi *English*

مع الأسف má:a l-ásaf *I'm sorry* (lit: with the-sorrow)

لا laa *not*

أتكلم atakállam *I speak*

فقط fáqaT *only*

Exercise 4
Listen again, and find the Arabic for the following:
a do you speak English?
b a little

Now listen to the second part of the dialogue.

تتكلمين **tatakallamiin** *you speak* (to a woman)

العربية **al-:arabíyyah** *Arabic, the Arabic language* (more formal than **:árabi**)

بطلاقة **bi-Taláaqah** *fluently*

قليلة **qalíilah** *a little, few* (fem.)

فقط **fáqaT** *only*

Exercise 5
The passenger thinks Julie speaks good Arabic. True or false?

3 ما عملك؟ **maa :ámal-ak?** *What do you do?*

During the flight the passenger asks Julie what she does. Listen to the recording or read the text a few times.

Exercise 6
a What does Julie do at the moment?
b Where does the passenger work?

راكب ما عملك؟

جولي أنا طالبة في جامعة لندن. وأنت؟

راكب أنا طبيب في عمان.

ما عملك؟ **maa :ámal-ik** *what do you do?* (to a woman)

جامعة لندن **jáami:at lándan** *University (of) London*

طبيب **Tabíib** *doctor*

Exercise 7
Find the Arabic equivalent for:
a What do you do?
b I am a doctor.

al-mulaaHaDHáat (Notes) الملاحظات

Talking about your occupation

When you refer to a woman's profession in Arabic, add **-ah** (ة) to the masculine.

Masculine	*Feminine*	
طبيب **Tabíib**	طبيبة **Tabíibah**	*doctor*
طالب **Táalib**	طالبة	*student*
مدرس **mudárris**	مدرسة	*teacher*
مهندس **muhándis**	مهندسة	*engineer*
مدير **mudíir**	مديرة	*manager*
رئيس **ra'íis**	رئيسة	*boss*

محمد مدير **muHámmad mudíir**	*Mohammed is a manager*
ليلى مدرسة **láylaa mudárrisah**	*Leila is a teacher*

🎧 4 هل لندن مدينة كبيرة؟ hal lándan madíinah kabíirah? *Is London a big city?*

The passenger asks Julie about London.

Exercise 8

Listen to the recording and answer the questions.
a Name one of the places Julie mentions in London.
b Which institution does the passenger ask her about?

راكب   هل لندن مدينة كبيرة؟

جولي   نعم، هي مدينة كبيرة جدا. هناك متاحف كبيرة كثيرة
                وجسور ومحلات.

راكب   أين الجامعة؟

جولي   هي في وسط المدينة، قريبة من المتحف البريطاني.

متحف، متاحف **mátHaf, matáaHif** *museum*

كثيرة **kathíirah** *many, much* (fem.)

جسر، جسور **jisr, jusúur** *bridge*

محل، محلات **maHáll, maHalláat** *shop, store*

جامعة **jáami:ah** *university*

وسط **wasT** *middle*

تعبيرات رئيسية **ta:biiráat ra'iisíyyah (Key phrases)**

Asking someone's nationality and replying

أَأَنت مصري؟ **a-ánta míSrii?** (masc.)   *Are you Egyptian?*

أَأَنت مصرية؟ **a-ánti miSríyyah?** (fem.)

أنا سوداني **ána suudáanii** (masc.)   *I am Sudanese*

أنا سودانية **ána suudaaníyyah** (fem.)

Asking whether people speak a language and replying

هل تتكلم/تتكلمين عربي؟   *Do you speak Arabic?*
hal tatakállam/tatakallamíin :árabi?   (to a man/woman)

أتكلم إنجليزي **atakállam ingliizi**   *I speak English*

لا أتكلم عربي **laa atakállam :árabi**   *I don't speak Arabic*

بطلاقة **bi-Taláaqah**   *fluently*

قليل **qalíil**   *a little*

يتكلم فرنساوي **yatakállam faransáawi***   *he speaks French*

تتكلم عربي **tatakállam :árabi**   *she speaks Arabic*

*A variant of **faránsi**, usually used when referring to the language.

Asking someone's occupation

‏ما عملك؟‎ maa :ámal-ak?   *What is your work?*

‏أنا طبيب‎ ána Tabíib   *I am a doctor.*

‏تراكيب اللغة‎ taraakíib al-lúghah (Structures)

1 Masculine and Feminine

All words in Arabic are either masculine or feminine in gender, as
in French and Spanish. Where we use the word *it* in English for
objects, Arabic uses *he* or *she* depending on the gender of the
object.

‏المكتب نظيف‎ al-máktab naDHíif   *the office is clean*

‏هو نظيف‎ húwa naDHíif   *it is clean*

‏الجامعة بعيدة‎   *the university is far (away)*
al-jáami:ah ba:íidah

‏هي بعيدة‎ híya ba:íidah   *it is far (away)*

2 Feminine Endings

There is no marker for masculine words, but most feminine words
are marked by the ending ‏ة‎ .

This is pronounced as a weak **h** sound, and is always preceded by
an **a**-vowel, which is not written. The ending has been transcribed
as **-ah** in this book.

Note

A few Arabic words for female family members, for example ‏أم‎
umm, *mother*, have no feminine gender marker, but are naturally
dealt with as feminine.

3 Agreement

Adjectives agree in gender, number and definiteness with the noun they are describing. This applies to all three types of construction you have already met: indefinite phrases, definite phrases and *is* sentences.

حقيبة ثقيلة **Haqíibah thaqíilah**   *a heavy bag*

الميدان الكبير **al-maydáan al-kabíir**   *the big square*

الغرفة وسخة **al-ghúrfah wásikhah**   *the room is dirty*

Unless otherwise stated, you can assume that the feminine of any word is formed by adding ة as shown above.

العربية لغة جميلة
al-:arabíyyah lúghah jamíilah
Arabic is a beautiful language

4 Nationality adjectives

To form a masculine adjective, add ـي (**-ii**) to the name of the country. To form a feminine adjective, add ـية (**-íyyah**):

مصر **miSr** *Egypt*   مصري/مصرية
                                       míSrii/miSríyyah *Egyptian*

لبنان **lubnáan** *Lebanon*   لبناني/لبنانية
                                       lubnáanii/lubnaaníyyah *Lebanese*

The final **-ii** of the masculine is technically **-iyy**, but this does not normally reflect in the pronunciation. Where the name of a country ends in **-aa** or **-ah**, this is omitted:

بريطانيا **briiTáanya** *Britain*   بريطاني/بريطانية
                                       briiTáanii/briiTaaníyyah *British*

أمريكا **amríikaa** *America*   أمريكي/أمريكية
                                         amríikii/amriikíyyah *American*

مكة **mákkah** *Mecca*   مكي/مكية
                                         mákki/makkíyyah *Meccan*

Many Arabic place names have the word *the* (**al-**) in front of them, as in English *Canada*, but *the United States*. When this occurs, the Arabic **al-** is omitted from the nationality adjective.

المغرب **al-mághrib** *Morocco*   مغربي/مغربية **mághribii/ maghribíyyah** *Moroccan*

الكويت **al-kuwáyt** *Kuwait*   كويتي/كويتية **kuwáytii/kuwaytíyyah** *Kuwaiti*

Note
Some of these adjectives take slightly different forms from those given above, but these will be pointed out as we come to them.

5 More than one

There are no particular rules for forming Arabic plurals, and they should be learned along with the singular, as they are given in the vocabulary. The word **al-** the does not change in the plural.

الغرفة **al-ghúrfah**   *the room*

الغرف **al-ghúraf**   *the rooms*

Important note
Arabic has a special formation for saying two of anything (see Unit 9).

6 Plurals of People and Objects.

Plurals of objects and abstracts are regarded in Arabic as feminine singular. So all adjectives agree by using their feminine singular and the pronoun **híya** she is used to refer to them.

كتب طويلة **kútub Tawíilah**   *long books*

الكتب الطويلة **al-kútub aT-Tawíilah**   *the long books*

الكتب طويلة **al-kútub Tawíilah**   *The books are long*

هي طويلة **híya Tawíilah**   *They are long*

7 Talking about one of something.

The word for *one* is an adjective, and therefore comes after its noun and agrees with it like any other adjective.

فندق واحد **fúnduq wáaHid**   *one hotel*

غرفة واحدة **ghúrfah wáHidah**   *one room*

8 The verb *to speak*

Here are the singular present tense forms of the verb *to speak*.

أتكلم **atakállam** *I speak*

تتكلم **tatakállam** *you speak* (masc)

تتكلمين **tatakallamíin** *you speak* (fem)

يتكلم **yatakállam** *he speaks*

تتكلم **tatakállam** *she speaks*

Note that the *you* masc. and *she* forms are identical.

هل يتكلم جون عربي؟   *Does John speak Arabic?*
hal yatakállam juun :árabi?

يتكلم عربي بطلاقة   *He speaks Arabic fluently*
yatakállam :árabi bi-Taláaqah

أوزان الكلمات awzáan al-kalimáat (Word shapes)

Pattern	Arabic example	Eng. sound-alike
maC¹C²uuC³	**mashgúul** مشغول	*Mam(e)luke*

This word pattern expresses something or someone to which an action has been done, called a *passive participle* in English.

mamlúuk is an Arabic word meaning *owned*, as the Mam(e)luke rulers in Egypt originally were, having been brought in as soldier slaves.

An example of this pattern is **mashghúul**, coming from the root **sh-gh-l**, *work/ occupation*; so **mashghúul** means *occupied/made to work,* i.e. *busy.*

The **ma-** never changes. It is a prefix, and can be applied to any root, but is not part of it.

Here are some more examples:

مكتوم **maktúum**	*concealed*
مكتوب **maktúub**	*written*
مسموح **masmúuH**	*permitted*
ممنوع **mamnúu:**	*forbidden*
مبصوط **mabSúuT**	*contented, happy*
مفروض **mafrúuDH**	*necessary, obligatory*

ممنوع التدخين

NO SMOKING

تمرينات tamriináat (Practice)

Exercise 9
Listen to the recording and work out which country these people say they come from. The countries are listed on page 65.

a مرحبا، أنا مغربية **márHaban, ánaa maghribíyyah**

b صباح الخير، أنا أردني **SabáaH al-khayr, ána úrdunii**

c أهلا، أنا عماني **áhlan, ánaa :umáanii**

d مرحبا، أنا بحرينية **márHaban, ánaa baHrayníyyah**

e وأنا كويتي wa-ánaa kuwáytii

١ عمان   ٢ الأردن   ٣ الكويت   ٤ المغرب   ٥ البحرين

Exercise 10

How many of the countries below do you recognise? Match them
with their corresponding nationality and language.

Country	Nationality	Language
a إيطاليا	**1** تونسي	**A** الأسبانية
b هولندا	**2** أسترالي	**B** العربية
c إسبانيا	**3** ألماني	**C** الهولندية
d أستراليا	**4** إيطالي	**D** الألمانية
e تونس	**5** فرنسي	**E** الإيطالية
f ألمانيا	**6** إسباني	**F** الفرنسية
g فرنسا	**7** هولندي	**G** الإنجليزية

Exercise 11

Michael is writing to an Arabic-speaking friend about someone he's
met. Read this excerpt from his letter, and answer the questions.

a What is her name?
b Where does she come from?

... اسمها سلمى وهي سورية من دمشق. تتكلم اللغة العربية
والانجليزية والفرنسية. هي مدرسة.

Find the Arabic for the following expressions:

c *her name is Salma*
d *she speaks Arabic*

Exercise 12

Read (or listen to) the following information about Martin Romano.

مارتن رومانو من أمريكا. هو طالب. يتكلم انجليزي و إيطالي
بطلاقة وعربي قليلا.

Martin is registering with a college in Cairo for an evening class. The secretary asks him some questions about himself. Imagine that you are Martin. How would you answer the following questions?

السكرتيرة ما اسمك؟

مارتن

السكرتيرة ما جنسيتك؟

مارتن

السكرتيرة ما عملك؟

مارتن

السكرتيرة هل تتكلم عربي؟

مارتن

السكرتيرة تتكلم إنجليزي بطلاقة طبعا؟

مارتن

السكرتيرة وأية لغة غير الإنجليزية؟

مارتن

أية (fem.) which
قليلا qaliilan slightly, a bit

Exercise 13
Supply the correct adjective endings from the masculine form given in brackets.

١ السكرتيرة (مشغول)
٢ الأهرام (المصري) (مشهور)
٣ الفيلم (جديد)
٤ السيارة (الكبير) (أمريكي)

٥ سميرة طالبة (جديد)

٦ هل اللغة (الانجليزي) (نافع)؟

٧ هناك في دبي فنادق (جديد) (كثير)

٨ هناك في الميدان صيدلية (واحد)

٩ فاطمة بنت (سعيد)

مشهور **mashhúur** *famous*

صيدلية، ـات **Saydalíyyah, -aat** *pharmacy*

فندق، فنادق **fúnduq, fanáadiq** *hotel*

سعيد **sa:íid** *happy, joyful*

Exercise 14

What are the professions of these people? Write a sentence using a
personal pronoun, as in the example.

 هو طبيب أسنان **húwa Tabíib asnáan**

He is a dentist

4 | هذا وذلك
háadhaa wa-dháalik
This and that

In this unit you will learn:
- how to tell the time
- how to ask about opening times
- the days of the week
- the numbers 11–20
- how to form phrases and sentences with *this, that, those,* etc.

🎧 1 أين المتاحف؟ áyna l-matáaHif? *Where are the museums?*

Bridget and Jim Hayes are visiting Sharjah, and an Arabic-speaking friend, Hassan, is showing them around. Today they plan to visit some of the new museums in the city.

Exercise 1
Listen to the recording several times. Then answer the questions.
a What does Hassan point out on the map first?
b Why don't they want to go to the Natural History Museum?
c Which museum do they decide to visit eventually?

حسن   هذه خريطة الشارقة. هذه هي المدينة القديمة،

          وهذا سوق السمك.

جيم   أين المتاحف؟

حسن   هذه هي المتاحف، هنا وهنا. هذا هو متحف الفنون،

    وهذا هو متحف التاريخ الطبيعي في شارع المطار.

بريجت　ذلك المتحف بعيد.

جيم　نعم، هذا صحيح. انظري، متحف الحصن هنا في شارع
البرج. هو متحف ممتاز، ومن الممكن أن نذهب إلى
المدينة القديمة بعد ذلك.

بريجت　حسنا. نذهب إلى متحف الحصن.

Exercise 2

Link the English phrases to their Arabic equivalents.

a This is the Old Town.

b That museum is far away.

c That's true.

d Maybe we can go to the Old Town.

١ من الممكن أن نذهب إلى المدينة القديمة.

٢ ذلك المتحف بعيد.

٣ هذا صحيح.

٤ هذه هي المدينة القديمة.

هذا/هذه **háadha/háadhihi** *this* (masc./fem.)

خريطة، خرائط **khariiTah, kharáa'iT** *map*

الشارقة **ash-sháariqah** *Sharjah*

سوق، أسواق **suuq, aswáaq** *market* (this word is sometimes
regarded as feminine)

سمك **sámak** *fish* (collective)

هنا **húnaa** *here*

تاريخ **taaríikh** *history*

طبيعي **Tabii:ii** *natural*

فن، فنون **fann, funúun** *art*

شارع، شوارع **sháari:, shawáari:** *street, road*

مطار، ـات **maTáar, -aat** *airport*

ذلك **dháalik(a)** *that* (masc.)

بـعيد **ba:iid** *far away, distant*

صحيح **SaHíiH** *true*

انظري **únDHuri** *look!* (to a woman)

حصن، حصون **HiSn, HuSúun** *fort, fortress*

برج، أبراج **burj, abráaj** *tower*

من الممكن أن **min al-múmkin an** *maybe* (before a verb)

نذهب **nádhhab** *we go*

بـعد **ba:d** *after*

🎧 **2** يقفل الساعة كم؟ **yáqfil as-sáa:ah kam?**
What time does it close?

Hassan, Jim and Bridget arrive at the museum. They ask the attendant about opening hours.

First look at the section on asking the time, then listen to the audio a few times.

Exercise 3
a What times does the museum close for lunch?
b When does it open again?
c What is the time now?
d What does the attendant give them?

حسن صباح الخير. المتحف يقفل الساعة كم؟

مسؤولة المتحف يقفل الساعة واحدة ويفتح الساعة

أربعة بعد الظهر.

بريجت كم الساعة الآن؟

حسن الساعة عشرة وربع.

بريجت حسنا، عندنا وقت كثير.

مسؤولة المتحف مرحبا، تفضلوا. هذا هو كتيّب عن المتحف.

حسن شكرا.

Exercise 4
Link the English phrases to the appropriate Arabic.

a It closes. ١ يفتح.

b It opens. ٢ الساعة عشرة وربع.

c What's the time? ٣ هذا هو كتيّب عن المتحف.

d It's a quarter past ten. ٤ يقفل.

e Welcome, come in. ٥ مرحبا، تفضلوا.

f This is a brochure of the museum. ٦ الساعة كم؟

يقفل **yáqfil** *he/it closes, shuts*

مسؤول، ـون **mas'úul, -uun** *official*

مسؤول المتحف **mas'úul al-mátHaf** *attendant, official of the museum*

ساعة، ـات **sáa:ah, -aat** *hour, time, watch, clock*

الساعة كم؟ **as-sáa:ah kam (at)** *what time?*

يفتح **yáftaH** *he/it opens*

أربعة **árba:ah** *four*

ظهر **DHuhr** *noon*

بعد الظهر **ba:d aDH-DHuhr** *(in) the afternoon*

الآن **al-'áan** *now*

عشرة **:áshrah** *ten*

ربع **rub:** *quarter*

عشرة وربع **:áshrah wa-rub:** *quarter past ten*

عندنا **:índ-naa** *we have*

وقت، أوقات **waqt, awqáat** *time*

كثير **kathíir** *much, many*

مرحبا **márHaban** *welcome*

تفضلوا **tafáDDaluu** *come in, here you are* (plural): used when inviting someone to come in, sit down, or when giving them something. The final *alif* is not pronounced.

كتيّب **kutáyyib** *booklet, brochure*

عن **:an** *concerning, about*

3 مواقيت المتحف mawaaqíit al-mátHaf

Museum opening times

Exercise 5
Read the notice for the museum opening
times, and answer the questions.

مـــــواقـــــيت المتـــحـــف
يوم السبت ٩،٠٠ – ١٣،٠٠ و١٧.٠٠ – ٢٠،٠٠
يوم الأحد ٩،٠٠ – ١٢،٠٠ و١٧.٠٠ – ٢٠،٠٠
يوم الاثنين إجازة
يوم الثلاثاء ٩،٠٠ – ١٣،٠٠ و١٧.٠٠ – ٢٠،٠٠
يوم الأربـعاء ٩،٠٠ – ١٣،٠٠ و١٧.٠٠ – ٢٠،٠٠
(الزيارة للنساء فقط)
يوم الخميس ٩،٠٠ – ١٣،٠٠ و١٧.٠٠ – ٢٠،٠٠
يوم الجمعة ١٦،٣٠ – ٢٠،٣٠

a When are women particularly welcome?
b Which day is the museum closed?
c When does the museum close on Friday evening?
d When does the museum usually open in the morning?
e On which day does the museum not open in the morning?
f How many days have the same opening times?

🎧 4 بكم...؟ bi-kam...? *How much does it cost?*

They go to the admission desk to buy tickets.

Exercise 6
Listen to the recording and answer the questions.
a How much does an adult ticket cost?
b How much does a child ticket cost?
c How much does Hassan have to pay?

السلام عليكم.	حسن
وعليكم السلام.	مسؤولة المتحف
التذكرة بكم من فضلك؟	حسن
البالغون بستة دراهم ، والأطفال بثلاثة دراهم.	مسؤولة المتحف
ثلاث تذاكر بستة دراهم من فضلك.	حسن
ثمانية عشر درهما من فضلك. شكرا. تفضلوا التذاكر.	مسؤولة المتحف
شكرا.	حسن

Exercise 7
Link the English to the appropriate Arabic expressions.

a How much is a ticket, please?

b Adults are six dirhams.

c Three six-dirham tickets, please.

d Here are the tickets.

١ البالغون بستة دراهم.

٢ ثلاث تذاكر بستة دراهم، من فضلك.

٣ تفضلوا التذاكر.

٤ التذكرة بكم، من فضلك؟

مسؤولة المتحف **mas'úulat al-mátHaf** *museum official*
(female)

تذكرة، تذاكر **tádhkirah,tadháakir** *ticket*

بكم **bi-kám** *how much* (lit. for how much)

بالغون **baalighúun** *adults*

ستة **sittah** *six*

درهم، دراهم **dírham, daráahim** *dirham* (unit of currency)

طفل، أطفال **Tifl, aTfáal** *child*

ثلاثة **thaláathah** *three*

ثمانية عشر **thamániyat :ashar** *eighteen*

تعبيرات رئيسية **ta:biiráat ra'iisíyyah (Key phrases)**

Asking and telling the time

الساعة كم؟ **as-sáa:ah kam?**   *What time is it?*

الساعة واحدة **as-sáa:ah wáaHidah** *It's one o'clock*

الساعة اثنين وربع/إلا ربع   *It's quarter past/*
as-sáa:ah ithnáyn wa-rub:/íllaa rub: *quarter to two*

الساعة ثلاثة و/إلا ثلث   *It's twenty past/to three*
as-sáa:ah thaláathah wa/íllaa thulth

الساعة عشرة ونصف   *It's half past ten*
as-sáa:ah :áshrah wa-níSf

Times of day

If it is not clear from the context whether the hour referred to is am or pm, Arabic has a set of words to indicate periods of the day which may be placed after stating the time:

الصبح aS-SúbH	*morning, forenoon*
الظهر aDH-DHúhr	*around noon*
بعد الظهر ba:d aDH-DHúhr	*afternoon*
العصر al-:áSr	*late afternoon* (about 4 pm)
المساء al-masáa'	*evening*
الليل al-layl	*night*

الساعة تسعة الصبح
as-sáa:ah tís:ah aS-SubH

nine o'clock in the morning

الساعة سبعة المساء
as-sáa:ah sáb:ah al-masáa'

seven o'clock at night

Asking about opening times

يفتح/يقفل الساعة كم؟
yáftaH/yáqfil as-sáa:ah kam

*What time does it
open/close?*

يفتح/يقفل الساعة سبعة
yáftaH/yáqfil as-sáa:ah sáb:ah

*It opens/closes at seven
o'clock*

The days of the week

يوم الأحد yawm al-áHad	*Sunday*
يوم الاثنين yawm al-ithnayn	*Monday*
يوم الثلاثاء yawm ath-thalaatháa'	*Tuesday*
يوم الأربعاء yawm al-arbi:áa'	*Wednesday*
يوم الخميس yawm al-khamíis	*Thursday*
يوم الجمعة yawm al-júm:ah	*Friday*
يوم السبت yawm as-sabt	*Saturday*

Sometimes the word **yawm** is omitted:

الغد الأحد **al-ghad al-áHad**   *tomorrow is Sunday*

More time-related words

اليوم **al-yawm**   *today*

الغد **al-ghad**   *tomorrow*

أمس **ams**   *yesterday*

بعد الغد **ba:d al-ghad**   *the day after tomorrow*

أمس الأول **ams al-áwwal**   *the day before yesterday*

قبل ثلاثة أيام   *three days ago*
qabl thaláathah ayyáam

بعد أربعة أيام   *in four days*
ba:d arba:ah ayyáam

Asking the price of something

التذكرة بكم؟   *How much is a ticket?*
at-taádhkirah bi-kám?

هذا بكم؟ **háadhaa bi-kám?**   *How much is this?*

هذا بخمسة دراهم   *This is five dirhams*
háadha bi-khámsah daráahim

بكم تلك المجلة؟   *How much is that*
bi-kám tílka l-majállah?   *magazine?*

هي بدينار واحد   *It is one dinar*
híya bi-diináar wáaHid

تراكيب اللغة taraakíib al-lúghah (Structures)

1 Demonstratives

The words *this, that*, etc. are called demonstratives. In English they behave in two ways.

• As an adjective: *This book is expensive*. The word *this* describes which book we mean.

• As a pronoun: *That was an excellent film*. Here the word *that* represents a noun (the film).

It will help you in the use of the Arabic demonstratives if you bear in mind that in Arabic they are always pronouns, and never adjectives. Arabic really says *this* (object, person) *the-big* (thing, one).

Singular

masc.	هذا المتحف **háadhaa l-mátHaf**	*this museum*
fem.	هذه الخريطة **háadhihi l-kharíiTah**	*this map*
masc.	ذلك الشارع **dháalika sh-sháari:**	*that street*
fem.	تلك المدينة **tilka l-madiinah**	*that town*

Plural*

هؤلاء الأطفال **haa'uláa'i l-aTfáal**	*these children*
أولائك البنات **uuláa'ika l-banáat**	*those girls*

*There is no difference between masculine and feminine in the plural words for *these* and *those*.

AGREEMENT

Demonstratives agree with their noun in gender:

háadhaa l-mátHaf

This(thing) the-museum

هذا المتحف

This museum (masc)

háadhihi l-madíinah

This(thing) the-town

هذه المدينة

This town (fem)

ADJECTIVES

Adjectives come after their nouns in the usual way.

háadha l-maktab al-jadíid

This(thing) the-office the-new(one)

هذا المكتب الجديد

This new office

háadhihi l-jaríidah t-tuunisíyyah

This(thing) the-newspaper
the-Tunisian(one)

هذه الجريدة التونسية

This Tunisian newspaper

DEMONSTRATIVE SENTENCES WITH INDEFINITES

háadhaa kitáab

this(thing) [is] book

هذا كتاب

This is a book

háadhihi sayyáarah

this (thing) [is] car

هذه سيارة

This is a car

dháalika qálam jadíid

that(thing) [is] pen new(one)

ذلك قلم جديد

That is a new pen

tílka jaríidah yawmíyyah

that (thing) [is] newspaper daily(one)

تلك جريدة يومية

That is a daily newspaper

DEMONSTRATIVE SENTENCES WITH DEFINITES

The pronoun agreeing with the subject noun is always put between the demonstrative and the rest of the sentence. This is necessary, as otherwise we would get a definite phrase (see Unit 1).

háadhaa sh-sháari:	هذا الشارع
this the-street	*This street*

háadhaa húwa sh-sháari:	هذا هو الشارع
this(thing) he [is] the-street	*This is the street*

tílka híya l-bint	تلك هي البنت
that(person) she [is] the-girl	*That's the girl*

The same procedure is often followed with names of people or places.

háadhaa húwa muHámmad	هذا هو محمد
This(person) he Muhammad	*This is Muhammad*

These/those with people:

haa'uláa'i l-awláad	هؤلاء الأولاد
	These boys

uuláa'ika l-banáat	أولاءك البنات
	Those girls

Remember that since plurals of inanimate objects are regarded in Arabic as being feminine singular, the demonstrative used is feminine singular and the pronoun used for *they* is actually *she*.

tílka híya l-kútub al-:arabíyyah	تلك هي الكتب العربية
These(things) they [are]	*These are the Arabic books*
the-books the-Arabic	

Spelling and pronunciation

a) Note that **háadhaa, haadhíhi** and **dháalika** are spelled with the dagger **alif** for the first long **a** (see page 21). This is usually omitted in print, but a normal **alif** <u>cannot</u> be used.

b) Although spelled long, the final vowel of **háadhaa** is usually pronounced short.

c) When these words – or any word ending in a vowel – come before **al-**, *the*, the **a** of the latter is omitted

هذا المتحف **háadhaa l-matHaf**

تلك المدرسة الكبيرة **tilka l-mádrasah l-kabíirah**

d) When **dháalika** comes at the end of a sentence, its final **a** is usually omitted.

2 Telling the time

The way of telling the time in Standard Arabic is complicated, and used only in the most formal situations. For this reason, the following section is given in the more common colloquial (transliterated) form, without Arabic script, except for the main terms.

as-sáa:ah wáaHidah

It's one o'clock

as-sáa:ah ithnáyn wa rúb:

the hour is two plus a quarter

as-sáa:ah thaláathah ílla thulth

the hour is three less a third of an hour, 20 minutes

s-sáa:ah iHdá:shar wa niSf

the hour is eleven and a half

Note that:

a) *one o'clock*, and in some dialects *two o'clock*, use the feminine form of the numeral (**wáaHidah, ithnáyn/thintáyn**)

b) *three o'clock* to *ten o'clock* inclusive use the independent form ending in **-ah**.

c) for *eleven* and *twelve o'clock* there is only one possible form.

d) **niSf**, *half*, is normally pronounced **nuSS**

e) For the English *past*, Arabic uses **wa** و, *and*

        as-sáa:ah iHdá:shar wa-rúb: *quarter past eleven*

f) For the English *to*, Arabic uses **ílla** إلّا, *except for, less*

        as-sáa:ah thaláathah ílla rúb: *quarter to three*

| **as-saa:ah sittah wa khams** | **as-saa:ah waaHidah wa nuSS** | **as-saa:ah arba:ah illa thilth** |

Twenty-five past and *twenty-five to* the hour are expressed in Arabic as 'the hour plus a half less five' and 'the hour plus a half plus five' respectively:

as-sáa:ah khámsah wa-niSf ílla khámsah *twenty five past five*

as-sáa:ah khámsah wa-niSf wa khámsah *twenty five to six*

More formally (and less commonly) all times can be stated using the preceding hour plus the number of minutes:

as-sáa:ah :ásharah wa khámsah wa-arba:íin daqíiqah *10:45*

دقيقة **daqíiqah** *minute*

This is the method used by speaking clocks and other automats, and also sometimes on official radio and television announcements. These, however, use the literary Arabic forms of the numbers, which differ significantly.

3 Saying at a particular time

Arabic requires no additional word, so **as-saa:ah khamsah** can mean *(it is) five o'clock* or *at five o' clock*.

4 Numbers 11–20

The numbers are given here in the colloquial form as they were in Unit 2.

11 iHdá:shar	**16 sittá:shar**
12 ithná:shar	**17 sab:atá:shar**
13 thalaathtá:shar	**18 thamantá:shar**
14 arba:atá:shar	**19 tis:atá:shar**
15 khamastá:shar	**20 :ishríin**

Note the common element (equivalent to English *-teen*) **á:shar**, which is a slightly altered form of the written **:áshar**.

Agreement with nouns

a) In written Arabic, the numbers must agree with their nouns in gender.

b) With the numbers 11–99 inclusive, the noun is in the accusative singular. This is shown on most nouns without an **-ah** ending by the **alif** accusative marker, and pronounced **-an** in formal speech (see Script and Pronunciation).

أربعة عشر كتابا **arba:atá:shar kitáaban** *14 books*, but

خمسة عشر تذكرة **khamastá:shar tádhkirah** *15 tickets*

c) In Arabic the noun is plural only after the numerals 3–10 inclusive.

خمسة بيوت **khámsah buyúut** *five houses*

5 Asking the price of something

Here Arabic uses the preposition **bi-**:

هذا بكم؟ **háadhaa bi-kám?**   *How much is this?*

هذا بخمسة دراهم
háadha bi-khámsah daráahim

This is five dirhams

بكم تلك المجلة؟
bi-kám tílka l-majállah?

*How much is that
magazine?*

هي بدينار واحد
híya bi-diináar wáaHid

It is one dinar

أوزان الكلمات awzáan al-kalimáat (Word shapes)

Pattern	Arabic example	Eng. sound-alike
maC¹C²aC³	máktab مكتب office, desk	*madman*

This shape usually represents a place where the action of the root
takes place.

The root **k-t-b** refers to *writing*, so **máktab** means *a desk* or *an
office*, i.e. a place where you write.

Sometimes this pattern adds a feminine ending **-ah**. Thus, from the
root **d-r-s** to do with *studying* we have **mádrasah** مدرسة,
meaning a place of study, i.e. *a school*. Occasionally the two forms
exist side by side:

 مكتب **máktab**   *office*

مكتبة **máktabah**   *library, bookshop*

Other examples:

مدخل **mádkhal**   *entrance*

مخرج **mákhraj**   *exit*

متحف **mátHaf**   *museum*

ملعب **mál:ab**   *playing field*

مسرح **másraH**   *theatre*

مسبح **másbaH**   *swimming pool*

مقبرة **máqbarah**   *cemetery*

تمرينات **tamriináat (Practice)**

Exercise 8

Listen to the times of day on the recording or read the transcript, and look at the times below. Decide in each case what the correct time is.

a as-sáa:ah wáaHidah wa-niSf

b as-sáa:ah sáb:ah ílla khámsah

c as-sáa:ah :ásharah wa-rub:

d as-sáa:ah khámsah

e as-sáa:ah tís:ah aS-SubH

a 1:15, 1:20 or 1:30?

b 6:25, 6:35 or 6:55?

c 10:15, 10:30 or 10:45?

d 4:55, 5:00 or 5:05?

e 9:00am or 9:00pm?

Exercise 9

Ask what time it is, and say the time shown on the clock. Listen to the recording or read the transcript to see if you are right.

Example:

as-sáa:ah kam? *What time is it?*

as-sáa:ah thamáanyah *It is eight o' clock*

Exercise 10

Do you remember the days of the week? See if you can fill in the gaps in these sentences in Arabic.

١ اليوم .... الثلاثاء

٢ الغد ....

٣ كان .... يوم الاثنين

٤ كان أمس الأول ....

٥ .... يوم الخميس

٦ .... بعد ثلاثة أيام

Exercise 11

Your Arabic-speaking friend is showing you some photographs of his home and family which you visited last year. Choose the correct demonstrative.

١ هذا/هذه هو البيت الجديد.

٢ هذا/هذه هي الأشجار في الحديقة.

٣ أولائك/ذلك هم الأولاد.

٤ هذا/هذه هي فاطمة.

٥ أولائك/تلك هم الجيران.

٦ ذلك/تلك هي القوارب في البحر.

شجرة، أشجار **shájarah, ashjáar** tree

حديقة، حدائق **Hadíiqah, Hadáa'iq** garden, park

جار، جيران **jaar, jiiráan** neighbour

قارب، قوارب **qáarib, qawáarib** (small) boat

بحر، بحار **baHr, biHáar** sea, large river

Exercise 12

Write out the following dates in English in numerical fashion, e.g.
10/6/1989 (day/month/year). Watch the direction of writing!

١ – ٣\١٢\١٩٥٢

٢ – ١٩\١١\١٩٦٧

٣ – ١\١\٢٠٠٠

٤ – ٢٨\٢\١٩٩٠

٥ – ١٧\٤\١٨٣٦

Exercise 13

You want to buy tickets for a performance at the National Theatre in Kuwait. Fill in your side of the dialogue, guided by the translation below.

أنت

كاتب   مساء النور.

أنت

كاتب   التذكرة بأربعة دنانير.

أنت

كاتب   ١٦ دينارا من فضلك.

أنت

كاتب   شكرا.

أنت

كاتب   يفتح الساعة سبعة، والمسرحية تبتدئ الساعة

سبعة ونصف.

أنت

1 Say good evening
2 Ask how much a ticket costs
3 Ask for four tickets
4 Offer the ticket clerk your money
5 Ask the ticket clerk when the theatre opens
6 Say thank you

مبلغ، مبالغ **máblagh, mabáaligh** *sum of money*

مسرحية، ـات **masraHíyyah, -aat** *play* (theatrical)

تبتدئ **tabtádi'** *she/it begins*

Now answer the following questions.

a How much does a ticket cost?

b When does the theatre open?

c When does the play begin?

Exercise 14

Write out the following times in transliteration, and practise saying them out loud.

a ٦:٣٥

b ٨:١٠

c ٩:٢٥

d ٧:٠٠

e ٣:٤٥

f ٥:٣٠

g ١:١٥

h ١٢:٥٥

i ٣:٢٠

j ١٠:٠٥

5 بيتنا بيتكم
báyt-naa báyt-kum
Our house is your house

In this unit you will learn:
- how to talk about your family
- how to say who things belong to
- how to describe them
- the numbers 21–100

🎧 1 هذه هي زوجتي háadhihi híya záwjat-ii
This is my wife

Hamed has invited his English friend Tom to his flat in Cairo for dinner. The whole family is there, so Tom has the chance to meet them all.

Exercise 1
Listen to the dialogue, and answer the following questions.
a Who does Hamed introduce to Tom first?
b How old is Tamiim?
c How old is their daughter?
d Are Tom's children older or younger than Hamed's?

حامد	تفضل يا توم!
توم	شكرا يا حامد.
حامد	هذه هي زوجتي سلمى. سلمى، هذا توم، من المكتب.
توم	مساء الخير يا سلمى، كيف حالك؟
سلمى	بخير الحمد لله. أهلا وسهلا. و كيف حالك أنت؟

توم   الحمد لله. هذه هدية لك!

سلمى   شكرا يا توم. هذا والدي، وهذه والدتي... وهذا ابننا تميم.
         تفضل، اجلس.

توم   تميم كم عمره؟

سلمى   عمره ١٥ سنة، وبنتنا فريدة عمرها ٢١ سنة.

حامد   أولادك أنت، كم عمرهم، يا توم؟

توم   أولادنا صغار – ابننا عمره ٥ سنوات، وبنتنا
         عمرها ٣ سنوات.

Exercise 2
Find the Arabic for:
a This is my father.
b Please sit down.
c This is our son.
d How old are your children?
e Our daughter is three years old.

زوجة **záwjah** wife

زوجتي **záwjat-ii** my wife (see below for possessive pronouns)

لك **lá-ki** for you (to a woman)

تفضل **tafáDDal** come in (to a man)

أهلا وسهلا **áhlan wa-sáhlan** welcome!

هدية، هدايا **hadíyyah, hadáayaa** present, gift

والد **wáalid** father

والدة **wáalidah** mother

ابن، أبناء **ibn, abnáa'** son

اجلس **ijlis** sit down! (to a man)

كم عمره **kam :úmr-uh** how old is he?

> سنة، سنوات **sánah, sanawáat** year
>
> بنت، بنات **bint, banáat** girl, daughter
>
> صغار **Sigháar** young, small (plural)

معلومات ثقافية ma:luumáat thaqaafíyyah (Cultural tips)

Within the framework of the Islamic way of life, customs vary widely in the Arab world. For example, in the more conservative areas, a man visiting a family will never see any of the women, and should not even ask about them. However, in more liberal countries, he can behave much as he would in a European country. It is best to err on the safe side until you are sure of your ground, taking your cue from your hosts.

In very traditional areas, if a man is invited with his wife, she may be taken to the women's quarters on arrival and be entertained and fed with the women, while her husband stays with the men. She will be reunited with her husband when they are leaving.

تعبيرات رئيسية ta:biiráat ra'iisíyyah (Key phrases)

Introducing people

هذا توم **háadha Tom**   *This is Tom* (for a man)

هذه هي زوجتي، سلمى   *This is my wife, Salma*
háadhihi híya záwjat-ii, sálma (for a woman)

Asking people how they are and saying how you are

كيف حالك **káyfa Háal-ak**   *How are you?* (to a man),

káyfa Háal-ik   (to a woman)

Note: Arabic spelling is the same.

أنا بخير الحمد لله   *I'm well, praise be to God*
ána bi-kháyr, al-Hámdu li-Láah

Welcoming people to your home

تفضل tafáDDal   *Come in*

اجلس íjlis   *Sit down*

أهلا وسهلا áhlan wa-sáhlan   *Welcome*

Asking and saying how old someone is

تميم كم عمره؟   *How old is Tamim?*
tamíim kam :umr-uh   (lit. how much his-life)

عمره ٨ سنوات umr-uh: 8 sanawáat   *He is eight years old*

Members of the family

والد/أب wáalid/ab*   *father*

والدة/أم wáalidah/umm   *mother*

ابن ibn   *son*

بنت bint   *girl, daughter*

أولاد awláad   *boys, children*

أخ akh*   *brother*

أخت، أخوات ukht, akhawáat   *sister*

زوج zawj   *husband*

زوجة záwjah   *wife*

عم/خال ámm/kháal: *uncle*

Note: Arabic distinguishes here. **:ámm** is your father's brother,
kháal is your mother's brother.

عمة/خالة ámmah/kháalah: *aunt* (see note above)

جد jadd	*grandfather*
جدة jáddah	*grandmother*
ابن عم/خال ibn :amm/khaal	*(male) cousin*
	(father's/mother's side)
بنت عم/خال bint :amm/khaal	*(female) cousin*

* The words **akh**, *brother*, and **ab**, *father*, are irregular nouns (see Unit 18 for details). All you need to know now is that they take a long vowel (usually **uu**) before most of the possessive pronouns given later in this lesson. For *father* you can also use the regular **wáalid**, but for *brother* there is no alternative.

🎧 Numbers 21–100

Exercise 3
Listen to the recording and repeat each number as you hear it, and fill in the blanks with the missing numbers.

.... 44/٤٤	:ishriin 20/٢٠
khamsiin 50/٥٠	wáaHid wa-:ishriin 21/٢١
wa-khamsiin wáaHid 51/٥١	ithnáyn wa-:ishriin 22/٢٢
.... 57/٥٧	thaláathah wa-:ishriin 23/٢٣
sittiin 60/٦٠	árba:ah wa-:ishriin 24/٢٤
thaláathah wa-sittiin 63/٦٣	khámsah wa-:ishriin 25/٢٥
.... 68/٦٨	síttah wa-:ishriin 26/٢٦
sab:iin 70/٧٠	sab:ah wa-:ishriin 27/٢٧
.... 76/٧٦	thamáaniyah wa-:ishriin 28/٢٨
thamaaniin 80/٨٠	tís:ah wa-:ishriin 29/٢٩
.... 85/٨٥	thalaathiin 30/٣٠
tis:iin 90/٩٠	wáaHid wa-thalaathiin 31/٣١
.... 99/٩٩	.... 33/٣٣
miiyah 100/١٠٠	arba:iin ....
	ithnáyn wa-arba:iin 42/٤٢

Tens with units

Units are placed before the tens:

٢٣/23 thaláathah wa-:ishríin   *three and-twenty*

٦٥/65 khámsah wa-sittíin   *five and-sixty*

Pronunciation

The tens have a slightly different written form ending in **-uun** ـون
in some contexts, but they are universally pronounced with the **-iin**
ending in everyday speech. They are easy to remember, as, with
the exception of *twenty*, they closely resemble the equivalent unit
numbers, with the addition of **-iin**.

تراكيب اللغة taraakíib al-lúghah (Structures)

Possessive pronouns

Possessives describe who or what something belongs to. English
expresses this in several ways:

This is my shirt.

This shirt is mine.

This shirt belongs to me.

There are several points to note in Arabic:

a) Written Arabic has only one way to express the possessive,
   using the equivalents of English *my, your, his,* etc. We call these
   words possessive pronouns. There is no equivalent in Arabic of
   the English *mine, yours,* etc. In Arabic these pronouns are
   suffixes, which are joined on to the object which is possessed:

> *their house* becomes in Arabic بيتهم **báyt-hum** house-their;
>
> *this is my car* becomes هذه سيارتي **háadhihi sayyáarat-i**
> this(-one) [is] car(-my) (see below for spelling)

b) Arabic distinguishes, in the case of *his* and *her, your* and *their*
   (but not *my* or *our*), whether the owner of the thing is a male or

female. In the following list (and throughout this book) some of these possessive pronouns are given in a slightly simplified form, much as they are used in spoken Arabic.

c) Since they are suffixes, the Arabic script versions of these pronouns have been given here as if they were joined to a word ending in a joining letter.

Singular		**Plural**	
ـي **-ii** *my*		ـنا **-na(a)** *our*	
ـك **-ak** *your* (masc.)		ـكم **-kum** *your* (masc.)	
ـك **-ik** *your* (fem.)		كن **kúnna** *your* (fem.)	
ـه **-uh** *his*		ـهم **-hum** *their* (masc.)	
ـها **-ha(a)** *her*		ـهن **-húnna** *their* (fem.)	

Pronunciation

1 **-haa** and **-naa** are generally pronounced short, although written with long vowels.

2 There are the following changes in pronunciation that are not reflected in the Arabic script:

After words ending in long vowels or **-ay**:

- **-ii**, *my*, becomes **-ya**.

   يداي **yadáa-ya** *my hands* (**yadaa** *hands*)

- **-ak** and **-uh** lose their vowels:

   يداك، يداه **yadáa-k, yadáa-h**

- **-ik** becomes **-ki**

   يداك **yadáa-ki**

When preceded by **i**, **ii** or **ay**:

- **-hum** and *-hunna* change to **-him** and **-hinna**:

   مبانيهم **mabaaníi-him** *their buildings*

The hidden *t*

You will remember that ة is the most common feminine ending in Arabic and is written with a hybrid letter, a cross between **h** and **t**. In possessives where the feminine word is the possessed or owned object, the ة **h** changes into an ordinary ت **t**.

السيارة الجديدة	-the-car the new-one
as-sayyáarah l-jadíidah	*the new car*
سيارته الجديدة	car-his the new-one
sayyáarat-uh al-jadíidah	*his new car*

Definites

All Arabic possessives are regarded as definite, and follow the agreement rules for definites. This is because if you say *my book*, you are referring to one specific book.

a-háadha báyt-ak?

أهذا بيتك؟

[?]This(thing) house-your?

Is this your house?

ná:am, háadha báyt-i.

نعم، هذا بيتي.

Yes, this(thing) house-my

Yes, this is my house

a-haadhíhi sayyaarát-haa?

أهذه سيارتها؟

[?]This(thing) car-her?

Is this her car?

laa, láysat haadhíhi sayyaarát-haa.

لا، ليست هذه سيارتها.

No, is-not this(thing) car-her

No, this is not her car

> ليست **láysat** *is not* (fem.)

أوزان الكلمات awzáan al-kalimáat (Word shapes)

Pattern	Arabic example	Eng. sound-alike
C¹uC²úuC³	بيوت **buyúut** houses	*Toulouse*

This shape usually represents one of two things:

a) The plural of simple nouns whose singular shape is C¹vC²C³.

b-y-t singular **bayt** *house* ➔ plural **buyúut** *houses*

فلس/فلوس **fils/fulúus** *piastre, small unit of currency*

شعب/شعوب **sha:b/shu:úub** *people, folk*

b) Nouns expressing the action of a verb – usually formed in English by adding the ending *-ing* (e.g. *do* ➔ *doing*, *think* ➔ *thinking*). In English we call this a verbal noun.

دخول **dukhúul** from **d-kh-l** *enter*, meaning *entering, entrance*

خروج **khurúuj** from **kh-r-j** *exiting, leaving*; *the act of going out*

Note that as is the case with many shapes, CuCuuC cannot be formed from every noun or verb root. The benefit of learning the shapes is in recognition, not formation. However, any noun which you come across in this form will be either a plural or a verbal noun.

تمرينات tamriináat (Practice)

Exercise 4

Put the following numbers into numerical order:

٦٧   ٣١   ٥٨   ٩٦   ٢٤   ٨٨   ٤٢   ٥٣   ٢٨   ١٤

Exercise 5

You are planning a camping trip with some Arab friends and see the following advertisement in an Arabic paper. You want to tell your friends about it. Read aloud the prices of the items below several times. Then listen to the recording to check that you were correct.

a ٩٩ درهم
b ٨٩ درهم
c ٦٥ درهم
d ٥٠ درهم
e ٤٢ درهم
f ٧٩ درهم
g ٢٥ درهم

Exercise 6

You have invited an Arab friend and her husband for dinner. Match the English phrases with the appropriate Arabic ones.

a Please come in.

b This is my husband.

c How are you? (to a man)

d This is a present for you. (to a woman)

e Sit down.

f Welcome.

١– هذا هو زوجي.

٢– أهلا وسهلا.

٣– كيف حالك؟

٤– تفضل.

٥– اجلس.

٦– هذه هدية لك .

Exercise 7

Fill in the gaps with a possessive, using the correct suffix endings.
The first one has been done for you.

١– قميص .... وسخ. (قميصك وسخ.)

٢– والدة .... إيطالية.

٣– هرم .... هو الكبير.

٤– هذه أخت .... مريم.

٥– ليست هذه السيارة سيارة ....

٦– أهذا مكتب .... الجديد؟

٧– جد .... من تونس.

٨– أين حقائب ....؟

1 Your shirt is dirty!
2 My mother is Italian.
3 My pyramid is the big one.
4 This is my sister Miriam.
5 This car is not mine.
6 Is this his new office?
7 Their grandfather is
  from Tunis.
8 Where are our suitcases?

 حقيبة، حقائب **Haqiibah, Haqáa'ib** bag, suitcase

Exercise 8

Study the family tree below, then answer the questions in Arabic.

i Imagine that you are Salma, and answer the questions.

Example: من أخوك **man akhúu-ki** *Who is your brother?*

Answer. أخي أحمد **ákh-ii áHmad** *My brother is Ahmed.*

من **man** *who?*

a Who is your husband?; b Who is your mother?; c Who are your children?

ii What relation are the following people to Ahmed?

Example: سميرة **samíirah**

Answer: هي زوجته **híya záwjat-uh** *She is his wife.*

a Bassam; b Fatima; c Suleiman; d Salma

iii Answer the following questions in Arabic.

a What relation is Fatimah to Fahad?; b What relation is Khalid to Bassam?; c What relation is Suleiman to Bassam, Noor and Fatima?

6 | أين وسط المدينة؟

áyna wásaT al-madíinah?

Where is the town centre?

In this unit you will learn:

- to give simple directions
- about more places in town and their location
- to say what belongs to whom

🎧 1 أين وسط المدينة من فضلك áyna wásaT al-madíinah, min fáDl-ak *Where is the town centre, please?*

Andy Fraser, a Scot working in Jordan, has to go to a small town near Amman to visit a client. He stops a passer-by to ask directions.

Exercise 1

Listen to the recording once, then answer these questions.

a What does Andy say to get the man's attention?

b Is the first thing Andy has to look out for:

    i   a mosque?

    ii   traffic lights?

    iii   King Hussein Street?

c In which direction should he turn at the traffic lights?

Listen to the recording again.

d How far should he go along the street?

e What is the office next to?

f Is the car park:

    i   on the left?

    ii   on the right?

    iii   behind the office?

Now read the dialogue.

أندي   عن إذنك! أين وسط المدينة؟

الرجل على طول. إلى أين تذهب؟

أندي   أذهب إلى مكتب علي المبروك. هل تعرفه؟ هذه هي خريطة المدينة.

الرجل نعم، أعرفه. خلني أفكر. نعم هو هنا. بعد الجامع الكبير لف شمال عند الإشارة. هذا شارع الملك حسين. إذهب على طول حوالي ١٠٠ متر.

أندي   نعم، أنا فاهم.

الرجل مكتب علي المبروك على اليمين، بجانب محطة البنزين، أمام سينما البلازا

أندي   نعم، أشكرك. هل هناك موقف للسيارات؟

الرجل نعم، هناك موقف كبير للسيارات وراء مكتب علي المبروك.

أندي   شكرا جزيلا!

الرجل عفوا!

Exercise 2
Link the English phrases with the equivalent Arabic expressions:

a Excuse me

b straight ahead

c let me think

d turn left

e on the right

f I understand

g Is there a car park there?

١ أنا فاهم

٢ على طول

٣ لف شمال

٤ هل هناك موقف للسيارات؟

٥ خلني أفكر

٦ على اليمين

٧ عن إذنك

عن إذنك :an ídhn-ak excuse me (lit. by your leave)

وسط wásaT centre (of town, etc.)

مدينة، مدن madíinah, múdun town, city

رجل، رجال rájul, rijáal man

على طول :ála Tuul straight ahead

تذهب tádh-hab you go (to a man)

أذهب ádh-hab I go

مكتب، مكاتب máktab, makáatib office

تعرفه tá:raf-uh you (masc.) know it/him

أعرفه á:raf-uh I know it/him

خلني أفكر khallí-nii ufákkir let me think

جامع، جوامع jáami:, jawáami: main mosque

لف liff turn!

شمال shamáal left

عند :ind at

إشارة، ـات isháarah, -aat (traffic) signal

ملك، ملوك málik, mulúuk king

إذهب idh-hab go! (to a man)

حوالي Hawáalii approximately, about

متر، أمتار mitr, amtáar metre

فاهم fáahim understanding

يمين yamiin right (hand)

بجانب bi-jáanib next to, beside

محطة، ـات maHáTTah, -aat station

بنزين banzíin petrol

أمام **amáam** *in front of*

سينما، سينمات **síinamaa, siinamáat** *cinema*

أشكرك **ashkúr-ak** *thank you* (lit. I thank you: to a man)

موقف، مواقف **máwqif, mawáaqif** *stopping, parking place*

وراء **waráa'** *behind*

شكرا جزيلا **shúkran jazíilan** *thank you very much; many thanks*

عفوا: **áfwan** *you're welcome*

2 في المدينة fi l-madiinah *In the town*

Look at the town map and read through the names of all the places.

Now listen to the recording to hear how they are pronounced.

---

1 سوق الذهب **suuq adh-dháhab** *gold market*

2 مطعم **máT:am** *restaurant*

3 فندق **fúnduq** *hotel*

4 محطة الباس **maHáTTat al-báaS** *bus station*

5 الخور **al-khoor** *the creek*

6 سوق السمك **suuq as-sámak** *fish market*

7 مركز الشرطة **márkaz ash-shúrTah** *police station*

8 بنك الشارقة **bank as-sháarqah** *Bank of Sharjah*

9 مستشفى **mustáshfaa** *hospital*

10 الحصن القديم **al-HiSn al-qadiim** *the old fort*

11 حديقة **Hadiiqah** *park, garden*

12 جسر **jisr** *bridge*

13 البلدية **al-baladíyyah** *town hall*

14 ميدان **maydáan** *square*

15 جامع **jáami:** *mosque*

16 برج الاتصالات **burj al-ittiSáalaat** *communications tower*

17 سويرماركت **suubarmáarkit** *supermarket*

18 مكتب البريد **máktab al-bariid** *post office*

19 صيدلية **Saydalíyyah** *chemist*

20 مركز التسوق **márkaz at-tasáwwuq** *shopping centre*

21 الكورنيش **al-koorniish** *the Corniche*

Exercise 3

Now listen to the recording while you read the text on page 107, and decide which places are being asked for.

a على الكورنيش، بين مطعم شهرزاد ومحطة الباص

b على اليمين في الميدان، بجانب برج الاتصالات

c قريب من الخور، بين الجسر وسوق الذهب

d بين السوبرماركت وصيدلية ابن سينا

e اذهب على طول في شارع جمال عبد الناصر وهو على
الشمال بعد الجسر

f في شارع الملك فيصل، وراء المستشفى

تعبيرات رئيسية ta:biiráat ra'iisíyyah (Key phrases)

Asking and giving simple directions

أين الفندق؟ áyna l-fúnduq	*Where is the hotel?*
لف يمين liff yamíin	*Turn right*
اذهب على طول ídh-hab :ála Tuul	*Go straight ahead*
على اليمين :ála l-yamíin	*On the right*
بجانب مكتب البريد bi-jáanib máktab al-baríid	*Beside, next to the post office*
أمام محطة الباص amáama maHáTTat al-baaS	*Opposite, in front of the bus station*
وراء البنك waráa' al-bank	*Behind the bank*
بين الصيدلية ومحطة البنزين báyna aS-Saydalíyyah wa-maHáTTat al-banzíin	*Between the chemist and the petrol station*
بعد الجسر ba:d al-jisr	*After the bridge*

تراكيب اللغة taraakíib al-lúghah (Structures)

Possessives with two nouns

Possessive constructions have two elements: the possessor or owner, and the thing possessed, or property. In 'the doctor's car' the doctor is the owner and the car is the property.

Owner (of)	Property
The doctor's	car

The most usual way to say this in English is by the use of an apostrophe s: 's, as above, in which case the order is *owner* before *property*. However, sometimes we use the word *of* and reverse the order:

Property	(of)	Owner
The title	of	the book
The Dogs	of	War

Arabic is similar to the above, except that:

a) no word for *of* is used

b) The first possessed noun (*title, Dogs*) never has the definite article **al-**. So the normal form in Arabic looks like this:

noun without **al-**	*followed by*	noun with **al-**
máktab		**al-mudíir**
office		(of) *the manager*
(the possessed object)		(the owner/possessor)

   *al-maktab al-mudíir** does not make sense to an Arab.

c) If the first (possessed) noun has the feminine ending ﺔ this is pronounced **-t** but – unlike with the possessive pronouns in Unit 5 – does not change its form when written. This is because it is still at the end of a word.

سيارة محمد sayyáarat muHámmad *Mohammed's car*

Saydalíyyat sáarah
Sarah's pharmacy

d) With the exception of the demonstratives *this*, *that*, etc, no word may be inserted between the two nouns, so any additional words such as adjectives have to come at the end. (see also below).

Pseudo possessives

Possessives are frequently used in Arabic to associate two concepts which in English would be expressed in another way.

márkaz ash-shúrTah

centre (of) the-police

مركز الشرطة

The police station

maHáTTat al-baaS

station (of) the-bus

محطة الباص

The bus station

Proper names

You will remember that all proper names are regarded as definite, whether or not they begin with the definite article **al-**, *the* such as القاهرة **al-qaahirah**, *Cairo*. In either case they refer to a specific person or place, and are therefore definite.

بيت أحمد **bayt áHmad**

Ahmed's house

جامعة القاهرة
jáami:at al-qáahirah

University of Cairo; Cairo University

Simple sentences

The formula *definite* + *indefinite* gives a simple sentence in Arabic (see Unit 2) implying the word *is/are* in English. Since nearly all possessive constructions are by nature definite (see above), you can use them in the same way. The last part of the sentence can be a simple adjective (e.g. *Muhammad's house is big*), but can also be a phrase with a preposition (using words such as *in, under, on,* etc.), telling you where something is located.

jáami:at al-qáahirah kabíirah	جامعة القاهرة كبيرة
university (of)(the) Cairo (is) big	*Cairo University is big*
bayt muHámmad qaríib	بيت محمد قريب
house (of) muHammad (is) near	*Muhammad's house is near*
bayt muHámmad fii wásaT al-madíinah	بيت محمد في وسط المدينة
house (of) muHammad (is) in (the) centre (of) the-town	*Muhammad's house is in the centre of town*

Word order and adjectives

Because nothing except the demonstratives can come between the two parts of a possessive, any other words introduced into the sentence must be placed elsewhere.

If any adjectives are applied to either of the terms in a possessive construction, these must come at the end. The possessive construction can never be split up.

If both possessive terms are of the same gender, it will strike you that these adjectives placed at the end of the phrase might describe either of the possessive terms. However, the context usually makes everything clear.

wazíir ad-daakhilíyyah al-jadíid	وزير الداخلية الجديد
minister (of) the-interior the-new	*The new minister of the interior*

wizáarat al-:adl al-jadíidah   وزارة العدل الجديدة

ministry (of) the-justice the-new   *The new ministry of justice*

kútub al-ustáadh al-jadíidah   كتب الأستاذ الجديدة

books (of) the-professor the-new   *The professor's new books*

Note

Ministries, embassies and government departments usually have the possessive construction, with the hidden -**t**.

وزارة **wizáarah**, *ministry* is derived from وزير **wazíir**, *minister*, and is the origin of the English word *vizier*:

وزارة السياحة   *Ministry of Tourism*

wizáarat as-siyáaHah

وزارة التعليم قريبة من الميدان   *the Ministry of Education*

wizáarat at-ta:líim qaríibah   *is near the square*

min al-maydáan

دائرة المرور **dáa'irat al-murúur**   *Traffic department*

An alternative is to place the nationality adjective after the noun, in which case there is no hidden -**t**:

سفارة **sifáarah**, *embassy* comes from سفير **safíir**, *ambassador* (which is derived in turn from **sáfar** travel, the origin of the word *safari*):

السفارة البريطانية   *the British embassy*

as-sifáarah al-briiTaaníyyah

السفارة الامريكية   *the American embassy*

as-sifáarah al-amriikíyyah

Demonstratives with possessives

Demonstratives (*this, that, those*, etc.) are the only words which can go between the two terms of a possessive:

a) If the *this*-word applies to the second (possessor) word, it goes between, usually taking the form:
noun without **al-** + *this* + noun with **al-**

qálam háadhaa t-tilmíidh قلم هذا التلميذ

pen (of) this(person) the-pupil *this pupil's pen*

b) If the *this* word applies to the first (possessed) word, it comes at the end:
noun without **al-** + noun with **al-** + *this*

sayyáarat al-mudíir haadhíhi سيارة المدير هذه

car (of) the-manager this (one) *This car of the manager's*

In both cases, the demonstrative must agree in gender with the word to which it applies.

أوزان الكلمات awzáan al-kalimáat (Word shapes)

Pattern	Arabic example	Eng. sound-alike
CiCaaCah	**wizáarah** وزارة ministry	*banana*

(See also note above.)

This type of noun is always derived from a word of the **CaCíiC** shape (see Unit 1), but which refers to a man. Its meaning is the place where he operates. Thus, as we have seen above, a وزير **wazíir**, *minister* operates from a وزارة **wizáarah**, *ministry*, and a سفير **safíir**, *ambassador* from a سفارة **sifáarah**, *embassy*.

In the Gulf, the Emirates (**imaaráat**, plural of إمارة **imáarah**) are so named because they were each originally ruled by an أمير **amíir**, *emir/prince*.

The shape is also used for some nouns derived from verbs, e.g. كتابة **kitáabah**, *writing* and قراءة **qiráa'ah**, *reading*.

تمرينات tamriináat (Practice)

Exercise 4
Fit the two words together to make places found around an Arab city.

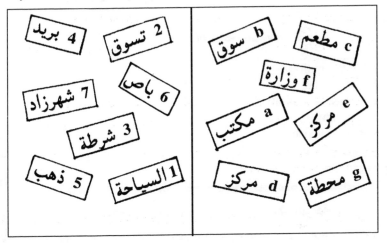

Exercise 5
Ask where the following places are. Check your answers with the recording or the transcript.
a the town hall
b the police station
c al-Bustan shopping centre
d King Faisal Street
e Shehrazade restaurant

Exercise 6
Now look at the town map on page 105 and imagine that you are walking down the street and someone asks you the way. Give directions to the places in Exercise 5, using the Key Phrases on page 106 to help you. Possible answers are given on the recording or transcript.

Exercise 7

Combine a noun from each column, to form a possessive construction.

Example: boy – bicycle

عجلة الولد **:ajalat al-walad**   *the boy's bicycle*

عجلة، ـات **ájalah, -aat** *bicycle*

a bank – manager
b town – centre
c country – capital
d company – office
e Rashid – sister
f Italy – embassy

عاصمة، عواصم **áaSimah, :awáaSim*** *capital* (political)

شركة، ـات **shárikah, -aat** *company* (commercial)

بلد، بلاد/بلدان **balad, biláad/buldáan** *country, state*

Exercise 8

Now make *is/are* sentences from the words below, making sure that the adjectives agree.

Example: *watch – Faisal – new* ➜ ساعة فيصل جديدة. (*Faisal's watch is new.*)

1 streets – Abu Dhabi – wide

2 University – Cairo – big

3 gardens – palace – beautiful

4 rooms – apartment – spacious

5 cuisine – Morocco – delicious

6 shops – market – small

عريض :**aríiD** *wide*

قصر، قصور **qaSr, quSúur** *palace*

غرفة، غرف **ghúrfah, ghúraf** *room*

شقة، شقق **sháqqah, shíqaq** *flat, apartment*

واسع **wáasi:** *roomy, spacious*

طبيخ **Tabíikh** *cooking, cuisine*

لذيذ **ladhíidh** *delicious, tasty*

دكان، دكاكين **dukkáan, dakaakíin** *small shop, stall*

Exercise 9

Saalim's mother is trying to tidy up the boys' bedroom and she asks Saalim what belongs to him and what to his brother Tamim. Complete the sentences using the correct possessive construction.

Example:

أهذا قميصك؟ لا، هذا قميص تميم.

Is this your shirt? No, it's Tamim's shirt.

قميص   حزام   جوارب   بنطلون

منديل   نظارة

a أهذا حزامك؟ نعم هذا ...

b أهذه جواريك؟ لا، هذه ...

c أذلك منديلك؟ نعم، ذلك ...

d أهذه نظارتك؟ نعم، هذه ...

e أهذا بنطلونك؟ لا، هذا ...

7 | ماذا فعلت؟
máadhaa fa:ált?
What did you do?

In this unit you will learn:

- how to talk about things which happened in the past
- about means of transport
- about Arabic verbs
- how to say *me, him, them,* etc.

1 أخي فهد **ákhii fahd** *My brother Fahd*

Samira, a Kuwaiti girl, writes to a friend to tell her about her brother who was working abroad.

Exercise 1

Listen to the recording while you read the letter, and say whether the following are true or false:

a Her brother went to Amman in May.
b He wrote to Samira every week.
c He returned to Kuwait in September.

سافر إلى عمان في شهر مارس وعمل في مكتب شركته في
الأردن. سكن عند عمي. كتبنا له رسالة كل أسبوع. رجع إلى
الكويت في شهر سبتمبر.

Exercise 2

Link the English phrases with the equivalent Arabic:

a He worked in the office.
b He stayed with my uncle.
c We wrote him a letter every week.

١ سكن عند عمي.
٢ كتبنا له رسالة كل أسبوع.
٣ عمل في المكتب.

سافر **sáafara** *travel*

شهر، شهور/أشهر **shahr, shuhúur/ásh-hur** *month*

مارس **maars** *March*

عمل: **ámila** *work, do*

سكن **sákana** *reside, live*

رسالة، رسائل **risáalah, rasáa'il** *letter, message*

كل **kull** *every, each*

رجع **rája:a** *return, come/go back*

سبتمبر **sabtámbar** *September**

*A full list of the Christian and Islamic months is given in Unit 11.

2 ماذا فعلت أمس؟ máadhaa fa:ált ams?

What did you do yesterday?

Zaki, a student at the college in Cairo, asks Sonya, an English friend, what she did the day before.

Exercise 3

Listen to the conversation, and answer the questions.
a How did Sonya go to Ahmed's house?
b Who lives with Ahmed and his wife?
c Do they live in:
  i Zamalek? **ii** Maadi? **iii** Helwan?

Listen to the recording again.
d Did they eat:
  i breakfast? **ii** lunch? **iii** dinner?
e Who cooked the meal?
f Did they have:
  i Arabic coffee? **ii** Turkish coffee? **iii** American coffee?
g Did Sonya get home:
  i by taxi? **ii** by bus? **iii** by car?

زكي   ماذا فعلت أمس؟

سونية   أمس ذهبت إلى بيت أحمد

زكي   كيف ذهبت إلى هناك؟

سونية   ذهبت بالتاكسي. هو وعائلته يسكنون في الزمالك.

زكي   ماذا فعلتم؟

سونية   قابلت والده ووالدته وأخواته. طبخت والدته الغداء. بعد
         الغداء شربنا قهوة عربية.

زكي   وهل أعجبتك؟

سونية   نعم، هي لذيذة.

زكي   هل رجعت بالتاكسي؟

سونية   لا، ما رجعت بالتاكسي. أحمد وصلني إلى البيت في سيارته.

Link the English phrases with the Arabic equivalents.

a yesterday	١ كيف ذهبت إلى هناك؟
b How did you go there?	٢ هل أعجبتك؟
c I went by taxi	٣ وصلني إلى البيت.
d Did you like it?	٤ أمس
e He gave me a lift home	٥ ذهبت بالتاكسي.

فعل **fá:ala** to do

أمس **ams** yesterday

ذهب **dháhab** to go

عائلة، ـات **:áa'ilah, -aat** family

يسكنون **yaskunúun** they live, reside, stay

قابل **qáabala** *to meet, encounter*

طبخ **Tábakha** *to cook*

غداء **ghadáa'** *lunch*

شرب **sháriba** *to drink*

قهوة **qáhwah** *coffee*

هل أعجبتك **hal a:jábat-ik** *did you* (fem.) *like it* (fem.)?

ما **maa** *not*

وصل **wáSSala** *to transport, take, give a lift*

🎧 تعبيرات رئيسية **ta:biiráat ra'iisíyyah (Key phrases)**

Talking about how you travelled

He travelled to Jeddah…	...سافر إلى جدة
by car	بالسيارة
by plane	بالطائرة
by bus/coach	بالباص
by train	بالقطار
by taxi	بالتاكسي
by ship	بالسفينة

Further expressions of time

I met him…	قابلته
last night	أمس بالليل
last week/month	الأسبوع/الشهر الماضي
last year	السنة الماضية

three years ago	قبل ثلاث سنوات
in 1995	في سنة ١٩٩٥
a week/month ago	قبل أسبوع/شهر
a year ago	قبل سنة

تراكيب اللغة   taraakíib al-lúghah (Structures)

The Arabic verb: general

The Arabic verb differs from the English verb in two ways:

a) It has only two tenses (i.e. ways to express when an action took place).

- The *past* tense is used for all *completed* actions.
- The *present* tense is used for all actions *not yet complete*.

b) Most verbs can be reduced to a *past stem* and a *present stem*, and a standard set of prefixes and suffixes can be added to these stems to form meaningful words.

Arabic verbs fit into a limited number of categories, but there are virtually no truly irregular verbs in Arabic – apparent irregularities can usually be explained by the occurrence of the weak letters **waaw** and **yaa'** as one of the letters in the stem. For further details, see Verb Tables.

The infinitive

There is no Arabic equivalent of the English infinitive *to do*, *to speak*, etc. Instead Arabic verbs are given in the *he*-form of the past tense, because this part is the simplest form of the verb, with no written suffixes or prefixes. It often also constitutes the past stem, from which which all other parts of the past tense can be formed.

So when we give a verb as, for example, **kátaba**, *to write*, the part we give actually means *he wrote*.

In the box below, we have given the suffix endings separated by a hyphen from the past stem of the verb **kátaba** so that you can learn them more easily. The verb **kátaba** belongs to Type **S-I** in the Verb Tables. The root **k-t-b** indicates *writing*.

Note: Study the following in conjunction with the S-section of the Verb Tables which contains further information.

Past tense

Singular	Plural
كتب **kátab(a)**	كتبوا **kátab-uu**
he wrote	*they* (masc.) *wrote*
كتبت **kátab-at**	كتبن **katáb-na**
she wrote	*they* (fem.) *wrote*
كتبت **katáb-t(a)**	كتبتم **katáb-tum**
you (masc.)*wrote*	*you* (masc.) *wrote*
كتبت **katáb-ti**	كتبتن **katab-túnna**
you (fem.)*wrote*	*you* (fem.) *wrote*
كتبت **katáb-t(u)**	كتبنا **katáb-na(a)**
I wrote	*we wrote*

Note: the final vowels in brackets are usually omitted in informal speech.

Here is a list of some commonly-used verbs. Remember that these are all in the *he*-form of the past tense, and in the past tense they can all be formed in the same way as **kátaba**.

Note: Some verbs must be used in conjunction with a preposition. This is given after the verb.

ذهب **dháhaba** go	وضع **wáDa:a** put, place
سافر **sáafara** travel	خبر **khábbara** tell, inform
وصل **wáSala** arrive	قابل **qáabala** meet
رجع **rája:a** return, go back	غسل **ghásala** wash
عمل **:ámila** do, work	غادر **gháadara** leave, depart
تفرج على **tafárraja :álaa** watch, spectate	كلم **kállama** speak to
فعل **fá:ala** do, act	وجد **wájada** find
ركب **rákiba** ride	قرأ **qára'a** read
سكن **sákana** live, reside	رقص **ráqaSa** dance
أكل **'ákala** eat	دخل **dákhala** enter
شرب **sháriba** drink	خرج **kháraja** go out (of)
لعب **lá:iba** play	كسر **kásara** break
طبخ **Tábakha** cook	تأخر **ta'ákhkhara** be late
شاهد **sháahada** see, look at	فتح **fátaHa** open
	قفل **qáfala** close

Noun and pronoun subjects

The subject of a verb is the person or thing which performs the action. It is important in Arabic to distinguish between noun and pronoun subjects.

1 Verbs with pronoun subjects

When you say *they arrived, he said, it opened*, you are using a pronoun subject, and the suffix ending of the verb indicates who or what the subject is. The separate pronouns which you learned in Unit 2 are not normally used with verbs, except for emphasis.

waSalat min al-maghrib ams　　وصلت من المغرب أمس

She-arrived from Morocco yesterday

She arrived from Morocco yesterday

saafara ila r-ribaaT al-usbuu: سافر إلى الرباط الأسبوع الماضي
al-maaDii

He-travelled to Rabat last week   *He travelled to Rabat last week*

2 Verbs with noun subjects

When the subject of a sentence is specified by means of a noun (*the workmen arrived, Ahmed said*):
a) the verb usually comes first, followed by the subject
b) the verb is always in the *he-* or *she-*form, no matter what the subject.

In English we usually say who or what we are talking about (the subject), then go on to say what the subject did (the verb), and follow this with any other information like who or what he did it to, where and when he did it (the object or predicate), so that the word order is usually *subject – verb – the rest*:

Subject	Verb	Object/predicate
The man	wrote	the letter.

The normal word order in Arabic is *verb – subject – the rest*.

Verb	Subject	Object/predicate
كتب الرجل الرسالة		
kataba	**r-rajul**	**ar-risaalah**
wrote(-he)	the man	the letter
سافرت المدرسة مع تلامذتها		
saafarat	**al-mudarrisah**	**ma:a talaamidhat-haa**
Travelled (-she)	the teacher	with her students
وصلت الطائرة الصبح		
waSalat	**aT-Taa'irah**	**S-SubH**
Arrived (-she)	the plane	in the morning
دخل الوزراء القصر		
dakhala	**l-wuzaraa'**	**al-qaSr**
entered (-he)	the ministers	the palace

The fact that the verb in these cases is either in the *he-* or *she-*form, i.e. always singular, never plural, should be noted carefully. Remember that the plural of things (inanimate objects or abstracts) is regarded as feminine singular, so that the rule for verbs which precede their subjects looks like this:

Subject	Example	Verb
One or more male human beings; singular inanimate noun of masc. gender	man, boys, book	he-form
one or more female human beings; singular inanimate noun of fem. gender; plural of inanimate noun of either gender	woman, girls, car, books, cars	she-form

Saying no

To negate something that happened in the past, the word **maa**, *not* can be placed before the verb.

maa sharibt al-qahwah

ما شربت القهوة

Not I-drank the-coffee

I didn't drink the coffee

Exercise 4

Turn the following sentences into negatives.

a The aeroplane was late   تأخرت الطائرة

b The workmen spoke to the boss   كلم العمال الرئيس

c I ate the bread   أكلت الخبز

طائرة، ـات **Táa'irah, -aat** aeroplane

عامل، عمال **áamil, :ummáal** workman

رئيس، رؤساء **ra'iis, ru'asáa'** boss, chief

خبز **khubz** bread

Sentences where the verb comes after the subject

The *verb–subject–rest* word order given above is the most common in Arabic, but it is possible to have verbs which come after their subjects. This occurs most frequently in sentences which have more than one verb, e.g. *The workmen arrived on the site and started to dig the foundations.*

If a sentence starting with a noun subject has more than one verb, the first one comes before the noun subject and obeys the *he-/she-* form agreement rule on page 125, and any subsequent verb comes *after* the subject and must agree with it completely, in number (singular or plural) and gender (male or female).

So if the subject refers to men, the second and any subsequent verbs must end in **-uu** (masculine plural). If it refers to women, it must end in **-na** (feminine plural). The plural of things, regarded as feminine singular, will have the ending **-at** on both verbs.

وصل العمال وصلحوا الباب	*The workmen arrived and*
wáSala l-:ummaal	*mended the door*
wa-SallaHuu l-baab	

دخلت البنات الغرفة وشربن القهوة	*The girls entered the room*
dakhalat al-banaat al-ghurfah	*and drank the coffee*
wa-sharibna l-qahwah	

وقعت الكتب من الرف وأصابت المدرس	*The books fell from the shelf*
waqa:at al-kutub min ar-raff	*and struck the teacher*
wa-aSaabat al-mudarris	

وقع **wáqa:a** *fall*

رف، رفوف **raff, rufúuf** *shelf*

أصاب **aSáaba** *hit, strike*

It, him, me – **object pronouns**

To say *me, it, them*, Arabic uses – with one exception – the same pronoun suffixes as the possessive pronoun suffixes which mean *my, his, our* (see Unit 5).

They are added to the verb to express the object of the sentence, to which the action of the verb is applied:

Singular	Plural
ني **-nii** *me*	ـنـا **-naa** *us*
ك **-ak** *you* (to a man)	ـكم **-kum** *you* (to men)
ك **-ik** *your* (to a woman)	ـكن **-kúnna** *you* (to women)
ـه **-uh** *him*	ـهم **-hum** *them* (men)
ـها **-haa** *her*	ـهن **-húnna** *them* (women)

As the above table shows, the only one which differs is the suffix for *me* which is ـني **-nii** after verbs (as opposed to ـي **-ii** after other types of word).

خبرني ناصر	*Nasser told me*
khabbara-nii naaSir	

كلمته أمس	*I spoke to him yesterday*
kallamt-uh ams	

قابلناهم في السوق	*We met them in the souq*
qaabalnaa-hum fi s-suuq	

When **-ak** and **-uh** come after a vowel, they are reduced to **-k** and

-h respectively and **-ik** becomes **-ki**. This is another example of elision.

شاهدناك **shaahadnáa-k/ki** *We saw you* (masc./fem.)

شربوه **sharibúu-h** *They* (masc.) *drank it*

Note: The masculine plural ending **-uu** is written with a 'silent' **alif** at the end (وا – see Verb Tables). This is omitted when any suffix is joined on to the verb.

Pronunciation – elision

Here are some more conventions of Arabic pronunciation. They will help to polish your Arabic.

1 Definition of elision

Elision usually means in Arabic that a preceding vowel swallows up a following one.

al- *the* becomes **l-** after vowels:

صلحوا الباب **SállaHuu l-baab** *They repaired the gate*

Elision also occurs with the sun letters (see Unit 1):

صلحوا السيارة **SállaHuu s-sayyáarah** *They repaired the car*

2 Elision of *fii*

When the word **fii**, *in* precedes **al-**, *the*, the a of **al-** omitted, and the vowel of **fii** is shortened to make **fi**. Technically this applies to all words ending in long vowels, but it is most noticeable with **fii**.

في البيت **fi l-bayt** *in the house*

3 Initial *i*

Standard Arabic does not allow words to begin with two consonants like English *trip, blank*. Instead it adds an **i-** vowel prefix (in Arabic expressed by an **alif** with an **i**-vowel below it. In practice, however, this vowel sign is rarely written.)

اِجتماع **ijtimáa:** *meeting*

When this vowel is preceded by a word ending in a vowel, the **i**-vowel is elided:

واجتماع **wa-ijtimáa:**, *and (a) meeting*, is pronounced **wa-jtimaa:**. This is a refinement in pronunciation, and it will do no harm if you fail to observe it meticulously.

Some words beginning with **alif** use this to carry a radical **hamzah** (i.e. one which is part of the root), and this should not be elided. This kind of **hamzah** is quite often – though not always – marked in print, and we have tried to follow the Arab convention.

أَكل **ákala** *he ate*

أمير **amíir** *prince, Emir*

أخذ **ákhadha** *he took*

أوزان الكلمات awzáan al-kalimáat (Word shapes)

Pattern	Arabic example	Eng. sound-alike
taC¹áaC²uC³	تعاون **ta:áawun** cooperation	*to our one*

More examples are:

تكاتب **takáatub** *correspondence, writing to each other*

تفاهم **tafáahum** *mutual understanding*

تضامن **taDáamun** *solidarity*

تبادل **tabáadul** *exchange, exchanging*

If you look at the nature of the meaning of all these nouns you will see that they all carry the idea of doing something with someone else.

تمرينات tamriináat (Practice)

Exercise 5
How did Mohammed travel to Cairo? Match the Arabic phrases to
the pictures .

سافر محمد إلى القاهرة...

١ بالسيارة

٢ بالطائرة

٣ بالسفينة

٤ بالباص

٥ بالتاكسي

Exercise 6
Who did what? Match the Arabic to the English sentences.

a We read the newspapers.   ١ دخلنا الغرفة.

b She put her bag on the table.   ٢ وجدت المفاتيح في جيبي.

c We entered the room.   ٣ وضعت حقيبتها على المائدة.

d You (masc. sing.) wrote a letter.   ٤ وصلوا إلى مطار البحرين.

e He lived in London.   ٥ خرجتن من الفندق.

f You (fem. pl.) came out of the hotel.   ٦ كتبت رسالة.

g I found the keys in my pocket.   ٧ سكن في لندن.

h They (masc.) arrived at Bahrain   ٨ قرأنا الجرائد.
Airport.

مفتاح، مفاتيح miftáaH, mafaatíiH *key*

جيب، جيوب jayb, juyúub *pocket*

مائدة، موائد máa'ida, mawáa'id *table*

جريدة، جرائد jariídah, jaráa'id *newspaper*

Exercise 7

In the following sentences, put the correct suffix endings on the verbs in brackets.

a They (masc.) travelled to Kuwait.   .(سافر) إلى الكويت

b She opened the door.   .(فتح) الباب

c Did you (m. sing.) watch the television?   هل (تفرج) على التلفزيون؟

d I arrived yesterday.   .(وصل) أمس

e She cooked and we ate the food.   .(طبخ) و(أكل) الطعام

Exercise 8

Jim went on holiday to Egypt.

a Match the drawings with the sentences. (See Key on page 132.)

b Write his postcard home for him, putting the verbs in brackets in the *I*-form.

٤ (ركب) جملا   ١ (لعب) على الشاطئ

٥ (شرب) عصير   ٢ (قابل) شباب مصريين

٦ (ذهب) إلى السوق   ٣ (جلس) في الكافيتريا

شاطئ **sháaTi'** shore, beach

جمل، جمال **jámal, jimáal** camel

شاب، شباب **shaabb, shabáab** youth/young person

كافيتريا **kaafitírya** cafeteria/café

عصير: **aSíir** juice

Exercise 9

Alter the underlined nouns in the following sentences to object pronouns.

Example: I met the manager. ➜ I met him.

قابلت المدير. ➜ قابلته.

٤ سألت السؤال   ١ كتبت الرسالة

٥ غسلن القمصان   ٢ أكلت التفاحة

٦ قابل فاطمة في عمان   ٣ كلم الرجال

تفاحة، تفاح **tufáaHah, tufáaH** apple

سأل **sá'ala** ask

سؤال، أسئلة **su'áal, ás'ilah** question

Exercise 10

Match the Arabic to the English sentences below

a My wife cooked the food.

b The driver took his boss to the airport.

c The students read books in the university library.

d The aeroplane arrived in Beirut.

e The secretaries drank coffee every day.

١ قرأ الطلاب الكتب في مكتبة الجامعة.

٢ شربت السكرتيرات قهوة كل يوم.

٣ طبخت زوجتي الطعام.

٤ وصل السائق رئيسه إلى المطار.

٥ وصلت الطائرة إلى بيروت.

سائق، ـون/ساقة **sáa'iq, -úun/sáaqah** driver

Exercise 11

Read the passage below and fill the gaps with the correct form of the past tense of the appropriate verb chosen from those in the box below the passage. You will find the Key Words on page 134.

ـــــ بيل وميري والأولاد من لندن ـــــ إلى دبي في شهر مارس سنة ١٩٩٧. ـــــ هناك لمدة أسبوع. ـــــ في شقة كبيرة قريبة من البحر، وـــــ ناسا كثيرين من الإمارات. يوم الاثنين ـــــ بيل تنس، وـــــ ميري إلى الشاطئ. يوم الثلاثاء ـــــ إلى بيت صديقهم منصور، وـــــ لهم زوجته طعاما عربيا.

ذهبوا	سافر	سكنوا	ووصلوا	ذهبت
	لعب	قعدوا	طبخت	قابلوا

> قعد **qá:ada** stay, remain, sit
>
> لمدة... **li-múddat...** for the period of...
>
> ناس **naas** people
>
> صديق، أصدقاء **Sadíiq, aSdiqáa'** friend
>
> لهم **lá-hum** for them

Exercise 12

The following sentences all have the verb (bold type) before the subject. Rewrite them with the verb after the subject, paying attention to the correct agreement.

Example:

رجع المدراء من الاجتماع. ← المدراء رجعوا من الاحتماع.

١ سافر محمد إلى القاهرة.

٢ رجع الأولاد من المدرسة.

٣ حضر المهندسون المؤتمر.

٤ طبخت البنات طعاما عربيا.

٥ وقعت الصحون من المائدة.

> مدير، مدراء **mudíir, mudaráa'** manager
>
> حضر **HáDara** attend, be present
>
> مهندس، ـون **muhándis, -úun** engineer
>
> مؤتمر، ـات **mu'támar, -áat** conference
>
> صحن، صحون **SaHn, SuHúun** dish

8 كان يا ما كان
kaan yaa maa kaan
Once upon a time

In this unit you will learn:

- how to say *was/were*
- how to say *is/are not*
- how to describe what something was like
- how to say *became*
- a new type of *is/are* sentence
- how to say you had done something

1 كان يا ما كان kaan yaa maa kaan
Once upon a time

In *The Arabian Nights*, or ألف ليلة وليلة **alf laylah wa-laylah** (lit. *a thousand nights and a night*), Princess Sheherazade kept the Sultan from executing her when, for 1001 nights, she told him one tale after another, always ending at an exciting point of the story, so that he had to let her live to tell the rest of the tale the next night.

This is how she introduced the stories of Sindbad the Sailor.

Exercise 1
Listen to the recording of the first part of the introduction below, and answer the questions.

a Was the porter called:
  i Harun al-Rashid? **ii** al-Hindbad? **iii** Sindbad?

b Where was the porter going?

c Why did he stop?

d Did he stop beside:

  i a house **ii** a door **iii** a market

e What did he ask the servant?

Now read the beginning of the story.

في أيام الخليفة هارون الرشيد كان في بغداد حمـال فقير اسمـه
الهندبـاد. و في يوم من الأيام كان الهندبـاد هذا يحمل حملا
ثقيلا إلى بيت تاجر في السوق. وكان ذلك في الصيف وكانت
حرارة الشمس شديدة جدا. وأصبح الهندباد تعبانا وعطشانا.
فوقف في الطريق عند باب قصر فخم للاستراحة من عمله.
ووضع حملـه على الأرض وجلس. وبينمـا هو جالس هكذا سمـع
موسيقى جميلة منبعثة من داخل القصر. وكان هناك خـادم واقف
أمـام باب القصر، فسأله الهندبـاد: من صاحب هذا القصر الفخم؟

Exercise 2

Link the English phrases with the appropriate Arabic expressions.

a beautiful music

b the heat of the sun was very strong

c that was in the summer

d in the days of the Caliph Harun al-Rashid

e in front of the gate of the palace

f al-Hindbad became tired

١ كان ذلك في الصيف

٢ أمـام باب القصر

٣ في أيام الخليفة هـارون الرشيد

٤ أصبح الهندبـاد تعبانا

٥ موسيقى جميلة

٦ كانت حرارة الشمس شديدة جدا

خليفة، خلفاء **khaliifah, khulafáa'*** *Caliph*, head of the Islamic state (obviously masc., despite its ending)

حمال، ـون **Hammáal, -uun** *porter*

فقير، فقراء **faqíir, fuqaráa'*** *poor, poor person*

في يوم من الأيام **fii yawm min al-ayyáam** *one day* (lit. 'in a day of the days')

كان ... يحمل **káana ... yáHmil** *he was carrying*

حمل، أحمال **Himl, aHmáal** *load, burden*

ثقيل **thaqíil** *heavy*

تاجر، تجار **táajir, tujjáar** *merchant*

صيف **Sayf** *summer*

حرارة **Haráarah** *heat*

شمس **shams** *sun*

شديد **shadíid** *strong, mighty*

أصبح **áSbaHa** *become*

تعبان **ta:báan** *tired*

عطشان **:aTsháan** *thirsty*

وقف **wáqafa** *stop, stand*

طريق، طرق **Taríiq, Túruq** *road, way*

باب، أبواب **baab, abwáab** *gate, door*

قصر، قصور **qaSr, quSúur** *palace*

فخم **fakhm** *magnificent*

للاستراحة **li-listiráaHah** *in order to rest* (lit. 'for the resting')

عمل، أعمال **:ámal, a:máal** *work, job, business*

الأرض **al-árD** *the ground, the earth* (fem.)

جلس **jálasa** *sit, sit down*

بينما **báynamaa** *while*

جالس **jáalis** *sitting, seated*

كـ **ka-** *like (joined to following word)*

سمع **sámi:a** *hear, listen*

موسيقى **muusiiqaa*** *music (fem.)*

منبعث **munbá:ith** *emanating*

داخل **dáakhil** *inside, the inside of something*

خادم، خدام **kháadim, khuddáam** *servant*

واقف **wáaqif** *standing, stationary*

صاحب، أصحاب **SáaHib, aS-Háab** *owner, master; also sometimes friend*

2 السندباد البحري **as-sindibaad al-baHrii** *Sindbad the Sailor*

Exercise 3

Who could own this magnificent palace? Listen to the rest of the story and answer the questions below.

a Why was the servant astonished?

b Had the sailor travelled:
   i for seven years? **ii** the seven seas? **iii** to seven countries?

c Did the porter become sad because:
   i Sindbad was rich and he was poor?
   ii the servant told him to leave?
   iii he was hungry?

d Who was with Sindbad:
   i a group of servants? **ii** his wife? **iii** a group of people?

e Did Sindbad give him:
   i gold? **ii** food? **iii** drink?

f What had he ordered his servants to do?

Listen to the story again, looking at the Key Words on page 140.

وقال له الخادم: إنه قصرالسندباد البحري. قال الحمال: ومن
هو؟ فدهش الخادم وقال: أنت ساكن في بغداد وما سمعت عن
السندباد البحري؟ قال الهندباد: لا. قال الخادم: هو الذي سافر
في البحار السبعة وشاهد عجائب الدنيا كلها. فعند ذلك أصبح
الحمال حزينا وسأل نفسه قال: لماذا السندباد هذا غني، وأنا
لست غنيا؟ وسمع السندباد هذا الكلام من داخل القصر وأرسل
خادما آخر إلى الباب. وخرج هذا الخادم من باب القصر و كلم
الهندباد وقال: تعال معي. فتبعه الحمال إلى داخل القصر وشاهد
هناك رجلا طويلا جالسا في وسط جماعة من الناس، وكان هذا
الرجل السندباد. وقال البحري للحمال: مرحبا، أهلا وسهلا.
وأجلسه بجانبه وقدم له أنواعا كثيرة من الأكل اللذيذ. وبعد ذلك
خبره عن رحلاته العجيبة. وكان السندباد قد أمر خدامه بنقل
حمل الهندباد إلى بيت التاجر.

Exercise 4

Link the English phrases with the appropriate Arabic expressions.

a he said	١ تعال معي
b (Indeed) it is the palace of Sindbad the Sailor	٢ سافر في البحار السبعة
c He has travelled the seven seas	٣ خبره عن رحلاته العجيبة
d I am not rich	٤ إنه قصرالسندباد البحري
e Come with me	٥ كان قد أمر خدامه
f Greetings and welcome!	٦ قال
g He told him about his amazing voyages	٧ مرحبا، أهلا وسهلا
h he had ordered his servants	٨ أنا لست غنيا

قال (له) **qáala lá-hu** *he said* (to him)

إنه **ínn-uh** *it is …* (see grammar section below)

من؟ **man** *who?*

دهش **dáhisha** *be surprised, astonished*

ساكن **sáakin** *living, residing*

الذي **alládhii** *who, the one who*

البحار السبعة **al-biHáar as-sáb:ah** *the seven seas*

عجيبة، عجائب **:ajíibah, :ajáa'ib*** *(object of) wonder*

الدنيا **ad-dúnya(a)** *the world* (fem.)

كلها **kúll-haa** *all of them*

حزين **Hazíin** *sad*

نفسه **náfs-uh** *himself*

لماذا؟ **li-máadha(a)** *why*

غني، أغنياء **ghánii, aghniyáa'** *rich, rich person*

لست **lástu** *I am not* (see grammar section below)

كلام **kaláam** *speech*

أرسل **ársala** *send*

آخر **áakhar*** *other* (*does not take accusative marker)

تعال **ta:áala** *come!*

مع **má:a** *(along) with*

تبع **tábi:a** *follow*

جماعة، ـات **jamáa:ah, -aat** *group, gathering*

انسان، ناس **insáan, naas** *human being;* pl. = *people*

أجلس **ájlasa** *seat, cause to sit down*

قدم **qáddama** *offer, present with*

نوع، أنواع **naw:, anwáa**: *kind, sort, type*

أكل **akl** *things to eat, food*

بعد **ba:d** *after*

رحلة، ـات **ríHlah, -aat** *journey, voyage*

عجيب **:ajiib** *wonderful*

أمر **ámara** *order, command* (بـ **bi-** *something*)

كان قد أمر **káana qad ámara** *he had ordered* (for **qad** see
  grammar section)

نقل **naql** *transport, transportation*

تعبيرات رئيسية **ta:biiráat ra'iisíyyah (Key phrases)**

Describing someone or something

كان ممثلا مشهورا   *He was a famous actor*
kaana mumaththilan mash-huuran

كانت تعبانة جدا بعد الرحلة   *She was very tired after*
kaanat ta:baanah jiddan   *the journey*
ba:d ar-riHlah

كان شعرها أسود   *Her hair was black*
kaana sha:r-haa aswad

(**aswad**, *black* does not take the accusative marker. See below and
Unit 16)

Talking about where something was

كان المفتاح في جيبه   *The key was in his pocket*
kaana l-miftaaH fii jayb-uh

كانت الجرائد على المائدة
kaanat al-jaraa'id :ala -l-maa'ida

*The papers were on the
table*

Talking about what someone or something is not

الفندق ليس كبيرا
al-funduq laysa kabiiran

The hotel is not large

lastu mariiDan لست مريضا

I am not ill

Talking about what you had done in the past

هل كنت قد شاهدت الفيلم من قبل؟
hal kunta qad shaahadta
l-fiilm min qabl?

*Had you seen the film
before?*

كنا قد وقفنا وجلسنا
kunna qad waqafnaa wa-jalasnaa

*We had stopped and sat
down*

تراكيب اللغة taraakíib al-lúghah (Structures)

1 Saying *was* and *were*

Arabic does not use a verb for *is/are*, but when you talk about the past, the verb **kaana** for *was/were* is necessary.

This verb differs slightly from the past tense verbs which you have met in that it has two stems (**kaan-** and **kun-**). The endings are the standard past tense suffixes used on all Arabic verbs (see page 364).

Singular		Plural	
he was	كان kaana	they (m.) were	كانوا kaan-uu
she was	كانت kaan-at	they (f.) were	كن kun-na
you (m.) were	كنت kun-t(a)	you (m.) were	كنتم kun-tum
you (f.) were	كنت kun-ti	you (f.) were	كنتن kun-tunna
I was	كنت kun-t(u)	we were	كنا kun-naa

Notes

a) The final vowels in brackets can be omitted in informal speech (see page 122).

b) The stem **kaan-** is used in the *he, she* and *they* (masc.) forms, and the stem **kun-** for the rest. It may help you to remember them if you notice that the shortened **kun-** stem is used before suffixes which begin with a consonant. **kaana** is a type **Mw-I** verb: see Verb Tables.

c) Since the last letter of the root of this verb is **n**, the usual short-hand spellings with the doubling sign is used when the suffix also begins with an **n** (كن **kunna** – *they* (fem.) *were*, and كنا **kunnaa** – *we were*).

كنا في تونس في الصيف   *We were in Tunisia in the summer*

kunnaa fii tuunis fi S-Sayf

Word order

The verb **kaana** usually comes first in the sentence, and the normal rules of agreement given in the previous unit apply.

kaana jamaal :abd an-   كان جمال عبد الناصر قائدا عظيما

naaSir qaa'idan :aDHiiman   *Jamaal Abd al-Nasir was a great*

(he-)was jamaal :abd an-   *leader*

naaSir (a) leader (a) great-one

kaana l-mudiir mashghuulan   كان المدير مشغولا

(he-)was the-manager busy   *The manager was busy*

kunt(u) mariiDan   كنت مريضا

I-was ill   *I was ill*

kaanat al-mumaththilah   كانت الممثلة مشهورة
mash-huurah

she-was the actress famous   *The actress was famous*

kaanat al-buyuut qadiimah   كانت البيوت قديمة

she-was the-houses old   *The houses were old*

2 The accusative marker

Formal Arabic has a set of (usually) three varying noun endings which show the part played by a word in a sentence, similar to case endings in Latin or German (see introduction). The words *he, him* and *his* show these cases in English:

1 Nominative	2 Accusative	3 Genitive
he	*him*	*his*

Most of these endings are only vowel marks which are omitted in modern written Arabic, and for the sake of simplification we have not included them in this book.

The only case ending appearing in print in contemporary written Arabic – except for a few special types of noun – is the *accusative* case.

How to form the accusative

This ending only affects the spelling of indefinite unsuffixed nouns or adjectives. The full form is actually ـً (pronounced **-an**), but only the **alif** is usually written after the noun/adjective.

Unsuffixed in this context normally means that the noun or adjective does not have the feminine ending ـة (**-ah**). Nouns and adjectives which have this ending never add the **alif**. The examples above illustrate this point.

Note

a) You may think that we could have said simply masculine nouns take the extra **alif**, but there are feminine nouns which do not have the ـة (**-ah**) ending, and these have to obey the **alif** law.

For example, أُم **umm**, *mother* is clearly feminine, but has no ـة (**-ah**) ending. Its accusative indefinite is therefore أمّا **umman**. There is also a handful of nouns signifying men which have the feminine ending, such as خليفة **khaliifa**, *caliph* in the text above. These are obviously regarded as masculine, but do not take the **alif** because of the presence of the ـة (**-ah**) ending.

b) A minority of Arabic unsuffixed nouns and adjectives do not add the **alif**. The commonest of these are the main colours, as well as some forms of the internal plural and many proper nouns. From this unit on, these are marked in the vocabulary boxes with an asterisk*, and also appear like this in the glossaries at the end of the book.

كان الكلب أبيض	*The dog was white*
kaana l-kalb abyaD	

قرأنا جرائد كثيرة أمس	*We read many newspapers*
qara'naa jaraa'id kathiirah ams	*yesterday*

قابلنا أحمد في السوق	*We met Ahmed in the souq*
qaabalnaa aHmad fi s-suuq	

When to use the accusative

In Arabic, the accusative is used in four instances:

1 When the second noun is the object of the sentence, i.e. the thing or person the verb applies to:

شاهدوا قصرا فخما	*They saw a magnificent*
shaahaduu qaSran fakhman	*castle*

2 After the verbs **kaana** *was, were/to be*, **laysa** *is not, are not/not to be*, **aSbaHa** *to become*, and a few other similar verbs*.

Note: **laysa** only can also take an alternative construction using the preposition **bi-** which does not take the accusative:

لست غنيا/لست بغني   *I am not rich*

lastu ghaniyyan/lastu bi-ghanii

3 In some common expressions and adverbs, when the ending is most commonly heard in spoken Arabic:

أهلا وسهلا **ahlan wa sahlan** *hello, greetings*

مرحبا **marHaban** *welcome*

شكرا **shukran** *thanks*

جدا **jiddan** *very*

أبدا **abadan** *never*

طبعا **Tab:an** *naturally*

4 After certain short words, known as particles, such as **inna** and **anna***.

*The Arabs refer to these words as '**kaana** and her sisters' and '**inna** and her sisters'.

3 Saying where something was

kaana can be used before prepositions (words which tell you where something is), and such sentences are the same as the those verbless sentences in the present, except that **kaana** is put at the beginning (and obeys the agreement rules given in Unit 7)

kaana qalam-ii fii jayb-ii   كان قلمي في جيبي

(he-)was pen-my in pocket-my   *My pen was in my pocket*

4 How to say *is/are not*

The word **maa**, *not* is used before normal verbs (see Unit 7, Unit 10), and can also be used before **kaana** in a past tense sentence.

To negate *is/are* sentences, the verb **laysa** is used. This verb is unique in Arabic, as it is only used in what looks like the past tense, with past tense suffixes, but the meaning is actually present.

Like **kaana** it has two stems (**lays-** and **las-**). As with **kaan-/kun-** you will see that in both verbs the first stem is used for the *he*, *she* and *they* (masc.) parts, and the second stem with the rest.

Remember that, although it looks like a past tense, it means *isn't/ aren't*.

Singular		Plural	
he isn't	ليس **lays-a**	*they* (m.) *aren't* ليسوا **lays-uu**	
she isn't	ليست **lays-at**	*they* (f.) *aren't* لسن **las-na**	
you (m.) *aren't*	لست **las-t(a)**	*you* (m.) *aren't* لستم **las-tum**	
you (f.) *aren't*	لست **las-ti**	*you* (f.) *aren't* لستن **las-tunna**	
I am not	لست **las-t(u)**	*we aren't* لسنا **las-naa**	

laysa l-walad mujtahidan   ليس الولد مجتهدا

(he-)is-not the boy diligent   *The boy is not diligent*

Accusative marker

laysa requires the accusative marker in the same way as **kaana**. (But see also alternative construction with **bi-** described above.)

5 How to say *to become*

There are several verbs in Arabic meaning *to become* but أصبح **aSbaHa** is by far the most common. Like **kaana** and **laysa** it requires the accusative marker on unsuffixed indefinites, but it has only one stem **aSbaH-**.

Note: The initial hamzah of **aSbaH** is never elided, so if you say *and he became* it is **wa-aSbaHa**, not **wa-SbaH**.

aSbaHa l-walad mariiDan   أصبح الولد مريضا

he-became the-boy ill   *The boy became ill*

aSbaHat al-bint mariiDah   أصبحت البنت مريضة

she-became the-girl ill   *The girl became ill*

بنت *bint* is an example of a feminine noun without the suffix ـة.
However the adjective **mariiDah** still has to have the suffix, as it
refers to a female.

These verbs have all been dealt with together here as they share the
common feature of using the accusative marker on what is not a
direct object.

6 Sentences with *inna* and *anna*

The particle **inna**, though frequently used, is virtually meaningless.
However, it is translated in this book where necessary as *indeed*,
just to show it is there (older Arabic-teaching manuals use the
biblical *verily*).

inna is usually used with *is/are* sentences which require no verb in
Arabic. When they are followed by an indefinite unsuffixed noun
– usually the name of a person or place – this noun takes the
accusative marker **-an**, and this time it is the first noun in the
sentence which has the accusative marker (unlike **kaana**, **laysa**
and **aSbaHa** sentences where it is attached to the second noun).

inna muHammadan :aamil   إن محمدا عامل مجتهد

mujtahid   *Muhammad is a hard*

indeed Muhammad worker hard   *worker*

anna is the conjunction *that* and follows the same rules as **inna**.

The Muslim Confession of Faith as heard from the minarets every
prayer time is a good example of the use of **anna**:

أشهد ألا إله إلا الله وأن محمدا رسول الله

**ash-hadu allaa ilaaha illa l-laah wa-anna muHammadan
rasuulu l-laah***

It is usually translated as '*I witness that there is no god but Allah,
and that Muhammed is His apostle*'

*The transliteration here reflects the Classical Arabic
pronunciation. **allaa** is a contraction of **an-laa** *that not, no*.

inna **and** *anna* **with pronouns**

Since **inna** requires an accusative after it, it has to use the suffixed pronouns (given in Unit 7)

إنه خبر جيد   *(Indeed) it is good news*

inna-h khabar jayyid

إنها بنت لطيفة   *(Indeed) she is a pleasant*

inna-haa bint laTiifah   *girl*

Summary of the Arabic sentence

These are the four types of Arabic sentence:

1 *Is/are* sentences with no verb:

(the) X [is/are] Y

السندباد رجل غني   *Sindbad is a rich man*

as-sindibaad rajul ghanii

2 Sentences with a verb (other than the **kaana** group below):

verb X Y

شرب محمد الشاي   *Mohammed drank the tea*

shariba muHammad ash-shaay

3 Sentences with **kaan, aSbaHa** and **laysa**

The second term of the sentence is accusative, marked with an **alif** when required:

kaana/aSbaHa/laysa *(the) X Y-accusative*

كان الهندباد فقيرا   *Hindbad was poor*

kaana l-hindibaad faqiiran

150 ARABIC

---

4 Sentences introduced by **inna** and its associates.

The first term of the sentence is accusative, marked as appropriate:

inna (the) X-accusative [is/are] Y

إن حسنا تلميذ مجتهد   Indeed Hassan is a hard-

inna Hasanan   working pupil

tilmiidh mujtahid

Remember:

a The accusative marker is only written after words which:
 i) do not have **al-** *the* in front of them
 ii) have no other suffix like the feminine ending **-ah** or are one of the minority of such words which never take the accusative marker (noted with an asterisk as they occur).

b The negative verb **laysa** *is/are not* is past in form, but present in meaning.

---

7 How to say *had done* something

Although there are only two tenses in Arabic, past and present, the verb **kaana** can be used to express the meaning of *had done something*, called the *pluperfect* tense in English.

The little word **qad** is commonly introduced between the subject and the main verb. It emphasises that the action has been well and truly completed, that it is over and done with.

The word order is as follows:

1. The *he-* or *she-* form of **kaana** (because it always precedes its noun – see Unit 7).

2. The subject of the sentence (i.e. who is doing the action) if this is stated. If it is a pronoun (*he, we,* etc) it will be implicit in the verb (see Unit 7).

3. The word **qad** (optional).

4. The fully-agreeing part of the main verb (i.e. the action which had been carried out) It is fully-agreeing because it comes after its subject (see Unit 7).

5. Any other information (when, where it happened, etc.).

kaana l-mudiir waSal	كان المدير وصل يوم السبت
yawm as-sabt	*The manager had arrived*
he-was the-manager he-	*on Saturday*
arrived day the-Saturday	

kaanuu qad saafaruu ila	كانوا قد سافروا إلى الهند من قبل
l-hind min qabl	*They had travelled to India*
they-were **qad** they-travelled	*before*
to the-India from before	

أوزان الكلمات awzáan al-kalimáat (Word shapes)

Pattern	Arabic example	Eng. sound-alike
C¹aC²C²aaC³	**Haddáad** حداد blacksmith	*had Dad* (as in *had Dad known* ...)

This is a formation often used for trades. In the Sindbad story we have حمال **Hammaal**, *porter,* from the root **H-m-l**, *carrying.*

Haddaad comes from حديد **Hadiid**, *iron.* Other examples are:

نجار **najjaar** *carpenter*

خباز **khabbaaz** *baker*

بناء **bannaa'** *builder*

خياط **khayyaaT** *tailor*

This type of word takes the ـون **-uun** plural

It is really an intensive form of **CaaCiC** (see Unit 2), in that it expresses the idea that somebody is always, habitually or professionally performing the action of the root.

The feminine ending **-ah** is often added to this word shape either to indicate a female member of the trade or profession:

خياطة **khayyaaTah** *tailoress, seamstress*

or a machine:

دبابة **dabbaabah** *a (military) tank* (lit. a crawling machine, from the root **d-b-b** *crawling*)

غسالة **ghassaalah** *washing machine* (from root **gh-s-l** *washing*)

سيارة **sayyaarah** *car* (lit. going-machine).

عصارة: **aSSáarah** *juicer*

دباسة **dabbáasah** *stapler*

These take the plural ات ـ **-aat**.

تمرينات **tamriináat (Practice)**

Exercise 5
Fill in the gaps in the following sentences with the appropriate form of **kaana**. Don't forget to add the accusative marker where necessary.

١ الآن درجة الحرارة ٣٥.
الصبح .... ١٨.

٢ هذه السنة سميرة في
الصف السادس. السنة
الماضية .... في
الصف الخامس.

٣ الآن الأولاد طوال، في سنة
١٩٩٥ .... قصارا.

٤ اليوم حامد سعيد، أمس
.... حزينا.

أمـس   اليـوم

الآن **al-áan** now

درجة، ـات **dárajah, -aat** step, degree

درجة الحرارة **dárajat al-Haráarah** temperature (lit. degree of heat)

صف، صفوف **Saff, Sufúuf** class (in school)

سادس **sáadis** sixth

خامس **kháamis** fifth

سعيد، سعداء **sa:iid, su:adáa'*** happy, joyful

Exercise 6

Write the sentences below in the past tense, remembering to put the
accusative marker where necessary (see page 144).

Example: Mahmoud is unhappy. → *Mahmoud was unhappy.*

محمود حزين.   ←   كان محمود حزينا.

٤ عمر الشريف ممثل مصري.	١ ذلك الطعام لذيذ.
٥ الأولاد سعداء.	٢ حدائق الفندق واسعة.
	٣ شركتنا مشهورة في الخليج.

ممثل، ـون **mumáththil, -uun** actor, representative

Exercise 7

Where are they?

Mahmoud and his wife Salma and their son Hamad and daughters Faridah and Sarah are staying at a hotel in Abu Dhabi. They have left a note at the desk to say where they can be found if friends or colleagues want to contact them. Answer the questions below in Arabic, using **laysa** and the accusative marker where necessary.

Example: *Is Salma in the Palm Court café?*

                 No, she is not at the Palm Court café.

هل سلمى في مقهى النخيل؟

لا، ليست في مقهى النخيل.

Where are you?   أين أنت؟

Name: ....   الاسم: محمود صالح

Date: ....   التاريخ: ....

Room number: ....   رقم الغرفة: ٥١٤/ ٥١٥/ ٥١٦

Time: ....   الساعة: ــ١١ ....

AL-BUSTAN RESTAURANT	☐	مطعم البستان
PALM COURT CAFÉ	☐	مقهى النخيل
LOBBY	☐	البهو
BUSINESS CENTRE	☑ محمود	مركز رجال الأعمال
CLUB HOUSE	☐	النادي
SWIMMING POOL	☐	المسبح
TENNIS COURT	☑ حمد وفريدة وسارة	ملعب التنس
GOLF COURSE	☑ سلمى	ملعب الجولف

١ هل الساعة ١٠,٣٠ الصبح؟

٢ هل محمود في البهو؟

٣ هل سلمى في مطعم البستان؟

٤ هل سلمى وفريدة وسارة في المسبح؟

٥ هل محمود في مركز الأعمال؟

٦ هل سلمى في ملعب الجولف؟

٧ هل أرقام الغرف ٥١١، ٥١٢ و٥١٣؟

٨ هل الأولاد في ملعب التنس؟

بهو **bahw** (hotel) lobby

بستان **bustáan** orchard

مسبح، مسابح **másbaH, masáabiH*** swimming pool

أعمال **a:máal** (plural) business, affairs, works

ملعب، ملاعب **mál:ab, maláa:ib*** pitch, court, course

Exercise 8

An Arabic proverb says:

الفهد منقط والنمر مخطط.

A leopard can't change his spots.

(lit. 'the leopard is spotted and the tiger is striped')

فهد، فهود **fahd, fuhúud** leopard

نمر، نمور **námir, numúur** tiger

منقط **munáqqaT** spotted

مخطط **mukháTTaT** striped

What is wrong with these two? Change the sentence below into the negative to make sense.

الفهد مخطط والنمر منقط.

Exercise 9

Change the following sentences into the negative, using the verb **laysa**.

١ علي طالب كسلان.

٢ أنا تعبان بعد رحلتي.

٣ الفنادق الكبيرة في وسط المدينة.

٤ هي مشهورة جدا.

٥ الطبيب مشغول في المستشفى.

٦ هذه القصة من ألف ليلة وليلة طويلة جدا.

كسلان **kasláan** lazy

مشغول **mashghúul** busy

مستشفى، مستشفيات **mustáshfaa, mustashfayáat** hospital

قصة، قصص **qíSSah, qíSaS** story, tale

Exercise 10

Change the sentences below into the pluperfect tense.

Example:

وجد الهندباد قصر السندباد.

كان الهندباد (قد) وجد قصر السندباد.

Note: The use of **qad** is optional. Watch out for the agreement of the main verb which comes after its subject in the pluperfect.

١ روت شهرزاد قصة جديدة كل ليلة.

٢ خرج الخدام من القصر.

٣ خبر البحري الحمال عن رحلاته العجيبة.

٤ تبعته الخادمات الى داخل القصر.

٥ أكل الناس الأكل اللذيذ.

روت **ráwat** *she told*

خادمة، ـات **kháadimah, -aat** (female) *servant*

٩ أكثر من واحد
akthar min waaHid
More than one

In this unit you will learn how to:
- look for a job in the paper
- look for a flat or a house
- talk about more than one person or thing
- say *these/those*
- talk about two people or things

1 وظائف شاغرة waDHáa'if sháaghirah
Situations vacant

Arabic newspapers carry classified advertisements, with all the usual sections for *Situations Vacant, For Sale, To Let,* and so on. When you are reading them, concentrate on picking out the key words, and learn to recognise words such as *Wanted* and *For Rent.*

Exercise 1

Read through the Key Phrases, then look at the job advertisements on page 159 and answer the questions. You don't need to understand every word.

a You are an experienced hairdresser looking for a job in Dubai. Which of these three jobs would suit you best?

وظائف شاغرة

i كـوافيرة درجـة اولى بـراتب مـغر
لصـــالـــون كـبير في الشارقـة

iii مـطـلـوب كـوافيرة درجـة اولى
لصـــالـــون راق بــــدبـــي

ii مطلوب كوافيرة ذات خبرة لتسريح
الشعر والمنكير والبـاديكر بـالعين

b Which picture is most appropriate for each of the job advertisements below?

iii

i

ii

a مدربة للرشاقة والايروبيك لمركز
ريـــاضـــي ت:٦٥١٣٩

b مـطـلـوب كـهـربـائـي سـيـارات
ومـــكـــيـــفـــات بــالــعـين
ت٠٣/٧٢١٢٨٨٤ –
٣٦١١٩

c مطلوب فنـي أجهـزة الكترونية
لتصليح هواتف متحركة فاكس
٧٤٧٥١

c What people are wanted for the jobs advertised on page 160? Match the people to the jobs.

1 labourers and builders

2 French teacher

3 manageress for a ladies' fashion shop

4 pharmacist

5 secretary (male or female)

6 employees for a restaurant

7 salesmen and saleswomen

8 saleswoman for a shoe shop

vii

مطلوب

مديرة

لمحل أزياء نسائي بدبي
خبرة وإجادة اللغة
الإنجليزية

نقال ٤٤٠٥٩
فاكس ٣١٩٣

viii

عمال + بنائيين الاتصال
٩١٥٥

ix

مندوب مبيعات خبرة في اجهزة
التبريد والتكييف لاتقل عن خمس
سنوات في الامارات مع لغة
انجليزية وعربية ارسال السيرة
الذاتية على الفاكس
٣٩٩٢١

x

مطلوب

سكرتير
أو سكرتيرة عربية

يجيد الطباعة عربي - انجليزي ولديه / لديها
معرفة في أمسور الهجرة والعمل

الاتصال ٣١٨٥٥
فاكس ٣٥٦١٣
الشارقة

v

مطلوب موظفات لمطعم بالعين
ت:٤٦٣٢٤

vi

مندوبات مبيعات ذوات خبرة مع
رخصة سواقة راتب ٥٠٠٠
٦٠٠٠ الرجاء ارسال السيرة
الذاتية على فاكس
٩١٨٥٥ لعناية المهندس
حسام

i مطلوب صيدلانية للعمل في
صيدلية بعجمان مرخصة من
وزارة الصحة
ت:١٨٢٦٠

ii مطلوب بائعة لمحل احذية نسائي
بدبي لديها خبرة ٣ سنوات
ت:٧٧١٧٣

iii مدرس لغة فرنسية مؤهل لمدرسة
هنديه ت:٢٧١٠٠
ف:٢٧٦٠٦

iv

شركة كبرى

تطلب :

بائعين وبائعات

لمحلاتها في دبي وأبوظبي

الشروط المطلوبة :

● خبرة في المبيعات
● إجادة اللغة الانجليزية محادثة وكتابة
● حسن المظهر

يرجى ارسال السيرة الذاتية
على فاكس رقم
٢٩٥٤٦

d Which of the advertisements on page 160 require:
   i   some previous experience?
   ii a driving licence?
   iii a knowledge of English?

e Name three requirements applicants need for this position as sales representative.

2 للإيجار li-l-iijáar *For rent*

Read through the Key Phrases to familiarise yourself with the new vocabulary, then answer the questions.

Exercise 2
Match the Arabic abbreviations to the English words.

a room, bedroom	١ ت
b bathroom	٢ ش
c telephone	٣ غ
d fax	٤ ح
e Post Office (PO) Box No.	٥ ف
f street	٦ ص ب

Exercise 3

You are looking for accommodation. Read the advertisements and answer the questions opposite.

a You want to rent somewhere for your large family. Which place has the most bedrooms and bathrooms?

b You are looking for two villas close to each other for your firm. Are there any which would be suitable?

c You want to rent a villa for just a few weeks. Is there anything available?

d You have found a villa that you like, but can only call the owner during office hours. Which one is it?

e You would like to rent a villa with a garden. Which one could you choose?

f Which flat could you rent if you needed to find somewhere immediately?

g You work for the *Gulf Times* newspaper. Which flat would be most convenient for you?

h Where could you find a villa to rent, which is not too expensive, with air conditioning if possible?

تعبيرات رئيسية ta:biiráat ra'iisíyyah (Key phrases)

Looking for a job

طلب **Talaba** *seek, want*

مطلوب **maTluub** *wanted, required*

وظيفة، وظائف* **waDHiifah, waDHaa'if*** *job, situation*

موظف، ـون **muwaDHDHaf, -uun** *employee, official* (m.)

موظفة، ـات **muwaDHDHafah, -aat** *employee, official* (f.)

كوافيرة، ـات **kwaafiirah, -aat** *hairdresser* (f.), *coiffeuse*

فني، ـون **fannii, -uun** *technician*

كهربائي، ـعر **kahrabáa'ii, -uun** *electrician*

مدربة، ـات **mudarribah, -aat** *trainer* (f.)

بنّاء، ـون **bannáa', -uun** *builder*

صيدلانية، ـات **Saydalaaniyyah, -aat** *pharmacist* (f.)

سكرتيرة، ـات **sikritayrah, -aat** *secretary*

مندوب مبيعات، مندوبو مبيعات **manduub mabii:aat, manduubuu mabii:aat** *sales representative* (**mumaththil** is also used instead of **manduub**)

بائع، ـون **baa'i:, -uun** *salesman*

بائعة، ـات **baa'i:ah, -aat** *saleswoman*

مبيع، ـات **mabii:, -aat** *selling, sales*

مكيف، ـات **mukayyif, -aat** *air conditioner*

محل، ـات **maHall, -aat** *(big) shop, store*

أحذية **aHdhiyyah** *footwear*

خبرة **khibrah** *experience*

رخصة سواقة **rukhSat siwaaqah** *driving licence*

إقامة **iqaamah** *residence; residence permit*

صالح **SaaliH** *valid;* (of people) *upright*

معرفة **ma:rifah** *knowledge*

راتب **raatib** *salary*

مغر(ي) **mughrii** *attractive, tempting* (for the spelling of this kind of adjective, see Unit 18)

سيرة ذاتية **siirah dhaatiyyah** *CV; resumé*

لعناية... **li-:inaayat...** *for the attention of...*

على الأقل **:ala l-aqáll** *at least*

Looking for accommodation

للبيع **li-l-bay:** *for sale*

للإيجار **li-l-iijáar** *for rent*

شقة، شقق **sháqqah, shíqaq** *flat, apartment*

فيلا، فيلل **fíilla, fíilal** *villa*

غرفة، غرف **ghúrfah, ghúraf** *room, bedroom*

صالة **Sáalah** *sitting room, lounge*

حمام، ـات **Hammáam, -aat** *bathroom*

دش **dushsh** *shower*

مطبخ **máTbakh** *kitchen*

طابق، طوابق **Táabiq, Tawáabiq*** *storey, floor*

سعر، أسعار **si:r, as:áar** *price*

متجاور **mutajáawir** *adjacent, neighbouring, next to each other*

مباشرة الخلو **mubáasharat al-khalw** *for immediate occupation*

أوقات العمل **awqáat al-:amal** *working/office hours*

فاكس **faaks** *fax*

صندوق بريد **Sandúuq bariid** *PO Box*

تراكيب اللغة taraakíib al-lúghah (Structures)

1 Talking about more than one of anything

a) Arabic plural formations are not often predictable, so they must be learned along with their singulars.

b) In Arabic, the plural of inanimate objects or abstracts is treated in all respects as a feminine singular, so verbs and adjectives must be in the feminine singular form.

c) In English, the word 'plural' refers to more than one (i.e. 1+).

However, Arabic has a special form for two of anything, called the dual, so the plural in Arabic refers to more than two (2+).

Plurals of nouns

There are three ways to form the plural in Arabic:

1 The external or suffix masculine plural.

2 The external feminine/neuter plural.

3 The internal plural.

1 The external or suffix masculine plural

Add the suffix ون- **-uun** to the singular noun. For the accusative form (see page 144), add ين- **-iin** to the singular.

This kind of plural can only be used on words which indicate male human beings, as opposed to females and things/abstracts. The common exception to this is سنة pl. سنون (**sanah, sinuun**) year, and even this word has an alternative plural (سنوات **sanawáat**).

HaDar al-mudarrisuun	حضر المدرسون المؤتمر
al-mu'tamar	*The teachers attended the*
he-attended the-teachers the-conference	*conference*
hum muqaawiluun	هم مقاولون
they contractors	*They are contractors*
kaana l-muhandisuun miSriyyiin	كان المهندسون مصريين
he-was the-engineers Egyptians	*The engineers were Egyptian*
aSbaHuu muHaasibíin	أصبحوا محاسبين
they-became accountants	*They became accountants*

2 The external feminine/neuter plural

Drop the ة (if there is one) and add ات- **-aat** to the singular word. This can be applied to words indicating females or things/abstracts, and there is no special accusative form.

waSalat aT-Taalibaat **yawm al-jum:ah** she-arrived the-[female]students day the-Friday	وصلت الطالبات يوم الجمعة *The (female) students arrived on Friday*
aSbaHna mudarrisaat they (f)-became teachers	أصبحن مدرسات *They became teachers*
a-antunna mumarriDaat? (?)-you (f.) nurses?	أأنتن ممرضات؟ *Are you nurses?*
ta:allam-naa kull al-kalimaat we-learned all the-words	تعلمنا كل الكلمات *We learned all the words*

3 The internal plural

This is formed in two ways: a) by altering the internal vowelling of the word (like English *foot* ➜ *feet*); and/or b) by adding prefixes or suffixes.

The internal plural is used mainly for males and things/abstracts, and rarely for females. There is no general relationship between the singular word shape and the plural word shape.

Some words indicating males form a plural with the feminine ending طالب، طلبة **Táalib, Tálabah**, *male student*. (This word also illustrates the fact that some words have alternative plurals, in this case طلاب **Tulláab**.) Such plurals are still regarded as masculine.

Tip: The Arabic internal plural system cannot generally handle words consisting of more than four consonants, excluding suffixes such as ـة **-ah**, but counting doubled consonants as two. It is therefore likely that 'short' words will take an internal plural, but this is not a rule.

dakhala r-rijaal al-ghurfah   دخل الرجال الغرفة

he-entered the-men the-room   *The men entered the room*

naHnu :ummaal fii sharikat   نحن عمال في شركة السيارت

as-sayyaaraat   *We are workers in the car*

we workers in company (of) the-cars   *company*

al-kutub :alaa l-maa'ida   الكتب على المائدة

the-books on the-table   *The books are on the table*

Plurals of adjectives

It is a good idea to think of adjectives in Arabic as another class of noun. They have the same choice as nouns in forming their plurals:

a) **-uun** or **-aat** ending

b) internal plurals, which which must be learned with their singulars.

If no adjective plural is given in the vocabulary, use the suffixed plurals according to the rules below. Internal plurals are given for those adjectives which have them.

Noun	*Adjective plural form*
male human beings	internal plural if it has one, otherwise + **-uun**.
female human beings	+ **-aat**
things/abstracts	+ **-ah** (fem. singular)

These rules hold for all adjectives with a few common exceptions, mainly relating to the primary colours (see Unit 16)

Common adjectives with internal plural forms

Adjective	Meaning	Male plural form
kasláan كسلان	lazy	kasáalaa كسالى
nashiiT نشيط	active	nisháaT نشاط
kabiir كبير	big	kibáar كبار
Saghiir صغير	small	Sigháar صغار
naHiif نحيف	thin	niHáaf نحاف
samiin سمين	fat	simáan سمان
Tawiil طويل	tall	Tiwáal طوال
qaSiir قصير	short	qiSáar قصار
dhákii ذكي	clever	adhkiyáa'* أذكياء
ghábii غبي	stupid	aghbiyáa'* أغبياء
jamiil جميل	handsome	jimáal جمال
sa:iid سعيد	happy	su:adáa'* سعداء
Hazíin حزين	sad	Huzanáa'* حزناء
ghariib غريب	strange	ghurabáa'* غرباء
ájnabii أجنبي	foreign	ajáanib* أجانب
:aDHiim عظيم	great, mighty	:uDHamáa'* عظماء
jadiid جديد	new	júdud جدد

(Note: Many of these plurals – marked with * – do not take the accusative marker. This applies to the plural only, not the singular as well.)

Remember: The plural of things in Arabic is regarded in all respects as feminine singular for the sake of grammatical agreement. Here are a few more mixed examples:

al-awlaad Tiwaal   الأولاد طوال

the-boys talls   *The boys are tall*

aT-Talabah mujtahiduun

the-students diligents

الطلبة مجتهدون

The students are diligent

al-mumaththilaat al-jadiidaat

the-actresses the-new(ones)

الممثلات الجديدات

The new actresses

al-buyuut al-qadiimah

the-houses the-old(one)

البيوت القديمة

The old houses

2 هؤلاء haa'uláa'(i)..., أولائك uuláa'ik(a)... these..., those...

You have already learned the demonstrative pronouns هذا/هذه *this* and ذلك/تلك *that* (see Unit 4) to describe singular words which are either masculine or feminine in gender. Because plurals of things/abstracts in Arabic are regarded as feminine singular, all verbs, adjectives and pronouns relating to them must be feminine singular.

When speaking of plural male/female human beings, use the forms هؤلاء haa'ulaa'(i) *these*, and أولائك uulaa'ik(a) *those* respectively. The final vowels are often missed out in informal situations.

With these plural forms, there is no distinction for gender, so both of them can apply to either males or females.

haa'ulaa'i T-Talabah HaaDiruun

these the-students presents

هؤلاء الطلبة حاضرون

These students are present

uulaa'ika l-banaat jamiilaat

those the-girls beautifuls

أولائك البنات جميلات

Those girls are beautiful

tilka l-buyuut kabiirah

this the-houses big

تلك البيوت كبيرة

These houses are big

3 Talking about two people or things.

Arabic has a special way of talking about two of anything, called the dual. This is obligatory in use for both people and things (i.e. you can't use the plural).

Formation of the dual

a) If the noun does not have the feminine ending **-ah**, add the suffix **-aan** to the singular. This changes to **-ayn** when an accusative marker is required.

al-waladaan Tawiilaan   الولدان طويلان

the(2)-boys tall (x2)   *The two boys are tall*

kaana l-waladaan Tawiilayn   كان الولدان طويلين

he-was the(2)-boys tall(x2)   *The two boys were tall*

This applies to the vast majority of nouns and adjectives.

b) If the noun has the **-ah** ending of the feminine singular, this changes to **-at** (spelled with an ordinary ت), and the suffix **-aan** is added to it.

as-sayyaarataan kabiirataan   السيارتان كبيرتان

the(2)-cars big(x2)   *The two cars are big*

kaanat as-sayyaarataan kabiiratayn   كانت السيارتان كبيرتين

she-was the(2)-cars big(x2)   *The two cars were big*

Since Arabic has this dual form for two, it is not usually necessary to insert the numeral word (see Unit 2). As with the personal pronouns and verbs, this is only used for emphasis.

(As with the masculine plural ending ون/ين- **-uun/-iin** the final ن of the dual is omitted if the word constitutes the first term of a possessive construction. See Unit 14).

Dual pronouns

Arabic does not need to distinguish between *one* and *two* for the person who is speaking, so where English says *we two*, Arabic says simply *we*.

you two أنتما **antumaa** (both masc. and fem.):

antumaa ta:baanaan   أنتما تعبانان

you-two tired(x2)   *You two are tired they two* هما **humaa** (both masc. and fem.):

humaa mashhuuraan	هما مشهوران
they-two famous(x2)	*They two are famous*

In practice, the dual is not common, except when speaking about things like hands, feet, etc., which always come in pairs.

يد **yad** *hand*

رجل **rijl** *foot*

أذن **udh(u)n** *ear*

عين **:ayn** *eye*

Note: These words – and indeed all parts of the body which occur in pairs – are feminine.

There are also special dual markers for the verb. These are given in the Verb Tables, but they occur so rarely that they need only to be noted at this stage.

أوزان الكلمات awzáan al-kalimáat (Word shapes)

Pattern	Arabic example	Eng. sound-alike
CuCaCCiC	**mudárris** مُدَرِّس *teacher*	*McCaskill*

This shape indicates the person or thing carrying out the action of Verb Form II (see Table S-II), grammatically known as the active participle. The verb دَرَّس **dárrasa** means *to teach*, so مُدَرِّس is a *teaching person*, i.e. *teacher*. This shape is also often used to indicate trades or professions (see Word shapes in Unit 8).

A similar shape with an **a**-vowel instead of an **i**-vowel after the middle radical is also common. This is the passive participle, i.e. the person or thing to which the action of the verb has been applied. An example of this is مُوَظَّف **muwáDHDHaf** *official*, *employee*. This comes from the verb وَظَّفَ **waDHDHafa** *to appoint to an official position, to employ*.

All these words can be made feminine by the addition of the ending ـة **-ah**. The male versions take the plural suffix ون، and the females ـات.

Remember that the point of learning word shapes is to be able to read and know something about Arabic words. It is not always possible to get an exact English sound-alike, but the pattern is usually easy to imitate. Say them aloud one after another until they become familiar.

مدرس **mudárris** *teacher*

مدرب **mudárrib** *trainer*

ممثل **mumáththil** *representative, actor*

محرر **muHárrir** *editor*

مفتش **mufáttish** *inspector*

ممرض **mumárriD** *nurse*

منجم **munájjim** *astrologer*

تمرينات **tamriináat (Practice)**

Exercise 4
Listen to the recording or read the transcript of four people describing where they live.

Then try to identify which person lives in which of the flats or houses described below.

a A villa with four bedrooms and two bathrooms, two living rooms and a kitchen

b A small villa with three bedrooms, living room, bathroom and kitchen c A flat with one room and salon

d A two-bedroomed apartment with living room.

١ أسكن في شقة صغيرة قريبة من وسط المدينة، فيها غرفة واحدة وصالة وحمام ومطبخ.

٢ نسكن في شقة جديدة. فيها غرفتان، واحدة لي أنا وزوجي وواحدة للأولاد، وصالة.

٣ نسكن في فيلا قريبة من البحر. هي جميلة جدا.عندنا أربع غرف وحمامان وصالتان وهناك مطبخ طبعا.

٤ نسكن في فيلا، فيلا صغيرة. هناك ثلاث غرف وصالة وحمام ومطبخ.

Exercise 5
Write the correct form of plural for the adjectives in brackets.

١ هؤلاء الأولاد (ذكي)
٢ بناتك (جميل)
٣ القمصان (مخطط)
٤ قرأنا الجرائد (الإنجليزي)
٥ البنوك (مقفول) بعد الظهر
٦ الرجال (المصري) (نشيط)

Exercise 6
Change the noun, adjective or pronoun in bold type in the following sentences into the correct plural form.

Example:

I bought a shirt last week.

I bought three shirts last week.

اشتريت قميصا الأسبوع الماضي.
اشتريت ثلاثة قمصان الأسبوع الماضي.

١ وجدنا مطعما جيدا في القاهرة.

٢ حضر المدير الاجتماع.

٣ هل أنت جوعان؟

٤ السكرتيرة مشغولة.

٥ بنتها طالبة في الجامعة.

٦ هو ممثل كويتي.

٧ كان الفيلم طويلا.

اشتريت **ishtaráyt** *I bought*

قميص، قمصان **qamíiS, qumSáan** *shirt*

جيد **jáyyid** *of good quality*

جوعان، جوعى **jaw:áan*, jáw:aa*** *hungry*

Exercise 7
Now change these whole sentences into the plural. Remember that verbs <u>preceding</u> their nouns remain singular, and that the -uun/-iin plural ending must show the correct case.

١ وصل العامل الجديد.

٢ أين الكتاب الفرنسي؟

٣ وجدته المدرسة على الرف.

٤ أصبح الولد سمينا.

٥ خرج الضيف من الفندق.

ضيف، ضيوف **Dayf, Duyúuf** *guest*

Exercise 8

Choose the correct ending for each of the sentences below.

١ هذه الشقق قريبة...

٢ هؤلاء نساء نحيفات...

٣ هذه الجرائد يومية...

٤ هؤلاء الطلبة اللبنانيون كثيرون...

a ولكن أولائك الطلبة المصريين قليلون.

b ولكن أولائك نساء سمينات.

c ولكن هذه الشقق بعيدة.

d ولكن هذه الجرائد أسبوعية.

ولكن **waláakin, walaakínna** *but* (the latter behaves like إن

inna. See Unit 8)

نساء **nisáa'*** *women* (pl.)

Exercise 9

Put the following sentences into the dual. (You can leave the verbs in the singular as they come before the noun.)

1 The office is closed.	١ المكتب مقفول.
2 The technician is not present.	٢ ليس الفني حاضرا.
3 The bathroom is spacious.	٣ الحمام واسع.
4 The employee (fem.) worked in the ministry.	٤ عمل الموظف في الوزارة.
5 The manageress spoke to the workman.	٥ كلمت المديرة العامل.

Exercise 10

Read (and if you have the recording, listen to) the following information about John Barker.

جون باركر انجليزي. عمره ٣٢ سنة. هو متزوج. يتكلم عربي. له خبرة ٥ سنوات في المبيعات في الإمارات. لديه رخصة سواقة وإقامة في الإمارات.

John is looking for a job as a salesperson in Abu Dhabi, and wants to register at an employment agency. He needs to fill in an application form.

Imagine that you are John, and fill out the application form for him. A possible reply is in the Key to the Exercises.

١ الاسم الكامل ....
٢ العمر..
٣ الجنسية ....
٤ أعزب/متزوج..
٥ العنوان ....
٦ رقم التلفون ....
٧ اللغات ....
٨ هل لديك رخصة سواقة صالحة؟ ....
٩ هل لديك رخصة إقامة صالحة في الإمارات؟ ....
١٠ خبرة ....

كامل **káamil** complete, whole

جنسية، ـات **jinsíyyah, -aat** nationality

أعزب **á:zab*** bachelor, single

متزوج **mutazáwwaj** married

عنوان، عناوين **:unwáan, :anaawíin*** address

لديك **ladáy-k** you have (lit. 'with you; in your possession')

10 | ؟ماذا تعمل maadhaa ta:mal?
What do you do?

In this unit you will learn:

- to say what you do every day
- to talk about your interests
- to say what you like or dislike
- to say what you will do in the future
- more about *not*

1 ماذا تعمل كل يوم؟ maadhaa ta:mal kull yawm? *What do you do every day?*

A women's magazine has sent Fawzia to interview Kamal, the sales manager of a local business. She asks him about what he does during the day. Listen to or read the interview several times, each time concentrating on a different point. Then answer the questions.

Exercise 1

a What does Kamal always eat in the morning?

b Does he telephone his
   i son? **ii** daughter? **iii** mother?

c Does he read reports for
   i 2–3 hours? **ii** 3–4 hours? **iii** 4–5 hours?

d Did he learn to use a computer
   i at school? **ii** at college? **iii** at work?

e Who does he sit with in the afternoon?

f How often does he meet the employees?

فوزية   ماذا تأكل الصبح؟

كمال   آكل الفواكه دائما، وأحيانا خبزا وجبنة وأشرب قهوة. وعادة أتكلم مع ابني بالتلفون. هو يعيش في أمريكا.

فوزية   وماذا تعمل بعد ذلك؟

كمال   أذهب إلى المكتب.السائق يوصلني الساعة ٨،٣٠ وأتكلم معه في السيارة عن أخبار اليوم.

فوزية   وبعد ذلك؟

كمال   السكرتيرة تطبع لي رسائل وأنا أقرأ التقارير المالية. هذا يستغرق ساعتين، ثلاث ساعات.

فوزية   هل تستخدم الآلة الحاسبة؟

كمال   نعم، طبعا. تعلمت استخدام الآلة الحاسبة في كلية التجارة.

فوزية   وماذا تعمل بعد الظهر؟

كمال   بعد الظهرأجلس مع المدير العام ونناقش شؤون الشركة، وأحضر اجتماعات يومية مع الموظفين.

Exercise 2

Now read the interview again. Link the English phrases to the corresponding Arabic expressions.

a I drink coffee.   ١ هو يعيش في أمريكا.

b He lives in America.   ٢ نناقش شؤون الشركة.

c I talk with him in the car.   ٣ أشرب قهوة.

d And what do you do in the afternoon?   ٤ وماذا تعمل بعد الظهر؟

e We discuss company affairs.   ٥ أتكلم معه في السيارة.

أكل، يأكل **ákala, yá'kul [S-I u]** *eat*[1]

فاكهة، فواكه **fáakihah, fawáakih*** *fruit*

خبز **khubz** *bread*

جبنة **júbnah** *cheese*

شرب، يشرب **sháriba, yáshrab [S-I a]** *drink*

تكلم، يتكلم **takállama, yatakállam [S-V]** *speak*

مع **má:a** *with, together with*

عاش، يعيش **:aash, ya:iish [My-I]** *live, reside*

عمل، يعمل **:ámila, yá:mal [S-I a]** *do, work*

ذهب، يذهب **dháhaba, yádh-hab [S-I a]** *go*

سائق، ـون **sáa'iq, -úun** *driver*

وصل، يوصل **wáSSala, yuwáSSil [S-II]** *connect, transport*

خبر، أخبار **khábar, akhbáar** *news*

طبع، يطبع **Tába:a, yáTba: [S-I a]** *print, type*

قرأ، يقرأ **qára'a, yáqra' [S-I a]** *read*

تقرير، تقارير **taqríir, taqaaríir*** *report*

مالي **máalii** *financial*

استغرق، يستغرق **istághraqa, yastághriq [S-X]** *take, use up,
occupy* (of time)

استخدم، يستخدم **istákhdama, yastákhdim [S-X]** *use*

آلة حاسبة **áalah Háasibah** *computer*[2]

تعلم، يتعلم **ta:állama, yata:állam [S-V]** *learn*

استخدام **istikhdáam** *use, employment*

كلية، ـات **kullíyyah, -aat** *college, faculty*

تجارة **tijáarah** *trade, commerce*

جلس، يجلس **jálasa, yájlis [S-I i]** *sit*

عام: **aamm** *general*

ناقش، يناقش **náaqasha, yunáaqish [S-III]** *discuss*

شأن، شؤون **sha'n, shu'úun** *matter, affair*

حضر، يحضر **HáDara, yáHDur [S-I u]** *attend*

1 آكل **aakul** *I eat.* Note spelling here. This sign over the **alif** (called **maddah**) is always used when (theoretically) two **hamzahs** come together, or a **hamzah** is followed by a long **a-**vowel (e.g. in the word for *computer* in the next note)

2 آلة حاسبة **aalah Haasibah** *computer.* This coinage – literally meaning *counting machine* – seems to have met with fairly general acceptance, although كمبيوتر **kambyuutir** is also common.

🎧 **2** ماذا تعمل في أوقات الفراغ؟ **maadhaa ta:mal fii awqaat al-faraagh?** *What do you do in your free time?*

Ruhiyyah and Hisham al-Musallam, on business from Jordan, are discussing with Ali, a Sudanese business contact, what they do in their free time.

Exercise 3
Listen to the discussion and answer the questions.

a What does Hisham not play any more?

b What do he and Ali have in common?

c Who likes to watch Egyptian television serials?

d What does Ruhiyyah invite Ali to do this evening?

e Who is the most active:
  i Hisham? **ii** Ruhiyyah? **iii** Ali?

علي   ماذا تفعل في أوقات الفراغ يا هشام؟

هشام   ألعب الجولف وأسبح. لما كنا عائشين في عمان، كنت
        ألعب التنس، لكن الآن لا ألعب. أقرأ كثيرا.

علي   أنا أقرأ كثيرا كذلك. أحب الشعر الحديث. هل تحبين الشعر
        يا روحية؟

روحية لا، أنا أفضل الروايات. أتفرج على التلفزيون كثيرا، وأحب
        المسلسلات المصرية

علي   أنا لا أحبها

هشام   ولا أنا. أكرهها فعلا. أفضل البرامج الثقافية أو الرياضة،
        لكن روحية لا تحب الرياضة.

روحية ولكننا نحب السينما نحن الاثنان. سوف نذهب إلى
        السينما في المساء. ستجيء معنا يا علي؟

Exercise 4

Read the dialogue again, and link the English phrases with the
appropriate Arabic expressions.

a I used to play tennis.   ١ كنت ألعب التنس.

b Do you like poetry?   ٢ سوف نذهب إلى السينما.

c I prefer novels.   ٣ روحية لا تحب الرياضة.

d Ruhiyyah doesn't like sport.   ٤ هل تحبين الشعر؟

e We are going to the cinema.   ٥ أفضل الروايات.

فعل، يفعل **fá:ala, yáf:al [S-I a]** *do*

وقت الفراغ **waqt al-faráagh** *free time*

لعب، يلعب **lá:iba, yál:ab [S-I a]** *play*

عائش: **áa'ish** *living*

سبح، يسبح **sábaHa, yásbaH [S-I a]** *swim*

جولف **guulf** *golf*

تنس **tánis** *tennis*

الآن **al-áan** *now*

شعر **shi:r** *poetry*

أحب، يحب **aHábba, yuHíbb [D-IV]** *like, love*

فضل، يفضل **fáDDala, yufáDDil [S-II]** *prefer*

رواية، ـات **riwáayah, -áat** *novel, story*

تفرج، يتفرج على **tafárraja, yatafárraj :ala [S-V]** *watch, look at*

مسلسل، ـات **musálsil, -áat** *serial, series*

ولا **wá-laa** *and not, nor*

كره، يكره **káriha, yákrah [S-I a]** *hate*

فعلا **fi:lan** *really, actually, in fact*

برنامج، برامج **barnáamij, baráamij*** *programme*

ثقافي **thaqáafii** *cultural*

رياضة **riyáaDah** *sport, sports*

جاء، يجيء **jáa'a, yajíi' [My-I]** *come*

 تعبيرات رئيسية **ta:biiráat ra'iisíyyah (Key phrases)**

Asking what others do and saying what you do

ماذا تأكل الصبح؟   *What do you eat in the morning?*

ماذا تعمل بعد الظهر؟	*What do you do in the afternoon?*
هل تقرأ كثيرا؟	*Do you read a lot?*
أذهب إلى المكتب	*I go to the office*
آكل الفواكه دائما	*I always eat fruit*
أشرب قهوة كثيرا	*I drink coffee a lot*
ألعب تنس/جولف	*I play tennis/golf*
أسبح	*I swim*

Asking what others like and saying what you like to do

ماذا تحب أن تفعل في أوقات الفراغ؟	*What do you like to do in your free time?*
أحب التلفزيون	*I like television*
هي لا تحب كرة القدم	*She doesn't like football*
نكره برامج الرياضة	*We hate sports programmes*

تحب أن تفعل **tuHíbb an táf:al** *you like to do* (lit. *you like that you do*)

كرة القدم **kúrat al-qádam** *football*

تراكيب اللغة taraakíib al-lúghah (Structures)

Talking about things in the present

This unit contains an overview of the Arabic verb system, placed here for ease of reference. Do not try to absorb all this information at once, as you will have ample opportunity to revise and consolidate your knowledge in future units. The overview should be studied in conjunction with Unit 7, which deals with the past tense, and, in particular, with the Verb Tables at the back of the book.

1 How to form the Present Tense

Look at the Present Tense column of Table 1 on page 364. You will see that the present tense is formed from a stem (whose vowels usually differ from those of the past stem), to which are added prefixes for all parts, plus suffixes for certain parts.

With only a few exceptions (see below), the same set of prefixes and suffixes apply to every Arabic verb, so it is obviously important to learn them thoroughly from the beginning.

Here is the present tense of *to write* in transliterated form, without the dual forms which occur rarely and can be learned later. The stem is given in bold type:

Singular	Plural
ya**ktub** *he writes, is writing*	ya**ktub**uun *they* (m.) *write*
ta**ktub** *she writes*	ya**ktub**na *they* (f.) *write*
ta**ktub** *you* (m.) *write*	ta**ktub**uun *you* (m) *write*
ta**ktub**iin *you* (f.) *write*	ta**ktub**na *you* (f.) *write*
a**ktub** *I write*	na**ktub** *we write*

Tips

To help you remember, here are some pointers:

Prefixes:
- The *you*-forms all have the prefix **ta-**, which is similar to the **t** in the pronouns **anta**, **anti**, etc.
- All the third person forms have the prefix **ya-** with the exception of the feminine singular.
- The *I*-form has **a-**; the pronoun is **anaa**.

•The *we*-form has **na-**; the pronoun is **naHnu**.

Suffixes:
• The *you* (fem. sing.) has suffix **-iin** to distinguish it from the masculine.
• The *they* and *you* (masc. pl.) have the external plural suffix **-uun**.
• The *they* and *you* (fem. pl.) have the suffix **-na**.

2 Vowelling of the prefixes

In the types of stems which we have marked II, III and IV (see Verb Tables), the vowel of all the prefixes changes to **u** (**yu-**, **tu-**, **u-**, etc.)

3 The present stem

In this unit, both tenses of the verb are given in Arabic script and transliteration in the *he*-form, plus the verb type in square brackets [S-III, Mw-I, etc.] to enable you to look them up in the verb tables.

Example:

	Past	Present	Type	Meaning
فضل، يفضل	**faDDala**	**yufaDDil**	[S-II]	*prefer*

In subsequent units, verbs will be given as follows and you should refer to the appropriate verb table to identify all the parts of the verb.

Past Ar.	Past Trans.	Type	Meaning
فضل	**faDDala**	[S-II]	*prefer*

4 Type S-I Verbs

Type S-I verbs are the only ones where the vowel on the middle radical is not predictable. In both tenses it can be any of the three Arabic vowels, **a**, **i** or **u**.

Since these vowels are never written in Modern Arabic, they have to be learned. In this book they are given in the following form:

Past Ar.	Past Trans.	Type	Meaning
كتب	**kataba**	[S-I u]	*write*

This should be interpreted as follows:

a) The Arabic gives the three root letters.

b) The transliterated past identifies the middle radical vowel – here **a** (**kat<u>a</u>ba**). *Note:* The vowel on the first radical is always **a** in the past tense, and this radical has no vowel in the present.

c) The verb type (here S-I) directs you to the appropriate verb table.

d) The vowel given after the verb type (here **u**) is the middle radical vowel in the present stem (**kt<u>u</u>b**).

The following scheme of things usually prevails, but there are always exceptions.

Past stem	Vowel on C²	➜	Vowel on C²	Present Stem
CaCaC	a	➜	u or i	**CCuC**
kataba *to write*				**ktub**
CaCiC	i	➜	a	**CCaC**
fahima *to understand*				**fham**
CaCuC	u	➜	u	**CCuC**
kabura *to be big*				**kbur**

Most S-I verbs are of the **CaCaC ➜ CCu/iC** type. There are quite a few **CaCiC ➜ CCaC** types, but **CaCuC ➜ CCuC** is rare, and usually indicates a state of being or becoming something.

Tip: You will usually still be understood if you get these vowels wrong, so don't worry too much about them at this stage.

5 Other types of verbs

Type D-I and type Fw-I verbs also have variable vowellings which will be indicated in the same way.

All other types of verbs (including S-II to X) fortunately have standard vowellings for both stems, so reference to the appropriate verb table will provide all parts automatically.

These will be explained as they are introduced, with reference to the verb tables, but there are some general pointers which you can learn about now.

You know already that there are no really irregular verbs in Arabic, with the exception of **laysa** (see Unit 8). The same prefixes and suffixes are used for all verbs, but some verbs have two stems, in one or both of the tenses.

An example of this is the verb **kaana**, (see Unit 8) which has the two past stems **kaan-** and **kun-**. This type of verb is usually known as a hollow verb, and is the subject of Table Mw-I. Although it should not be used in *is/are* sentences, **kaana** has a 'present' tense which is used in certain contexts to express doubt or uncertainty. This also has two stems: **kuun-** and **kun-**. Again refer Table Mw-I.

6 Function of the present tense

Arabic has only two simple tenses, the past and the present. Just as the past tense serves for *did*, *has done*, the present tense fulfils the functions of *does*, *is doing* and, in questions *does do*, as in *Does he live here?* Common sense will tell you how to translate from Arabic.

يعيشون في شقة كبيرة في أبو ظبي

ya:iishuun fii shaqqah kabiirah fii abuu DHabi

they-live in apartment big in Abu Dhabi

They live in a big apartment in Abu Dhabi

تنشر الحكومة الإحصائيات في أول الشهر

tanshur al-Hukuumah al-iHSaa'iyaat fii awwal ash-shahr

she-publishes the-government the-statistics in first the month

The government publishes the statistics at the beginning of the month

ماذا تأكل في الصباح؟

maadhaa ta'kul fi S-SabaaH?

what you-eat in the-morning

What do you eat in the morning?

7 The past continuous

The *past continuous* is what we call a verb-phrase such as *was studying, used to study,* and so on.

In Arabic this is expressed with the aid of the verb **kaana** (type Mw-I), in the same way as the *had done* type verb explained in Unit 8, except that the main verb this time is in the present tense.

In all other respects, including agreement and word order, this tense behaves like its sister in Unit 8.

kaana + present tense verb	= past continuous *was studying*
kaana + past tense verb	= pluperfect *had studied*

كانت فاطمة تدرس في جامعة لندن

kaanat faaTimah tadrus fii jaami:at landan

she-was Fatimah she-studies in university [of] London

Fatimah was studying at the University of London

كنا نذهب إلى السوق كل يوم

kunnaa nadhhab ilaa s-suuq kull yawm

we-were we-go to the-market every day

We used to go to the market every day

8 Talking about what you will do in the future

There is no future tense in Arabic.

Actions which have not yet happened are expressed by placing the word سوف **sawfa**, or the prefix ـس **sa-** before a present tense verb. Since it consists of only one Arabic letter, **sa-** is joined to the word which follows it.

سوف يصل الوزير غدا

sawfa yaSil al-waziir ghadan

[future] he-arrives the-minister tomorrow

The minister will arrive tomorrow

سأسافر الأسبوع القادم

sa-usaafir al-usbuu: al-qaadim

[future] - I-travel the-week the-coming

I shall travel next week

وصل، يصل **wáSala, yáSil [Fw-I i]** *to arrive*

---

9 The complete *not*

Arabic has several ways of expressing *not* which must be used in different contexts.

Negative	Context	Formation
ليس **laysa***	*is/are* sentences	second noun/adjective, if indefinite, has accusative marker
لا **laa**	present verb	verb takes normal form
ما **maa**	past verb	verb in the past tense
لن **lan**	future verb	**sa-/sawfa** omitted, and verb in the subjunctive**
لم **lam**	past actions	verb in the present jussive** form, but with past meaning

* Unlike the other negatives, **laysa** is actually a verb and has to be used accordingly. (See Unit 8)

** For these terms see later in this unit.

---

a) **laysa** is used for negating *is/are* sentences:

laysa r-rajul kabiiran   ليس الرجل كبيرا

is-not the-man old   *The man is not old*

b) **maa** negates a past verb:

maa saafarat ila l-maghrib

ما سافرت إلى المغرب

not she-travelled to the-Morocco *She did not go to Morocco*

c) **laa** negates sentences with a present tense verb :

laa ya:rafuun al-lughah

لا يعرفون اللغة الفرنسية

l-faransiyyah

They (masc.) *don't know*

not they-know the-language the-French *French*

d) **lan** negates the future. The **sa-** or **sawfa** future marker is omitted when **lan** is used.

lan taSilii qabl aDH-DHuhr

لن تصلي قبل الظهر

not you-will-arrive before the-noon *You* (fem. sing.) *will not*

arrive before noon

e) **lam** negates verbs which refer to the past, although, as will be discussed below, the actual verb used is a form of the present.

lam ya'kuluu l-laHm

لم يأكلوا اللحم

not they-ate the-meat *They didn't eat the meat*

Note: **maa** + past verb and **lam** + present verb convey exactly the same meaning. Literary Arabs regard the latter construction more elegant.

10 Altered forms of the present verb

If you look carefully at examples d) and e) above, you will note that the verbs used are slightly different from those you have learned (they have no final ن for example).

Historically, in addition to the normal form, Arabic had two so-called moods of the present (not the past) tense, called the *subjunctive* and the *jussive* respectively.

These altered forms must be used after certain words in Arabic. Two of these are **lan**, which requires the subjunctive, and **lam**, which requires the jussive.

Fortunately, for many verbs, the subjunctive and the jussive are identical in writing. They are given in full in Table 1 on page 364 but, for convenience, here are the parts which show a difference. Other parts of the verb remain unchanged.

Verbs which show further deviations will be explained as they occur.

تكتبين **taktubiin** *you write* (fem. sing.) ➜ **taktubii** تكتبي

يكتبون **yaktubuun** *they write* (masc. pl.) ➜ **yaktubuu** يكتبوا

تكتبون **taktubuun** *you write* (masc. pl.) ➜ **taktubuu** تكتبوا

The Arabs call this 'the omission of the **nuun**'.

An unpronounced **alif** is added at the end. You will remember that the same thing happened in the past tense. In fact it is a convention that any verb which has a **-uu** suffix adds this redundant letter. Nobody knows why.

Remember to use these forms after both **lan** and **lam**.

11 Prepositions and pronoun suffixes

Prepositions tell you where something is in relation to something else, such as *on*, *behind*, *in*, etc.

However they often, in both English and Arabic, form an essential part of what are known as phrasal verbs. English examples of phrasal verbs are *call up*, *call on*, *call in*, all essentially different meanings derived from the simple verb *call*.

In Arabic, for instance, you don't 'need something', you 'need *towards* something'.

Here are some examples:

احتاج، يحتاج إلى **iHtaaja, yaHtaaj ilaa** [Mw-VIII] *to need something*

احتفل، يحتفل بـ **iHtafala, yahtafil bi-** [S-VIII] *to celebrate something*

رغب، يرغب في **raghiba, yarghab fii** [S-I a] *to want, desire something*

رحب، يرحب بـ **raHHaba bi-** [S-II] *to welcome someone*

Prepositions required after verbs are given in the vocabularies.

When prepositions are used with pronouns (*towards him, by her*, and so on), they use the same possessive pronouns suffixes as are used with nouns (see Unit 5):

كتابها **kitaab-ha** *her book*

منها **min-ha** *from her*

Pronunciation

Arabic prepositions alter slightly when they are attached to a suffix, and some of them affect certain suffixes.

i) Prepositions ending in **-a** lose the **-a** with the suffix **-ii**, *me*: **ma:a** *with* +-**ii** *me* = معي **ma:ii** *with me*

ii) Prepositions ending in **-n** double this with the suffix **-ii**: **min** *from* + **-ii** *me* = مني **minn-ii** *from me*

akhadhuu l-jariidah min-nii أخذوا الجريدة منّي

they-took the-newspaper from-me   *They took the newspaper from me*

(*Note:* This is different from منّا **min-naa**, *from us*, where one **n** belongs to the suffix.)

iii) After long vowels and **-ay**, **-ii** *me* is pronounced **-ya**:

فيَّ **fiiya** (or **fiyya**) *in me*

علىَّ **:alayya** *on me*

iv) After **-i**, **-ii** or **-ay**, **-hu**, **-hum** and **-hunna** change **-u** to **-i** (not visible in the written form):

فيه **fii-hi** *in him*

بهم **bi-him** *with them*

v) Prepositions ending in long **-aa** written as a **-y** without dots (see page 21) change their endings into **-ay**:

إلى **ilaa**, *towards* becomes ‫إليـ‬ **ilay-**: ‫إليكم‬ **ilay-kum**, *towards you*

على **alaa**, *on* becomes ‫عليـ‬ **:alaay-** : ‫علينا‬ **:alay-naa**, *on us*

‫يضحك علينا‬   **yaD-Hak :alay-naa**

he-laughs on-us   *He's laughing at us*

vi) ‫لـ‬ **li-**, *to, for* becomes **la-** before all the suffixes except **-ii** (see i) above). This change is again not apparent in the written form:

‫لهم‬ **la-hum** *for them*

sa-adfa: la-haa l-mablagh   ‫سأدفع لها المبلغ المضبوط‬

al-maDbuuT   *I'll pay her the exact*

(future)I-pay to-her the-sum   *amount*

the-exact

Note: **li-**, as a one letter word (see page 22) is attached to the word after it. If this has **al-** *the*, the **alif** is omitted:

‫للولد‬ **li-l-walad** *for the boy*

In addition, if the noun itself begins with **laam**, the doubling sign is used

‫للّغة‬ **li-l-lughah** *to the language*

‫أوزان الكلمات‬ awzáan al-kalimáat (Word shapes)

Pattern	Arabic example	Eng. sound-alike
CuCaCáa'*	**wuzaráa'** ‫وزراء‬ ministers	*to a rat* (Cockney/ Glaswegian pron. of the *t* as a glottal stop)

This shape is mainly used for the plural of certain male human beings which have the singular shape **CaCiiC**. In fact it is relatively safe to guess plurals of such nouns using this shape. It does not take the accusative marker.

🎧 سفراء **sufaraa'*** from سفير **safiir** *ambassador*

أمير، أمراء *prince, emir*

وزير، وزراء *minister*

مدير، مدراء *director, manager*

It is also used with some adjectives of the same shape:

سعيد، سعداء **sa:iid, su:adaa'*** *happy, joyful*

and some nouns with the singular shape **CaaCiC**:

شاعر، شعراء **shaa:ir, shu:araa'*** *poet*

تمرينات **tamriináat (Practice)**

Exercise 5
Nafisah plays tennis, and enjoys going to the cinema and swimming. She would like to make friends with someone who has the same interests as she does. She sees the following entries in the newspaper. Who has most in common with her?

كن صديقي **kun Sadiiq-ii!** *Be my friend!*

٣ اسمي حميد وأنا طالب. هواياتي السينما والتنس والسباحة.

٢ أنا سلطان. ألعب كرة، وأحب الألعاب الكمبيوترية والسينما والموسيقى العربية.

١ اسمي خميس. أحب لعب السنوكر والتنس وكرة القدم.

ألعاب la:b, al:áab *playing, game* لعب، ألعاب

هواية، ـات hawáayah, -áat *hobby*

سباحة sibáaHah *swimming*

Exercise 6

Change the following sentences into the negative, using one of the words in the box below. Use each word only once.

١ هذا الجمل قبيح.

٢ البيوت رخيصة في الرياض.

٣ سوف نسافر إلى الهند في الشهر القادم.

٤ ذهبنا إلى المسبح يوم الجمعة.

٥ أختي تعمل في صيدلية.

٦ درس صالح في أمريكا.

ما	ليس	لن	ليست	لا	لم

جمل، جمال jámal, jimáal *camel*

قبيح qabíiH *ugly*

الهند al-hind *India*

درس، يدرس dárasa, yádrus [S-I u] *study*

Exercise 7

Fill the gaps using the prepositions from the box below.

١ المدير يدفع ....ـها راتبا شهريا.

٢ ستسافر............ـه في الطائرة.

٣ هل تضحك ....ـنا؟

٤ أخذت الجريدة ....ـي.

٥ أهذا كتاب جيد؟ زوجتي تحتاج ....ـه.

من	مع	ل	على	إلى

Exercise 8

Hameed is an active person. Make up complete sentences about him, saying what his sports are and what he likes and dislikes, and using the information in the table below. The first one is done for you.

حميد يلعب كرة.

Hameed plays football.

يكره	لا يحب	يحب	يلعب
السينما	القراءة	تنس	كرة
التلفزيون	الكتب	السباحة	سكواش

Exercise 9

The verbs in brackets in the following sentences are all in the *he-*form. Referring to the translation below, substitute the correct present tense forms.

١ الأولاد القطريون (يتعلم) اللغة الانجليزية في المدرسة الثانوية.

٢ (يتصل) بأمها كل يوم.

٣ (يشرب) شاي عند رجوعنا من العمل.

٤ (يكتب) رسالة إلى صديقتي نورة.

٥ الموظف يريد أن (يكلمـ)ـنا فورا.

٦ هل (يعرف) ذلك الرجل؟

٧ (يقفل) الصيدليات الساعة ٦.

٨ سوف (يصل) إلى نيو يورك يوم الخميس.

٩ كانت البنات (يلعب) مع أولاد الجيران.

١٠ كان محمود وإخوانه (يكسب) كثيرا في الكويت.

Translation:

1 *Qatari children learn English in secondary school*
2 *She telephones her mother every day.*
3 *We drink tea on our return from the work*
4 *I am writing a letter to my friend Nourah*
5 *The official wants to talk to us immediately.*
6 *Do you (fem. sing.) know that man?*
7 *The pharmacies close at six o'clock*
8 *They (fem.) will arrive in New York on Thursday*
9 *The girls used to play with the neighbours' children.*
10 *Mahmoud and his brothers used to earn a lot in Kuwait.*

Exercise 10

Change the following past tense verbs (in brackets) into the present tense.

١ (سأل) سكرتيره سؤالا.

٢ (حملت) البنت القهوة إلى الصالة.

٣ (فحص) الطبيب عيون المريض.

٤ صاحب الدكان (قدم) لنا شاي.

٥ ما (فهمت) هذا الكتاب.

٦ إلى أين (ذهبت)؟

Translation:

1 *He asked his (male) secretary a question.*
2 *The girl carried the coffee to the living room.*
3 *The doctor examined the eyes of the patient.*
4 *The shopkeeper offered us tea.*
5 *I didn't understand this book.*
6 *Where did you (masc. sing.) go?*

فحص **fáHaSa, yáfHaS [S-I a]** to examine

مريض، مرضى **maríiD, márDaa*** (adj.) ill; (noun) patient

Exercise 11
Read the article below about the Dubai Shopping Festival, and
answer the following questions.
a When does it take place?
b Why do so many people come to the festival?
c Name two of the attractions.
d Where is the firework display held?

جوائز قيمة في سحويات منها   يقام مهرجان دبي للتسوق في

سيارات وكيلوغرامات ذهب.   شهر مارس ويحضر الناس

وهناك أيضا فعاليات ثقافية،   بالآلاف من الإمارات والعالم كله

وفنية ورياضية مثل سباق   إلى دبي ليستفيدوا من التنزيلات

الخيول وعروض فخمة من   الكبيرة في أسعار البضائع في

الألعاب النارية فوق خور دبي   المراكز التجارية والأسواق.

المشهور.   وإضافة إلى ذلك تقدم الشركات

يقام **yuqáam** is held, takes place (passive verb)

مهرجان، ـات **mahrajáan, -áat** festival

تسوق **tasáwwuq** shopping

استفاد، يستفيد **istafáada, yastafiid [My-X]** benefit

تنزيل، ـات **tánziil, -áat** lowering, reduction

سعر، أسعار **si:r, as:áar** price

بضائع **baDáa'i:*** goods, merchandise

تجاري **tijáarii** commercial

إضافة إلى ذلك **iDáafatan ílaa dháalik** *in addition to that*

قدم، يقدم **qáddama, yuqáddim [S-II]** *offer, present*

جائزة، جوائز **jáa'izah, jawáa'iz*** *prize, reward*

قيم **qáyyim** *valuable, expensive*

سحب، سحوبات **saHb, suHuubáat** *lottery*

ذهب **dháhab** *gold*

أيضا **áyDan** *also*

فعالية، ـات **fa:aalíyyah, -aat** *activity, event*

فني **fánnii** *artistic; technical*

رياضي **riyáaDii** *sporting*

مثل **mithl** *like*

سباق **sibáaq** *racing*

خيل/خيول **khayl/khuyúul** *horses (both with plural meaning)*

عرض، عروض **:arD, :urúuD** *show, display*

ألعاب نارية **al:áab naaríyyah** *fireworks*

فوق **fawq(a)** *above, over*

خور **khawr** *creek*

11 | الأعياد الإسلامية
al-a:yaad al-islaamiyyah
Islamic Festivals

In this unit you will learn:
- about the main Islamic festivals
- special greetings used on festival days
- the Islamic calendar
- how to say *what?/where?/who?*
- how to say *to have*

Introduction

The emphasis of the book changes slightly from this unit onwards. Units 1–10 contain all the essential basics of Modern Standard Arabic, so now we can go on to more advanced and realistic texts and dialogues. These use more complex sentence structures, so make sure you have mastered the principles given in Units 1–10 before going on. Individual words can be looked up in the glossaries. However, it is less easy to refer back to half-absorbed constructions, so some revision now will pay dividends later.

The Arabic texts and dialogues will be given as they would appear in a modern book or newspaper; that is, with only occasional vowelling. Only a literal word-for-word translation of the texts will be given in the Key to the Exercises to help you to concentrate on the Arabic structures. You should try to convert this into normal English.

Major new grammatical features are given in special sections just as before, and minor points and reminders of things already dealt with are given in the Notes after the texts.

Where there is no realistic alternative, data which has to be learned mechanically (for instance parts of the verb) can be referred to in the tables at the back of the book. We suggest that, while you refer to these as much as possible, you should not allow yourself to become discouraged if you can't take them all in at once. Rather keep coming back to them as you work through the units.

الأعيـاد الإسلامية al-a:yaad al-islaamiyyah

Islamic festivals

Jack and Fran, visiting Egypt during the month of Ramadan, ask their friend Ahmed about Islamic festivals.

Exercise 1
Look carefully through the new words before you begin. Listen to the recording several times, and answer the questions.
a How many festivals do all Muslims celebrate?
b Which month comes before the first festival?
c What should people abstain from during the month of Ramadan?

Exercise 2
Listen to the recording again and answer these questions.

a The great festival of the pilgrimage begins:
  i on the first day ii on the last day iii in the middle

b People travel:
  i to Mecca ii to Medina iii from Mecca

c They visit:
  i the Kaabah ii the mosque

d How do they celebrate the festival?

e Which Muslim celebration resembles a Christian festival?

Now read the dialogue.

جاك   كم عيدا عند المسلمين؟

أحمد   الأعياد المهمّة عندنا إثنان.

فران   وما هما؟

أحمد   الأوّل هو العيد الصغير واسمه عيد الفطر.

جاك   وفي أيّ شهر هو؟

أحمد   العيد الصغير في أوّل يوم من شهر شوال.

فران   وما مناسبته؟

أحمد   مناسبته أنّ شهر شوال يعقب شهر رمضان الكريم،   وهو شهر الصوم عند المسلمين.

جاك   وما معنى الصوم عندكم؟

أحمد   الصوم معناه أنّ الناس لا يأكلون ولا يشربون في النهار. هذا هو معنى الصوم.

فران   وما هو العيد الآخر؟

أحمد   هو العيد الكبير أو عيد الأضحى.

جاك   وما مناسبته؟

أحمد   مناسبته الحجّ وهو يبدأ في آخر يوم من أيّام الحج. والحج معناه أنّ الناس يسافرون الى مكّة المكرّمة ويزورون الكعبة.

فران   وكيف يحتفلون بهذا العيد؟

أحمد   هم يذبحون فيه ذبائح.

جاك   وما هي الذبيحة؟

أحمد   الذبيحة هي خروف يذبحونه ويأكلونه في نهاية الحج. وهذا عادة عند المسلمين.

فران   فأعيادكم اثنان فقط إذا؟

أحمد   لا، في بعض الأقطار يحتفلون بعيد ثالث.

جاك   وما هو؟

أحمد   هو مولد النبي، صلّى الله عليه وسلّم، في شهر ربيع الأوّل.

فران   نعم، هذا مثل عيد الميلاد عندنا نحن المسيحيّين.

Exercise 3

Read the text again, referring to the notes below, and link the English phrases with the equivalent Arabic expressions.

a We have two important festivals.	١ في أوّل يوم من شهر شوال.
b Which month is it in?	
c The first day of the month of Shawal.	٢ كيف يحتفلون بهذا العيد؟
	٣ فأعيادكم اثنان فقط إذا؟
d What do you mean by fasting?	٤ ما معنى الصوم عندكم؟
e People don't eat or drink in the daytime.	٥ هذا مثل عيد الميلاد عندنا نحن المسيحيّين.
f How do they celebrate this festival?	٦ الأعياد المهمّة عندنا إثنان.
g What is the sacrifice?	٧ هذا عادة عند المسلمين.
h It is a custom among the Muslims.	٨ الناس لا يأكلون ولا يشربون في النهار.
i So you only have two festivals?	٩ ما هي الذبيحة؟
j This is like our Christian Christmas.	١٠ في أيّ شهر هو؟

عيد، أعياد **:iid, a:yáad** festival; anniversary

مسلم، ــون **múslim, -uun** Muslim

مهم **muhímm** important

فطر **fiTr** breaking of a fast

شوال **shawáal** name of an Islamic month. See list later in this unit.

مناسبة، ــات **munáasabah, -aat** occasion

عقب **:áqaba S-1 u** come after, follow

كريم، كرام **kariim, kiráam** noble, generous (here used as an honorific adjective for the month Ramadan, often translated holy)

صوم **Sawm** fast, fasting

معنى **má:naa*** meaning

نهار **naháar** *daytime, hours of daylight*

آخر **áakhar*** (fem. أخرى **úkhraa***) *other*

عيد الأضحى **iid al-áD-Haa:** *Festival of the Sacrifice* (see below)

الحج **al-Hajj** *the Pilgrimage*

آخر **áakhir** *last* (of something)

يوم، أيّام **yawm, ayyáam** *day*

مكة المكرمة **mákkah l-mukárramah** *Holy (City of) Mecca*

زار **záara Mw-I** *visit*

الكعبة **al-ká:bah** *the Kaabah* (Holy Shrine in Mecca)

احتفل بـ **iHtáfala bi- S-VIII** *celebrate*

ذبح **dhábaHa S-I** *a slaughter*

ذبيحة، ذبائح **dhabíiHah, dhabáa'iH*** *sacrificial animal*

خروف، خرفان **kharúuf, khurfáan** *sheep*

نهاية **niháayah** *end*

عادة، ـات **:áadah, -aat** *custom, habit*

إذا **ídhan** *so, therefore*

بعض **ba:D** *some, part of something*

قطر، أقطار **quTr, aqTáar** *region, zone, area*

ثالث **tháalith** *third* (adj.)

مولد النبي **máwlid an-nábii** (festival of) *the Prophet's Birthday*

صلى الله عليه وسلم **Sállaa l-Láahu :aláy-hi wa-sállam**
  Prayers and Peace be upon Him (said after mentioning the
  name of the Prophet)

مثل **mithl** *like*

عيد الميلاد **iid al-miiláad:** *Christmas*

مسيحي، ـون **masíiHii, -uun** *Christian*

al-mulaaHaDHáat (Notes) الملاحظات

- **kam** *how many*. This word takes the singular of the noun, which is also marked with the accusative ending **-an** if there is no other suffix (see Unit 8).

- **muslimiin**. The masculine plural ending **-uun** becomes **-iin** after all prepositions (in this case **:ind**), and also when the noun is the possessing item of a possessive construction (see Unit 14). For **:ind** expressing *to have*, see later in this Unit.

- Note the dual pronoun **humaa** *they-two* for two things or persons (see Unit 9)

- **awwal yawm** *the first day*. The adjective **awwal** *first* can be used in the normal way, but frequently precedes its noun which then does not have **al-** *the*.

- **shahr shawwaal** is a possessive construction (*the month of Shawwal*), so the word **shahr** cannot have **al-**.

- **anna** *that* (conjunction), like **inna** (Unit 8) is always followed by a noun showing the accusative marker if applicable, or a pronoun suffix.

- معناه **ma:naa-h** *its meaning*. Words ending in **-aa** but written with ى change to **alif** when anything is added. ى can only exist as the final letter of an Arabic word or word combination, the same as ة (which becomes ت when anything is added).

- The verbs *eat* and *drink* are in their full plural agreeing forms because they come after their subject **an-naas** *the people* (see Unit 7).

- **aakhir** *last* behaves in the same way as **awwal**. See above.

- **yazuuruun** *they visit*. This kind of verb, called by the Arabs a hollow verb, has two stems for both present and past tenses. This one is vowelled like **kaana**, but there are two other vowel patterns. Study these in Tables **Mw**, **My** and **Ma**, and you can always refer back to them in the future. Like all verbs, these occur usually in the *he* or *she* forms (because of the agreement rules), so are often recognizable from their long **aa** vowel in the past. In the present tense the long vowel is (in order of statistical frequency) **uu**, **ii** or (infrequently) **aa**.

■ **fii-h**. The use of prepositions in both English and Arabic is very idiomatic and therefore unpredictable. We would say *on it*, but the Arabs say *in it*. A similar idiosyncracy in English would be: *on Tuesday*, but *in March*.

■ **kharuuf yadhbaHuun-uh** *a sheep which they slaughter*. English would supply the word *which*, and ignore the ending **-uh** on the verb. See relative clauses, Unit 13.

■ **haadhaa :aadah** *this is a custom*. You will recognise this as an *is/are* sentence. The **haadhaa** does not agree with the feminine noun, as it refers back to the preceding sentence as a whole.

■ **faqaT** *only*. This word always follows what it refers to.

■ **yaHtafiluun** *they celebrate*. The verb is plural here, because no subject is stated, it being the *they* implied within the verb.

■ **naHnu** *we* is for emphasis or contrast here.

🎧 تعبيرات رئيسية **ta:biiráat ra'iisíyyah (Key phrases)**

What to say at feast times and birthdays

The most universal greeting at festival times:

عيد مبارك: **:iid mubaarak**   *May the festival be blessed (for you)*

The reply:

الله يبارك فيك   *God bless you*

Al-laah yubaarik fii-k (fii-ki to a woman, **fii-kum** to several people)

A greeting which can be used for any annual occasion such as a birthday:

كل عام وأنت بخير   *Every year and [may] you*

kull :aam w-anta bi-khayr   *[be] well*

(fem. **anti**, plural **antum**)

The reply:

وأنت بخير   *And [may] you [be] well*

wa anta/anti/antum bi-khayr

Cards are often sent, usually bearing one of the congratulatory phrases given above.

معلومات ثقافية ma:luumáat thaqaafíyyah (Cultural tips)

The main religious festivals celebrated by all Muslims, regardless of sect or country of origin, are:

عيد الفطر **:iid al-fiTr** (or *Lesser Bairam*, at the end of Ramadan)

Date: 1st of Shawwal (see calendar, page 211)

This is a holiday of about three days, marking the end of the fast of the month of Ramadan, during which Muslims allow nothing to pass their lips (food, drink, smoke) between sunrise and sunset.

On the first day of the feast there are special prayers in the mosque, and the rest of the holiday is traditionally spent visiting family and friends, offering congratulations, and making up for lost time with large feasts. Children usually receive gifts of money and new clothes.

As you can imagine, total abstention from food and drink during the daytime in Ramadan causes considerable hardship. Working hours are reduced, but you will find that people tend to be listless. Lack of sleep is another problem, as a sustaining meal has to be prepared and consumed before the dawn deadline. If you are in a

Muslim country during Ramadan, it is polite to show consideration by not eating or drinking in front of local people.

عيد الأضحى :iid al-aD-Haa (or *Korban Bairam*)

Date: 10th of Dhuu l-Hijjah (see calendar)

This is the major feast of Islam, and again merits a holiday of several days. Even for those not on the pilgrimage, a large feast is in order, those who can afford it slaughtering (usually) a sheep and sharing it with the family, often giving some of the meat to the poor. The richer and more important you are, the bigger the feast that is expected. Members of the family visit each other's houses, offering congratulations, and again gifts are made to the children.

مولد النبي muulid an-nabii *Prophet's Birthday*

Date: 12th of Rabii: al-awwal (see calendar)

The Prophet Muhammad's Birthday is often just called **muulid**. Although not officially prescribed by Islam, this is celebrated in varying local forms in many parts of the Arab world.

Muslims of the Shi'ah persuasion have additional festivals of their own.

The Islamic calendar

Although nowadays it is only used in most countries for religious purposes (such as festival dates), you should be familiar with the Islamic calendar.

The Islamic date is calculated from the date of the Prophet Muhammad's flight (in Arabic **hijrah**) from Mecca to Medinah, which took place on July 16, 622 AD. For this reason, Islamic dates are specified as هجري **hijrii**, often abbreviated to هـ. The English abbreviation is AH.

Apart from starting more than six centuries later than the Western calendar, the Islamic year consists of 12 lunar months, adding up to only 354 days. Consequently, the years are not synchronised with our solar calendar, so festivals creep forward according to our dating system. For instance in 2000 AD (1420–21 هـ) Ramadan started about 5 December.

For most secular transactions, Arabic versions of the Western month names are used. The Arabs call the AD year ميلادي **miilaadii** *pertaining to the birth* (i.e. of Christ), abbreviated to م.

٢٠٠٠ م — ١٤٢٠ هـ

Below is a table for the two sets of months. For the reasons given above, these do not, of course, correspond except in the order in which they come.

Western calendar	Islamic calendar
ينايـر **yanaayir**	محرم **muHarram**
فبرايـر **fabraayir**	صفر **Safar**
مـارس **maaris**	ربيع الأول **rabii: al-awwal**
أبريل **abriil**	ربيع الثاني **rabii: ath-thaanii**
مـايو **maayuu**	جمـادى الأولى **jumaada l-uulaa**
يونيو **yuunyuu**	جمـادى الآخرة **jumaada l-aakhirah**
يوليو **yuulyuu**	رجب **rajab**
أغـسطس **aghusTus**	شَعبان **sha:baan**
سبتمبر **sabtambar**	رمضـان **ramaDaan**
أكتوبر **uktuubir**	شوال **shawwaal**
نوفمبر **nuufambar**	ذو القعدة **dhuu l-qa:dah**
ديسمبر **diisambar**	ذو الحجة **dhuu l-Hijjah**

There is a third set of month names, starting with **kaanuun ath-thaani** 'the second Kanoon', used mainly in the Syria–Iraq region, and you should try to learn these if you are going to that area.

تراكيب اللغة taraakíib al-lúghah (Structures)

1 Question words

These question words differ from the question markers هل **hal** and أ **a** given in Unit 2, which merely turn statements into *yes/no* questions. The words referred to here are more specific.

What?

There are two words for *what*:

ما **maa** is used before nouns and subject pronouns:

ما هو؟ *What [is] it (he)?*

ما هذا؟ *What [is] this?*

ما اسمه؟ *What [is] his/its name?*

ماذا **maadhaa** is used before verbs:

ماذا أكلوا؟ *What they ate? (What did they eat?)*

ماذا يحمل؟ *What he-carries? (What is he carrying?)*

Note: ما is a very versatile word in Arabic, and its meaning depends on the context. You have already seen it meaning *not* in Units 7 and 10, and it has other usages too.

Note also the common construction in the text:

ما هي الذبيحة؟ *What [is] she the-sacrifice-animal?*

We would say *What is a sacrifice animal?*

Who?

مَن **man** is used before both nouns and verbs. In unvowelled Arabic this looks identical to **min** *from*. You have to decide from the context, which does not usually present any difficulty.

من هم؟ *Who [are] they?*

مَن فتح الباب؟ *Who he-opened the-door? (Who opened the door?)*

Also note:

مَن هو المدير؟ *Who he [is] the-manager? (Who is the manager?)*

Which?

أيّ **ayy** (masc.), أيّة **ayyah** (fem.)

This is followed by a singular noun without **al-** and agrees with it in gender.

أيّ رجل؟ *Which man?*

أيّة بنت؟ *Which girl?*

How many?

كَم **kam**

This is followed by a singular noun which requires the accusative marker **-an**, unless it has a feminine ending.

كم عيدا؟ *How many festivals?*

كم سيّارة؟ *How many cars?*

How?

كَيْف **kayf(a)** is used before nouns and verbs. The final **-a** is often omitted.

كيف سافرت؟ *How you-travelled?*

كيف حالك؟ *How [is] condition-your?* (i.e. *How are you?* – a very common greeting).

Where?

أين **ayna**

Note that when **ayna** means *where to?* and *where from?* it is preceded by إلى *to* and من *from* respectively.

أين المتحف؟ *Where [is] the-museum?*

إلى أين تذهب؟ *To where you-go?*

من أين حضروا؟ *From where they-came?*

When?

متى **mataa** usually used with verbs.

متى وصلتم؟ *When you-arrived?*

Why?

لماذا **li-maadhaa** used before verbs.

لماذا سافرت الى مسقط؟ *Why she-travelled to Muscat?*

2 How to say *to have*

Arabic has no actual verb meaning *to have*, but uses a combination of a preposition and a noun or pronoun.

Three common prepositions are used:

لـ **li-** *to, for*

عند **:ind(a)** *with* (equivalent of French *chez*)

لدى **ladaa** *with* – this is slightly archaic, though still used. When a pronoun suffix is added, it behaves like **ilaa** (see Unit 10). It has not been used much in this book.

So, to say *Muhammad has a new car* we say:

لمحمد سيارة جديدة *to-muHammad car new*

عندي كتاب ممتاز *with-me book excellent (I have an excellent book)*

Note: **li-** and **:ind** are more or less interchangeable. The former is considered more elegant, but in spoken Arabic the latter is used almost exclusively.

To say *had*, Arabic uses **kaana** *was/were* + **li-/:ind**:

كانت لمحمد سيارة جديدة *she-was to-muHammad car new*

كان عندي كتاب ممتاز *was with-me book excellent*

In the first example above, it is not always necessary for the verb **kaana** to agree with its subject (here **sayyaarah** feminine). **kaana** would be just as acceptable.

To say *will have* use **yakuun** (the present tense of **kaana**) + **li-/:ind**. With this verb the future marker **sa-** or **sawfa** is optional:

سيكون عندكم ضيف غد *[future marker] he-is with-you guest tomorrow*

(You will have a guest tomorrow)

To say *have not* in the present, use the verb **laysa** (see Unit 8) + **li-/:ind**, and in the past and future by applying the appropriate words for *not* (see Unit 10).

3 Thematic sentences

A type of sentence which is often encountered in Arabic is the *thematic* or *topical* sentence.

The topic of the sentence, that is the person or thing the sentence is about, is stated first, followed by what you want to say about the topic. The part of the sentence which comes after you have mentioned the topic must be able to stand independently, and very often has a real or implied pronoun which refers back to that topic.

There are a number of these in the text, and we have given below a few examples with literal translation to help you understand the concept. There is no need to spend a lot of time learning how to use this construction, but the Arabs regard it as an elegant construction and you will come across it frequently.

It is more or less equivalent to English sentences beginning with *as for*, as in *As for Peter, he's rarely at home.* Note that the part of the sentence following the topic (*Peter*) makes complete sense on its own by including the pronoun *he*.

الأول هو العيد الصغير *the-first he [is] the-festival the-small*

الصوم معناه أن... *the-fasting meaning-his [is] that...*

4 The ordinal numbers 1–20

These are adjectives which tell you the order things come in. With the exception of *first* and *sixth*, they are easily related to the cardinal numbers, using the root of the number and the word shape **CaaCiC** (see Unit 2). Apart from *first*, they all form the feminine in the usual way by adding ة **-ah**.

first	أول **áwwal**, fem. أولى **úulaa**	
second	ثان، الثاني **thaanin, ath-thaanii****	
third	ثالث **thaalith**	

fourth	رابع **raabi:**	
fifth	خامس **khaamis**	
sixth	سادس **saadis**	
seventh	سابع **saabi:**	
eighth	ثامن **thaamin**	
ninth	تاسع **taasi:**	
tenth	عاشر **aashir:**	
eleventh	حادي عشر **Haadii :ashar** (fem. حادية عشرة)	
twelfth	ثاني عشر **thaanii :ashar** (fem. ثانية عشرة)	
thirteenth	ثالث عشر **thaalith :ashar** (fem. ثالثة عشرة)	

...and so on up to *nineteenth*.

twentieth   the cardinal number (عشرون/عشرين) is used.

** For this kind of word, see Unit 18.

أوزان الكلمات awzáan al-kalimáat (Word shapes)

Pattern	Arabic example	Eng. sound-alike
CaCaa'iC*	**jaraa'id** جرائد *newspapers*	*examine*

This is another internal plural shape, usually coming from feminine singulars of the shape **CaCiiCah**, e.g. جريدة **jariidah**, singular of the above example. It does not show the accusative marker.

 ضرائب from ضريبة *tax*

حقائب from حقيبة *bag, suitcase*

حدائق from حديقة *garden, park*

Note: If the singular refers to a female human being, the **-aat** plural is used:

زميلة (female) *colleague*; pl. زميلات

تمرينـات tamriináat (Practice)

Exercise 4
Match the questions below with the appropriate answers.

a	ثلاثة: حميد وناصر وسعيد.	١	من مؤلف هذا الكتاب؟
b	سأشرحها لك.	٢	أين مدينة الاسكندرية؟
c	في مصر.	٣	ماذا تعمل الآن؟
d	هي هدية لك.	٤	متى رجع من جدة؟
e	تذهب إلى المكتب.	٥	كم ولدا عندك؟
f	نجيب محفوظ.	٦	لماذا تحب هذه البنت؟
g	أول بيت على اليمين.	٧	كيف تلعب هذه اللعبة؟
h	أقرأ الجرائد.	٨	أي بيت بيت فريدة؟
i	يوم الجمعة.	٩	ما هذا؟
j	لأنها جميلة جدا!	١٠	إلى أين تذهب يا مريم؟

مؤلف، ـون mu'állif, -uun *author*
شرح sháraHa S-I a *explain*

Exercise 5
Rearrange the months of the year into the correct order.

٧	ديسمبر	١	سبتمبر
٨	مايو	٢	أبريل
٩	نوفمبر	٣	فبراير
١٠	أغسطس	٤	أكتوبر
١١	يونيو	٥	يوليو
١٢	مارس	٦	يناير

Exercise 6

Make complete *to have* sentences in the present tense, using either **li-** or **:ind**.

Example:

هو .... ثلاثة أولاد. ⟵ هو له ثلاثة أولاد.

(He .... three sons. → He has three sons.)

٦ نحن .... سيارة ألمانية.	١ الملك .... قصور كثيرة.
٧ هم .... حقائب ثقيلة.	٢ أنت .... أخت طويلة.
٨ الشركة .... ٥ فروع.	٣ أنتم .... أولاد صغار.
٩ محمد .... شقة واسعة.	٤ أنا........... آلة حاسبة جديدة.
١٠ سميرة .... فستان جميل.	٥ المدرس .... ٥٠ تلميذا.

تلميذ، تلامذة **tilmíidh, taláamidhah** *pupil*

فرع، فروع **far:, furúu:** *branch* (of a tree, company, etc.)

فستان، فساتين* **fustáan, fasaatíin*** *frock, dress*

Now change the sentences 1–5 above into the past tense, using **kaana**.

Exercise 7

Prayer is the second of the five pillars of Islam, and Muslims are called to prayer five times a day. The daily calls are:

الفجر **al-fajr** *dawn*

الظهر **aDH-DHuhr** *midday*

العصر **al-:aSr** *mid-afternoon*

المغرب **al-mághrib** *sunset*

العشاء **al-:isháa'** *late evening*

Prayer times vary according to sunrise and sunset and are always listed in the daily newspapers. Look at the prayer times here from the month of April. Which day came first?

Exercise 8

Listen to the recording or read the transcript to find out which floor of the apartment block these people live on.

Then record the information about them.

Example: *Ali lives on the third floor.*

١ اسمي علي. أسكن في الطابق الثالث.

٢ اسمي حمدان. أسكن في الطابق السادس.

٣ اسمي سهام. أسكن في الطابق الثاني.

٤ اسمي مصطفى. نسكن في الطابق التاسع.

٥ اسمي عبد الله. نسكن في الطابق الثامن.

٦ اسمي نورة. نسكن في الطابق العاشر.

٧ اسمي حميد. أسكن في الطابق الأول .

Exercise 9

Abdullah takes his family shopping to a large superstore out of town. Everyone is looking for something particular, and the store is so big that they have to ask at the information desk where to go.

Look at the store guide and say which row each of them needs to go to.

Example: *Abdullah needs a pair of shoes and a fax machine.*

يذهب إلى الصف الخامس والصف التاسع عشر.

He goes to the fifth row and the 19th row.

a Qasim (aged13) wants a shirt, a video game and batteries.

b Nadia needs a greetings card for a friend, some coloured pens and a cassette.

c Miriam (17) wants a hair dryer, jeans and a new game.

d Ali (18) wants a T-shirt, a CD and a computer.

e Sarah wants towels, some chairs for the balcony and clothes for the baby.

	English		Arabic
1	Household linen	مفارش منزلية	١
2	Men's clothing	ملابس رجالية	٢
3	Women's clothing	ملابس نسائية	٣
4	Children's clothing & shoes	ملابس وأحذية أطفال	٤
5	Men's & women's shoes	أحذية رجالية ونسائية	٥
6	Baby garments	ملابس حديثي الولادة	٦
7	Bicycles	دراجات	٧
8	Toys	لعب	٨
9	Games/Sports accessories	ألعاب/ مستلزمات رياضية	٩
10	Stationery	قرطاسية	١٠
11	Books/Greetings cards	كتب / بطاقات معايدة	١١
12	Hardware/Batteries	أدوات/بطاريات	١٢
13	Tables/Chairs	موائد/كراسي	١٣
14	Home Appliances/CDs	أدوات منزلية/أقراص مدمجة	١٤
15	Video tapes/Cassettes	أشرطة فيديو/أشرطة كاسيت	١٥
16	Electrical accessories/ Video games	أدوات كهربائية/ألعاب فيديو	١٦
17	Luggage	حقائب	١٧
18	Computers/Software	أجهزة كمبيوتر/ برامج	١٨
19	Phones/Fax machines	هواتف/فاكس	١٩
20	Cameras/Radio cassette recorders	كاميرات/مسجلات راديو كاسيت	٢٠

12 صفحة المرأة
SafHat al-mar'ah
Woman's page

In this unit you will learn:
■ how to express nationalities such as *English, Lebanese,* etc.

صفحة المرأة SafHat al-mar'ah *Woman's page*

The following interview was given to a women's magazine by a well-known fashion model, Leila. Look through the vocabulary given below, and listen to the interview a few times before answering the questions.

Exercise 1
Say if the following sentences are true or false.
a Leila comes from Jordan.
b She is 28 years old.
c She was interested in fashion as a child.
d She specialised in literature at university.

Exercise 2
Listen to the interview again, looking again through the new words underneath, and answer the following questions.
a Does she want to found an agency which:
  i is worldwide? **ii** shows world fashions?
b Does she hope to employ:
  i male models? **ii** female models? **iii** male and female models?
c What else does she hope to do?
d What two things help her to keep slim?
e What kind of beauty look does she try to achieve?
f How does she feel about make-up?

الصحفية أهلا وسهلا.

ليلى   أهلاً بك.

الصحفية أوّلا، ما جنسيتك؟

ليلى   أنا لبنانية من بيروت.

الصحفية وعمرك؟

ليلى   عمري ٢٨ سنة.

الصحفية كيف بدأت في مهنة عرض الأزياء؟

ليلى   منذ طفولتي. أحب عرض الأزياء لأنها نوع من أنواع الفن. لذلك دخلت في هذا المجال.

الصحفية هل درست الفنون؟

ليلى   نعم، درست الفنون في الجامعة وتخصّصت في تصميم الأزياء.

الصحفية وماذا تطمحين إليه في مهنتك؟

ليلى   طموحي هو إنشاء وكالة عالمية لعرض الأزياء تضم عارضين وعارضات غربيّين وعرب.

الصحفية وشيء غير هذا؟

ليلى   نعم، تصميم أزياء تحمل ماركة دولية باسمي.

الصحفية وكيف تحافظين على رشاقتك؟

ليلى   أتبع حمية وأمارس الرياضة الخفيفة.

الصحفية وجمالك؟

ليلى   إنّي أفضّل الجمال الطبيعي، ولذلك أترك شعري على طبيعته، ولا أحب وضع الماكياج إلا لضرورات العرض فقط.

الصحفية شكرا لك.

ليلى   شكرا.

Exercise 3

Now read the dialogue again, and link the English phrases to the Arabic expressions.

a How did you begin in the fashion modelling profession?

b because they are a kind of art

c that is why I entered this field

d I studied arts at university.

e male and female Western and Arab models

f How do you keep slim?

g I prefer natural beauty.

١ لذلك دخلت في هذا المجال

٢ درست الفنون في الجامعة.

٣ أفضّل الجمال الطبيعي.

٤ كيف بدأت في مهنة عرض الأزياء؟

٥ كيف تحافظين على رشاقتك؟

٦ عارضين وعارضات غربيّين وعرب

٧ لأنها نوع من أنواع الفن

صحفي **SúHufii** *reporter/journalist* (fem. **SuHufíyyah**)

أوّلا **áwwalan** *firstly*

بدأ **báda' S-I a** *begin*

مهنة، مهن **míhnah, míhan** *job, trade, profession*

عرض **:arD** *showing, displaying*

زي، أزياء **zíyy, azyáa'** *clothes, fashion, style*

منذ **múndhu** *since*

طفولة **Tufúulah** *childhood*

لأن **li'ánna** *because*

لذلك **li-dháalik** *because of that, for this reason*

مجال، ـات **majáal, -áat** *field, sphere of activity*

تخصّص **takháSSaSa S-V** *specialise*

تصميم **taSmiim** *design, designing*

طمح إلى **TámaHa ilaa S-I a** *aspire to, have the ambition to*

طموح **TumúuH** *aspiration, ambition*

إنشاء **insháa'** *foundation, setting up*

وكالة، ـات **wakáalah, -áat** *agency*

عالمي: **áalamii** *worldwide*

ضم **Dámma D-1 u** *include, comprise*

عارض، ـون **áariD, -úun** *(male) model*

عارضة، ـات **áariDah, -áat** *(female) model*

غربي، ـون **ghárbii, -úun** *western*

شيء، أشياء **shay', ashyáa'*** *thing*

غير **ghayr** *other than, apart from*

ماركة **máarkah** *marque, label*

دولي **dúwalii** *or* **dáwlii** *international*

حافظ على **HáafaDHa :alaa S-III** *keep, preserve*

رشاقة **rasháaqah** *shapeliness, elegance, slim figure*

حمية **Hímyah** *diet*

مارس **máarasa S-III** *practise*

خفيف **khafiif** *light*

جمال **jamáal** *beauty*

ترك **táraka S-I u** *leave, let be*

شعر **sha:r** *hair*

طبيعة **Tabii:ah** *nature*

وضع **waD:** *putting*

ماكياج **maakyáaj** *make-up*

ضرورة، ـات **Durúurah, -áat** *necessity, requirement*

معلومات ثقافية **ma:luumáat thaqaafíyyah** (Cultural tips)

As is obvious from the interview above, Leila is a thoroughly modern, professional young woman. A role and lifestyle such as hers could only be viable in one of the more liberal Arab states, where a near western attitude prevails.

Indeed every country has its own ideas, running the whole gamut from the above to obligatory veiling and virtual purdah.

The role of women is prescribed to some extent in the Koran and other Islamic texts, and Islamic law (**shariiah**) defines many of their rights and privileges. In most Islamic countries it is still legal for a man to take up to four wives. Westerners are inevitably shocked by this, but the practice is not in fact widespread – not least because it is very expensive in terms of dowries and general upkeep. The rules require each wife to be treated equally. Another semi-myth prevalent in the west is that, to obtain a divorce, a man simply has to say to his wife 'I divorce you' three times. This is partly true, but there are numerous conditions which in most cases inhibit abuse of this practice. For instance, men in many Arab countries have to pay a very large sum of money (dowry) to the bride's family, and, depending on the timing and situation of the divorce, some or all of this has to be paid back. This can easily run into tens of thousands of pounds.

---

al-mulaaHaDHáat (Notes) الملاحظات

■ **awwalan** *firstly*. For this and other adverbs, see Unit 16.

■ **:umr-ik**. **:umr** *life* is also used for age.

■ **28 sanah**. For compound numbers see Unit 5. Meanwhile, note that numbers above 10 take the singular noun, not the plural.

■ **uHibb**. This is a Form IV doubled verb. A doubled verb has the second and third radicals (vowels) the same, and some parts of this verb are written with the doubling sign. (See table **D-IV**). Remember that in all Form II, III and IV verbs, the present tense prefixes are vowelled with **u** instead of **a**.

■ **li'anna-haa**. **li'anna** *because* is a combination of **li-** *for* and **'anna** *that* (see Unit 8). **-haa** refers to the inanimate plural *fashions*.

■ **naw: min anwaa:**. An Arabic idiom for one of something.

■ **li-dhaalik** *for that,* i.e. *for this reason.* Another combination with **li-**.

■ **taTmaHiin**. Feminine verb, as a woman is being addressed.

■ For the form **ilay-h**, see Unit 10.

■ وكالة عالمية لعرض الأزياء تضم... (**wikaalah :aalamiyyah li-:arD al-azyaa' taDumm...**) *An agency for fashion modelling (which) will include...* Arabic does not use a word for *which* after an indefinite noun (see Unit 13).

■ **gharbiyyiin wa-:arab**. When adjectives describe a group of mixed males and females, the masculine plurals are used.

■ باسمي *in my name.* This is pronounced **bi-smii**.

■ **inn-ii**. The use of **inna** + the suffix pronoun lends a very slight emphasis to the statement (see Unit 8).

تراكيب اللغة taraakíib al-lúghah (Structures)

Forming adjectives from nouns

To describe persons or things associated with the noun, English uses a variety of suffixes:

history – historic
man – manly
America – American
Japan – Japanese

Arabic adds the following endings to the noun:

Gender	Transliteration	Arabic
masc. sing.	**-ii**	ـــي
fem. sing.	**-iyyah**	ـــية
masc. plural	**-iyyuun**	ـــيون/ـــيين
fem. plural	**-iyyaat**	ـــيات

They should all have the doubling sign over the ي, but this is almost always omitted.

Remember also that the ending ـــيون changes to ـــيين when affected by the possessive or the requirement for an accusative marker (see Unit 14).

There are irregular plurals (masculine only) which will be given with the singulars where required.

The noun sometimes has to be altered slightly:

a) If it has **al-** in front – as in some countries and places – this is dropped:

المغرب – مغربي   *Morocco – Moroccan*

b) The feminine ending ـة and certain other endings are dropped:

صناعة – صناعي   *industry – industrial*
أمريكا – أمريكي   *America – American*

c) Some words change their internal vowelling before the ending:

مدينة – مدني   **madiinah – madanii** *city – urban, civilian*

Like all Arabic adjectives, these can freely be used as nouns:

إنجليزي *English, an Englishman*

أوزان الكلمات awzáan al-kalimáat (Word shapes)

Pattern	Arabic example	Eng. sound-alike
taCCiiC	**tartíib** ترتيب arrangement	*tartine* (French)

This is the verbal noun of all Form II (except the **Lw, Ly** types which have a slightly different form), and therefore always expresses the action of a verb. In English, this can be expressed by adding *-ing* to the verb, but there are often parallel words with a slightly different nuance (e.g. *arranging, arrangment; presenting, presentation*). In these cases the one Arabic form usually serves for both.

رتب **rattaba S-II** *to arrange, put in order* ➜ ترتيب **tartiib** *arranging, arrangement*

صمم **Sammama S-II** *to design* ➜ تصميم *designing, design*

مول **mawwala Mw-II** *to finance* ➜ تمويل *financing*

درس **darrasa S-II** *to teach* ➜ تدريس *teaching*

حول **Hawwala Mw-II** *to convert* ➜ تحويل *converting, conversion*

تمرينات **tamriináat (Practice)**

Exercise 4

Here are some common word combinations, many of which you will see on road signs, in shops etc.

We give you two nouns, e.g. مركز **markaz** *centre* – تجارة **tijaarah** *commerce*, and your task is to put them together, making the second noun into an adjective: مركز تجاري **markaz tijaarii** *commercial (shopping) centre*

Some are given in the definite form.

a منطقة **minTaqah** *area, zone* – زراعة **ziraa:ah** *agriculture*

b المطار **al-maTaar** *the airport* – الدولة **ad-dawlah** *the state*

c قمر **qamar** *moon* – صناعة **Sinaa:ah** *manufacturing***

d السوق **as-suuq** *the market* – المركز **al-markaz** *the centre*

e البنك **al-bank** *the bank* – الوطن **al-waTan** *the nation*

f السفارة **as-sifaarah** *the embassy* – الهند **al-hind** *India*

g الشؤون **ash-shu'uun** *the affairs* – الخارج **al-khaarij** *the exterior*

h الأزياء al-azyaa' *the fashions* – النساء an-nisaa' *the women*

i منطقة minTaqah *zone* – صناعة Sinaa:ah *industry*

j طبيخ Tabiikh *cuisine* – عرب: arab *Arabs*

k المتحف al-matHaf *the museum* – الشعب ash-sha:b *the people, folk*

l البريد al-bariid *the post* – الجو al-jaww *the air*

m القنصلية al-qunSuliyyah *the consulate* – أمريكا amriikaa *America*

n الإدارة al-idaarah *the administration* – البلد al-balad *the town, municipality*

o منطقة minTaqah *area, zone* – عسكر: askar *army, troops*

p بريد bariid *post* – خارج khaarij *exterior*

q الآثار al-aathaar *the remains* – التاريخ at-taariikh *the history*

r الدراسات ad-diraasaat *the studies* – الأدب al-adab *the literature*

s العلوم al-:uluum *the sciences* – الطبيعة aT-Tabii:ah *the nature*

t الألعاب al-al:aab *the games* – النار an-naar *the fire*

u القصر al-qaSr *the palace* – الملك al-malik *the king*

v المستشفى al-mustashfaa *the hospital* – المركز al-markaz *the centre*

w بريد bariid *post* – داخل daakhil *interior*

x الأجهزة al-ajhizah *equipment* (pl.) – الكهرباء al-kahrabaa' *the electricity*

y الديوان ad-diiwaan *diwan, personal office* – الأمير al-amiir *the emir*

**Here, the adjective means *artificial*: 'artificial moon', i.e. satellite.

13 | الخليج العربي
al-khaliij al-:arabi
The Arabian Gulf

In this unit you will learn:
- more about describing places
- how to use the relative pronouns *who, which, that,* etc.
- about passive verbs

ابتسم، أنت في الشارقة ibtasim, anta fi sh-shaariqah *Smile, you're in Sharjah*

The passage below is from a tourist brochure about Sharjah, describing its role in the Emirates. Listen to the audio and read the passage carefully several times, referring to the vocabulary given below.

Exercise 1
Now answer these questions.
a What phrase welcomes the visitor to Sharjah?
b Where is Sharjah's geographical location?
c What kind of activity is Sharjah a centre for?
d How many inhabitants did Sharjah have at the last census?
e Name three areas in which Sharjah pursues scientific development projects.
f What capital of the Emirates is Sharjah considered to be?
g What does Sharjah have a number of?
h What type of programmes are transmitted from the television station?

ابتسم أنت في الشارقة!

بهذه العبارة الترحيبية التي تفيض بكل مشاعر الود الصادق تستقبل الشارقة ضيوفها. وإمارة الشارقة هي إحدى إمارات دولة الإمارات العربية المتحدة التي تحتل موقعا جغرافيا متميزا على الخليج العربي. وهو موقع جعل الشارقة تتمتع على امتداد العصور بدور قيادي بين بلدان الخليج العربي كمركز من أهم مراكز النشاط التجاري.

ويقدر عدد السكان حسب أحدث الإحصاءات التي أجريت عام ١٩٩٥ بحوالي نصف مليون نسمة أي بكثافة تقدر بحوالي ١٩٠ نسمة للكيلومتر المربع.

تعتبر الشارقة من الإمارات الأولى على مستوى منطقة الخليج التي انتهجت أسلوب التخطيط العلمي الشامل فيما يتعلق بمشاريع التنمية الاقتصادية والزراعية والسياحية والاجتماعية والثقافية الخ.

وتوصف الشارقة بأنها العاصمة الثقافية لدولة الإمارات، وهناك دائرة خاصة ترعى تنفيذ الأنشطة الثقافية بالإمارة ، كما تضم الإمارة عددا من المتاحف العلمية والتاريخية الفخمة ومحطة من أحدث محطات الإرسال التلفيزيوني تذيع الكثير من البرامج الثقافية والتعليمية.

Exercise 2

Link the English phrases to the Arabic expressions on page 233.

a which expresses the feelings of true friendship
b the latest census which was carried out
c which looks after the implementation of cultural activities
d a number of magnificent scientific and historical museums
e Sharjah is described as the cultural capital
f 190 people to the square kilometre
g one of the most important centres for commercial activity
h many cultural and educational programmes

١ التي تفيض بكل مشاعر الود

٢ عددا من المتاحف العلمية والتاريخية الفخمة

٣ ١٩٠٣ نسمة للكيلومتر المربع

٤ الكثير من البرامج الثقافية والتعليمية

٥ أحدث الإحصاءات التي أجريت

٦ من أهم مراكز النشاط التجاري

٧ ترعى تنفيذ الأنشطة الثقافية

٨ توصف الشارقة بأنها العاصمة الثقافية

ابتسم **ibtásama [S-VIII]** smile

عبارة، ـات **:abáarah, -áat** phrase, expression

ترحيبي **tarHíibii** welcoming (adj.)

الذي **alládhii** who, which, that (fem. التي **allátii**)

أفاض بـ **afáaDa bi- [My-IV]** flood, overflow with

كل **kull** each, every, all

مشاعر **masháa:ir*** feelings, sentiments

ود **wadd** love, friendship

صادق **Sáadiq** truthful, true

استقبل **istáqbala [S-X]** receive, meet

إحدى **iHdaa** one (fem. of أحد **áHad**)

دولة، دول **dáwlah, dúwal** country, state

الإمارات العربية المتحدة **al-imaaráat al-:arabíyyah al-muttáHidah** The United Arab Emirates

احتل **iHtálla [D-VIII]** occupy

موقع، مواقع **máwqi:, mawáaqi:*** site, situation, place

جغرافي **jughráafii** geographical

متميز **mutamáyyiz** distinctive, prominent

الخليج العربي **al-khaliij al-:árabii** the Arabian Gulf

جعل **já:ala [S-I a]** cause, make do something

تمتع بـ **tamátta:a [S-V]** enjoy

على امتداد العصور **:ala imtidáad al-:uSúur** over the ages

دور، أدوار **dawr, adwáar** role, turn

قيادي **qiyáadii** leading

بين **báyna** among, between

كـ **ka-** as, like

مركز، مراكز **márkaz, maráakiz*** centre

أهم **ahámm** more/most important

نشاط **nasháaT** activity

تجاري **tijáarii** commercial

يقدر **yuqáddar** (passive of S-2) is estimated

عدد، أعداد **:ádad, a:dáad** number

ساكن، سكان **sáakin, sukkáan** inhabitant, resident

حسب **Hasb** according to

أحدث **áHdath** newest, latest

إحصاء، ـات **iHSáa', -áat** count, census

أجريت **újriyat** was carried out (passive of Ly-IV)

عام، أعوام **:aam, a:wáam** year

نصف، أنصاف **niSf, anSáaf** half

نسمة **násamah** individual (used in population counts only)

أي **ay** that is

كثافة **katháafah** density

مربع **murábba:** square (adj.)

تعتبر **tu:tábar** is considered (passive of S-VIII)

مستوى **mustáwaa** level, context

منطقة، مناطق **minTáqah, manáaTiq*** region, area

انتهج **intáhaja [S-VIII]** follow, pursue (a path, method, etc.)

أسلوب، أساليب **uslúub, asaaliib*** style, method

تخطيط **takhTíiT** planning

علمي **:ilmii** *scientific*

شامل **sháamil** *comprehensive*

فيما يتعلق ب **fii-maa yata:állaq bi-** *as regards, with regard to*

مشروع ، مشاريع **mashrúu:, masháarii:*** *project*

تنمية **tanmíyah** *development*

اقتصادي **iqtiSáadii** *economic*

زراعي **ziráa:ii** *agricultural*

سياحي **siyáaHii** *tourist* (adj.), *touristic*

اجتماعي **ijtimáa:ii** *social*

ثقافي **thaqáafii** *cultural*

الخ *etc.* (abbreviation, pronounced **ila áakhirih(i))**

توصف ... بأنها **túuSaf ... bi-ánna-haa** ... *is described as*

دائرة، دوائر **dáa'irah, dawáa'ir*** *department, directorate*
(government)

خاص **khaaSS** *special; private*

رعى **rá:aa [Lh-I]** *take care of, look after*

تنفيذ **tanfiidh** *implementation, execution*

كما **ka-maa** *just as, also*

تاريخي **taaríikhii** *historical*

إرسال **irsáal** *transmission, sending*

أذاع **adháa:a [My-IV]** *to broadcast*

الكثير من... **al-kathíir min...** *many, a great number of...*

برنامج، برامج **barnáamij, baráamij*** *programme*

تعليمي **ta:líimii** *educational*

معلومات ثقافية **ma:luumáat thaqaafíyyah** (Cultural tips)

The literary Arabic form of the name Sharjah is **ash-shaariqah**.
The English version omits the Arabic definite article, and the **j**

comes from a local pronunciation of the Arabic letter **q**.

The United Arab Emirates (UAE) was formed in December 1971 as a federation of seven sheikhdoms, of which Sharjah ranks third in size and wealth (after Abu Dhabi and Dubai). Although their economies are ultimately based on oil production, all the Emirates have made efforts to diversify. Sharjah has concentrated on promoting and encouraging social, educational and cultural projects, resulting in its being named Arab City of Culture in 1998.

---

al-mulaaHaDHáat (Notes) الملاحظات

- **ja:ala** The original meaning of this verb is *to put*. However, it is very frequently used with a following imperfect verb (here **yatamatta:**) *to express to cause, to make do something*, also sometimes *to begin*.

- **yuqaddar** *is estimated, evaluated*. This is a passive verb (see grammar section below). Other examples in the text are the feminine form of the same verb – **tuqaddar**, **ujriyat** *were carried out*, **tu:tabar** *is considered* and **tuuSaf** *is described*.

- **nasamah** a person, individual. This is is a special word only used in population counts.

- **uulaa** is the feminine of **awwal** *first*.

- الخ *etc*. Abbreviations are not very common in Arabic. The pronunciation is given in the vocabulary above and the literal meaning is *to its last* or *to its end*.

- **kamaa**, literally *just as*, is often used to join sentences and can usually be translated simply as *also*.

- **baraamij**. The singular **barnaamij** has – according to the Arab interpretation – five root letters (**b-r-n-m-j**). Such words are rare, and almost always of foreign derivation. Since the Arabic internal plural system cannot cope with 5-consonant words, one is arbitrarily ignored in the plural formation.

تعبيرات رئيسية ta:biiráat ra'iisíyyah (Key phrases)

قابلت رجلا يعمل في مصنع الأجهزة الكهربائية

qaabalt rajulan ya:mal fii maSna: al-ajhizah al-kahrabaa'iyyah

I-met a-man he-works in factory [of] the-equipments the-electrical

I met a man who works in the electrical appliances factory

الصديق الذي زرته أمس يسكن في تونس

aS-Sadiiq alladhii zurt-uh ams yaskun fii tuunis

the-friend who I-visited-him yesterday he-lives in Tunisia

The friend whom I visited yesterday lives Tunisia

الضابط الذي سيارته هناك جالس في المقهى

aD-DaabiT alladhi sayyaarat-uh hunaak jaalis fi l-maqhaa

the-officer who his-car [is] there [is] sitting in the-café

The officer whose car is there is sitting in the café

البذلة الجديدة التي اشتريتها مصنوعة في الصين

al-badhlah al-jadiidah allatii ishtarayt-haa maSnuu:ah fi S-Siin

the-suit the-new which I-bought-it [is] manufactured in the-China

The new suit which I bought is made in China

تراكيب اللغة taraakíib al-lúghah (Structures)

1 Relative clauses

Relative clauses in English are the second half of sentences such as:

I replied to the letter which arrived last week.

They are usually introduced by linking words such as *which, who, whom, whose, that*, called relative pronouns. The person or thing which the relative clause describes (here *letter*) is called the *antecedent*.

There are two important things to decide in Arabic:

1 Whether the antecedent is:

a) definite (with *the* or the name of a person or place):

The train which we were supposed to catch was cancelled.
Mr Smith who lives next door lent me his lawn mower.
Muscat which was once a small town is now a large metropolis.

b) indefinite (usually with *a*):

He is a character who always has an answer to everything.
Books which you have already read should be thrown out or given away.

Arabic has two different structures, according to the indefinite/definite status of the antecedent.

2 The antecedent's role in the first part of the sentence, i.e. whether:

a) it is doing something (*subject*);

b) something is being done to it (*object*);

c) it belongs to someone or something (*possessive*).

English makes slight alterations to some of the relative pronouns:

- *who* shows that the antecedent is the subject;
- *whom* shows that the antecedent is the object, or having something done to it;
- *whose* shows a possessive relationship.

Sometimes the relative pronoun is omitted in informal speech:
The woman [whom] I love...
The films [that] I like...

Forming relative clauses in Arabic

a) those with definite antecedents require the use of relative pronouns (the equivalents of *who, which, whom* etc.)

b) those with indefinite antecedents do not use relative pronouns.

Otherwise, the methods of forming both types are identical.

Arabic relative pronouns

Form	Arabic pronoun	Used with antecedent types
masc. sing.	الَّذي **alládhi**	one male one object of masc. gender
fem. sing.	الَّتي **alláti**	one female one object of fem. gender plural objects of either gender
masc. plur.	الَّذين **alladhíina**	plural males only
fem. plur.	الآتي **alláati**	plural females only
dual (masc.)	اللذان **alladháani**	two men
dual (fem.)	اللتان **allatáani**	two women/objects

Notes:
1 Duals change their endings to ـين **-ayni** when they are governed by another word. (See Unit 14).
2 In most varieties of spoken Arabic, all the above are reduced to **illi**.

There is no distinction in Arabic between *who, whom* or *which* as there is in English. The relative pronouns agree only in number and gender with the antecedent.

As well as deciding whether to put the relative pronoun in or not, the Arabic relative clause differs from that of English in two ways:
a) it must constitute a complete and independent sentence on its own. English ones do not; *which I bought yesterday* does not make independent sense.
b) it must contain some stated or implied pronoun which refers back to the antecedent. This pronoun is called the *referent*.

Definite antecedent
English: *The film that I saw...*

Arabic: *The film* (masc. sing.) +
　　　　that (antecedent is definite, so relative pronoun required; select from box) +
　　　　I saw (referent required to show that what you saw refers to the film)

This gives the model:
The film – that – I saw it

Because *film* is masculine in Arabic, it requires the appropriate masculine relative, and it is expressed by masculine **-uh** *him*.

So in Arabic we say:

الفيلم – الذي – شاهدته

al-fiilm – alladhi – shaahadt-uh

In both English and Arabic the relative clause makes independent sense. The relative pronoun is simply a joining word.

Indefinite antecedent
For indefinite antecedents the process is identical, except that there is no relative pronoun:

A film which I saw

A film – I saw it (him)

فيلم – شاهدته

fiilm – shaahadt-uh

Relationship between verb and antecendent
In the above examples, the antecedent film is the object of the verb, i.e. the action of the verb is being applied to it. There are three other possible common relationships between the antecedent and the verb:

1 *Subject*. The antecedent is performing the action of the verb. Remember that in Arabic, all verbs are regarded as having built-in pronoun subjects. **yaktub** does not just mean *writes*, it means *he writes*.

The official who works in the customs ➜

The official – who – he-works in the customs (definite, so needs relative pronoun)

الموظف – الذي – يعمل في الجمارك

al-muwaDHDHaf – alladhi – ya:mal fi l-jamaarik

An official who works in the customs... ➜

(an) official – he-works in the customs (indef. – no relative pronoun)

موظف – يعمل في الجمارك

muwaDHDHaf – ya:mal fi l-jamaarik

2 *Possessive.* This is almost always expressed with the relative pronoun *whose* in English.

Maryam, whose sister lives in London

Maryam – who – her sister lives in London (relative pronoun required after proper name, in this case feminine)

مريم – التي – تسكن أختها في لندن

maryam – allati – taskun ukht-haa fii landan

A girl whose sister lives in London

(a) girl – her sister lives in London

بنت – تسكن أختها في لندن

bint – taskun ukht-haa fii landan

3 *Prepositional phrases*

The contractors to whom I paid a large sum

The contractors – who – I-paid to-them a large sum

المقاولون – الذين – دفعت لهم مبلغا كبيرا

al-muqaawiluun – alladhiina – dafa:t la-hum mablaghan kabiiran

Contractors to whom I paid a large sum

Contractors – I-paid to-them a large sum

مقاولون – دفعت لهم مبلغا كبيرا

muqaawiluun – dafa:t la-hum mablaghan kabiiran

All the above examples have verb sentences as the relative clause, but similar combinations are possible with *is/are* verbless sentences. The same rules regarding inclusion or omission of the relative pronoun apply.

The manager, whose name is Qasim...

The manager – who – his-name Qasim

المدير – الذي – اسمه قاسم

al-mudiir – alladhi – ism-uh qaasim

An official whose name is Muhsin

Official – his-name Muhsin

موظف – اسمه محسن

muwaDHDHaf – ism-uh muHsin

2 Passive verbs

A passive verb is one whose subject suffers the action, rather than carries it out (known as an *active verb*). English uses the auxiliary verb *to be* for the passive:

Active: *A bolt of lightning struck the tree*
Passive: *The tree was struck by a bolt of lightning*

The use of the passive is much more restricted in Arabic than in English. In many verbs it is identical in writing to the active, as the only changes are in the vowelling which is not shown.

The rules for forming it for the various verb types are given in the Verb Tables.

There are five examples in the text. Three of these look identical to the active forms, but differ in (unseen) vowelling:

يقدر **yuqaddar** (active **yuqaddir**) *is estimated* and its feminine **tuqaddar** [S-II verb]

تعتبر **tu:tabar** (active **tu:tabir**) *is considered* (fem. form) [S-VIII]

أجريت **ujriyat** (active أجرت **ajrat**) *was carried out* (fem. form) [Ly-IV]

توصف **tuuSaf** (active تصف **taSif**) *is described* (fem. form) [Fw-I]

Some of these verbs are among the most frequently-used passive forms in newspaper Arabic, so look out for them. In the case of those which are identical to the active in spelling, your only guideline is the context. For instance (after you have looked up all the words), the subject of the first example is **:adad** *number*. Since numbers can not carry out estimations, the verb must be passive.

أوزان الكلمات awzáan al-kalimáat (Word shapes)

Pattern	Arabic example	Eng. sound-alike
maCaaCiC*	**maraakiz** مراكز centres	*maraccas*

This is a plural form for many words in Arabic which begin with the prefix **ma-** or (less commonly) **mi-**, some of which have the feminine ending ة. One of the few mainly reliable rules for forming internal plurals is that, if the vowel after the middle radical of the root is short, then they will almost invariably take this plural shape, e.g. the example in the box above is the plural of **markaz** (short **a** after middle radical **k**).

This word pattern does not take the accusative marker.

Other examples from the text are:

موقع **mawqi:** ← *situations* **mawaaqi:*** مواقع

منطقة **minTaqah** ← *regions* **manaaTiq*** مناطق

Here are a few more common ones:

مدرسة **madrasah** ← *schools* **madaaris*** مدارس

مصنع **maSna:** ← *factories* **maSaani:*** مصانع

مكتب **maktab** ← *offices, desks* **makaatib*** مكاتب

منزل **manzil** ← *residences* **manaazil*** منازل

تمرينـات tamriináat (Practice)

Exercise 3
There are eight relative clauses in the tourist brochure above, four definite and four indefinite. Can you spot them?

Exercise 4
Rewrite the following sentences, supplying the correct relative pronouns (if any) to put into the gaps.

١ هذا هو البيت .... سنستأجره.

٢ زارني عامل .... يعمل في مصنع.

٣ شاهدت الطبيب .... عيادته في وسط المدينة.

٤ خالد .... قرأت كتابه يدرس في المدرسة الثانوية.

٥ كان الكرسي .... جلست عليه مكسورا.

٦ الطلبة .... يدرسون في الجامعة من الإمارات.

٧ رسالة .... كتبها الأسبوع الماضي وصلت اليوم.

٨ القمصان .... يبيعونها في السوق مصنوعة في الصين.

٩ مغنية .... كانت مشهورة قبل سنوات كثيرة ستزور سورية.

١٠ ابني له صديق .... أصله اسكتلندي.

Translation
1 *This is the house* which *we are going to rent.*
2 *An employee* who *works in a factory visited me.*
3 *I saw the doctor* whose *clinic is in the middle of town.*
4 *Khalid* whose *book I read teaches at the secondary school*
5 *The chair* which *she sat on was broken*
6 *The students* who *study at the university are from the Emirates.*

7 *A letter* which *he sent last week* arrived today.

8 *The shirts* which *they sell in the souk* are made in China.

9 *A singer (f)* who *was famous many years ago* will be visiting Syria.

10 *My son has a friend* who *is originally* [his origin is] *Scottish*.

استأجر **istá'jara [S-X]** *to rent, be a tenant of*

عيادة، ـات **:iyáadah, -aat** *clinic*

وسط **wasT** *middle*

باع **báa:a [My-I]** *sell*

مغنية **mughánniyyah** (female) *singer*

Exercise 5

Read the following excerpts from a Gulf tourist brochure and look
out for passive verbs and relative clauses. These are marked in the
answer key with bold type and underlining respectively.

١– لقد أعيد بناء منزل
الشيخ صقر الكائن في
هذه المنطقة.

٢– في هذه المنطقة
يمكن مشاهدة أول
أشكال تكييف الهواء،
البرجيل، الذي كان
يستخدم لتبريد البيوت
في الخليج. جددت
القلعة التي شيدت في
القرن الماضي، وحولت
إلى متحف.

٣– الطرق الضيقة
تأخذ الزائر إلى سوق

التوابل التي تنبعث
منها روائح أنواع
التوابل كلها مثل
القرنفل والهال والقرفة
التي تباع إلى الزوار من
الأكياس التي تحيط
المتاجر.

٤– سباقات الهجن
رياضة شعبية تقام
أيام الجمعة أثناء أشهر
الشتاء.

أعاد **a:áada [Mw-IV]** to repeat, renew

بناء **bináa'** building, construction

كائن **káa'in** being, existing, situated

أمكن **ámkana [S-IV]** to be possible

مشاهدة **musháahadah** seeing, viewing

شكل، أشكال **shakl, ashkáal** kind, type, form

هواء **háwaa'** air

برجيل، براجيل **barjiil, baráajiil** traditional wind tower

تبريد **tabríid** cooling

جدد **jáddada [D-II]** renew, restore

قلعة، قلاع **qál:ah, qiláa:** fort, fortress, citadel

شيد **sháyyada [My-II]** erect, construct

قرن، قرون **qarn, qurúun** century

ضيق **Dáyyiq** narrow

زائر، زوار **záa'ir, zuwwáar** visitor

تابل، توابل **táabil, tawáabil** spice

انبعث **inbá:atha [S-VII]** emanate, be sent out

رائحة، روائح **ráa'iHah, rawáa'iH*** smell, scent, perfume

قرنفل **qurúnful** cloves

هال **haal** cardamom

قرفة **qírfah** cinnamon

كيس، أكياس **kiis, akyáas** bag, sack

أحاط **aHáaTa [Mw-IV]** surround

متجر، متاجر **mátjar, matáajir*** trading place, shop, stall

سباق، ـات **sibáaq, -aat** race

هجين، هجن **hajiin, hújun** racing camel

شعبي **shá:bii** folk, popular

أقام **aqáama [Mw-IV]** (here) to hold (of an event)

شتاء **shítaa'*** winter

Exercise 6

Link the two sentences together using a relative clause.

١ عمر الشريف ممثل مصري. لعب أدوارا مشهورة كثيرة.

٢ ذهبنا إلى مدينة البتراء القديمة. اكتشفت في سنة ١٨١٨.

٣ في مصر آثار فرعونية مهمة. يزورها سواح كثيرون.

٤ يعمل زوجي في الشارقة. تقع الشارقة في الخليج العربي.

٥ نستأجر شقة في دمشق. يسكن صاحبها في الرياض.

٦ سافروا إلى عدن بطائرة الصبح. وصلت الطائرة الظهر.

البتراء **al-batráa'** Petra

اكتشف **iktáshafa [S-VIII]** discover (here passive)

فرعوني **far:úunii** pharaonic

دمشق **dimáshq*** Damascus

Exercise 7

Many adjectives in Arabic are derived from nouns, and there are several examples of them in the text above. See if you can find the nouns in the box on page 248 in transliteration in the wordsearch.

i	t	a	:	l	ii	m	l	a	d
r	i	a	h	kh	ii	r	aa	t	a
i	j	t	i	m	aa	:	a	l	h
y	aa	u	r	a	d	a	h	h	m
aa	r	m	gh	S	i	i	a	m	:
D	a	a	ii	r	q	f	:	u	i
a	h	t	b	t	aa	b	aa	t	l
h	a	a	i	q	i	f	r	i	m
b	s	S	a	l	S	q	i	H	a
t	aa	th	k	u	t	a	z	y	w
d	h	a	H	aa	y	i	S	i	aa

جغرافيا	*geography*
تاريخ	*history*
تجارة	*commerce*
علم	*science*
اقتصاد	*economy*
زراعة	*agriculture*
سياحة	*tourism*
اجتماع	*meeting; sociology*
رياضة	*sports*
تعليم	*education*
ثقافة	*culture*

14 | السمع والطاعة
as-sam: wa T-Taa:ah
Hearing is obeying
(The Arabian Nights)

In this unit you will learn:

- to follow a recipe
- how to tell people to do something
- more ways of addressing people or attracting their attention
- about duals and masculine plurals in possessive constructions

الكشري al-kushari *Koshari*

Koshari is a popular Egyptian dish of lentils and rice, often sold from carts in the streets. Look at the Key Phrases below, and read through the recipe. It will help if you listen to the recording at the same time.

Exercise 1

Now answer these questions.

a How many people does the koshari serve?
b What proportion of rice is used to lentils?
c How long must the lentils be soaked?
d How long do they cook with the rice?
e What else is layered with the rice, lentils and macaroni?
f What is added to the dish before it is served?

(الكمية تكفي ٦ أشخاص)

المقادير

- ٤ أكواب ونصف أرز، يغسل ويصفى
- كوب عدس أسود
- نصف كوب زيت
- ملح حسب الرغبة
- ٧ أكواب ونصف الكوب ماء للأرز
- ١٠ أكواب ماء لسلق المعكرونة
- كوبا معكرونة
- ملعقتا طعام زيت للمعكرونة
- ٦ بصلات مقطعة الى شرائح طويلة

الصلصة

- ملعقتا طعام سمن
- ٦ حبات طماطم مقشرة ومفرومة
- ملعقة صغيرة فلفل أحمر حار مطحون
- ملعقتا طعام من معجون الطماطم
- ملح حسب الرغبة

الطريقة

١ انقعي العدس بالماء لمدة ٦ ساعات وصفيه.

٢ حمري البصل بالزيت ثم ارفعيه واتركيه جانبا. اسكبي الماء فوقه واتركيه حتى يغلي قليلا، ثم أضيفي الأرز والعدس واتركيه على نار هادئة لمدة ٤٠ دقيقة.

٣ اسلقي المعكرونة بالماء ثم أضيفي الزيت.

٤ حمري الطماطم في الزيت، ثم أضيفي الفلفل ومعجون الطماطم والملح.

٥ أثناء التقديم ضعي خليط الأرز والعدس أولا، ثم طبقة من المعكرونة ثم طبقة من البصل، ورشي فوقه الصلصة الحارة أو قدميها إلى جانب الطبق.

Exercise 2

Link the English phrases to their Arabic equivalents.

a fry the onions in the oil

b leave them on a low heat

c add the pepper and the tomato paste

d then add the rice and lentils

e pour the hot sauce over it

١ أضيفي الفلفل ومعجون الطماطم

٢ رشي فوقه الصلصة الحارة

٣ ثم أضيفي الأرز والعدس

٤ حمري البصل بالزيت

٥ اتركيه على نار هادئة

كشري **kúshari** name of an Egyptian dish

كمية، ـات **kammíyyah, -aat** amount

كفى **káfaa [Ly-I]** to suffice, be sufficient for

شخص، أشخاص **shakhS, ashkháaS** person

مقدار، مقادير **miqdáar, maqáadiir*** quantity, measure

كوب، أكواب **kuub, akwáab** glass, cup (in recipes)

أرز **áruzz** rice

غسل **ghásala [S-I i]** wash

صفى **Sáffaa [Ly-II]** drain, strain

عدس: **ads** lentils

أسود **áswad*** black, here meaning brown (lentils)

زيت **zayt** (edible) oil

ملح **milH** salt

رغبة، ـات **rághbah, -áat** desire, wish

ماء **maa'** water

سلق **salq** boiling, the action of boiling something

معكرونة **ma:karúunah** macaroni

ملعقة، ملاعق **mil:áqah, maláa:iq*** spoon, spoonful

طعام **Ta:áam** food

ملعقة طعام **mil:áqat Ta:áam** tablespoon

بصل **báSal** onions

مقطع **muqáTTa:** chopped

شريحة، شرائح **shariiHah, sharáa'iH*** slice

صلصة **SálSah** sauce

سمن **sáman** ghee, clarified butter

حبة. ـات **Hábbah, -áat** grain, seed; also used for counting
  units of certain fruits and vegetables

طماطم **TamáaTim*** tomatoes

مقشر **muqáshshar** peeled, skinned

مفروم **mafrúum** minced, ground

فلفل **fúlful/filfil** pepper

أحمر **áHmar*** red

حار **Haarr** hot (chilli)

مطحون **maT-Húun** ground, milled

معجون **ma:júun** paste

طريقة، طرائق **Taríiqah, Taráa'iq*** method, way

نقع **náqa:a [S-I a]** to soak, steep

مدة **múddah** (period of) time

حمر **Hámmara [S-II]** to brown, fry

ثم **thúmma** then

رفع **ráfa:a [S-I a]** raise, lift

جانبا **jáaniban** aside, to one side

سكب **sákaba [S-I u]** to pour out

فوق **fáwqa** above, over

حتى **Háttaa** until

غلى **ghálaa [Ly-I]** to boil, come to the boil

أضاف **aDáafa [My-IV]** to add

نار **naar** fire (fem.)

هادئ **háadi'** gentle, quiet

دقيقة، دقائق **daqíiqah, daqáa'iq*** minute

أثناء(ا) **athnáa'(a)** during, while

تقديم **taqdíim** presentation, serving

وضع **wáDa:a [Fw-I a]** to put, place

خليط **khalíiT** mixture

طبقة، ات **Tábaqah, -áat** layer

رش **ráshsha [D-I u]** sprinkle, spray

أو **aw** or

قدم **qáddama [S-II]** to present, serve

جانب، جوانب **jáanib, jawáanib*** side

طبق، أطباق **Tábaq, aTbáaq** plate

معلومات ثقافية ma:luumáat thaqaafíyyah (Cultural tips)

Arabic cookery

The recipe given is for koshari, a simple, nutritious (vegetarian) dish from Egypt. Instructions in Arabic recipes are usually written in the feminine singular, on the assumption that Arab men stay out of the kitchen!

Although all Arab countries have their delicacies, the most highly regarded are those of Lebanon and Syria, which have much in common with the cuisines of other Eastern Mediterranean countries.

North Africa has many tasty dishes, many of them long-simmered stews eaten with couscous (polenta).

Cookery in the Gulf is much influenced by Indian cuisine, with the extensive use of spices. The staple in the Gulf is rice, and there is a wonderful selection of freshly-caught fish and shellfish available from local souks at reasonable prices.

There are many good books on Middle Eastern cookery, but those by Claudia Roden and Anissa Helou are especially worth seeking out.

تعبيرات رئيسية ta:biiráat ra'iisíyyah (Key phrases)

Describing how to prepare the ingredients

The ingredients should be...

مقشر **muqashshar** *peeled*

مقطع **muqaTTa:** *chopped*

مطحون **maT-Huun** *milled, ground*

Quantities

ملعقة طعام **mil:aqat Ta:aam** *tablespoon*

ملعقة شاي **mil:aqat shaay** *teaspoon*

كوب **kuub** *glass, cup* (in recipes)

مئة غرام **mi'at ghraam** *100 grams*

ليتر **liitir** *litre*

Instructions

All instructions are feminine singular (see above).

انقعي **inqa:ii** *soak*

صفي **Saffii** *strain*

اخلطي **ikhliTii** *mix*

حمري **Hammirii** *brown, fry*

اسلقي **usluqii** *boil*

ارفعي **irfa:ii** *lift*

اتركي **utrukii** *leave*

اسكبي **uskubii** *pour*

أضيفي **aDiifii** *add*

رشي **rushshii** *sprinkle*

غطي **ghaTTii** *cover*

قدمي **qaddimii** *serve*

تراكيب اللغة taraakíib al-lúghah (Structures)

Giving instructions and directions

The type of verb used for giving someone instructions or directions is called the *imperative*. In English this does not usually differ from the ordinary present tense verb:

Present tense: *You <u>work</u> hard*

Imperative: *<u>Work</u> hard!*

Arabic uses a special adaptation of the variant form of the present tense called the *jussive*, which you can find in the Verb Tables at the end of this book.

Forming the imperative

This is also explained in the section on verbs at the end of the book, but it is simply constructed as follows:

a) Look up in the verb tables the *you* form, or 2nd person singular, jussive form of the present tense, e.g.:

تقدم **tuqaddim** *you present, serve*

b) Remove the prefix **ta-** or **tu-**, to get قدم **qaddim**.

c) If the result, as in the above example, begins with:
   - a consonant followed by any of the vowels, you have formed the imperative masculine singular (قدم **qaddim** *Present!*)
   - two consonants (Arabic letters **dh** (ذ), **kh** (خ), etc. counting as only one consonant), supply an **alif** at the beginning and pronounce it in most cases as the vowel **i**.

تستعلم **tasta:lim** *you enquire*

➜ ستعلم **sta:lim**

➜ استعلم **ista:lim** *enquire!*

d) Form I verbs, as usual, show vowel variation. With sound Form I verbs (see Table S-I), removing the prefix always results in a two-consonant beginning, so an **alif** must be prefixed. Note the vowel following the second consonant, which can be **a**, **i** or **u**.

- If it is **a** or **i**, the above rules for two consonants apply:

تغسل **taghsil** *wash* → غسل **ghsil** → اغسل **ighsil** *Wash!*

- If it is **u**, the **alif** must also be given a **u**-vowel:

تترك **tatruk** *leave (aside)* → ترك **truk** → اترك **utruk** *Leave!*

In practice this is not too important, as these vowels are very often elided unless the imperative comes at the beginning of a sentence.

Note: The one exception to the above rules is the Form IV verb (all types; see Tables). In these verbs, an **alif** with an **a**-vowel is always prefixed to the shortened jussive form, whether this begins with two consonants or not. This initial **a**-vowel is never elided, and is often written with a **hamzah** as below:

ترسل **tursil** (from أرسل S-IV *to send*) → رسل **rsil** → أرسل **arsil** *Send!*

تضيفي **tuDiifii** (fem. sing. from أضاف.My-IV *to add*) → ضيفي **Diifii** → أضيفي **aDiifii** *Add!* (fem. sing.). The **alif** is added even though the shortened jussive begins with a consonant followed by a vowel.

Irregular imperatives

The only common irregular imperatives are:

تعال **ta:aal** *Come!* (no phonetic relation to the verb جاء **jaa'a**)

خذ **khudh** *Take!* from أخذ **akhadha** *to take*

هات **haat** *Give!*, probably from the verb أتى **ataa**

كل **kul** *Eat!*, from أكل **akala** *to eat*

Feminine and plural imperatives

Feminine and plural imperatives obey the rules above, using the relevant parts of the jussive:

ـي **-ii** fem. sing. (addressed to one female)

وا- **-uu** masc. pl.

ن- **-na** fem. pl.

For *come!* these same endings are added to تعال giving تعالي، تعالوا etc. The same is true for the other irregular imperatives listed above

Note: The dual imperatives for addressing two people occur rarely and have been omitted from this section. However, they can be deduced from the jussive form in exactly the same way.

Negative imperatives

Use the negative word لا **laa**, *not* followed by the appropriate part of the jussive, retaining its prefix:

لا تترك **laa tatruk** *don't leave* (to a man)

لا تغسلي **laa taghsilii** *don't wash* (to a woman)

لا تستعلموا **laa tasta:limuu** *don't enquire* (to several men)

معلومات ثقافية **ma:luumáat thaqaafíyyah (Cultural tips)**
A situation in which you often see imperatives are road signs telling you to do something (*slow down, stop*, etc.)

However, many common signs are expressed in a different way, for instance with the word الرجاء **ar-rijaa'** which means *the request*, i.e. *it is requested, please do/don't do something.* This is followed

by a noun indicating the action requested. Such signs often feature the word عدم **:adam** *lack of, absence of* when the request is a negative one, i.e *not to do something*.

2 More ways to address people

As we have already seen, all forms of Arabic use the vocative particle يا **yaa** when addressing people or attracting attention:

يا سامي! **yaa saamii** *Sami!*

A slightly different form is used when the person addressed has the definite article:

يا ايها الأمير! **yaa ayyuhaa al-amiir!** *O Emir!*

This construction is commonly found in political and other emotive speeches with a plural noun:

يا ايها الإخوة العرب!   *O Arab brothers!*

yaa ayyuhaa l-ikhwah al-:arab

يا ايتها السيدات!   *Ladies!*

yaa ayyatuhaa (fem.) **as-sayyidaat**

3 Masc. plurals and duals in possessive constructions

As you know these endings all end in the letter **nuun** ن:

Masculine plural:

ـون **-uun** (subject)

ـين **-iin** (object and possessive)

Dual:

ـان **-aan** (fem.ـتان **-ataan**) (subject)

ـين **-ayn** (fem. ـتين **-atayn**) (object and possessive)

However, when any of these types of word form the first part of a possessive construction, the letter **nuun** of the endings is dropped. There are several examples of such duals in the recipe:

كوبا معكرونة   *two cups of macaroni*

ملعقتا طعام زيت   *two tablespoons of oil*

(this is a double possessive, the Arabic literally reading

two-spoons [of] food [of] oil)

Examples of the masculine plural are:

حضر موظفو الحكومة   *The officials of the govern-*

HaDara muwaDHDHafuu   *ment attended*

l-Hukuumah

تطلب الشركة مندوبي مبيعات   *The company is seeking sales*

taTlub ash-sharikah manduubii *representatives*

mabii:aat

أوزان الكلمات awzáan al-kalimáat (Word shapes)

Pattern	Arabic example	Eng. sound-alike
istiCCaaC	**istinkaar** استنكار *rejection*	*(m)ist in car* (omitting first letter)

This is the verbal noun of S-X verbs.

🎧 استخدام **istikhdaam** *using, usage, use*

استعمال **isti:maal** *same meaning as above*

استعلام **isti:laam** *enquiring, enquiry*

استقبال **istiqbaal** *reception* (of guests, etc.)

استثناء **istithnaa'** *excepting, exception*

تمرينـات tamriináat (Practice)

Exercise 3
You are in an aeroplane and are served a meal. Match each of these packs of food and seasoning to the appropriate English word.

a salt **b** pepper **c** sugar **d** butter **e** water

Exercise 4
Look at these road signs and match them with the English.

a Turn left **b** Stop **c** Slow down **d** Turn right

Exercise 5

You are in a car park in Dubai and have to pay the parking fee. Read the instructions on the ticket machine and answer the questions on page 262.

a Match the following English with the Arabic:

    i *Payment by coins*   ١ الدفع بالبطاقة

    ii *Payment by card*   ٢ الدفع بالنقود المعدنية

b Which coins can you use?

c On what day do you <u>not</u> need to pay a fee?

d What is the longest time you can park?

e How much does it cost to park for two hours?

f Find the word for *press*

Exercise 6

Find an appropriate response to the cues in the right-hand column.
(Note: Some of these are in the feminine singular.)

a جربه، هو لذيذ	١ أنا جوعان
b هات واحد جديد	٢ أنا تعبانة
c رده إليه	٣ تاكسي! تاكسي!
d كل شيئا!	٤ هذا الكوب مكسور
e خذها إلى المستشفى	٥ عمري ما أكلت الكسكس
f اجري!	٦ هذا الكتاب لأحمد
g المحطة	٧ أختي مريضة
h نامي	٨ تأخرت!

عمري ما **úmrii maa …** *I have never …*

جرب **járraba [S-II]** *try out, taste*

رد إلى **rádda [D-I u]** *return something to someone*

جرى **járaa [Ly-I]** *run*

نام **náama [Ma-I]** *sleep*

Exercise 7

A local supermarket has special offers on some food items which are announced over the loudspeaker. Listen to the recording, and answer the questions.

a How much is the minced lamb per kilo?
b What do they want you to see?
c What do they suggest you make for a meal?
d How long does the cheese offer last?
e Listen to the recording again, and select an appropriate word from the box to put into the gaps below, putting it into the imperative form.

.... إلى قسم اللحوم! .... بأسعار مذهلة! تنزيلات في لحم الغنم المفروم الكيلو بـ ٨ دراهم.

.... تشكيلة الجبن من فرنسا وإيطاليا. .... وجبة معكرونة للعائلة اليوم. .... جبنة الحلوم اللذيذة. أسعار خاصة لليوم فقط.

شاهدوا	جربوا	تعالوا	أطبخوا	اشتروا

قسم، أقسام **qism, aqsáam** section, division	
لحم، لحوم **laHm, luHúum** meat	
غنم **ghánam** sheep (collective)	
تشكيلة، ـات **tashkiilah, -áat** selection	
وجبة، ـات **wájabah, -áat** meal	
جبنة الحلوم **júbnat al-Hallúum** Halloumi cheese	

Exercise 8

a Read the following exchange between Fawzi and his assistant Karim. (Note that where English says *shall I...*, Arabic uses the simple present tense)

كريم   أفتح هذه الرسالة؟

فوزي   نعم، افتحها.

Instruct Karim to do what he offers to do, using an imperative verb
(with suffix pronoun if necessary).

١ أرسل الفاكس الآن؟

٢ أكتب الرسالة فورا؟

٣ اتصل بالمكتب؟

b Fatimah's new maid is helping her with the lunch. Can you tell
her to do what she is offering?

١ أضع الماء على الطاولة؟

٢ أترك الأرز في المطبخ؟

٣ أغسل الصحون؟

الآن **al-áan** now

أرسل **ársala [S-IV]** send

فورا **fáwran** immediately

15 العرب في هوليوود
al-:arab fii huuliiwuud
Arabs in Hollywood

In this unit you will learn:

- to make comparisons
- to say how things are done
- more about shopping

العرب في هوليوود al-:arab fii huuliiwuud
The Arabs in Hollywood

The best-known Arab actor to have achieved stardom in the Western cinema is the Egyptian-born Omar Sharif, famous for his celebrated roles in the films *Lawrence of Arabia* and *Dr Zhivago*. However, in the 1990s competition came along in the shape of Salma Hayek.

Read the magazine article about Salma, looking carefully through the new vocabulary.

Exercise 1

Now answer the questions.

a What was Salma Hayek the first Arab woman to do?
b What aspect of her beauty appeals particularly to the West?
c Which stars does she compete with in Hollywood?
d When was she born?
e Where does her mother come from originally?
f How old was she when she was spotted by producers?
g What film did she work in with Quentin Tarantino?
h What will her most recent film give her?

سلمى... العربية التي قهرت هوليوود

في الشرق نعتبرها سفيرة الجمال العربي التي استطاعت ان تكون أول امرأة تخترق أسوار هوليوود وتفرض نفسها على أعلى قائمة نجمات السينما.

وفي الغرب يعتبرونها رمزا لسحر الشرق بما تحمله من ملامح شرقية غاية في الجمال الذي يناظر السحر. ولهذا أعطوها البطولات في أكبر أفلامهم مفضلينها على أكثر نجمات هوليوود جمالا. وإذا سلمى الحايك اليوم تزاحم شارون ستون وديمي مور وغيرهما من نجمات هوليوود.

وسلمى الحايك، أو اسطورة الشرق في الغرب، المولودة سنة ١٩٦٦، هي ابنة مهاجر لبناني مقيم بالمكسيك والدتها اسبانية الأصل. وإذا اجتمع الجمال اللبناني والاسباني تكون الثمرة في حلاوة سلمى الحايك. ولأنها جميلة جدا فقد رصدتها عين المنتجين وهي في الثالثة عشر من عمرها واختيرت وقتها كأجمل الوجوه التلفزيونية. ثم أخذها المنتج تارانتينو إلى لوس انجليس لتشترك في الفيلم «ديسبيرادو» الى جانب انطونيو بانديراس وأعطت للفيلم مذاقا خاصا جدا جلب لها اهتمام شركات الإنتاج الكبرى وسرعان ما قدموا لها العقود الكثيرة بل إنها أخذت مؤخرا دورا كان من المفترض أن يسند لمغنية شهيرة امريكية ولكن منتجي هوليوود فضلوا سلمى عليها ومن الأكيد أن هذا الفيلم سيعطي لسلمى انطلاقة أكثر قوة وانتشارا.

Exercise 2

Match the English phrases to the Arabic expressions.

a the first woman

b the leads in their greatest films

c most of the stars of Hollywood in terms of beauty

d the most beautiful television personality

e greater eminence as regards power and popularity

١ أكثر نجمات هوليوود جمالا

٢ انطلاقة أكثر قوة وانتشارا

٣ أول امرأة

٤ أجمل الوجوه التلفزيونية

٥ البطولات في أكبر أفلامهم

قهر **qáhara [S-1 a]** to conquer

اعتبر **i:tábara [S-VIII]** to consider, regard

سفيرة، ـات **safiirah, -áat** ambassador (female)

استطاع **istaTáa:a [Mw-X]** to be able

امرأة، نساء **imrá'ah, nisáa'** (irregular plural) woman

اخترق **ikhtáraqa [S-VIII]** to breach (wall, defences, etc.)

سور، أسوار **suur, aswáar** wall, fence

فرض **fáraDa [S-I i]** impose

نفس، نفوس **nafs, nufúus** self; soul (fem.)

أعلى **á:laa** highest; the highest point, top

قائمة، ـات **qáa'imah, -áat** list

نجمة، ـات **nájmah, -áat** star, (female) film star

رمز، رموز **ramz, rumúuz** symbol, code

سحر **siHr** magic

ملامح **maláamiH*** features

غاية **gháayah** extreme, most

ناظر **náaDHara [S-III]** to equal, compete with

أعطى **á:Taa [Ly-IV]** to give

بطولات **buTúulaat** leading roles

فيلم، افلام **fiilm, afláam** *film*

مفضل **mufáDDil** *preferring*

زاحم **záaHama [S-III]** *to jockey for position with*

غير **ghayr** *other than*

اسطورة، اساطير **usTúurah, asáaTiir*** *legend*

مولود **mawlúud** *born*

ابنة، بنات **íbnah, banáat** *daughter*

مهاجر، ـون **muháajir, -úun** *emigrant*

مقيم **muqíim** *residing, resident*

المكسيك **al-maksíik** *Mexico*

اسباني **isbáanii** *Spanish*

أصل، أصول **aSl, uSúul** *origin, basis*

إذا **ídhaa** *if*

اجتمع **ijtáma:a [S-VIII]** *meet, come together*

ثمرة **thámrah** *fruit*

حلاوة **Haláawah** *sweetness; also beauty*

رصد **ráSada [S-I u]** *observe, watch, monitor*

عين، عيون **:ayn, :uyúun** *eye; also spring (of water) (fem.)*

منتج، ـون **múntij, -úun** *producer*

ثالثة عشر **tháalithah :áshar** *thirteenth*

عمر **:umr** *age, life*

اختار **ikhtáara [My-VIII]** *to choose*

وقتها **waqtá-haa** *then, at that time*

كـ **ka-** *as, like*

أجمل **ájmal*** *more/most beautiful*

وجه، وجوه **wajh, wujúuh** *face, (media) personality*

تلفزيوني **tilifizyúunii** *television (adj.), televisual*

أخذ **ákhadha [S-I u]** *to take*

لـ **li-** *for, in order to*

اشترك **ishtáraka [S-VIII]** *to participate, subscribe*

مذاق **madháaq** *flavour*

جلب **jálaba [S-I i]** *attract, bring*

اهتمام **ihtimáam** *attention, concern, interest*

انتاج **intáaj** *production*

الكبرى **al-kúbraa** *the largest* (see grammar notes)

سرعان ما **sur:áan maa** *quickly, before long*

بل **bal** *rather;* (here) *in fact, indeed*

مؤخرا **mu'ákhkhiran** *recently, lately*

مفترض **muftáraD** *assumed, supposed*

أسند لـ **ásnada [S-IV]** *entrust to, vest in*

مغنية، ـات **mughánniyah, -áat** *singer* (female)

شهير **shahíir** *famous*

أكيد **akíid** *certain*

انطلاقة **inTiláaqah** (here) *eminence, brightness*

أكثر **ákthar*** *more/most*

قوة، ـات **qúwwah, -áat** *force, power, strength*

انتشار **intisháar** *spread, currency;* (here) *popularity*

---

al-mulaaHaDHáat (Notes) الملاحظات

■ **awwal imra'ah** *the first woman.* **awwal** *first* is treated in Arabic as a superlative adjective. See below.

■ **imra'ah** *woman* is an irregular noun:
   1 When it has the definite article, it drops both the initial **alif**; (المرأة) and the vowel after the **r** and is pronounced **al-mar'ah**
   2 It has the phonetically-unrelated plural **nisaa'**, also with the variant **niswaan** (نساء، نسوان).

■ **an takuun**. Although no verb *to be* is used in simple statements equating to *is/are*, certain conjunctions, including **an** *that*, require the present subjunctive tense after them. See below.

■ **bi-maa** is a common conjunction, usually translated as *for, in that, as, because*.

■ **salmaa (al-)Haayik**. The Arab press seems to be unsure whether Salma's family name should have the article or not. Both usages appear.

■ **ghayr-humaa** lit. *and other than them-two*. The dual suffix is used because two people (Stone and Moore) have been named.

■ **ibnah** is used for daughter in isolation. If you say *daughter of Rashid*, the form is **bint**, which also means *girl*.

■ **takuun** *will/would be*. When the present tense of **kaana** is used, it implies future or uncertainty instead of straight fact.

■ **fa-qad** This is **fa-** *so* with the past marker **qad** (see Unit 8)■ **ath-thaalithah :asharah min :umr-haa**. This phrase is feminine to agree with the unstated word **sanah** *year*. See Ordinal numbers, Unit 11.

■ **ukhtiirat**. Past tense passive of a My-VIII verb. See verb tables.

■ **waqt-haa** *soon, quickly*. Lit. *her time* means *then* with a sense of immediacy, *there and then*

■ **wujuuh** *faces* also has the extended meaning of *(show business) personalities*.

■ **bal** is an emphatic word, meaning *not only this but...*

■ **muntijii huuliiwuud**. For the dropping of the final **nuun** of the first word, see Unit 14.

🎧 تعبيرات رئيسية **ta:biiráat ra'iisíyyah (Key phrases)**

Comparatives and superlatives

محمود أطول من ناصر	*Mahmoud is taller than Nasir*
هذه هي المشكلة الأصعب	*This is the hardest problem*

هل شاهدت البرنامج الأول؟   *Did you see the first programme?*

هي أجمل امرأة في هوليوود   *She is the most beautiful woman*
in Hollywood

تراكيب اللغة taraakíib al-lúghah (Structures)

1 Forming comparatives and superlatives

Comparative adjectives in English usually end in *-er* and are
followed by the word *than*: *larger than life*.

Superlatives usually end in *-(e)st* : *the greatest show on earth.*

Comparatives

Because they involve internal changes, true comparatives in Arabic
can only be formed from simple adjectives with three root
consonants, often plus a long vowel (usually *aa*, *ii*, e.g. *waasi:*,
kabiir). The comparative of such adjectives can be constructed
taking the following steps:

a) Identify the three root consonants, e.g.: **kabiir ➔ k-b-r**.

b) Prefix an **alif** (pronounced **a**) and re-vowel the root letters as
follows:

   1st radical – no vowel

   2nd radical – an **a**-vowel.

   e.g. كبير ➔ radicals ك–ب–ر ➔ أكبر **akbar**

Note: Although it is not always written, the prefixed **alif**
technically has a hamzah on it (أ), so the **a**-vowel is never elided.

This form does not change and is used for all genders and numbers.

The word for *than* is من **min**:

الفيل أكبر من الفأر   *The elephant is bigger than the mouse*

al-fiil akbar min al-fa'r

Look at the following common adjectives and their comparatives:

طويل *tall*	أطول *taller*
قصير *short*	أقصر *shorter*
كبير *big*	أكبر *bigger/older* (humans)
صغير *small*	أصغر *smaller/younger* (humans)
قديم *old*	أقدم *older* (things)
رخيص *cheap*	أرخص *cheaper*
جميل *beautiful*	أجمل *more beautiful*

طارق سليم　　　　　　　　أمي　اختي

سليم أطول من طارق　　　　　اختي اقصر من أمي

saliim aTwal min Taariq　　**ukht-ii aqSar min umm-ii**

Salim is taller than Tariq　　*My sister is shorter than my mother*

Pronunciation notes:

1 If the adjective has the same second and third root letters, the **a**-vowel is shifted back from the second radical to the first, and the second and third radicals are written as one (technically with the doubling sign **shaddah**, but this is usually omitted):

شديد **shadiid** *strong, violent* → radicals ش–د–د → أشد **ashadd**

هـام **haamm** *important* → radicals هـ–م–م → أهم **ahamm**

2 If it ends in one of the weak letters و or ي, this becomes a long **aa** (written ى) in the comparative:

حلو **Hulw** *sweet, beautiful* → radicals ح–ل–و → أحلى **aHlaa**

الغالي **al-ghaalii**** *expensive* → radicals غ–ل–ي → أغلى **aghlaa**

** given here with the definite article, as indefinites of this type have an irregular spelling (see Unit 18).

3 For polysyllabic words which cannot conform to the above system, Arabic uses أكثر **akthar** *more* and أقل **aqall** *less* followed by an adverbial accusative (see below), ending in a marked or unmarked **-an**.

Superlatives

Superlatives are formed in exactly the same way as comparatives, but take different sentence structures. All of the examples below are taken from the article above.

1 Superlative + indefinite singular noun (technically in the genitive)

أول امرأة **awwal imra'ah**   *the first woman*

first is regarded as a superlative.

2 Superlative + definite plural noun

أجمل الوجوه التلفزيونية   *the most beautiful television personality*

ajmal al-wujuuh at-tilifizyuuniiya

This equates with the English parallel *the most beautiful of [the] television personalities*.

3 Definite noun + definite superlative

شركات الانتاج الكبرى   *the biggest production companies*

sharikaat al-intaaj al-kubraa

In the last example, the first word **sharikaat** is definite because it is the first term in a possessive: see Unit 6.

Note:
a) this is actually more of an intensive than a superlative, probably better translated as *the great production companies*.
b) a few common adjectives have a feminine form when required by agreement (here for a neuter plural). This is derived from the three root letters and vowelled and spelled as in **kubraa**. This is the least common of the three constructions, but is often encountered in set phrases, e.g.:

الشرق الأوسط   **ash-sharq al-awsaT** *The Middle East* (masc.)
بريطانيا العظمى   **briiTaanyaa l-:uDHmaa** *Great Britain* (fem., from عظيم *mighty*).

c) أول **awwal** *first* functions exactly as a superlative. When used after the noun, as in construction 3 above, it takes the feminine form أولى **uulaa**, e.g. المرة الأولى or أول مرة. *[for] the first time.*

Note that none of these comparatives or superlatives take the **alif** accusative marker.

2 The adverbial accusative

The adverbial accusative is often associated with the comparative or superlative, and there are several examples in the article above. We will look at adverbs themselves in more detail in Unit 16.

Use of the adverbial accusative

The adverbial accusative tells us to what respect or characteristic the comparative refers. In English we might say:
He is better off than me in terms of/as regards possessions, but he is worse off for money.

Modern colloquial English often uses the suffix *-wise*:
She has done less well career-wise, but her personal life is more satisfying.

Formation

The adverbial accusative is always indefinite, and is formed from a noun or adjective with the ending **-an** (marked by an **alif** on most masculines; unmarked in the feminine). This ending is usually pronounced, even in informal spoken Arabic.

Therefore, you need only remember to put in the **alif** when required. Examples from the passage are:

أكثر نجمات هوليوود جمالا

lit. *the greatest of the Hollywood stars in terms of beauty*

(marked accusative **jamaalan**)

انطلاقة أكثر قوة وانتشارا

prominence greater in terms of strength and popularity

(unmarked **quwwatan**, marked **intishaaran**)

This construction is frequently used with the two words **akthar** *more, most*, and **aqall** *less* to form comparatives and superlatives where the adjective is too long or complex to use the direct formation. In this case the equivalent noun of the adjective is used. This takes experience, but here are two examples.

a) The adjective مجتهد **mujtahid** *diligent, hard working* has far too many letters to form a direct comparative. The equivalent noun is اجتهاد **ijtihaad** *diligence*. Adding the accusative ending, we get:

أكثر اجتهادا **akthar ijtihaadan** *more diligent* (lit. *more in terms of diligence*)

b) The adjective مفيد **mufiid** *beneficial* comes from the noun افادة **ifaadah** *benefit*:

اقل افادة **aqall ifaadatan** *less beneficial, of less benefit*

Here the noun has a feminine ending, so there is no **alif**

3 Conjunctions

Conjunctions join parts of sentences, explaining the relationship of one part to another. Common examples are *and* expressing a direct link, and *or* which expresses an alternative. Others express a more complex link, for instance purpose, reason and so on.

These latter in Arabic fall into two distinct categories, depending on the type of word which comes after them. Here are some examples of the most commonly encountered conjunctions from the interview above:

1 Conjunctions followed by verbs

أن **an** *that*. The verb following is usually in the present subjunctive (see Verb Tables):

استطاعت أن تكون أول امرأة	*she was able to be the first*
(Lit. she was able that she be…)	*woman…*
كان من المفترض أن يسند لمغنية شهيرة	*…should have been entrusted*
(lit. …was of the supposed that	*to a famous singer*
it be entrusted)	

لـ **li** *to, in order that.* The verb following is always in the subjunctive. (Note that this should be distinguished from the identical word meaning *to*, for use with nouns, which is a preposition, not a conjunction.)

لتشترك في الفيلم   *(in order) to take part in the film*

Other conjunctions in this category will be pointed out as we come across them.

2 Conjunctions followed by nouns or pronouns
These are technically in the accusative:

أن **anna** *that*

ومن الأكيد أن هذا الفيلم   *and it is certain that this film...*
(followed by a noun with the demonstrative pronoun)

لأن **li'anna** *because*

ولأنها جميلة جدا   *and because she is very beautiful*
(followed by the suffix – i.e. accusative – pronoun)

ولكن، لكن **walaakinna, laakinna** *but* (no difference in meaning)

ولكن منتجي هوليوود.... *but the Hollywood producers...*
(lit. *producers of Hollywood*) showing accusative masculine plural noun with final **nuun** dropped (see Unit 14)

Note: Although not really a conjunction, the slightly emphatic particle إن **inna** also belongs to this category; see Unit 8)

أوزان الكلمات **awzáan al-kalimáat (Word shapes)**

Pattern	Arabic example	Eng. sound-alike
CaCaaCiiC*	**maqaadiir** مقادير *quantities*	*magazine*

This is another internal plural shape. This one derives from singulars which have four consonants, with a long vowel between the third and the fourth. The accent is always on the last syllable. Presence of the feminine suffix ة **-ah** makes no difference. This is a pretty safe bet for any such word, but there are a few exceptions. These plurals do not take the accusative marker. In the text for this unit we have:

أساطير، اسطورة **usTuurah, asaaTiir*** *legend* (the hamzah counts as a radical)

Here are some other examples. Watch for the long vowels (any of them) between the third and the fourth radicals:

مفتاح **miftaaH** *key* ➜ مفاتيح **mafaatiiH***

مقدار **miqdaar** *amount, quantity* ➜ مقادير **maqaadiir***

منديل **mandiil** *handkerchief* ➜ مناديل **manaadiil***

صندوق **Sunduuq** *box, chest* ➜ صناديق **Sanaadiiq***

عصفور **uSfuur** *sparrow, small bird* ➜ عصافير: **aSaafiir***

There are not many exceptions to this rule. Some adjectives take the ون_ **-uun** ending, and note the following nouns:

أستاذ، أساتذة **ustaadh, asaatidhah** *professor*

تلميذ، تلامذة **tilmiidh, talaamidhah** *pupil* (but also تلاميذ **talaamiidh**)

معلومات ثقافية **ma:luumáat thaqaafíyyah** (Cultural tips)

There are quite a few English words which derive ultimately from Arabic, often via Spanish and hence French (the Arabs ruled most of Spain for about 500 years). *Magazine* – originally in the military sense – is one of them. It comes from مخازن **makhaazin***, plural of مخزن **makhzan** *storehouse* (a slightly different Word Shape from that given above). Here are a few others:

- both *zero* and *cypher* ultimately derive from صفر **Sifr** *zero*, the concept of which the Arabs invented

- *calibre* derives from قالب **qaalib** *mould* (for bullets, etc.);

- *algorithm* derives from the name of a famous Arab philosopher الخوارزمي **al-khawaarizmii;**

- *algebra* is from another famous Arabic name الجابر **al-jaabir;**

- *chemise* is from قميص **qamiiS**, mentioned in the Koran (7th century AD);

- more subtle is *arsenal* from دار الصناعة **daar aS-Sinaa:ah**, and *admiral* from أمير البحر **amiir al-baHr** (with the last word omitted).

تمرينات tamriináat (Practice)

Exercise 3
The adverts below all offer bargains to the shopper. Look at the ads and answer the questions about each one on page 279. The key vocabulary is on page 280.

a

b

c

التعاون + التعاون
زيت زيتون ٥٠٠مل **مجاناً** إسباجيتي ٤٠٠ج

d

e

a What do you have to do to win a prize?
b i When does the offer end at the Co-op?
  ii How long have they been serving their customers?
c What do you get free if you buy the oil?
d What are the two main prizes to be won
e What does Western Union promise you?
f How do you obtain the discount offered at Bou Khalil?

ربح rábaHa [S-I a] *to win, gain, profit*	
فاضل fáaDil *favourable, good*	
عرض، عروض :arD, :urúuD *offer, deal*	
زبون، زبائن zabúun, zabáa'in* *customer, client*	
مجانا majjáanan *free, gratis*	
نقد، نقود naqd, nuqúud *cash, money*	
مكان، أمكنة makáan, ámkinah *place*	
حسم Hasm *discount*	
بطاقة، ـات buTáaqah, -áat *card*	
امتياز imtiyáaz *distinction, privilege*	

Exercise 4

You are thinking of buying a computer, and have narrowed the
choice down to two possibilities. Look at the two specifications
below.

B

■ شاشة ١٧ بوصة

■ مشغل القرص الثابت ١٠ غيغابيت

■ ذاكرة وصول عشوائي ٦٤ ميغابيت

■ موديم فاكس ٥٦ ك

■ ٤٤٩٩ درهم

A

■ شاشة ١٥ بوصة

■ مشغل القرص الثابت ٨ غيغابيت

■ ذاكرة وصول عشوائي ٣٢ ميغابيت

■ موديم ٤٤ ك

■ سهل الاستعمال

■ ٣٣٩٠ درهم

a Select appropriate adjectives from the box to fill in the gaps, changing them to the comparative form.

١ هذا الكمبيوتر له شاشة ....

٢ له موديم ....

٣ له ذاكرة ....

٤ له قرص ثابت ....

٥ هو .... استعمالا.

٦ هو ....

سريع **sarii:** *fast*	سهل **sahil** *easy*
صغير **Saghiir** *small*	حسن **Hasan** *good*
كبير **kabiir** *big*	رخيص **rakhiiS** *cheap*

شاشة **sháashah** *screen*

موديم **múudiim** *modem*

ذاكرة **dháakirah** *memory*

قرص ثابت **qarS tháabit** *hard disk*

استعمال **isti:máal** *use, usage*

b Which computer does each of the specifications in part **a** above refer to?

16 | صفحة الرياضة
SafHat ar-riyaaDah
Sports page

In this unit you will learn:
- about sports and leisure activities
- about colours
- to describe how or when you have done something

🎧 الليلة السوداء al-laylah s-sawdaa' *The black night*

Listen to the recording of this report of a football match between Morocco and Tunisia. The vocabulary is given for you below, so look through that carefully first, and then attempt the exercises.

Exercise 1
a For which side is it a black night?
 i Morocco **ii** Tunisia
b Which round of the competition is it?
 i the first **ii** the fourth **iii** the final
c Where did the match take place?
d How many spectators were there?

Listen to the recording again and answer these questions.
e How many goals did Mahmoud al-Turki score?
f Which side scored first?
g Who scored at the end of the first half?

Listen to the recording one more time.
h When was the last goal scored?
i What happened to Suleiman al-Fasi?
j Which team was he playing for?

Now read the report.

ليلة سوداء للكرة المغربية

تأهل الفريق التونسي الى الدور النهائي من مسابقة كأس العرب لكرة القدم في ليلة سوداء للكرة المغربية. وعلى ملعب الزمالك في القاهرة امس، وأمام ٤٢ الف متفرج قاد محمود التركي الفريق التونسي الى الفوز. وسجل التركي وحده ثلاثة اهداف في المباراة التي انتهت ٥-١.

وافتتح الفريق التونسي التسجيل عن طريق لاعب وسطه جعفر ابو عادل بتسديدة رائعة من خارج المنطقة خدعت الحارس المغربي في الدقيقة التاسعة من المباراة. وكانت نتيجة الفرصة الاولى للفريق

المغربي هدفهم الوحيد في اخر الشوط الأول عندما سدد طارق الأحمر كرة قوسية دخلت ركن المرمى التونسي وأدرك التعادل. ولكنه بدا ان اللاعبين المغاربة قد رفعوا الراية البيضاء في الشوط الثاني وسيطر التونسيون على اللعب سيطرة تامة. وجاءت الأهداف بسرعة، آخرها في الدقيقة الأخيرة من المباراة عندما أودع القائد التونسي الكرة في الشبكة المغربية للمرة الثالثة بعد ما احتسب الحكم ركلة ركنية وطرد المدافع المغربي سليمان الفاسي لنيله البطاقة الصفراء الثانية.

Exercise 2

Link the English phrases below with the Arabic expressions.

a a black night for Moroccan football

b al-Turki himself scored three goals

c the Moroccan players raised the white flag

d for the third time

e the referee awarded a corner kick

f for getting his second yellow card

١ ... اللاعبين المغاربة قد رفعوا الراية البيضاء

٢ للمرة الثالثة

٣ لنيله البطاقة الصفراء الثانية

٤ ليلة سوداء للكرة المغربية

٥ احتسب الحكم ركلة ركنية

٦ سجل التركي وحده ثلاثة أهداف

ليلة، ـات، ليال **láyla, -áat, layáalin** night

أسود، سوداء **áswad*, fem. sawdáa'*** black

كرة، ـات **kúrah, -áat** ball, also used as a shortened form of
كرة القدم **kúrat al-qádam** football

مغربي، مغاربة **mághribii, magháaribah** Moroccan

تأهل **ta'áhhala [S-V]** to qualify (إلى **ilaa** for)

فريق، فرق **fariiq, firaq** team

نهائي **niháa'ii** final (adj.)

مسابقة، ـات **musáabaqah, -áat** competition

كأس، كؤوس **ka's, ku'úus** cup, trophy

الزمالك **az-zamáalik** Zamalek (an area of Cairo)

ألف، آلاف **alf, áalaaf** thousand

متفرج، ـون **mutafárrij, -úun** spectator

قاد **qáada [Mw-I]** to lead

فوز **fawz** victory

سجل **sájjala [S-II]** to score, to register

وحده **wáHduh** himself

هدف، أهداف **hádaf, ahdáaf** goal, target, aim

مباراة، مباريات **mubáaraah, mubaarayáat** match (sport)

انتهى **intáhaa [Ly-VIII]** to come to an end, finish

افتتح **iftátaHa [S-VIII]** to commence, open

تسجيل **tasjiil** registration, scoring

عن طريق **:an Tariiq** by way of

لاعب، ـون **láa:ib, -úun** player

لاعب وسط **lúa:ib wasT** midfield player (football)

تسديدة، ـات **tasdíidah, -áat** shot (football)

رائع **ráa'i:** splendid, brilliant, marvellous

خارج **kháarij** outside

منطقة، مناطق **mínTaqah, manáaTiq*** area (football: penalty area)

خدع **kháda:a [S-I a]** to deceive

حارس، حراس **Háaris, Hurráas** guard (football: *goalkeeper*)

تاسع **táasi:** *ninth*

نتيجة، نتائج **natíijah, natáa'ij*** result, outcome

فرصة، فرص **fúrSah, fúraS** chance, opportunity

وحيد **waHíid** sole, only, singular

شوط، أشواط **shawT, ashwáaT** half (football), *heat* (athletics, etc.), *race*

عندما **:índamaa** when

سدد **sáddada [S-II]** to aim (football: *shoot*)

قوسي **qáwsii** curved, bowed

دخل **dákhala [S-I u]** to enter

ركن، أركان **rukn, arkáan** corner

مرمى **mármaa** goal, goalmouth

أدرك **ádraka [S-IV]** to attain, achieve

تعادل **ta:áadul** balance, equality (football: *draw, equal score*)

بدا **bádaa [Lw-I]** to appear, seem, show

راية، ـات **ráayah, -áat** flag, banner

أبيض، بيضاء **ábyaD***, fem. **bayDáa'*** white

الثاني **ath-tháani** the second

سيطر على **sáyTara :álaa [Q-I]** to dominate

لعب **la:b** play, game

سيطرة **sáyTarah** domination

تام **taamm** complete

سرعة **súr:ah** speed

اخير **akhíir** last

أودع **áwda:a [Fw-IV]** to place

شبكة، شباك **shábaka, shibáak** net, netting

مرة، ـات **márrah, -áat** time, occasion

بعد ما **ba:d maa** after (before a verb)

احتسب **iHtásaba [S-VIII]** to award, grant

حكم، حكّام **Hákam, Hukkáam** *referee, umpire*

ركلة، ـات **ráklah, -áat** *kick*

ركني **rúknii** *corner* (adj.)

طرد **Tárada [S-I u]** *to banish, drive away* (football: *send off*)

مدافع، ـون **mudáafi: , -úun** *defender*

نيل **nayl** *getting, receiving*

بطاقة، ـات **buTáaqah, -áat** *card*

أصفر، صفراء **áSfar*, fem. Safráa'*** *yellow*

---

al-mulaaHaDHáat (Notes) الملاحظات

■ **sawdaa'** *black*, fem. For this and other basic colour adjectives, see grammar notes below.

■ **sajjala** *scored*. This and other words take on special meanings in football contexts. Its usual meaning is *to register, record*.

■ **ahdaaf**, pl. of **hadaf** *goals scored*. The word for the physical **goal** (*posts* and *net*) is **marmaa** which occurs later in the text.

■ **sayTara ... sayTarah taammah** *dominated ... completely*. See section on adverbs below.

■ **akhiir** and **aakhir** both mean *last*, but they are used differently:
  – **akhiir** is a normal adjective coming after the noun:
  الفصل الأخير **al-fasl al-akhiir** *the last section*.
  – **aakhir** is a noun meaning *the last part of something* and is usually used as the first term of a possessive construction:
  آخرها **aakhir-haa** *the last of them*, i.e. *the goals*.

■ **awda: ... al-kurah ash-shubbaak** *placed the ball in the net*. Arabic does not use the preposition *in* with this verb.

■ **ba:d maa** *after*. When **ba:d**, **qabl** *before* and certain other words relating to time are followed by a verb, it is necessary to interpose this (meaningless) **maa**.

■ **li-nayl-uh** *getting, obtaining*. **nayl** here is a verbal noun, and the phrase can be paraphrased *because of his getting, for getting*. This type of construction is quite common in Arabic.

تعبيرات رئيسية ta:biiráat ra'iisíyyah (Key phrases)

السيارة الحمراء as-sayyaarah l-Hamraa'	*the red car*
قميص أزرق qamiiS azraq	*a blue shirt*
زهرة صفراء zahrah Safraa'	*a yellow flower*
الجبل الأخضر al-jabal al-akhDar	*the green mountain*

تراكيب اللغة taraakíib al-lúghah (Structures)

1 Irregular adjectives

As you learned in Unit 3, most Arabic adjectives form their feminine by adding ة -ah to the masculine form.

There is an important set of adjectives which behave differently. The most common of these refer to the basic colours, and some physical disabilities.

These adjectives have three forms:
a) masculine singular
b) feminine singular
c) plural for human beings

a) Masculine Singular
Identical in all respects to the comparative adjective (see Unit 15), and following the same rules regarding doubled and weak radicals.

Does not take the **alif** accusative marker.

b) Feminine Singular.
The first radical takes an **a**-vowel, the second no vowel, and the suffix **-aa'** ـاء is added after the third radical.

Again this does not take the accusative marker.

c) Plural Form
Used only when referring to several human beings. The first radical takes **u-**, and the second no vowel.

This form does take the accusative marker when required.

English	Masculine	Feminine	Plural
black	أسود **aswad**	سوداء **sawdaa'**	سود **suud**
white	أبيض **abyaD**	بيضاء **bayDaa'**	بيض **biiD**[2]
red	أحمر **aHmar**	حمراء **Hamraa'**	حمر **Humr**
green	أخضر **akhDar**	خضراء **khaDraa'**	خضر **khuDr**
yellow	أصفر **aSfar**	صفراء **Safraa'**	صفر **Sufr**
blue	أزرق **azraq**	زرقاء **zarqaa'**	زرق **zurq**
lame	أعرج **a:raj**	عرجاء **:arjaa'**	عرج **:urj**
blind	أعمى **a:maa**[1]	عمياء **:amyaa'**	عميان **:umyaan**[3]

---

1 root ends with ى. (See rules for comparatives in Unit 15)

2 Arabic will not accept the combination **uy** so the vowel changes to **ii**.

3 An alternative form, usually used with this adjective

2 Other colours

The above rules apply only to what Arabic regards as the basic colours. Other colours are formed from nouns with the adjectival ending ـي **-ii** (see Unit 12) and behave normally:

Noun	*Adjective*
برتقال **burtuqaal** *orange*	برتقالي *orange*
بن **bunn** *coffee beans*	بني *brown*
بنفسج **banafsaj** *violet*	بنفسجي *violet*
ورد **ward** *roses*	وردي *pink*

Examples from the text are:

ليلة سوداء *a black night*

الراية البيضاء *the white flag*

البطاقة الصفراء *the yellow card*

طارق الأحمر *Taariq al-aHmar* (here used as a proper name)

3 Adverbs

Adverbs describe how, when or where the action of a verb is performed. In both English and Arabic, there are two ways to form them:

Accusative marker

In English by adding the suffix -ly to the adjective: *She sings beautifully*. The Arabic equivalent of this is to add the accusative marker to an adjective, or sometimes a noun. This is written with an **alif** unless the word has the feminine ending, and is always pronounced **-an**. Such common words as *very, always, never* are also formed in this way.

So we have شخصيا **shakhSiyyan** *personally*, from **shakhSii** *personal*, which is itself derived from **shakhS** *person*.

Here are some other common examples:

a) From adjectives:	b) From nouns:
كثيرا **kathiiran** *frequently, a lot, often*	عادة: **:aadatan** *usually*
نادرا **naadiran** *rarely*	فجأة **faj'atan** *suddenly*
قريبا **qariiban** *promptly, soon*	صدفة **Sudfatan** *by chance, fortuitously*
سريعا **sarii:an** *quickly*	جدا **jiddan** *very*
يوميا **yawmiyyan** *daily*	أبدا **abadan** *never*
شهريا **shahriyyan** *monthly*	أحيانا **aHyaanan** *sometimes*
أولا **awwalan** *firstly*	فورا **fawran** *immediately*
(also the other ordinal numerals:)	مباشرة **mubaasharatan** *directly*
ثانيا **thaaniyan** *secondly*	طبعا **Tab:an** *naturally, of course*
ثالثا **thaalithan** *third*, etc.	حقا **Haqqan** *really, truly, in fact*
أخيرا **akhiiran** *lastly, at last*	
دائما **daa'iman** *always*	
رسميا **rasmiyyan** *officially*	

Prepositional

The second way to form adverbs in English is to use a preposition (usually *with*, *in* or *by*) plus a noun: *I am writing this in haste*.

The same applies to Arabic, the usual preposition being **bi-**: بالضبط **bi-DH-DHabT** *with exactness, exactly*

In Arabic, as in English, both methods can be used, often with a slight change in meaning – *hastily/in haste*. سريعا **sarii:an** *quickly* can also be expressed as بسرعة **bi-sur:ah** *with speed*.

Common examples of this type are:

ببطء **bi-buT'** *slowly*

بجد **bi-jadd** *seriously*

بوضوح **bi-wuDuuH** *clearly*

Verbal nouns

A common adverbial construction in Arabic is *verb* + *its verbal noun* (accusative) + *an adjective* (also accusative) qualifying the verbal noun. This will be familiar to readers of the King James Bible where phrases like *They rejoiced a great rejoicing* are quite frequent in the Old Testament (presumably because it was translated from Hebrew, a sister Semitic language to Arabic). This has exactly the same meaning as *They rejoiced greatly*.

There is one example in the text:

سيطر التونسيون على اللعب سيطرة تامة

The Tunisians dominated the play completely (lit. a complete domination)

أوزان الكلمات awzáan al-kalimáat (Word shapes)

Pattern	Arabic example	Eng. sound-alike
CaCCaCah	**barbarah** بربرة barbarism	*Barbara*

This is the verbal noun shape from QI-verbs (see Verb Tables). In the football text we have:

سيطرة **sayTarah** *domination*

Here are a few more:

ترجم Q-I ➜ ترجمة **tarjamah** *translating, translation*

فلسف Q-I ➜ فلسفة **falsafah** *philosophising, philosophy*

زلزل Q-I ➜ زلزلة **zalzalah** *quaking, earthquake*
(also sometimes زلزال *zilzaal*)

تلفز Q-I ➜ تلفزة **talfazah** *televising, television*

تمرينات **tamriináat (Practice)**

Exercise 3
See if you can work out which of these sports corresponds to the pictures on page 292:

٧ التزلج على الثلج	١ ايروبيك
٨ بولينغ	٢ تنس الطاولة
٩ الغوص بالسكوبا	٣ كرة اليد
١٠ صيد السمك	٤ كرة القدم
١١ التزلج على الماء	٥ جولف
١٢ الزوارق الشراعية	٦ باليه

ثلج **thalj** *ice*
زورق، زوارق **záwraq, zawáariq*** *boat*

معلومات ثقافية ma:luumáat thaqaafíyyah (Cultural tips)

Some of the sports mentioned in the exercise are transliterations into Arabic of English terms. If these contain the letter *g*, which Arabic does not have, various spellings arise. جولف *golf* is written with a ج. Most Egyptians pronounce ج as a hard *g*, and this spelling is fairly general. However, in بولينغ *bowling* we have a spelling with the nearest Arabic sound غ **gh**.

There are unfortunately no hard and fast rules. It seems to be down to the whim of the writer/typesetter. In fact you often even see the same word spelled in two different ways (ج and غ) in the same document. More rarely, ق is used, as this is pronounced hard *g* in the spoken dialects of many Arab countries, including nearly the whole of the Arabian Peninsula.

The other (main) letters which Arabic lacks, *p* and *v* are usually transcribed as ب **b** and ف **f** respectively. Occasionally you will see the adopted Persian letters پ **p** and ڤ **v** with three dots, but this is not very common.

Foreign words in Arabic often have a liberal sprinkling of long vowels, as their word shapes do not conform to the usual guidelines.

Exercise 4

Read the prospectus for this Women's Club, and answer the questions.

نادي الفتيات

العضوية في النادي مفتوحة لكافة الجنسيت للسيدات والأطفال.
(البنات من جميع الأعمار أما الأولاد الذكور حتى ١٠ سنوات فقط)

عضوية نادي الفتيات:

عضوية فردية	....	٢٧٠٠ درهم سنويا
عضوية عائلية (الأم + ٣ أبناء)	....	٣٧٠٠ درهم سنويا
عضوية المكتبة	....	٢٦٠ درهم شهريا

عضوية يومية للزوار

الكبار (أكثر من ١٣ سنة)	....	٥٠ درهم
الصغار (حتى ١٢ سنة)	....	٢٠ درهم

تسهيلات النادي:

● منتجع الصحة	● حجرة الألعاب الرياضية *
● قاعة التزلج *	● سونا
● كافتريا *	● الأيروبيك *
● مركز الفن	● المسبح*
● ملاعب التنس	● المكتبة *

* الاستخدام للعضوات مجانا

النادي مفتوح طوال اليوم من الساعة ٩ صباحا حتى الساعة ١٠ مساء.

a How much does annual membership cost?
b Up to how many children may accompany a mother free?
c Until what age are boys allowed to accompany their mothers?
d The club is open from:
   i 9am ii 10am
e The club closes at:
   i 9pm ii 10pm
f How much does monthly membership of the Library cost?
g Name three facilities which are free for members.

 Exercise 5

Five people are talking about how often they take part in sporting activities. Listen to the recording and write down in the columns below who likes to do what and how often. We've done the first one for you.

سؤال: ماذا تحب من الرياضات؟

جواب: ألعب كرة القدم كثيرا

أبدا	نادرا	أحيانا	كثيرا	يوميا
١			football	
٢				
٣				
٤				
٥				

مارس **máarasa [S-III]** *to practise, carry out, perform*

Exercise 6

Select an appropriate adverb from the box to fill in the gaps in the sentences. You may only use each adverb once.

١ افتح الباب .... عندنا ضيف.

٢ ذهبت إلى السوق وقابلت أحمد هناك........... .

٣ كان ذلك البرنامج مهما ....

٤ كنا جالسين في البيت، وقام زيد .... وخرج.

٥ تسافر هذه الطائرة إلى الرياض............ .

٦ يا أولاد، العبوا .... ، الوالد نائم.

جدا	مباشرة	بهدوء	بسرعة	فجأة	صدفة

نائم **náa'im** *sleeping, asleep*

Exercise 7

You are shopping for clothes with some Arabic-speaking friends.
How would you say what they are looking for? Make up complete
sentences like this one:

Yunis – blue coat   يحتاج يونس إلى معطف أزرق.

جوارب

حزام

معطف   قميص

فستان

جزمة   حقيبة

بنطلون

a Ali – black shoes   **e** Faridah – red trousers

b Sonia – yellow dress   **f** Hamed – brown belt

c Saeed – green shirt   **g** Anisa – pink handbag

d Khalid – white socks

17 | إن شاء الله
in shaa' Al-laah
If God wills

In this unit you will learn to:
- talk about what you hope to do
- make suggestions

🎧 1 إن شاء الله in shaa' Al-laah *If God wills*

Listen to the recording of a radio news item about the Arabic language.

Exercise 1
Answer the following questions:
a What has the Egyptian company produced?
b What does Professor Ibrahim specialise in?
c Who are the cassettes intended for?

Listen to the recording again.
d What was the Arabic Language Academy discussing in 1925?
e What do they hope to achieve by producing the tapes?
f Who do they particularly hope will like them?

المذيعة   هنا صوت العرب من القاهرة. أنتجت شركة مصرية ثلاثة
أشرطة تعليمية لتبسيط قواعد النحو في اللغة العربية. وقد
أسهم في إعداد الأشرطة الأستاذ إبراهيم محمود من كلية
الآداب في جامعة القاهرة والمتخصص في تدريس اللغة
العربية. مرحبا يا أستاذ إبراهيم.

الأستاذ   شكرا.

المذيعة   أولا هل هذه الأشرطة للعرب ام الاجانب؟

الأستاذ   للعرب.

المذيعة   لكن العرب يعرفون اللغة العربية. أليس كذلك؟

الأستاذ   طبعا يعرفونها، ولكنه هناك في اللغة العربية الفصحى صعوبات لا يفهمها إلا المثقفين. وحتى في عام ١٩٢٥ كان مجمع اللغة العربية يناقش بعض هذه الصعوبات و أصدر قراراته العلمية.

المذيعة   وقصدكم إذا في انتاج هذه الأشرطة ان تساعدوا العامة في العالم العربي على الكتابة الصحيحة والاسلوب الجيد؟

الأستاذ   بالضبط، وبطريقة حديثة نتمنى أن تجلب اهتمام الشباب إن شاء الله.

المذيعة   إن شاء الله. شكرا لك يا استاذ ابراهيم.

الأستاذ   عفوا.

Exercise 2

Match the English with the appropriate Arabic phrases.

a an Egyptian company produced three educational cassettes

b participated in preparing the cassettes

c Are these cassettes for Arabs?

d don't they?

e we hope that it will attract the interest (of)

f if God wills

g thank you, Professor Ibrahim

h you're welcome

١ أليس كذلك؟

٢ عفوا

٣ نتمنى أن تجلب اهتمام

٤ إن شاء الله

٥ أنتجت شركة مصرية ثلاثة أشرطة تعليمية

٦ شكرا لك يا أستاذ إبراهيم

٧ هل هذه الأشرطة للعرب؟

٨ أسهم في إعداد الأشرطة

مذيعة، ـات mudhíi:ah, -áat (female) *broadcaster*

صوت، أصوات Sawt, aSwáat *voice, sound*

أنتج ántaja [S-IV] *to produce*

شريط، أشرطة shariiT, ashríTah *tape, cassette*

تبسيط tabsiiT *simplification*

قاعدة، قواعد* qáa:idah, qawáa:id* *rule*

النحو an-naHw *grammar*

أسهم ás-hama [S-IV] *contribute, take part*

اعداد i:dáad *preparation*

أستاذ، أساتذة ustáadh, asáatidhah *professor*

أدب، آداب ádab, aadáab *literature, arts*

متخصص، ـون mutakháSSiS, -uun *specialist*

تدريس tadríis *teaching*

أجنبي، أجانب ajnábii, ajáanib *foreign, foreigner*

عرف: árafa [S-I i] *to know*

أليس كذلك؟ a-láysa ka-dháalik *is it not (so)?*

الفصحى al-fúS-Haa *literary, classical (adj. used only with the Arabic language)*

صعوبة، ـات Su:úubah, -áat *difficulty*

فهم fáhima [S-I a] *to understand*

إلا illaa *except*

مثقف، ـون mutháqqaf, -úun *cultured, educated person*

مجمع اللغة العربية májma: al-lúghah al-:árabiyyah *the Arabic Language Academy*

ناقش náaqasha [S-III] *to discuss*

أصدر áSdara [S-IV] *to publish*

قصد qaSd *aim, goal, intent*

إذا ídhan *so, therefore*

ساعد sáa:ada [S-III] *to help*

العامة al-:áammah *the general public*

العالم **al-:áalam** *the world*

كتابة **kitáabah** *writing*

صحيح **SaHíiH** *correct, true*

تمنى **tamánnaa [Ly-V]** *to hope, wish*

شاب، شباب **shaabb, shabáab** *young person, youth*

إن **in** *if*

شاء **sháa'a [Ma-I]** *to wish, will*

الله **Al-láah** *God, Allah*

عفوا: **áfwan** *don't mention it* (reply to thanks)

معلومات ثقافية **ma:luumáat thaqaafíyyah** (Cultural tips)

Literary Arabic is rarely spoken outside the media, and everyday communication is carried out in the many varieties of colloquial Arabic. Although these are all basically Arabic, they differ widely from area to area. As a consequence, Arabs have to learn the grammatical rules of the literary language, called **al-:arabiyyah al-fuS-Haa**, or simply **al-fuS-Haa**, meaning literally *the most eloquent Arabic*, at school.

Many of the rules, and much of the vocabulary, are different from those of spoken Arabic, so the acquisition of good **fuS-Haa** Arabic is not a simple matter. In addition, education and even literacy are still by no means universal in many Arab countries. Hence the need for the cassette programmes discussed in the radio programme.

Arabic also has problems coining words for new inventions, which tend to originate in the West. English and other Western languages usually borrow or concoct a word based on Latin and/or Greek. For instance *television* is half Greek- and half Latin-based. While many foreign words – such as **tilifizyuun** – have become established in Modern Literary Arabic, there is the feeling among the establishment that this is diluting the Arabic language. Arabic is the language of the Koran, goes the argument, so should be able to express anything.

The Arab Language Academies were therefore founded early in the 20th century, and took upon themselves the task of preserving linguistic purity. One of the main processes, known as **ta:riib** *Arabisation*, means extending the meaning of an existing Arabic root, or creating new forms from it. Some of these have been a total success, others partially successful, and others a virtually total failure. For example:

طائرة **Taa'irah** *aeroplane*, from the verb to fly, [lit. flying thing].

هاتف **haatif** *telephone*, has achieved partial success and co-exists with the competing import تلفون **tilifuun**.

تلفزيون **tilifizyuun** has resisted all efforts to replace it with a word of pure Arabic origin, as have many other European words relating to modern technological achievements.

---

al-mulaaHaDHáat (Notes) الملاحظات

■ صوت العرب *The Voice of the Arabs* is a radio service broadcasting from Cairo

■ أليس كذلك Lit. *Is it not like that?* For **laysa** see Unit 8.

■ ولكن **walaakinna**. The suffix here is a connecting word and is not translated.

■ الفصحى See cultural notes above.

■ كان ... يناقش When the past of **kaana** is followed by a present verb (here **yunaaqish**) the meaning is past continuous, translated *was/were doing something*. The subject usually comes between the two verbs. (see Unit 10)

■ بعض **ba:D** *some* is actually a noun meaning a part (of something). It always occurs as the first part of a possessive construction, followed by a noun or a pronoun suffix.

■ أن تساعدوا **an tusaa:iduu. an** is followed by a subjunctive, here marked by the dropping of the final **nuun**. See Verb Tables.

■ إن **in** *if*. See below.

■ عفوا **:afwan**. In English, thanks can be acknowledged in various ways, such as *Don't mention it*. In all levels of Arabic, it is virtually obligatory to use **:afwan**.

المشروع ناجح al-mashruu: naajiH 2

The project is successful

A few months later there is further news of the project, which looks like being a success.

Exercise 3

Listen to or read the article below, and answer the questions.

a In which country did the company start to market the tapes?
b Who gave them a good reception?
c How many of the tapes were sold?

Listen to the recording again.

d Where do they hope to sell the tapes next?
e What is the special feature of these tapes?
f Who produced a similar programme ten years ago?

وبدأت الشركة توزيع الأشرطة في الأسواق المصرية مع بداية العام
الجاري ٢٠٠٠، ولاقت استقبالا حسنا من التلامذة والمدرسين في
شتى مراحل التعليم الابتدائي والإعدادي والثانوي، وقد بيعت خلال
الشهرين الماضيين نصف الكمية المستهدفة. وتنوي الشركة في
الفترة القريبة المقبلة النزول إلى الأسواق العربية بهذه الأشرطة، سواء
في معارض الكتب أو المكتبات المختلفة. وتقول مصادر الشركة أن
هذه هي المرة الأولى التي تبسط فيها قواعد اللغة العربية بهذا الشكل
في العالم العربي، وإن كان التلفزيون العراقي قد أنتج قبل أكثر من
١٠ سنوات برنامجا لنفس الغرض.

Exercise 4

Match the English phrases to the equivalent Arabic expressions.

a At the beginning of the current year 2000
b from pupils and teachers in various stages of education
c half of the projected quantity was sold in the past two months
d either at book exhibitions or in various bookshops
e the rules of the Arabic language are simplified
f Iraqi television had produced a programme
g more than ten years ago

١ قد بيعت خلال الشهرين الماضيين نصف الكمية المستهدفة

٢ تبسط قواعد اللغة العربية

٣ قبل أكثر من ١٠ سنوات

٤ كان التلفزيون العراقي قد أنتج برنامجا

٥ مع بداية العام الجاري ٢٠٠٠

٦ سواء في معارض الكتب أو المكتبات المختلفة

٧ من التلامذة والمدرسين في شتى مراحل التعليم

توزيع **tawzíi:** distribution

بداية **bidáayah** beginning

الجاري **al-jáarii** the current

لاقى **láaqaa [Ly-III]** to meet with

استقبال، ــات **istiqbáal, -áat** reception

حسن **Hásan** good, beautiful, handsome

تلميذ، تلامذة\تلاميذ **tilmíidh, taláamidhah/talaamiidh** pupil

مدرس، ــون **mudárris, -úun** teacher

شتى **sháttaa** various

مرحلة، مراحل **márHalah, maráaHil*** stage, level

تعليم **ta:líim** education

ابتدائي **ibtidáa'ii** elementary

اعدادي **i:dáadii** preparatory

ثانوي **tháanawii** secondary

خلال **khaláal** during

الماضي **al-máaDii** the past

نصف، أنصاف **niSf, anSáaf** half

مستهدف **mustáhdaf** aimed for

نوى **náwaa [Ly-I]** to intend

فترة، ــات **fátrah, -áat** period, time, spell

مقبل **múqbil** coming, next

نزول **nuzúul** descent, descending

سواء **sawáa'an** equally, whether

معرض، معارض **má:raD, ma:áariD*** *exhibition, fair*

كتاب، كتب **kitáab, kútub** *book*

مكتبة، ـات **máktabah, -áat** *library, book shop*

مختلف **mukhtálif** *different, various*

قال **qáala [Mw-I]** *to say*

مصدر، مصادر **máSdar, maSáadir*** *source*

بسط **bássaTa [S-II]** *to simplify*

وإن **wa-'in** *though, even though*

غرض، أغراض **gháraD, aghráaD** *purpose, goal, end*

---

al-mulaaHaDHáat (Notes) الملاحظات

- الجاري **al-jaari**. Adjectives of this shape derive from a root ending in one of the weak letters ي or و, which is omitted in the indefinite, which would here be جارٍ **jaarin**, the final syllable consisting of a vowel mark, usually omitted. This is a source of confusion even to Arabs and, since the words are usually pronounced with a final **-ii**, they have been given in the definite.

- شتى **shattaa** *various* behaves in a similar way as **ba:D** above.

- بيعت **bii:at** *was sold*. This is a passive verb. See Verb Table My-I.

- الشهرين الماضيين **ash-shahrayn al-maaDiyayn** *the past two months*. This is a dual (see Unit 9). **al-maaDii** is the same sort of adjective as **al-jaarii** above.

- إن هذه... **inna haadhihi...** *that this...* Uniquely after the verb **qaal** *to say*, *that* is expressed by **inna** instead of the expected **anna**.

- تبسط **tubassaT** *is simplified*. A passive verb (Table S-II).

- وإن **wa-'in** *even though*. **wa** *and* + **in** (see below).

- كان ... قد أنتج **kaana ... qad antaja** ... *had produced*. **kaan** + another perfect verb translates the English pluperfect tense. As with the past continuous (see above) the subject comes between the two verbs, the second of which is frequently preceded with the past marker **qad** (see Unit 8).

- نفس الغرض **nafs al-gharaD** *the same purpose*. When **nafs** is followed by a definite noun, it translates as *the same ...*

تعبيرات رئيسية ta:biiráat ra'iisíyyah (Key phrases)

Saying what you will do if something happens

إن شاء الله in shaa' Al-laah   *God willing*

إن جئت بيتي، أكرمتك   *If you come to my house,*
in ji'ta bayt-ii, akramta-ka   *I'll treat you generously*

Saying what you would do if things were different

لو كنت غنيا لاشتريت مجوهرات كثيرة لزوجتي
law kunt ghaniyan la-ishtarayt mujawharaat kathiirah li-zawjatii
If I were rich, I'd buy lots of jewellery for my wife

> أكرم **ákrama [S-IV]** *honour, be hospitable/generous to*
> اشترى **ishtáraa [Ly-VIII]** *buy*
> مجوهرات **mujawharáat** *articles of jewellery*

تراكيب اللغة taraakíib al-lúghah (Structures)

1 *If* sentences

Such sentences are technically known as *conditionals* because the second half of the sentence depends on the fulfillment of a condition imposed by the first part. *If you go, then I'll go too*, i.e. I will only go on the condition that you go too.

The word *then* in such sentences is often optional, but in relation to Arabic it is useful to include it and to name the two parts of the sentences the *if*-part and the *then*-part.

The verbs in both parts of the conditional sentence are usually in the past tense – even if the reference is clearly to the future. In the phrase **in shaa' Al-laah**, uttered by Muslims whenever any reference is made to a future event, the verb **shaa'(a)** is past tense.

There are three words for *if*: لو **law**, إن **in** and إذا **idhaa**.

law

law is used in Arabic *if*-sentences where it is thought impossible or unlikely that the condition will be fulfilled – impossible including the category of past events which have already rendered the condition unfulfillable.

All **law** sentences require the word **la-** *then* to introduce the second part.

لو كنت أنا المدير لوظفتك

If I were the manager, I would employ you

(Impossible because I am not the manager and unlikely to become the manager)

وظف **wáDHDHaf [S-II]** *to hire, employ*

لو كان صديقي سمع الأخبار لخبرني

If my friend had heard the news, he would have told me

(He obviously didn't hear it. The use of **kaana** with the perfect of the main verb is common to place the action firmly in the past.)

خبر، أخبار **khábar, akhbáar** *item of news* (plural *news*)

سمع **sámi:a [S-I a]** *to hear*

خبر **khábbara [S-II]** *to tell, inform*

لو لم يكتب لي تلك الرسالة لما ذهبت إلى بيته

If he had not written me that letter, I would not have gone to his house

In negative conditions with **law** it is common to use **lam** with the jussive in the first part, and **maa** with the past in the second (see negatives, Unit 10).

idhaa/in

These two words are nowadays more or less interchangeable, and are used when fulfillment of the condition is regarded as possible or likely. Again the verbs are mostly in the past.

إن سألته أجابك   *If you ask him, he will answer you*

> سأل **sá'ala [S-I a]** *to ask*
> أجاب **ajáaba [Mw-IV]** *to answer*

إن رأيناها خبرناها   *If we see her, we shall tell her*

> رأى، يرى **rá'aa, yáraa** *to see* (irregular verb: see tables)

إذا سافرت أختي سافرت الوالدة معها

If my sister travels, mother will travel with her

> أخت، اخوات **ukht, akhawáat** *sister*
> سافر **sáafara [S-III]** *to travel*

إذا جعت أكلت شيئا   *If I get hungry, I'll eat something*

> جاع **jáa:a [Mw-I]** *to become hungry*

The *then*-part can be introduced by ف **fa-** *so*. This is obligatory in another type of conditional sentence, where the *then*-part is either:

a) an imperative verb:

إذا أردت العلم فاقرأ   *If you want knowledge, read!*

أراد **aráada [Mw-IV]** *want, wish for*
علم، علوم **:ilm, :ulúum** *knowledge, science*

or (b) an *is/are* sentence (without a verb):

إذا فعلوا ذلك، فالنجاح أكيد *If they do that, then success is certain*

فعل **fá:ala [S-I a]** *to do, make*
نجاح **najáaH** *success*

أوزان الكلمات awzáan al-kalimáat (Word shapes)

Pattern	Arabic example	Eng. sound-alike
iCCaaC	إنكار **inkaar** *denial*	*in car*

This is the verbal noun of S-IV and D-IV verbs. There is only one example in the texts in this unit:

اعداد **i:daad** *preparation*

However, there are several other Form IV verbs.

Exercise 5
See if you can generate the verbal noun form from the following. Answers in the Key or on the recording:

a أنتج **antaja** *to produce*

b أصدر **aSdara** *to publish*

c أكرم **akrama** *to treat hospitably*

d أسلم **aslama** *to accept the Islamic religion*

e أرسل **arsala** *to send*

f أجبر **ajbara** *to compel, force*

g أقبل **aqbala** *to approach*

h ألهم **alhama** *to inspire*

i أغلق **aghlaqa** *to close, lock*

j أفسد **afsada** *to spoil*

معلومات ثقافية ma:luumáat thaqaafíyyah (Cultural tips)

Arab food is wholesome and delicious. It is excellent food to eat in company, because such a variety of foods is put on the table that there is something for everyone to enjoy.

As appetisers (مزة **mazzah**), a selection of salads (سلطات **salaaTaat**) and dips, stuffed vine leaves (ورق عنب **waraq :inab**), savoury pastries such as سمبوسك **sambuusak**, fried meat and cracked wheat rissoles (كبة **kibbah**) or grilled meatballs (كفتة **kuftah**) is placed on the table to be eaten with flat Arab bread (خبز **khubz**).

The most popular dips are حمص بالطحينة **HummuS bi-T-TaHiina** (chick peas with sesame paste, garlic and lemon), متبل **mutabbal** (aubergine puree with sesame paste), and لبنة **labnah** (strained yoghurt) with olives. تبولة **tabbuulah** (cracked wheat salad with chopped parsley, tomato and lemon juice) and فتوش **fattuush** (a Lebanese mixed salad with sumac and toasted Arab bread sprinkled on top) are favourite salads, as well as خضريات **khuDriyyaat**, from أخضر **akhDar** *green*, meaning a simple dish of raw vegetables.

The next course may be something grilled (مشوي **mashwii**), either lamb kebabs, chicken (دجاج **dajaaj**) or fish (سمك **samak**), with rice (أرز **aruzz**)or potatoes (بطاطس **baTaaTas**).

Desserts (حلويات **Halawiyyaat**) might be an assortment of Lebanese pastries (بقلاوة **baqlaawah**), filled with nuts and soaked in syrup, which most people buy only from specialist shops, or sometimes a milky pudding, such as مهلبية **muhallabiyyah** or أم علي **umm :alii**, is offered.

تمرينات tamriináat (Practice)

Exercise 6

Mohammed and Fatimah are reading the menu of a Lebanese restaurant, but they only have Dhs 100. They are trying to decide what they can afford to order. Look at the menu and their projections of what they would have to pay if they ordered various dishes.

Kasbah Restaurant

مطعم القصبة

Starters			المقبلات
Labneh	8	٨	لبنة
Hummus	8	٨	حمص
Moutabbal	8	٨	متبل
Waraq Enab	12	١٢	ورق عنب
Sambousek	12	١٢	سنبوسك
Kibbeh	15	١٥	كبة
Salads			السلطات
Tabbouleh	12	١٢	تبولة
Fattoush	10	١٠	فتوش
Salad of the Season	8	٨	سلطة الموسم
Grills*			المشاوي
Fish	20	٢٠	الأسماك
Chicken	15	١٥	الدجاج
Meat Kebabs	20	٢٠	كباب لحم
Halloumi Cheese	18	١٨	حلوم مشوي
* With rice or potatoes			مع الأرز والبطاطا
Sweets			الحلويات
Baklava	12	١٢	بقلاوة
Mouhalabiyyeh	8	٨	مهلبية
Ice Cream	6	٦	أيس كريم
Creme Caramel	8	٨	كريم كراميل
Drinks			المشروبات
Coffee	4	٤	القهوة
Tea	4	٤	الشاي
Orange juice	8	٨	عصير برتقال
Mineral water	4	٤	المياه المعدنية

a Link the suggestions on page 310 to the appropriate prices they would pay. **b** Do they have enough money to pay?

إن طلب محمد الحمص والفتوش ١ a دفعت ٢٤ درهما
إذا طلبت فاطمة ورق عنب وتبولة ٢ b دفع ٨ دراهم
إذا طلبت فاطمة الدجاج المشوي ٣ c دفعت ١٦ يرهما
مع الأرز d دفعا أكثر من ١٠٠ درهم
إن طلب محمد سمكا مع البطاطس ٤ e دفعت ١٥ درهما
إذا طلب محمد المهلبية ٥ f دفع ١٨ درهما
إن طلبت فاطمة بقلاوة وقهوة ٦ g دفع ٢٠ درهما
إذا طلبا الأطباق كلها ٧

Exercise 7

Translate these conditional sentences into Arabic.

a If I were rich, I would buy a new car.

b If she had learned to type, she would earn a higher salary.

c If I had had the number, I would have telephoned him.

d If you (fem. sing.) had been more diligent in your studies, you would have passed the exams.

e If they (masc.) had visited their mother yesterday, she would have told them about her illness.

f If the officer hadn't stopped the thieves in the customs, they would have got on the plane.

طباعة **Tibáa:ah** *typing*

كسب **kásaba [S-I i]** *earn, gain, win*

دراسة، ـات **diráasah, -aat** *study*

نجح **nájaHa [S-I a]** *succeed in* في *something; pass (an exam)*

امتحان، ـات **imtiHáan, -áat** *exam*

مرض، أمراض **máraD, amráaD** *illness, disease*

وقف **wáqqafa [Fw-II]** *stop, bring to a halt*

لص، لصوص **liSS, luSúuS** *thief*

ضابط، ضباط **DáabiT, DubbáaT** *officer*

جمرك، جمارك **júmruk, jamáarik** *customs, excise*

ركب **rákiba [S-I a]** *ride, mount, get into* (a vehicle)

18 | من كل بلد خبر
min kull balad khabar
News from every country

In this unit you will learn:
- to talk about *each, every, all* and *some*
- to use some irregular nouns and adjectives

1 مصر miSr *Egypt*

Exercise 1
Read the passage and answer the questions.
a Who made a statement welcoming the UN resolution?
b What has been smuggled abroad?
c Which famous Egyptian pieces are in the British Museum?

مصر

الآثار المصرية في الخارج

اعرب رئيس دائرة الآثار المصرية أمس عن ترحيبه بقرار الجمعية
العمومية للأمم المتحدة بالسماح للدول التي لها آثار مهربة في
الخارج باستردادها. وقال إنه هناك حوالي ١٢ مليون قطعة أثرية
مصرية مسروقة في الغرب أشهرها ذقن أبو الهول وحجر رشيد
الموجودان في المتحف البريطاني في لندن.

Exercise 2
Now find the Arabic for the following expressions:
a the head of the department of Egyptian antiquities
b approximately 12 million
c the beard of the Sphynx
d the Rosetta Stone

أثر، آثار **áthar, aatháar** sing. *track, trace*, pl. also
   archaeological remains, antiquities

الخارج **al-kháarij** *abroad, the outside*

أعرب عن **á:raba :an [S-IV]** *to state, express*

ترحيب **tarHiib** *welcome, welcoming* (noun)

قرار، ـات **qaráar, -áat** *decision, resolution*

جمعية، ـات **jam:íyyah, -áat** *group, assembly, society*

عمومي **:umúumii** *general*

أمة، أمم **úmmah, úmam** *nation*

متحد **muttáHad** *united*

سماح **samáaH** *permission*

مهرب **muhárrab** *smuggled*

استرداد **istirdáad** *getting back, reclaiming*

قطعة، قطع **qíT:ah, qiTá:** *piece*

أثري **átharii** *archaeological*

مسروق **masrúuq** *stolen*

الغرب **al-gharb** *the West*

أشهر **ásh-har*** *more/most famous*

ذقن، ذقون **dhaqn, dhuqúun** (fem.) *beard*

أبو الهول **abuu l-hawl** *the Sphynx* [lit. *Father of Terror*]

حجر، أحجار **Hájar, aHjáar** *stone*

رشيد **rashiid** *Rosetta, a town in Egypt; Rashid* (man's name)

موجود **mawjúud** *found, situated, existing*

بريطاني **briiTáanii** *British*

لندن **lándan** *London*

---

al-mulaaHaDHáat (Notes) الملاحظات

■ **a:raba** *to express* requires the preposition **:an**.

■ **tarHiib** and its verb **raHHab** *to welcome* require **bi-**.

■ **samaaH** *permission* also requires **bi-**.

■ **inna-h(u)**. The verb **qaala** *to say* uniquely is followed by **inna** for *that*. All other verbs use **anna** (see Unit 8).

■ **ash-har** is the comparative/superlative of **mash-huur**. This is an irregular formation, actually taken from another word. See Unit 15.

■ **abuu l-hawl** *the Sphynx*. For the irregular noun **abuu** see below.

■ **al-mawjuudaan**. The adjective here is in the dual as it refers to two objects (the Sphinx's beard and the Rosetta Stone).

---

2 اليمن al-yaman *The Yemen*

Exercise 3
Read the passage and answer the questions
a What arrived in the port of Aden?
b Who was it carrying?
c What do the tourists hope to visit?

اليمن

٤٥٠ سائح أوروبي في عدن

استقبل ميناء عدن أمس الأول سفينة سياحية ألمانية تحمل أكثر من ٤٠٠ سائح وسائحة من مختلف الجنسيات الأوروبية. وسيزور هؤلاء السواح بعض المدن اليمنية التاريخية.

Exercise 4
Find the Arabic for the English expressions.
a of various nationalities
b The tourists will visit some Yemeni towns.

اليمن **al-yáman** *Yemen*

سائح، سواح **sáa'iH, suwwáaH** *tourist*

أوروبي، ون **urúubii** *European*

عدن: **ádan** *Aden*

ميناء، الموانى **miináa', al-mawáanii** (sometimes fem.) *harbour, port*

أمس الأول **ams al-áwwal** *the day before yesterday*

سفينة، سفن **safíinah, súfun** *ship*

سياحى **siyáaHii** *tourist* (adj.), *touristic*

ألمانى **almáanii** *German*

مختلف **mukhtálif** *different, various*

تاريخى **taaríikhii** *historical, historic*

---

al-mulaaHaDHáat (Notes) الملاحظات

■ **miinaa'** *harbour*. The plural of this word is a defective noun (see below).

■ **ams al-awwal** lit. *yesterday the-first*. Also occurs in the form **awwal ams**, both meaning *the day before yesterday*.

■ **mukhtalif** *various* when, as here, used as the first part of a possessive construction. When used as an ordinary adjective, it means *different*.

■ **ba:D** *some*. See below.

🎧 3 أمريكا **amriikaa** *America*

Exercise 5
Read the passage and answer the questions.
a How old is the millionaire's prospective bride?
b How old is he?
c What aids does he need?
d How much does he love his fiancée?

أمريكا

أعلن مليونير أمريكي من ولاية كاليفورنيا في الأسبوع الماضي أنه
سيتزوج فتاة في الخامسة والعشرين من عمرها. وهذا بعد احتفاله
بعيد ميلاده المئوي بأيام قليلة. وهو يستخدم منظما لضربات القلب
ويتنقل على كرسي بعجلات. وقال انه يحبها من كل قلبه وهي
تبادله الحب.

Exercise 6

Find the Arabic for the following English expressions.

a He will marry a girl.
b he said that he loves her
c with all his heart

أعلن **á:lana [S-IV]** *to announce, state*

مليونير **malyoonáyr** *millionaire*

ولاية، ـات **wiláayah, -aat** *administrative division of a country;*
here *state*

تزوج **tazáwwaja [Mw-V]** *to marry*

فتاة، فتيات **fatáah, fatayáat** *girl, young woman*

احتفال، ـات **iHtifáal, -áat** *celebration*

مئوي **mí'awii** *centennial, hundredth*

منظم، ـات **munáDHDHim, -áat** *regulator*

ضربة، Darabáat **Dárbah, Darabáat** *a beat, blow*

قلب، قلوب **qalb, qulúub** *heart*

تنقل **tanáqqala [S-V]** *to be transported*

كرسي، كراسي **kúrsii, karáasii** *chair*

عجلة، ـات **:ájalah, -áat** *wheel*

بادل **báadala [S-III]** *to return, reciprocate to someone*

---

al-mulaaHaDHáat (Notes) الملاحظات

- **al-maaDii** *the past.* Defective adjective. See page 324.

- **al-khaamisah wa-l-:ishriin** *the 25th.* Note that in compounds of tens and units, only the unit takes the ordinal form. For basic rules see Unit 11. The adjective applies to the implied/understood feminine noun **sanah** *year.*

- **iHtifaal** *celebration* and its verb require **bi-**.

- **mi'awii** *hundredth.* This is not a true ordinal number, rather an adjective meaning *centennial* from مئة **mi'ah** – *hundred* – irregular but most common spelling – or مائة *hundred.*

- **munaDHDHim(an) li-Darabaat al-qalb** *regulator for beats of the heart,* i.e. *a pacemaker.*

- **min kull qalb-uh** *with all his heart.* For **kull** see grammar section below.

- **tubaadil-uh** *she reciprocates* [to him]. Many of such Form III verbs take a direct object, where in English a preposition is required. See Verb Tables.

🎧 4 أبو ظبي abuu DHabii *Abu Dhabi*

Exercise 7

Read the passage, and answer the questions.

a Who is Fairuz?

b Why is she in Abu Dhabi?

أبو ظبي

وصلت إلى الإمارات اليوم المطربة اللبنانية المشهورة فيروز في زيارة خاصة، ستزور خلالها أخاها الذي يقيم في أبو ظبي.

Exercise 8

Now find the Arabic for the following English expressions.

a She arrived in the Emirates today.

b She will visit her brother

أبو ظبي **abuu DHábi** Abu Dhabi

وصل **wáSala [Fw-I i]** to arrive (**ilaa** إلى at)

مطربة، ـات **múTribah, -aat** (female) singer, musician

فيروز **fayrúuz** Fairuz (female name); turquoise (gem)

زيارة، ـات **ziyáarah, -áat** visit

خلال **khaláal** during

أخ، إخوان/ إخوة **akh, ikhwáan** or **ikhwah** brother

---

al-mulaaHaDHáat (Notes) الملاحظات

■ **abuu DHabii**. Literally 'father of gazelle'. For **abuu** see grammar section below.

■ **waSal** to arrive requires the preposition **ilaa**.

■ **akhaa-haa** her brother. See grammar section below.

5 نيو يورك **nyuu yuurk** New York

Exercise 9

Read the passage, and answer the questions.

a What special day has UNESCO chosen to commemorate on March 21?

b Who is Ali al-Allaq?

c What is poetry greater than?

نيو يورك

اختارت منظمة اليونسكو يوم ٢١ مارس يوما عالميا للشعر. ورحب الشعراء العرب بهذا، بينهم الشاعر العراقي علي جعفر العلاق الذي قال إنه «مؤمن إيمانا لا حدود له أن الشعر أكبر من الزمان كله، وأكثر اتساعا من الأمكنة جميعا. إنه مالئ اللحظات والفصول والقرون بجمال المعنى ومعنى الجمال».

Exercise 10

Find the Arabic for the following English expressions.

a Arab poets welcomed this.   **b** Poetry is greater than all time.

c It fills the moments … with the beauty of meaning.

أقام **aqáama [Mw-IV]** *to reside*

منظمة، ـات **munáDHDHamah, -áat** *organisation*

شعر **shi:r** *poetry*

رحب بـ **ráHHaba [S-II]** *to welcome* (requires **bi-**)

شاعر، شعراء **sháa:ir, shu:aráa'*** *poet*

عراقي: **:iráaqii** *Iraqi*

مؤمن، ـون **mú'min, -úun** *believing, a believer* (in something)

إيمان **iimáan** *belief, faith*

حد، حدود **Hadd, Hudúud** *limit, border*

زمان، أزمنة **zamáan, azmínah** *time*

اتساع **ittisáa:** *extent, compass*

مكان، أمكنة **makáan, amkínah** *place*

جميعا **jamii:an** *all together*

مالئ **máali'** *filling, filler*

لحظة، ـات **láHDHah, laHaDHáat** *moment*

فصل، فصول **faSl, fuSúul** *section, season* (of the year)

قرن، قرون **qarn, qurúun** *century*

معنى، المعاني **má:naa, al-ma:áanii** *meaning*

---

al-mulaaHaDHáat (Notes) الملاحظات

- **yawman :aalamiyyan** *as a world day.* Adverbial accusative of respect. See Unit 15.

- **mu'min iimaanan.** Adverbial accusative. See Unit 15.

- **laa Huduud la-h(u)** Lit. *no limits to it.* Here the word **laa** is used to negate a noun. For its other uses see Unit 10.

- **ittisaa:an** *in extent* and **jamii:an** *all together* are examples of the adverbial accusative. See also below.

تعبيرات رئيسية ta:biiráat ra'iisíyyah (Key phrases)

كل يوم **kull yawm**	*every day*
كل عام وأنت بخير **kull :aam wa-anta bi-khayr**	*Happy Birthday/Eid*, etc.
من كل قلبي **min kull qalb-ii**	*with all my heart*
بعض الناس **ba:D an-naas**	*some of the people*

تراكيب اللغة taraakíib al-lúghah (Structures)

1 *Each*, *every* **and** *all*

All these English words are expressed using the Arabic كل **kull**, but with different constructions according to the specific meaning required.

each, every	**kull** + indefinite singular
all	**kull** + definite plural def. plural + **kull** + suffix pronoun

Each, every

The construction used for both of these is the same:

kull followed by an indefinite singular noun (without the definite article **al-**).

من كل بلد خبر	*from every country news*
كل عام وأنت بخير	lit. *every year and you in well-being*

the Arabic congratulatory phrase used in connection with all anniversaries, particularly birthdays.

> خير **khayr** (state of) *well-being*

كل مشكلة لها حل	every problem has a solution
	(lit. every problem for it a solution)

> مشكلة، مشاكل **múshkilah, masháakil*** problem
>
> حل، حلول **Hall, Hulúul** solution

All

a) **kull** followed by a noun with the definite article, usually plural. This is a possessive construction and obeys the rules given in Unit 6.

كل المتاحف مقفولة يوم الجمعة

all [of] the museums are closed on Friday

كان كل العساكر يحملون أسلحة

all [of] the soldiers were carrying arms

> عسكري، عساكر **:askárii, :asáakir** soldier
>
> سلاح، أسلحة **siláaH, aslíHah** weapon, arm

كل البنات حاضرات	all [of] the girls are present

> حاضر **HáaDir** present, here

The noun can be replaced by a suffix pronoun:

كلهم أخذوا قطعة كعك

all of them (they all) took a piece of cake

> كعك **ka:k** cake

b) A plural noun with the definite article, followed by **kull** with a suffix pronoun agreeing with the noun. This construction is slightly more common. To make it clear, here are the same examples as above in the new format. The meaning is exactly the same.

المتاحف كلها مقفولة يوم الجمعة

the museums all-of-them are closed on Friday

كان العساكر كلهم يحملون أسلحة

the soldiers all-of-them were carrying arms

البنات كلهن حاضرات   *the girls all-of-them are present*

When used with a singular noun or pronoun suffix, the translation can be *all* or *the whole*, e.g. from the text:

الزمان كله *all time, the whole of time*

أكلت الكعك كله *She ate all the cake, the whole cake.*

An alternative word for all is جميع **jamii:**, used either with a plural in the same way as **kull** or, as we have in the text, with the accusative marker as an adverb (see Unit 16):

وأكثر اتساعا من الأمكنة جميعا

and greater in compass than all places

Some

The word for some is بعض **ba:D**, a noun meaning *a part of something*. This is used in the same way as kull when it means all as explained above.

بعض المدن اليمنية التاريخية

some of the historic Yemeni towns

بعضهم عرب وبعضهم إنجليز

some of them are Arabs, and some English

Summary

kull is a noun meaning *the whole*, *totality* of something.

ba:D is a noun meaning *a part* of something. They are both sometimes used independently:

قال البعض إنها مجنونة   *some said that she was mad*

من كل قلبه   *with all his heart*

مجنون، مجانين **majnúun, majaaníin** *mad*

2 Irregular nouns

There are two classes of irregular nouns and adjectives which must be mentioned as the variations in their endings show up in print, i.e. they do not consist entirely of unmarked vowel endings.

Remember that Literary Arabic recognises three cases of the noun/adjective, depending on its function in the sentence:

Nominative, used for the subject of all sentences and the compliment of verbless sentences; also for the complement of **inna**-type sentences (see Unit 8)

Accusative, used for the object of verb sentences, the subject of inna, the complement of **kaana** sentences (Unit 8), and for many adverbial expressions (Unit 16).

Genitive, used for the second part of possessive constructions (i.e. for the possessor) and after all prepositions. The genitive is unmarked except in the nouns mentioned below.

Two common nouns behave differently when they form the first part of a possessive phrase, either with another noun or a pronoun suffix:

أب، آباء **ab, aabaa'** *father*

أخ، إخوان\إخوة **akh, ikhwaan** or **ikhwah** *brother*

These behave normally when they do not form the first part of a possessive:

له أخ واحد *he has one brother*

In possessives they show the nominative case with a و, the accusative with an ا, and the genitive with a ي.

For example, take *her brother/father*, using the possessive suffix **-haa**.

Case	her father	her brother
Nominative	أبوها **abuu-haa**	أخوها **akhuu-haa**
Accusative	أباها **abaa-haa**	أخاها **akhaa-haa**
Genitive	أبيها **abii-haa**	أخيها **akhii-haa**

Here is an example from the article above:

ستزور خلالها أخاها   *during which she will visit her brother*
                            (accusative, object of a verb)

Examples of the other two cases are:

يعمل أبوهم في شركة كبيرة   *their father works in a big company*
                            (nominative, subject of a verb)

نسكن مع أبينا   *we live with our father*
                            (genitive after a preposition)

Notes

a) When the suffix ي- **-ii** *my* is added to these words, the various long vowel endings are omitted, and all cases are أبي **ab-ii** and أخي **akh-ii**.

b) Technically, in formal Standard Arabic, the same varying forms should be used before another noun, but this seems to be dropping out of modern press Arabic, and the nominative **-uu** form is used in all contexts. This is important, as **abuu** especially occurs in many personal and place names. For instance, in the text we have في أبو ظبي *in Abu Dhabi*, which should technically be أبي **abii** after the preposition في *in*.

c) **abuu** is frequently used to express a possessor of something, rather than a strictly biological father, e.g. أبو الهول *possessor of terror; that which holds terror*, i.e. *the Sphynx* (see also below).

d) A common word ذو، ذا، ذي **dhuu, dhaa, dhii** *possessor* is only used with a following noun, e.g. كان رجلا ذا شأن *he was a man of importance* (lit. *possessor of importance*)

Tip: You can avoid using **abuu** etc. in many situations by substituting the regular noun والد **waalid** which also means *father*, but this is not permissible in proper names. You can't do anything about **akh**, though.

3 Defective nouns and adjectives

Another class of irregular words are the so-called defective nouns and adjectives. The defect is that, in certain cases as explained below, they lose their final letter, which is always ى. These are perfectly regular in the definite, but the indefinite works as follows, using the word **qaaDii** *judge* as a model:

Definite	all cases:	القاضي **al-qaaDii**
Indefinite	Nominative	قاض **qaaDin**
	Accusative:	قاضيا **qaaDiyan**
	Genitive:	قاض **qaaDin**

The class also includes adjectives such as الماضي، ماض، ماضيا **al-maaDii, maaDin, maaDiyan** *past, former*.

These words are a common source of error to Arabs when writing, perhaps because in spoken Arabic, the final **-ii** is pronounced, and native speakers feel instinctively that there is something missing or unnatural if they drop it.

Important note: To save confusion, and because they look peculiar in isolation in their truncated form, words of this class have been given in the vocabularies and glossaries with the definite article, e.g.:

القاضي، قضاة **al-qaaDii, quDaah** *judge*

الماضي **al-maaDii** *past* (adj.)

Note that it can be the singular which is defective, as in the examples above, or the plural as in the following examples:

معنى، المعاني **ma:naa, al-ma:aanii** *meaning*

ميناء، الموانئ **miinaa', al-mawaanii** *harbour*

Here are another couple of common defective adjectives:

ماء صاف **maa' Saafin** *pure water*

السد العالي **as-sadd al-:aali** *the High Dam* (in Egypt)

ماء، مياه **maa, miyaah** *water*

الصافي **aS-Saafii** *pure, clear*

سد، سدود **sadd, suduud** *dam*

العالي **al-:aalii** *high*

أوزان الكلمات awzáan al-kalimáat (Word shapes)

Exercise 11

The following is a revision exercise, covering the word shapes given in all the previous units. You are given an Arabic root, along with its basic meaning. Refer back to the relevant unit and create the required word shape. The answers, along with their meanings, are given in the key and on the recording.

Unit 1   و–ح–د *to be one, unique*

Unit 2   ب–ر–د *being cold*

Unit 3   ض–ب–ط *being exact, accurate*

Unit 4   ل–ع–ب *playing*

Unit 5   ف–ط–ر *breaking one's fast*

Unit 6   ط–ب–ع *printing, typing*

Unit 7   ف–هـ–م *understanding*

Unit 8   ر–س–م *drawing*

Unit 9   ع–ل–م *knowing*

Unit 10 ع–ل–م *knowing*

Unit 11 ف–ض–ل *being preferable, good, excellent*

Unit 12 ف—س—ر *explaining, elucidating*

Unit 13 ن—ظ—ر *seeing, looking at*

Unit 14 ك—ش—ف *uncovering, discovering*

Unit 15 ف—ت—ح *opening*

Unit 16 ل—خ—ب—ط *being mixed up, in a mess*

Unit 17 ق—ن—ع *convincing (someone of something)*

تمرينات tamriináat (Practice)

Exercise 12
Find the odd one out:

١ أخي – عمي – أمي – أبي

٢ أب – مطرب – مدير – شاعر

٣ أبو صالح – أبو ظبي – أبو الهول

٤ كرسي – طاولة – غسالة – رئيس

٥ ميناء – قلب – سفينة – ماء

غسالة، ـات **ghassáalah, -áat** *washing machine*

Exercise 13
Here is part of a Hotel Guide for Algiers. Look at the key to the hotel facilities, and decide whether these statements referring to the four hotels described below are true or false.

١ كل غرفة في فندق الخليج فيها تلفزيون وراديو وعرض أفلام.

٢ بعض الفنادق فيها ملعب تنس.

٣ كل الفنادق تقبل بطاقات التسليف.

٤ بعض الفنادق لها مواقف سيارات.

٥ كل فندق فيه تكييف.

٦ كل الفنادق فيها صالون تجميل.

٧ كلها فيه مسبح.

٨ بعض الغرف في فندق «اللؤلؤة» فيها حمـام.

٩ في كل فندق خدمة تنظيف الملابس.

١٠ ليس في كل الغرف في فندق «اسبلنديد» هاتف.

قبل **qábila [S-I a]** *to accept*

بطاقة التسليف **buTáaqat at-tasliif** *credit card*

تكييف **takyíif** *air conditioning*

صالون تجميل **Sáaluun tajmíil** *beauty salon*

خدمة، ـات **khídmah, -áat** *service*

تنظيف **tanDHíif** *cleaning*

ملابس **maláabis** *clothes*

Exercise 14

Add the word *all* to the plural nouns (underlined) in the following
sentences, using **kull** with a suffix pronoun agreeing with the noun.

Example:

لعب الأولاد في الحديقة *The children played in the garden.*

لعب الأولاد كلهم في الحديقة *All the children played in the garden.*

١ درس الطلبة للامتحانات.

٢ وصل السواح من ألمانيا.

٣ تفتح الدكاكين في المساء.

٤ رحب الموظفون بتقرير المدير.

٥ استقبلته أخواته في المطار.

٦ وضعت الكتب على الرف.

1 *The students studied for their examination.*

2 *The tourists arrived from Germany.*

3 *The shops open in the evening.*

4 *The employees welcomed the director's report*

5 *His sisters met him in at the airport.*

6 *I put the books on the shelf.*

KEY TO THE EXERCISES

Script and Pronunciation Guide
1 Volvo, Honda, Jeep, Toyota, Chrysler

Unit 1

1 a السلام b عليكم
2 أهلا بك
3 a الخير b صباح c مساء d النور
4 a صباح الخير b كيف حالك؟ c مساء الخير d عليكم السلام e وعليكم السلام
5 a حالك b وأنت؟ c الحمد لله d أهلا بك/أهلا وسهلا d كيف حالكم e شكرا، تفضل
6 1c; 2b; 3a
7 1c; 2b; 3a
8 a صغير b شاي بسكر c المصباح d الأهرام e سندوتش
9 Aladdin and the magic lamp
10 Sun: a, c, d, e, g; Moon: b, f
12 id; iib; iiie; ivc; va
13 ١g; ٢a; ٣b; ٤c; ٥i; ٦j; ٧h; ٨d; ٩e; ١٠f
a Rabat; b Algiers *or* Algeria; c Cairo; d Riyadh; e Manamah; f Baghdad; g The Middle East; h Saudi Arabia; i (The) Sudan; j Jordan
14 a coffee; b lemon; c small Coca Cola; d chocolate ice-cream; e the cinema; f the bank
15 a as-sandwíitsh; b at-tilifúun; c al-bayt; d aT-TamáaTim; e as-síinima; f al-bíirah aS-Saghiirah; g al-bárgar al-kabíir; h ar-ráadyo al-jadíid
16 1g; 2d; 3h; 4c; 5e; 6b; 7a; 8f
17
١ السينما الجديدة ٢ بنت صغيرة ٣ كتاب جميل٤ فيلم طويل ٥ البيت الكبير الواسع
18
١ ص-غ-ر ٢ ط-و-ل ٣ ب-ع-د ٤ ق-ر-ب ٥ ج-د-د ٦ ق-د-م ٧ ج-م-ل
٨ ل-ط-ف ٩ ك-ر-م ١٠ ص-ح-ح
1 S-gh-r; 2 T-w-l; 3 b-:-d; 4 q-r-b; 5 j-d-d; 6 q-d-m; 7 j-m-l; 8 l-T-f; 9 k-r-m; 10 S-H-H

Unit 2

Dialogue 1 min áyna ánta? *Where are you from?*
Translation:

Suad Well. My name is Suad. What's your name?
Michael My name is Michael.
Suad Welcome, Michael. Where are you from?
Michael I am from Manchester, in England. And you?
Suad I am from Alexandria in Egypt.

Transliteration:

su:áad Hásanan. ána ísm-ii su:áad. maa ísm-ak?
máaykal ána ísm-ii máaykal
su:áad áhlan wa-sáhlan yaa máaykal. min áyna anta?
máaykal ána min manshastar fii inglatárra. wa-ánti?
su:áad ána min al-iskandaríyyah fii miSr.

1 a Suad; b Michael
2 a Manchester; b Alexandria
3 a مـانشستر من أنا b وأنت؟

Dialogue 2 miSr jamíilah *Egypt is beautiful*
Translation:

Egypt is very beautiful. Cairo is a big city, and it is very old. The Egyptian Museum is in Tahrir Square close to the Nile Hotel. There is an excellent restaurant in the Nile Hotel in Tahrir Square. And of course there are the pyramids in Geezah.

Transliteration:

miSr jamíilah jíddan. al-qáahirah madíinah kabíirah, wa-híya qadíimah jíddan. al-mátHaf al-míSrii fii maydáan at-taHríir qaríib min fúnduq al-níil. hunáaka máT:am mumtáaz fii fúnduq al-níil fii maydáan at-taHríir. wa-Táb:an hunáaka l-ahráam fi l-gíizah.

4 a that it is big, beautiful and very old; b in Tahrir Square; c an excellent restaurant

Dialogue 3 raqm tilifúun-ak kam? *What's you phone number?*
Translation:

Zaki What's your phone number, Hamid?
Hamid My phone number is 6347211. And your phone number?
Zaki My phone number is 6215500. Marie, what's your phone number?
Marie My phone number is 6207589.

Transliteration:

zákii ráqam tilifóon-ak kam, yaa Háamid?

Háamid ráqam tilifóon-ii síttah thaláathah árba:ah sáb:ah ithnáyn wáaHid wáaHid. wa-ráqam tilifóon-ak ánta?

Zaki ráqam tilifóon-ii síttah ithnáyn wáaHid khámsah khámsah Sifr Sifr. yaa maarii, ráqam tilifóon-ik kam?

maarii ráqam tilifóon-ii síttah ithnáyn Sifr sáb:ah khámsah thamáanyah tís:ah

5 a 6215500 b 6207589 c رقم تلفون d ... رقم تلفوني

6 م–ل–س/ح–ل–ص/ع–ف–ن/م–ك/ف–ش–ن/م–ز/ل/ل–د–ع

7 a المدير الجديد b السيارة الجميلة c الولد الطويل d البيت الصغير e المدير المشغول

8 a السكرتير جديد b جميلة c السيارة طويل d الولد صغير e البيت مشغول المدير

9 a هو جديد b هي جميلة c هو طويل d هو صغير e هو مشغول

10

١ أأنت من مصر؟ ٢ هل محمد في دبي؟ ٣ أهي أمريكية؟ ٤ هل الكتاب جديد؟
٥ هل يتكلم عربي؟

11

١ السيارة جديدة ٢ هي مشغولة ٣ الفندق قريب من الأهرام ٤ محمد هنا ٥ هو مشغول

12 1 Tunis; 2 Lebanon; 3 Paris; 4 Scotland; 5 Abu Dhabi; 6 Italy

13 a Dubai; b Ras al-Khaimah; c Abu Dhabi

14 a973; b20; c1; d974; e966; f39

Unit 3

Dialogue 1 á-ánta suudáani? *Are you Sudanese?*

Translation:

Husáam Hello! Are you Egyptian?

Záki No, I'm Sudanese, from Khartoum. And you?

Husáam I'm Egyptian, from Tanta.

Záki Where is Tanta?

Husáam Tanta is near Cairo.

Transliteration:

Husáam márHaban. 'a-ánta míSrii?

záki laa, ána suudáanii min al-kharTúum. wa-ánta?

Husáam ána míSrii min TánTaa

záki áyna TánTaa?

Husáam TánTaa qaríibah min al-qáahirah

1 a Sudanese; b Khartoum

2 a Egypt; b England; c Australia; d Lebanon; e France

Translation:

Suad I am Egyptian, and you, Mike?

Michael I am English.
Kylie I am Australian.
Yuunis I am Lebanese. I am from Beirut.
Marie I am French.

Transliteration:
su:áad ána miSríyyah, wa-ánta yaa máayk?
máayk ána inglíizii
káaylii ána ustraalíyyah
yúunis ána lubnáanii. ána min bayrúut
maarii ána faransíyyah

Dialogue 2 hal tatakállam inglíizii? *Do you speak English?*
Translation:
Passenger Excuse me. Where are you from?
Julie I am from England. And you?
Passenger I am from Amman. I am Jordanian.
Julie Do you speak English?
Passenger No, I am sorry, I don't speak English. I only speak Arabic.

Transliteration:
ráakib :an ídhn-ik. min áyna ánti?
júulii ána min ingiltárra. wa-ánta?
ráakib ána min :ammáan. ána úrdunii
júulii hal tatakállam inglíizii?
ráakib laa, má:a l-ásaf, laa atakállam inglíizii. atakállam :árabi fáqaT

3 a English; **b** Arabic
Translation:
Passenger You speak Arabic fluently!
Julie No, only a little
Transliteration
ráakib tatakallamíin al-:arabíyyah bi-Taláaqah!
júulii laa, qalíilah fáqaT
4 a هل تتكلم إنجليزي؟ **b** قليلة
5 true

Dialogue 3 maa :ámal-ak? *What do you do?*
Translation:
Passenger What is your occupation?
Julie I am a student, at London University. And you?
Passenger I am a doctor in Amman.

Transliteration:
ráakib maa :ámal-ik?

júulii ána Táalibah fii jáami:at lándan. wa-anta?
ráakib ána Tabíib fii :ammáan

6 a student; b in Amman
7 a ما عملك؟ b أنا طبيب

Dialogue 4 hal lándan madíinah kabíirah? *Is London a big city?*
Translation:
Passenger Is London a big city?
Julie Yes it is a very big city. There are many big museums and bridges and shops.
Passenger Where is the university?
Julie It is in the middle of the town, near the British Museum.

Transliteration:
ráakib hal lándan madíinah kabíirah?
júulii ná:am híya madíinah kabíirah jíddan. hunáaka matáaHif kabíirah kathíirah wa-jusúur wa-maHalláat
ráakib áyna l-jáami:ah?
júulii híya fii wasT al-madíinah, qaríibah min al-mátHaf al-bríiTáanii

8 a museums/ bridges/ shops; b the university
9 a Morocco; b Jordan; c Oman; d Bahrain; e Kuwait
10 a4E; b7C; c6A; d2G; e1B; f3D; g5F
11 a Salma; b Damascus, Syria c اسمها سلمى d تتكلم اللغة العربية
Translation:
....her name is Salma and she is Syrian, from Damascus. She speaks Arabic, English and French. She is a teacher.

Transliteration:
... ísm-haa sálmaa wa-híya suuríyyah min dimáshq. tatakállam al-lughah al-:arabíyyah wa l-ingliizíyyah wa l-faransíyyah. híya mudárrisah.
12

٤ قليل	١ اسمي مارتن رومانو
٥ نعم، طبعا!	٢ أنا أمريكي
٦ نعم، اللغة الإيطالية ... قليل.	٣ أنا طالب

Translation:
Martin Romano is American. He is a student. He speaks English, fluent Italian, and a little Arabic.

Transliteration:
máartin ruumáanuu min amríikaa. huwa Táalib. yatakállam inglíizii, iiTáalii bi-Taláaqah wa :árabi qalíilan.

13

١ مشغولة ٢ المصرية، مشهورة ٣ جديد ٤ الكبيرة، أمريكية ٥ جديدة ٦ الانجليزية،
نافعة ٧ جديدة، كثيرة ٨ واحدة ٩ سعيدة

14 a مدرسة هي b طالب هو c مهندس هو d مديرة هي e طالبة هي f طبيبة هي

Unit 4

Dialogue 1 áyna l-matáaHif? *Where are the museums?*
Translation:

Hassan This is the map of Sharjah. This is the Old Town, and this is the fish market.

Jim Where are the museums?

Hassan These are the museums here, and here. This is the Arts Museum, and this is the Natural History Museum, on the Airport road.

Bridget That museum is far away.

Jim Yes, that's true. Look, the Fort Museum is here, in Tower (Burj) Street. It's an excellent museum, and maybe afterwards we can go to the Old Town.

Bridget Good. We'll go to the Fort Museum.

1 a The Old Town; b It's too far; c The Fort Museum
2 a4; b2; c3; d1

Dialogue 2 yáqfil as-sáa:ah kam? *What time does it close?*
Translation:

Hassan Good morning. At what time does the museum close?

Attendant Good morning. It closes at one o'clock, and opens at four o'clock in the afternoon.

Bridget What is the time now?

Hassan It's a quarter past ten.

Bridget Good. We have plenty of time.

Attendant Welcome, come in. This is a brochure of the museum.

Hassan Thank you

3 a 1pm; b 4pm; c 10:15 am; d a brochure
4 a4; b1; c6; d2; e5; f3
5 a Wednesday evenings; b Monday; c 8:30pm; d 9am; e Friday; f 5

Dialogue 4 bi-kam...? *How much does it cost?*
Translation:

Hassan Hello!

Female Attendant Hello!

Hassan How much is a ticket, please?

Female Attendant Adults are six dirhams, and children three dirhams.
Hassan Three tickets at six dirhams please.
Female Attendant Eighteen dirhams please. Thank you. Here are the tickets.
Hassan Thank you.

6 a 6 Dhs; b 3Dhs; c 18 Dhs
7 a4; b1; c2; d3
8 a 1:30; b 6:55; c 10:15; d 5:00; e 9:00am
9 see transcript
10

١ يوم؛ ٢ يوم الأربعاء؛ ٣ أمس؛ ٤ يوم الأحد؛ ٥ بعد غدٍ؛ ٦ يوم الجمعة

11

١ هذا؛ ٢ هذه؛ ٣ أولئك؛ ٤ هذه؛ ٥ أولئك؛ ٦ تلك

12 3/12/1952; 19/11/1967; 1/1/2000; 28/2/1990; 17/4/1836
13

٤ تفضل.	١ مساء الخير
٥ المسرح يفتح الساعة كم؟	٢ التذكرة بكم؟
٦ شكرا	٣ أربعة تذاكر من فضلك.

a 4 dinars; b 7 o' clock; c half past seven
14 see transcript

Unit 5

Dialogue 1 háadhihi híya záwjat-ii *This is my wife*
Translation:
Hamed Tom, come in, please.
Tom Thank you, Hamed.
Hamed This is my wife, Salma. Salma, this is Tom, from the office.
Tom Good evening, Salma, how are you?
Salma I'm well, praise God. Welcome. And how are you?
Tom Praise God. This is a present for you. (*He gives Salma some flowers*)
Salma Thank you Tom. Come in. Welcome. This is my father, and this is my
mother.... and this is our son Tamiim. Please, sit down.
Tom How old is Tamiim?
Salma He is 15 years old, and our daughter Farida is 21.
Hamed How old are your children, Tom?
Tom Our children are small – our son is 5, and our daughter is 3 years old.

1 a Salma; b 15; c 21; d younger
2 a والدي هذا b اجلس c ابننا هذا d كم عمرهم؟ e سنوات ٣ عمرها بنتنا أولادك أنت،
3 33 thaláathah wa-thalaathíin; 40 arba:íin; 44 árba:ah wa-arba:íin; 57 sáb:ah

wa-khamsíin; 68 thamáanyah wa-sittíin; 76 síttah wa-sab:íin; 85 khámsah wa-thamaaníin; 99 tís:ah wa-tis:íin.

4 ١٤ ٢٤ ٢٨ ٣١ ٤٢ ٣٥ ٥٨ ٧٦ ٨٨ ٩٦

5 a Lantern Dhs.99; b Barbecue Dhs.89; c Relax chair Dhs.65; d Tow rope Dhs.50; e Sleeping bag Dhs.42; f Ice chest Dhs.79; g Charcoal Dhs.25

6 a4; b1; c3; d6; e5; f2

7

١ قميصك وسخ ٢ والدتي إيطالية ٣ هرمي هو الكبير

٤ هذه أختي مريم ٥ ليست هذه السيارة سيارتي

٦ أهذا مكتبه الجديد؟ ٧ جدهم من تونس ٨ أين حقائبنا ؟

8 i a خالد b مريم c وخميس وفهد سلمان

ii a ابنه b بنته c والده d أخته

iii a خاله بنت b عمته زوج c جدهم

Unit 6

Dialogue 1 áyna wásaT al-madíinah, min fáDl-ak?
Translation:

Andy Excuse me, where is the centre of town?

Man Straight ahead. Where are you going to?

Andy I'm going to the office of Ali al Mabrouk. Do you know it? Here is a map of the town. (*Andy produces a map of the town*)

Man Yes, I know it. Let me think. Yes, it's here. (*He shows Andy on the map*) After the big mosque, turn left at the traffic lights. This is King Hussein Street. Go straight ahead for about 100 metres.

Andy Yes, I understand.

Man The office of Ali al Mabrouk is on the right, beside the petrol station, opposite the Plaza cinema.

Andy Oh, yes. Thank you. Is there a car park there?

Man Yes, there is a big car park behind the office of Ali al Mabrouk.

Andy Thank you very much.

Man You're welcome.

1 a اذنك! عن b i; c left; d 100m; e petrol station; f iii

2 a٧; b٢; c٥; d٣; e٦; f١; g٤

3 a hotel; b mosque; c fish market; d post office; e park; f old fort

4 a4; b5; c7; d2; e3; f1; g6

5 see transcript

6 see transcript

7

١ مدير البنك ٢ وسط المدينة ٣ عاصمة البلاد ٤ مكتب الشركة ٥ أخت راشد ٦ سفارة ايطاليا

8

١ شوارع أبو ظبي عريضة ٢ جامعة القاهرة كبيرة ٣ حدائق القصر جميلة ٤ غرف الشقة واسعة ٥ طبيخ المغرب لذيذ ٦ دكاكين السوق صغيرة

9 a حزامي b جوارب تميم c منديلي d نظارتي e بنطلون تميم

Unit 7

Dialogue 1 ákhii fahd *My brother Fahd*
Translation:
He travelled to Amman in March, and worked in the Jordanian office of his company. He stayed with my uncle. We wrote a letter to him every week. He returned to Kuwait in September.

1 a False b False cTrue
2 a3; b1; c2

Dialogue 2 máadhaa fa:ált ams? *What did you do yesterday?*
Translation:
Zaki What did you do yesterday?
Sonya Yesterday I went to the house of Ahmed.
Zaki How did you go there?
Sonya I went by taxi. He and his family live in Zamalek.
Zaki What did you do?
Sonya I met his father and his mother and his sisters. His mother cooked lunch. After lunch we drank Arabic coffee.
Zaki And did you like it?
Sonya Yes, it is delicious.
Zaki Did you return by taxi?
Sonya No, I didn't come back by taxi. Ahmed gave me a lift home in his car.

3 a by taxi; b his family; c i; d ii; e Ahmed's mother; f i; g iii; h a٤; b١; c٥; d٢; e٣
4

١ ما تأخرت الطائرة ٢ ما كلم العمال الرئيس٣ ما أكلت الخبز

5 1b; 2c; 3d; 4e; 5a
6 a٨; b٣; c١; d٦; e٧; f٥; g٢; h٤

طبخت، أكلنا e وصلتd تفرجت c فتحت b سافروا a **7**

8 a a٢; b٥; c٦; d١; e٤; f٣
   b

١ لعبت؛ ٢ قابلت؛ ٣ جلست؛ ٤ ركبت؛ ٥ شربت؛ ٦ ذهبت

9

١ كتبتها ٢ أكلتها ٣ كلمهم ٤ سألته ٥ غسلنها ٦ قابلها

10 a٣; b٤; c١; d٥; e٢
11 *Translation:*

Bill and Mary and the children *travelled* from London and *arrived* in Dubai in
March 1997. They *stayed* there for a week. They *lived* in a big flat near the sea,
and *met* many people from the Emirates. On Monday Bill *played* tennis, and
Mary *went* to the beach. On Tuesday they *went* to the house of their friend
Mansour, and his wife *cooked* Arabic food for them.

سافر بيل وميري والأولاد من لندن ووصلوا إلى دبي في شهر مارس سنة ١٩٩٧.
قعدوا هناك لمدة أسبوع. سكنوا في شقة كبيرة قريبة من البحر، وقابلوا ناسا
كثيرين من الإمارات. يوم الاثنين لعب بيل تنس، وذهبت ميري إلى الشاطئ. يوم
الثلثاء ذهبوا إلى بيت صديقهم منصور، وطبخت لهم زوجته طعاما عربيا.

12

٤ البنات طبخن طعاما عربيا	١ محمد سافر إلى القاهرة
٥ الصحون وقعت من المائدة	٢ الأولاد رجعوا من المدرسة
	٣ المهندسون حضروا المؤتمر

Unit 8

1 kaana yaa maa kaan *Once upon a time*
Translation:

In the days of the Caliph Harun al-Rashid there was, in Baghdad, a poor porter
whose name was Hindbad. One day this Hindbad was carrying a heavy load to
the house of a merchant in the market. And that was in the summer, and the heat
of the sun was very strong. Hindbad became tired and thirsty. So he stopped in
the road at the gate of a magnificent palace to rest from his work. He put his
burden on the ground and sat down. And while he was sitting like that, he heard
beautiful music emanating from inside the palace. And there was a servant
standing in front of the gate of the palace, so Hindbad asked him: Who is the
owner of this magnificent palace?

1 a ii; **b** to a merchant's house in the market; **c** he was tired and thirsty; **d** ii;
e Whose palace is this?
2 a٥; b٦; c١; d٣; e٢; f٤

2 as-sindibaad al-baHrii *Sindbad the Sailor*

Translation

And the servant said to him: Verily it is the palace of Sindbad the Sailor. And the porter said: And who is he? And the servant was astonished and said: You are living in Baghdad, and you have not heard of Sindbad the Sailor? Hindbad said: No. The servant said: He is the one who has travelled the seven seas, and has seen all the wonders of the world. And the porter became sad, and asked himself, saying: Why is this Sindbad rich and I am not rich? And Sindbad heard this from inside the palace and despatched another servant to the gate. This servant came out of the palace gate and said to Hindbad: Come with me. So the porter followed him inside the palace and he saw there a tall man, sitting in the midst of a group of people, and this man was Sindbad. And the Sailor said to the porter: Greetings and welcome. And he seated him next to himself and offered him many kinds of delicious food. And after that he told him about his amazing voyages, and he had already ordered his servants to take Hindbad's load to the merchant's house.

3 a because Hindbad hadn't heard of Sindbad the Sailor; b ii; c i; d iii; e ii; f to deliver the load to the merchant

4 a٦; b٤; c٢; d٨; e١; f٧; g٣; h٥

5

١ كانت؛ ٢ كانت؛ ٣ كانوا؛ ٤ كان

6

١ كان ذلك الطعام لذيذا ٢ كانت حدائق الفندق واسعة ٣ كانت شركتنا مشهورة في الخليج ٤ كان عمر الشريف ممثلا مصريا ٥ كان الأولاد سعداء

7

١ لا، ليست الساعة ١٠.٣٠ الصبح ٢ لا، ليس محمود في البهو ٣ لا، ليست في مطعم البستان ٤ لا، لسن في المسبح ٥ نعم، هو في مركز الأعمال ٦ نعم، هي في ملعب الجولف ٧ لا، ليست أرقام الغرف ٥١١، ٥١٢ و٥١٣ ٨ نعم، هم في ملعب التنس

8

ليس الفهد مخططًا وليس النمر منقطًا

9

١ ليس علي طالبا كسلانا ٢ لست تعبانا بعد رحلتي ٣ ليست الفنادق الكبيرة في وسط المدينة ٤ ليست مشهورة جدا ٥ ليس الطبيب مشغولا في المستشفى ٦ ليست هذه القصة من ألف ليلة وليلة طويلة جدا

10

١ كانت شهرزاد روت قصة جديدة كل ليلة ٢ كان الخدام قد خرجوا من القصر ٣ كان البحري خبر الحمال عن رحلاته العجيبة ٤ كانت الخادمات قد تبعنه الى داخل القصر ٥ كان الناس قد أكلوا الأكل اللذيذ

Unit 9

1 waDHáa'if sháaghirah *Situations vacant*

1 a iii/ b ic; iia; iiib/ c 1viii; 2iii; 3vii; 4i; 5x; 6v; 7iv; 8ii/ d i: vii, ix, x, vi, ii, iv; d ii: vi; d iii: vii, ix, x, iv/ e 3 years experience in UAE food sales; good English; valid convertable residence permit; aged 24–28 years; Emirates driving licence

2 c ١; f ٢; a ٣; b ٤; d ٥; e ٦

3 a ix; b vii; c iv; d ii; e vi; f iv; g x; h v

4 a٣; b٤; c١; d٢

5

١ هؤلاء الأولاد أذكياء ٢ بناتك جميلات ٣ القمصان مخططة ٤ قرأنا الجرائد الإنجليزية ٥ البنوك مقفولة بعد الظهر ٦ الرجال المصريون نشاط

6

١ وجدنا مطاعم جيدة في القاهرة ٢ حضر المدراء الاجتماع ٣ هل أنتم جوعى؟ ٤ السكرتيرات مشغولات ٥ بناتها طالبات في الجامعة ٦ هم ممثلون كويتيون ٧ كانت الأفلام طويلة

7

١ وصل العمال الجدد ٢ أين الكتب الفرنسية؟ ٣ وجدته المدرسات على الرف ٤ أصبح الأولاد سمانا ٥ خرج الضيوف من الفنادق

8 c١; b٢; d٣; a٤

9

١ المكتبان مقفولان ٢ ليس الفنيان حاضرين ٣ الحمامان واسعان ٤ عمل الموظفان في الوزارتين ٥ كلمت المديرتان العاملين

10

١ جون باركر ٢ ٣٢ سنة ٣ إنجليزي ٤ متزوج ٥ ص ب ٥٦٧، أبو ظبي ٦ ١٢٣٤٥٦٧ ٧ الإنجليزية، العربية ٨ نعم ٩ نعم ١٠ ٥ سنوات

Unit 10

1 maadhaa ta:mal kull yawm? *What do you do every day?*
Translation

Fawzia What do you eat in the morning?

Kamal I always eat fruit, and sometimes bread and cheese, and I drink coffee. I usually telephone my son. He lives in America.

Fawzia And then what do you do?

Kamal I go to the office – my driver takes me at eight thirty, and I talk with him in the car about the day's news.

Fawzia And then?

Kamal The secretary types letters for me while I read financial reports. This takes two to three hours.

Fawzia Do you use a computer?

Kamal Yes, of course. I learned the use of a computer at the College of Commerce.

Fawzia And what do you do in the afternoon?

Kamal In the afternoon I sit with the general manager and we discuss company affairs, and I attend daily meetings with the employees.

1 a fruit; b i; c i; d ii; e the general manager; f daily

2 b١; e٢; a٣; d٤; c٥

2 maadhaa ta:mal fii awqaat al-faraagh? *What do you do in your free time?*
Translation:

Ali What do you do in your leisure time, Hisham?

Hisham I play golf, and I swim. When we lived in Amman I used to play tennis, but I don't play now. I read a lot.

Ali I read a lot too. I like modern poetry. Do you like poetry, Ruhiyyah?

Ruhiyyah No, I prefer novels. I watch television a lot, and I like the Egyptian serials.

Ali I don't like them.

Hisham Me neither. I really hate them. I prefer cultural programmes, or sports, but Ruhiyyah doesn't like sport.

Ruhiyyah But we both like the cinema. We are going to the cinema this evening. Will you come with us, Ali?

3 a tennis; b reading a lot; c Ruhiyyah; d Go to the cinema; e i

4 a١; e٢; d٣; b٤; c٥

5 Hameed, 3

6

١ ليس هذا الجمل قبيحا ٢ ليست البيوت رخيصة في الرياض ٣ لن نسافر إلى الهند في الشهر القادم ٤ ما ذهبنا/لم نذهب إلى المسبح يوم الجمعة ٥ أختي لا تعمل في صيدلية ٦ ما درس/ لم يدرس صالح في أمريكا

7

١ لها ٢ معه ٣ علينا ٤ مني ٥ إليه

8

حميد يلعب كرة وسكواش. يحب التنس والسباحة لا يحب القراءة والكتب. يكره السينما
والتلفزيون.

9

١ يتعلمون ٢ تتصل ٣ نشرب ٤ أكتب ٥ يكلمـنا ٦ تعرفين ٧ تقفل ٨ يصلن ٩ يلعبن
١٠ يكسبون

10

١ يسأل ٢ تحمل ٣ يفحص ٤ يقدم ٥ (لا) أفهم ٦ تذهب

11 a March; b price reductions and valuable prizes; c cultural events/artistic
events/sporting events/horse races/fireworks; d above the famous Dubai creek

Unit 11

al-a:yaad al-islaamiyyah *Islamic festivals*
Literal translation:

Jack *how-many festival with the-muslims?*
Ahmad *the-festivals the-important with-us [are] two.*
Fran *and-what [are] they-two?*
Ahmad *the-first he [is] the-festival the-small and-name-his [is] festival [of]
the-fast-breaking*
Jack *and in which month he?*
Ahmad *festival [of] the-fast-breaking he [is] in first day [of] month [of]
Shawal*
Fran *and what [is] occasion-his?*
Ahmad *occasion-his [is] that [the] month [of] Shawal he-follows [the] month
[of] Ramadan the-holy, and-he [the] month [of] the-fasting with the-Muslims*
Jack *and what [is] meaning [of] the-fasting with-you?*
Ahmad *the-fasting, his-meaning [is] that the-people not they-eat and-not they-
drink in the-daytime. This he [is] meaning of the-fasting*
Fran *and what [is] he the-festival the-other?*
Ahmad *he [is] the-festival the-great or festival [of] the-sacrifice*
Jack *and what [is] occasion-his?*
Ahmad *occasion-his [is] the-pilgrimage and he-begins in last day of [the] days
[of] the pilgrimage. And the-pilgrimage, meaning-his [is] that the-people they-
travel to Mecca the-Holy and-they-visit the-Kaabah*
Fran *and how they-celebrate (for) this the-festival?*

Ahmad *they they-slaughter in-him [i.e. it] sacrifice (animals)*

Jack *and what [is] she the-sacrifice(animal)?*

Ahmad *the sacrifice (animal) she [is a] sheep [which] they-slaughter-him and-they-eat-him in [the] end [of] the-pilgrimage. And he [i.e. it] [is a] custom with the-muslims*

Fran *so festivals-your two only then?*

Ahmad *no, in some [of] the-regions they celebrate (with) festival third*

Jack *and what [is] he?*

Ahmad *he [is] birthday [of] the-prophet* PBUH* *in [the] month [of] Rabii the-first*

Fran *yes, this [is] like [the] festival [of] the-birth with-us we the Christians*

* Peace and Prayers be Upon Him (said after the name of the Prophet)

1 a two; b Ramadan; c eating and drinking in the daytime;

2 aii; bi; ci; d they sacrifice a sheep; e the Prophet's birthday

3 c١; f٢; i٣; d٤; j٥; a٦; h٧; e٨; g٩; b١٠

4 f١; c٢; h٣; i٤; a٥; j٦; b٧; g٨; d٩; e١٠

5 ٦، ٣، ١٢، ٢، ٨، ١١، ٥، ١٠، ١، ٤، ٩، ٧

6

١ الملك له قصور كثيرة ٢ أنت عندك أخت طويلة ٣ أنتم عندكم أولاد صغار ٤ أنا عندي آلة حاسبة جديدة ٥ المدرس عنده ٥٠ تلميذا ٦ نحن عندنا سيارة ألمانية ٧ هم عندهم حقائب ثقيلة ٨ الشركة لها ٥ فروع ٩ محمد عنده شقة واسعة ١٠ سميرة عندها فستان جميل

١ الملك كان له قصور كثيرة ٢ أنت كان عندك أخت طويلة ٣ أنتم كان عندكم أولاد صغار ٤ أنا كان عندي آلة حاسبة جديدة ٥ المدرس كان عنده ٥٠ تلميذا

7 a

8 ١ Ali–3rd; ٢ Hamdan–6th; ٣ Siham–2nd; ٤ Mustafa–9th; ٥ Abdullah–8th; ٦ Noora–10th; ٧ Hameed–1st

9

a يذهب إلى الصف الرابع، والصف السادس عشر والصف الثاني عشر

b تذهب إلى الصف الحادي عشر والصف العاشر والصف الخامس عشر

c تذهب إلى الصف السادس عشر والصف الثالث والصف التاسع

d يذهب إلى الصف الثاني والصف الرابع عشر والصف الثامن عشر

e تذهب إلى الصف الأول والصف الثالث عشر والصف السادس

Unit 12

SafHat al-mar'ah Woman's page
Literal translation:
Journalist (female) *welcome*
Leila *welcome to-you*
Journalist *firstly what [is] nationality-your?*
Leila *I (am) Lebanese from Beirut*
Journalist *and-age-your?*
Leila *age-my 28 year*
Journalist *how you-began in profession (of) showing the-fashions?*
Leila *since childhood-my. I-like showing the-fashions because-they (are a) kind (of the) kinds (of) the-art. for-that I-entered into this field.*
Journalist *(?) you-studied the-arts?*
Leila *yes I-studied the-arts in the-university and-I-specialised in designing (of) the-fashions*
Journalist *and-what you-aspire to-it in profession-your?*
Leila *ambition-my he (is the) founding (an) agency world(wide) for-showing the-fashions (which) it-includes (male-)models and (female-)models western and-Arab*
Journalist *and-thing other-than this?*
Leila *(the) designing (of) fashions (which) they-carry (a) label international in-name-my*
Journalist *and-how you-keep slimness-your?*
Leila *I-follow (a) diet and-I-practise the-exercise the-light*
Journalist *and-beauty-your?*
Leila *indeed-I I-prefer the-beauty the-natural, and-for-this (reason) I-leave hair-my to nature-its, and-not I-like putting (on) the-make-up except for-(the)-requirements (of) modelling only*
Journalist *thanks to-you*
Leila *thanks*

1 a false; b true; c true; d false
2 a i; b iii; c have her own international label; d diet and light exercise; e natural beauty; f she only uses it for work
3 c١; d٢; g٣; a٤; f٥; e٦; b٧
4

a منطقة زراعية؛ b المطار الدولي؛ c قمر صناعي؛ d السوق المركزي/المركزية؛ e البنك الوطني؛
f السفارةالهندية؛ g الشؤون الخارجية؛ h الأزياء النسائية؛ i منطقة صناعية؛ j طبيخ عربي؛
k المتحف الشعبي؛ l البريد الجوي؛ m القنصلية الأمريكية؛ n الإدارة البلدية؛ o منطقة عسكرية؛
p بريد خارجي؛ q الآثار التاريخية؛ r الدراسات الأدبية؛ s العلوم الطبيعية؛ t الألعاب النارية؛
u القصر الملكي؛ v المستشفى المركزي؛ w بريد داخلي؛ x الأجهزة الكهربائية؛ y الديوان الأميري

Unit 13

ibtasim, anta fi sh-shaariqah *Smile, you're in Sharjah*
Literal translation:
With this the-phrase the-welcoming which overflows with-all the-feelings [of]
the-friendship the-true she-greets [the-]Sharjah her-guests. And Emirate [of]
the-Sharjah she [is] one [of] emirates [of the] state [of] the-Emirates the-Arab
the-United which she-occupies [a] situation geographical prominent on-the-Gulf
the-Arab. And-he [is a] situation [which] has-caused the-Sharjah she-enjoys [i.e.
to enjoy] over [the] extent [of] the-ages [a] role leading among [the] countries
[of] the-Gulf the-Arab as [a] centre [of the] most-important [of] centres [of]
the-activity the-commercial.
And-he-is-estimated [the] number [of] the-inhabitants according-to [the] latest
the-census which was-carried-out [in] year 1995 at-about half million individual
that [is] in-density [which] is-estimated at-about 190 individual to-the-kilometre
the-square.
Sharjah is-considered [to be] of the-Emirates the-first on [the] level [of the]
region [of] the-Gulf which she-pursued [the] method [of] the-planning the-
scientific the-comprehensive in-what is-concerned with-projects [of] the-
development the-economic and-the-agricultural and-the-touristic and-the-social
and-the cultural etc.
And-Sharjah she-is-described by-that-she [is] the-capital the-cultural for-[the]
state [of] the-Emirates, and-there [is a] department special [which] she-looks-
after [the] implementation [of] the-activities the-cultural in the-Emirate, also
she-comprises the-Emirate [a] number [of] the-museums the-scientific and-the-
historical the-magnificent and [a] station from [the] most-modern [of] stations
[of] the-transmission the-televisual [which] she-broadcasts the-many of the-
programmes the-cultural and-the-educational.

1 a Smile you are in Sharjah; b on the Arabian Gulf; c commercial; d half a
million; e economic/ agricultural/ touristic/ social / cultural; f cultural;
g museums; h cultural and educational
2 a١; d٢; f٣; h٤; b٥; g٦; c٧; e٨
3 *definite:*

التي تفيض بكل مشاعر الود... / التي تحتل موقعا... /التي انتهجت أسلوب التخطيط... /
التي أجريت عام ١٩٩٥....

indefinite:

دائرة خاصة ترعى... / موقع جعل الشارقة تتمتع... /بكثافة تقدر بحوالي ١٩٠ نسمة
للكيلومتر المربع... / تذيع الكثير من البرامج...

4

١ هذا هو البيت الذي سنستأجره

٢ زارني عامل يعمل في مصنع

٣ شاهدت الطبيب الذي عيادته في وسط المدينة

٤ خالد الذي قرأت كتابه يدرس في المدرسة الثانوية

٥ كان الكرسي الذي جلست عليه مكسورا

٦ الطلبة الذين يدرسون في الجامعة من الإمارات

٧ رسالة كتبها الأسبوع الماضي وصلت اليوم

٨ القمصان التي يبيعونها في السوق مصنوعة في الصين

٩ مغنية كانت مشهورة قبل سنوات كثيرة ستزور سورية

١٠ ابني له صديق أصله اسكتلندي

5

١ لقد أعيد بناء منزل الشيخ صقر الكائن في هذه المنطقة

٢ في هذه المنطقة يمكن مشاهدة أول أشكال تكييف الهواء، البرجيل، الذي كان يستخدم لتبريد البيوت في الخليج. جددت القلعة التي شيدت في القرن الماضي، وحولت إلى متحف.

٣ الطرق الضيقة تأخذ الزائر إلى سوق التوابل التي تنبعث منها روائح أنواع التوابل كلها مثل القرنفل والهال والقرفة التي تباع إلى الزوار من الأكياس التي تحيط المتاجر.

٤ سباقات الهجن رياضة شعبية تقام أيام الجمعة أثناء أشهر الشتاء.

6

١ عمر الشريف ممثل مصري لعب أدوارا مشهورة كثيرة

٢ ذهبنا إلى مدينة البتراء القديمة التي اكتشفت سنة ١٨١٨.

٣ في مصر آثار فرعونية مهمة يزورها سواح كثيرون.

٤ يعمل زوجي في الشارقة التي تقع في الخليج العربي.

٥ نستأجر شقة في دمشق يسكن صاحبها في الرياض.

٦ سافروا إلى عدن بطائرة الصبح التي وصلت الظهر.

7

Unit 14

Koshari

Literal translation:
The-Koshari
(the-amount she-suffices 6 persons)
The-Quantities
4 cups and-half rice, it-is-washed and-it-is-strained
Cup [of] lentils black
Half cup [of] oil
Salt according-to the-desire
7 cups and-half [of] the-cup [of] water for-the-rice
10 cups [of] water for-boiling [of] the-macaroni
two-cups [of] macaroni
two spoons [of] food (i.e. tablespoons) [of] oil for-the-macaroni
6 onions cut into slices long
The-sauce
two-spoons [of] food [of] ghee
6 fruits [of] tomato peeled and-chopped
[a] spoon small [of] pepper red hot milled
two-spoons [of] food of paste [of] the-tomatoes
salt according-to the-desire
The- method
1- soak the-lentils in-the-water for-period [of] 6 hours and strain-it
2- fry the-onions in-the-oil then lift-them and-leave-them aside. Pour the-water over-them and-leave-them until they-boil a-little, then add the-rice and-the-lentils and-leave-them on fire gentle for-period [of] 40 minute.
3- boil the-macaroni in-the-water then add the-oil
4- fry the-tomatoes in-the-oil, then add the pepper and the paste [of] the-tomatoes and-the-salt.
5- during the-presenting (i.e. serving) place [the] mixture [of] the-rice and-the-lentils firstly, then [a] layer of the-macaroni then [a] layer of the-onions, and-sprinkle over-it the-sauce the-hot or present-it to [the] side [of] the-plate.

1 a 6; b four and a half times as much; c 6 hours; d 40 minutes; e onions; f tomato sauce

2 c١; e٢; d٣; a٤; b٥

3 ic; iid; iiib; iva; ve

4 ic; iia; iiid; ivb

5 a i٢/ii١; b 1 Dirham, 50 fils; c Fridays & holidays; d 4 hours; e 5 Dirhams; f اضغط

6 d١; h٢; g٣; b٤; a٥; c٦; e٧; f٨

7 a 8 dirhams; b selection of cheeses; c macaroni; d today only

7 e

تعالوا، اشتروا، شاهدوا، اطبخوا. جربوا

8 a

١ ارسله ٢ اكتبها ٣ اتصل

b

١ ضعيه ٢ اتركيه ٣ اغسليها

Unit 15
al-:arab fii huuliiwuud *Arabs in Hollywood*
Literal translation:

Salma the-Arab [girl] *who she-conquered Hollywood*
In the-East we-regard-her [as the] *ambassadress* [of] *the-beauty the-Arab who she-was-able that she-be* [the] *first woman* [who] *she-penetrates* [the] *walls* [of] *Hollywood and-she-imposes self-her on* [the] *top* [of the] *list* [of the] *stars* of] *the-cinema.*

And-in the-West they-regard-her [as a] *symbol of-*[the]*-magic* [of] *the-East by-what she-bears-it of features oriental* [the] *extreme in the-beauty which it-equals the-magic and-for-this they-gave-her the-leads in* [the] *greatest* [of] *films-their preferring-her to most* [of the] *stars* [of] *Hollywood beauty-wise and-so Salma Hayek today she-competes* [with] *Sharon Stone and-Demi Moore and-other-*[than]*-them-two of* [the] *stars* [of] *Hollywood.*

And-Salma al-Hayek, or [the] *legend* [of] *the-East in the-West, the-born* [in the] *year 1966 she* [is the] *daughter* [of an] *emigrant Lebanese residing in-Mexico mother-her Spanish* [of] *the-origin and-if came-together the-beauty the-Lebanese and-the-Spanish will-be the-fruit in* [the] *beauty* [of] *Salma al-Hayek. And-because-she* [is] *beautiful very so-*[past marker] *spotted-her* [the] *eye* [of] *the-producers and-she in the-thirteenth* [year] *of age-her and-she-was-chosen at-that-time as-*[the]*-most-beautiful* [of] *the-faces the-television. Then he-took-her the-producer Tarantino to-Los Angeles so-she-participates in the-film Desperado at* [the] *side* [of] *Antonio Banderas and-she-gave to-the-film* [a] *flavour special very* [which] *it-attracted to-her* [the] *interest* [of the] *companies* [of] *the-production the-great and-soon they-offered to-her the-roles the-many in-fact indeed-she she-took recently* [a] *part it-was of the-assumed that it-be-entrusted to-*[a]*-singer famous American but* [the] *producers* [of] *Hollywood they-preferred Salma to-her and-*[it is]*-of the-certain that this the-film it-will-give to-Salma eminence greater power-wise and-popularity-wise.*

1 a breach the walls of Hollywood; b her oriental features; c Sharon Stone and Demi Moore; d 1966; e Spain; f 13; g Desperado; h Power and popularity
2 c١; e٢; a٣; d٤; b٥

3 a spend more than 250 Dirhams; **b i** 8th April; **ii** more than 20 years; **c** spaghetti; **d** gold and cash; **e** your money will arrive in minutes; **f** use the Privilege card
4 a

٤ له قرص ثابت أحسن.	١ هذا الكمبيوتر له شاشة أكبر
٥ هو أسهل استعمالا.	٢ له موديم أسرع.
٦ هو أرخص.	٣ له ذاكرة أصغر.

b 1B; 2B; 3A; 4B; 5A; 6A

Unit 16

al-laylah s-sawdaa'

Literal translation:
Night black for-the [foot]*ball the-Moroccan*
Qualified the-team the-Tunisian for-the-round the-final of (the)competition (of the) Cup (of) the-Arabs in night black for-the [foot]*ball the-Moroccan. And-on (the) pitch of-the-Zamalek in the-Cairo yesterday, and-before 42 thousand spectator led Mahmoud al-Turki the-team the-Tunisian to-the-victory. And-scored al-Turki [on] own-his three goals in the-match which ended 5-.1*
And-opened the-team the-Tunisian the-scoring by way (of) its-centre Jaafar Abu Adil with (a)shot splendid from outside the-area (which) deceived the-goalkeeper the-Moroccan in-the-minute the-ninth of-the-match. And-was (the)-result of the-opportunity the-first for-the-team the-Moroccan their-goal the-sole in (the) end (of) the-half the-first when shot Tariq al-Ahmar (a) ball curved (which) entered (the) corner (of) the-goal the-Tunisian and gained the-equality.
But-it appeared that the-players the-Moroccan [past marker] raised the-flag the-white in-the-half the-second and-dominated the-Tunisians [on] the-play domination complete. And-came the-goals with-speed, (the) last-(of)-them in the-minute the-last of-the-match when placed the-captain the-Tunisian the-ball [in] the-net the-Moroccan for-the-time the-third after awarded the-referee kick corner and-sent-off the-defender the-Moroccan Suleiman al-Fasi for-his-getting the-card the-yellow the-second.

1 a i; **b** iii; **c** Cairo; **d** 42,000; **e** three; **f** Tunisia; **g** Tariq al-Ahmar (Morocco); **h** the last minute of the match; **i** he got a 2nd yellow card and was sent off; **j** Morocco.

2 c١; **d**٢; **f**٣; **a**٤; **e**٥; **b**٦

3 1g; 2e; 3d; 4l; 5a; 6j; 7h; 8f; 9c; 10k; 11b; 12i

4 a Dhs. 2700; **b** 3; **c** 10yrs; **d** i; **e** ii; **f** Dhs. 260; **g** any three of: gym, aerobics, library, swimming pool, ice-skating, café

5 see transcript

Never	Rarely	Sometimes	Frequently	Daily
1		tennis	golf	
2				gym
3	swim		skating	
4		swim, sail		
5	sail		aerobics	

6

١ افتح الباب بسرعة. عندنا ضيف.

٢ ذهبت إلى السوق قابلت أحمد هناك صدفة.

٣ كان ذلك البرنامج مهما جدا.

٤ كنا جالسين في البيت، وقام زيد فجأة وخرج.

٥ تسافر هذه الطائرة إلى الرياض مباشرة.

٦ يا أولاد، العبوا بهدوء، الوالد نائم.

7

١ يحتاج علي إلى جزمة سوداء.

٢ تحتاج سونية إلى فستان أصفر.

٣ يحتاج سعيد إلى قميص أخضر.

٤ يحتاج خالد إلى جوارب بيضاء.

٥ تحتاج فريدة إلى بنطلون أحمر.

٦ يحتاج حامد إلى حزام بني.

٧ تحتاج أنيسة إلى حقيبة وردية.

Unit 17

in shaa' Al-laah

Literal translation:

The broadcaster: *Here (is) Voice (of) the-Arabs from Cairo. Produced (a) company Egyptian three cassettes educational for-simplification (of the) rules (of) the-grammar in the-language the-Arabic. And* [past marker] *participated in preparation (of) the-tapes the-Professor Ibrahim Mahmoud from Faculty (of) the-Arts in University (of) Cairo and-the-specialist in teaching (of) the-language the-Arabic. Welcome to Professor Ibrahim.*

Professor Ibrahim *Thanks.*

B *Firstly,* [question marker] *these the-cassettes for-the-Arabs or the-foreigners?*

P *For-the-Arabs*

B *But the-Arabs they-know the-language the-Arabic,* [question marker]-*is-not like-that?*

P *Naturally they-know-her, but-[it] there (are) in the-language the-Arabic the-literary difficulties (which) not understands-them except the-cultured. And-even in year 1925 was Academy (of) the-language the-Arabic he-discusses* [i.e. was discussing] *some (of) these the-difficulties and-they-published their-resolutions the-scientific.*

B *And-your-aim therefore in production (of) these the-tapes that you-help the-*

public in the-world the-Arab in the-writing the-correct and-the-style the-good?
P *With-the-exactness* [exactly], *and-in-way modern (which) we-hope that-it attract interest (of) the-youth, if God willed.*
B *If God willed. Thanks to-you O Professor Ibrahim.*
P *You're welcome.*

1 a 3 educational cassettes; b teaching Arabic; c for the Arabs; d the difficulties of literary Arabic; e to help people write correctly and with a good style; f young people
2 1d; 2h; 3e; 4f; 5a; 6g; 7c; 8b

al-mashruu: naajiH

Literal translation:
And-began the-company distribution (of) the-tapes in the-markets the-Egyptian with beginning (of) the-year the-current 2000, and-found reception good from the-pupils and-the-teachers in variety (of) stages (of) the-education the-elementary and-the-preparatory and-the-secondary and-[past marker] *was-sold during the-two-months the-past half (of) the-quantity the-projected.*
And-intends the-company in the-period the-near the-future the-descent to-the-markets the-Arab with-these the-cassettes, whether in exhibitions (of) the-books or the-bookshops the-various. And-says sources (of) the-company that this she (is) the-time the-first which is-simplified in-it rules (of) the-language the-Arabic in-this the-form in the-world the-Arab, although was the-television the-Iraqi [past marker] *produced* [i.e. had produced] *before more than 10 years programme for-same purpose.*

3 a Egypt; b pupils and teachers; c half of them; d to the Arab market, at book exhibitions or bookshops; e it's the first time the rules of Arabic have been simplified in this way; f Iraqi television
4 1c; 2e; 3g; 4f; 5a; 6d; 7b
5 a إنتاج **intaaj** *production, producing*
b إصدار **iSdaar** *publishing, publication*
c إكرام **ikraam** *hospitality*
d إسلام **islaam** *Islam*
e إرسال **irsaal** *sending, broadcasting*
f إجبار **ijbaar** *compelling, forcing, compulsion*
g إقبال **iqbaal** *approaching*
h إلهام **ilhaam** *inspiration*
i إغلاق **ighlaaq** *locking, shutting*
j إفساد **ifsaad** *spoiling*
6 a: 1f; 2a; 3e; 4g; 5b; 6c; 7d
b no

7

١ لو كنت غنيا، لاشتريت سيارة جديدة.

٢ لو كانت تعلمت الطباعة كانت كسبت راتبا أعلى.

٣ لو كان عندي الرقم، لكنت اتصلت به.

٤ لو كنت أكثر اجتهادا في دراساتك، لنجحت في الامتحانات.

٥ لو كانوا زاروا أمهم أمس لكانت خبرتهم عن مرضها.

٦ لو لم يوقف الضابط اللصوص في الجمرك، لكانوا ركبوا الطائرة.

Unit 18

1 miSr *Egypt*

Literal translation:

Egypt

The-antiquities the-Egyptian in the-abroad

He-stated head [of the] department [of the] antiquities the-Egyptian yesterday about welcoming-his of-resolution [of] the-assembly the-general to-the-Nations the-United to-the-allowing to-the-states which to-them antiquities smuggled in the-abroad for-reclaiming-them. And-he-said that-it there approximately 12 million piece archaeological Egyptian stolen in the-West most-famous-[of]-them beard [of] Father of Terror [i.e. the Sphinx] and stone [of] Rosetta the-situated in the-Museum the-British in London.

1 a the head of the Egyptian Antiquities Department; b antiquities; c the sphinx's beard and the Rosetta stone

2

c ذقن أبو الهول	a رئيس دائرة الآثار المصرية
d حجر رشيد	b حوالي ١٢ مليون

2 al-yaman *Yemen*

Literal translation:

the-Yemen

450 tourist European in Aden

Received port [of] Aden yesterday the-first [i.e. the day before yesterday] ship touristic German [which] she-carries more than 400 tourist[male] and-tourist [female] from various [of] the-nationalities the-European. And-[future marker]-visit these the-tourists some [of] the-towns the-Yemeni the-historical

3 a a German tourist ship; b more than 400 tourists; c visit some of Yemen's historical towns

4

b سيزور هؤلاء السواح بعض المدن اليمنية   a من مختلف الجنسيات

3 amriikaa America
Literal translation:
America
Announced millionaire American from state [of] California in the-week the-past
that-he [future marker] marry [a] girl in the-fifth and-the-twenty of life-her. And-
this after celebrating-his of-anniversary [of] birth-his the-hundredth by-days few.
And-he he-uses regulator for-beats [of] the-heart and-he- is transported on chair
with-wheels. And-he-said that-he he-loves-her from all [of] his-heart and-she
returns-him the-love

5 a 25; b 100; c pacemaker, wheelchair; d with all his heart
6

c من كل قلبه   a سيتزوج فتاة
b قال انه يحبها

4 abuu DHabii Abu Dhabi
Literal translation:
Abu Dhabi
She-arrived to The-Emirates today the-singer the-Lebanese the-famous Fairuz in
visit private, [future marker]- she-visits during-it brother-her who he-resides in
Abu Dhabi.

7 a Lebanese singer; b for a private visit
8

b ستزور أخاها   a وصلت الى الامارات اليوم

5 nyuu yuurk
Literal translation:
New York
Chose organisation [of] the-UNESCO [the] day 21 March [as a] day world-wide
for-the-poetry. And-welcomed the-poets the-Arab [with]-this, among-them the-
poet the-Iraqi Ali Jaafar al-Allaq who he-said that-he [was] "Believing belief not
limits to-it that the-poetry [is] bigger than the-time all-[of]-it, and-more extent-
wise than the-places totally. Indeed-it [is] filler [of] the-moments and-the-seasons
and-the-centuries with-beauty [of] the-meaning and meaning [of] the-beauty".

9 a World poetry day; b an Iraqi poet; c all time
10

a رحب الشعراء العرب بهذا

b الشعر أكبر من الزمان كله

c انه مالئ اللحظات بجمال المعنى

11
Unit 1: وحيد **waHiid** *unique*
Unit 2: بارد **baarid** *cold*
Unit 3: مضبوط **maDbuuT** *exact, accurate*
Unit 4: ملعب **mal:ab** *playing field/court/pitch*
Unit 5: فطور **fuTuur** *breakfast*
Unit 6: طباعة **Tibaa:ah** *printing, typing*
Unit 7: تفاهم **tafaahum** *(mutual) understanding*
Unit 8: رسام **rassaam** *artist*
Unit 9: معلم **mu:allim** *teacher, instructor, master*
Unit 10: علماء **:ulamaa'** *scholars, religious leaders*
Unit 11: فضائل **faDaa'il** *advantages, good points*
Unit 12: تفسير **tafsiir** *explanation, interpretation*
Unit 13: مناظر **manaaZir** *views, sights*
Unit 14: استكشاف **istikshaaf** *discovery, act of trying to discover*
Unit 15: مفتاح **miftaaH** *key*
Unit 16: لخبطة **lakhbaTah** *mix up, mess*
Unit 17: إقناع **iqnaa:** *convincing, conviction*
12

١ أمي

٢ أب

٣ أبو صالح

٤ رئيس

٥ قلب

13
1 F; 2 T; 3 T; 4 F; 5 T; 6 F; 7 F; 8 T; 9 T; 10 F
14

١ درس الطلبة كلهم للامتحانات.

٢ وصل السواح كلهم من ألمانيا.

٣ تفتح الدكاكين كلها في المساء.

٤ رحب الموظفون كلهم بتقرير المدير.

٥ استقبلته أخواته كلهن في المطار.

٦ وضعت الكتب كلها على الرف.

LISTENING TRANSCRIPTS

Unit 4

Exercise 9
(all preceded by **as-sáa:ah...**)

a **tis:ah**

b **thalaatha wa-niSf**

c **ithna:shar illaa rub:**

d **arba:ah wa-thulth**

e **ithna:shar wa-:asharah**

f **ithnayn illa khamsah**

Exercise 14
(all preceded by **as-sáa:ah...**)

a **síttah wa-nuSS (niSf) wa-khámsah**

b **thamáanyah wa-:ásharah**

c **tís:ah wa-nuSS (niSf)ílla khámsah**

d **sáb:ah**

e **árba:ah ílla rub:**

f **khámsah wa-nuSS**

g **wáaHidah wa-rub:**

h **wáaHidah ílla khámsah**

i **thaláathah wa-thulth**

j **:ásharah wa-khámsah**

Unit 5

Exercise 5

a **tis:ah wa-tis:iin dirham**

b **tis:ah wa-thamaaniin dirham**

c **khamsah wa-sittiin dirham**

d **khamsiin dirham**

e **ithnain wa-arba:iin dirham**

f **tis:ah wa-sab:iin dirham**

g **khamsah wa-:ishriin dirham**

Unit 6

Exercise 5

a أين البلدية؟

b أين مركز الشرطة؟

c أين مركز التسوق «البستان»؟

d أين شارع الملك فيصل؟

e أين مطعم شهرزاد؟

Exercise 6

a على شمال الميدان، أمام سوق السمك

b وراء الميدان، بين سوق السمك والبنك

c أمام برج الاتصالات على شمال الصيدلية

d بين الكورنيش وشارع جمال عبد الناصر

e وراء مركز الشرطة بين سوق الذهب والفندق

Unit 14
Exercise 7

تعالوا إلى قسم اللحوم! اشتروا بأسعار مذهلة!
تنزيلات في لحم الغنم المفروم الكيلو بـ ٨ دراهم.
شاهدوا تشكيلة الجبن من فرنسا وإيطاليا.
أطبخوا وجبة معكرونة للعائلة اليوم. جربوا جبنة الحلوم اللذيذة.
أسعارخاصة لليوم فقط.

Unit 16
Exercise 5

Example:

سؤال   ماذا تحب من الرياضات؟
جواب ألعب كرة القدم كثيرا

١   ماذا تلعب يا يونس؟
ألعب تنس أحيانا، لكن ألعب جولف كثيرا

٢   وأنت يا سعيد؟
أذهب إلى القاعة الرياضية يوميا

٣   هل تمارسين السباحة يا فريدة؟
لا، أمارس السباحة نادرا. أفضل التزلج. أمارس التزلج كثيرا

٤   هل تمارس السباحة يا حامد؟
نعم، أسبح أحيانا، وأحيانا أركب الزوارق الشراعية

٥   يا سونية، هل ركبت الزوارق الشراعية؟
لا أبدا. أمارس الايروبيك كثيرا

GLOSSARY OF LANGUAGE TERMS

Accent See stress.

Adjectives Adjectives describe a person or thing, e.g. a *huge* building, I am *tired*. In Arabic these have the same properties as nouns, and must agree with them in number, gender and definiteness.

Adverbs Adverbs describe how, when or where the action of a verb occurs or has occurred. In English they usually end in *-ly*, e.g. *quickly*. In Arabic they either end in **-an** or are phrases such as *with speed*, i.e. *quickly*.

Agreement This term describing changes in one word caused by another mainly applies to nouns and adjectives, and verbs, which must agree with their subjects, e.g. feminine subject requires feminine verb.

Articles The words *a* or *an* (*indefinite* article), and *the* (*definite* article). Arabic has no indefinite article, so to say *a book* you just say *book*. The definite article **al-** is attached or prefixed to the following word.

Comparative Adjectives which compare two things. In English they often end in *-er* or are preceded by the word *more,* e.g. *brighter/more intelligent*.

Conjunctions Words which join parts of sentences, e.g. *and*, *or*, *but*.

Consonants The non-vowel letters, e.g. **b, d, g, dh, DH**.

Demonstratives See pronouns.

Dual A special form in Arabic to refer to *two* of anything, as opposed to one (singular) and more than two (plural).

Elision Where part of a word – usually a vowel – is omitted to smooth speech.

Gender Masculine or feminine. See nouns and adjectives.

Hidden t The feminine ending of a noun **-ah**, which in certain contexts changes to **-at**.

Imperative The form of a verb used when telling someone to do something.

Interrogatives Question words. See also under pronouns.

Negatives These are words used to negate or deny something, e.g. *no*, *not*. Arabic uses different words with nouns/adjectives and verbs.

Nouns A noun is the name of a person, thing, place or an abstract concept, e.g. *Hassan, boy, book, Dubai, economics*. In Arabic a noun has three important properties:

1. It is either *masculine* or *feminine*. There is no 'neuter', or *it*, used in English to describe inanimate objects or abstracts. This is called *gender* .

2. It is either *singular* (one only), *dual* (two only) or *plural*(more than two). English does not have a dual. This is called *number*.

3. It is either *definite* or *indefinite*. The noun refers either to an unspecified person or thing or to a specific one. In English indefinites are often preceded by *a* or *an*, but this is omitted in Arabic. Definites are often preceded by *the*, *this*, *that* etc., or *his*, *her*. Names of people, places (words with capital letters in English) are automatically definite, e.g. *Ahmed, Bahrain*. The concept of definiteness is very important in Arabic as it affects other words in the sentence. (Note that pronouns are always definite.)

Number See nouns and adjectives.

Numbers The numbers or numerals divide into two sets, *cardinal*, e.g. *one, two, three* and *ordinal*, e.g. *first, second, third*.

Object The object of a verb is the thing or person which the action of the verb affects. It contrasts with the subject, e.g. *the dog* (subject) *chased the cat* (object).

Phrase A phrase is a part of a sentence, not necessarily making sense on its own, but useful for describing features of a language, e.g. *the big house* .

Plural More than one. See nouns and adjectives.

Possessive When something owns or possesses something else. In English we either add *s* to the noun, e.g. *Charlie's aunt*, or use a possessive pronoun, e.g. *my father,* or the word *of*, e.g. *the manager of the company*.

Prefix A short part of a word added to the beginning of a noun or verb, e.g. English *un-*, *dis-* or *pre-*. In Arabic prefixes alter the meaning of a verb.

Prepositions Usually short words relating a noun to its place in space or time, e.g. *in*, *on*, *with*. In Arabic a few common prepositions are prefixed to the following word.

Pronouns Pronouns are used as substitutes for nouns. The English personal pronoun *he* has three forms: subject *he*, object *him*, and possessive *his* (in other pronouns such as *you* some of these forms have fused together), e.g. *He* isn't at home (subject pronoun), We saw *him* (object pronoun)and It is *his* house (possessive pronoun). *Subject* pronouns have equivalent words in Arabic. *Object* pronouns and *possessive* pronouns share the same form in Arabic, and are not separate words, but endings or suffixes attached to their nouns.

Other types of pronoun are demonstratives, e.g. *this*, *that*, relatives, e.g. *who*, *which*, *that* (in phrases like *the one that I like best*) and interrogatives *who*, *what* and *which* (used in questions like *who goes there?*).

Relatives See pronouns.

Sentence A sentence is a complete utterance making sense on its own, e.g. *he is in his room*. In English these must contain a verb, but sentences with *is* and *are* do not have a verb in Arabic. For instance, the sentence above would be *he in his room* in Arabic.

Stem See verbs

Stress Also called accent. This is the part or syllable of a word which is most emphasised, e.g. the first *o* in English *photograph*. In the first few units of this book, stress has been marked with an accent: á,ú etc.

Subject The subject of a sentence is the person or thing which is carrying out the action. It can be a noun, pronoun or a phrase as in: *Bill* lives in Abu Dhabi, *He* works for the oil company, *The best picture* will win the prize.

Suffix An ending attached to a word which alters its meaning.

Superlatives Applied to adjectives when they express the highest level of a quality. In English they end in *-est* or are preceded by *most* , e.g. *the brightest/most intelligent boy*. See also comparatives.

Tense See verbs.

Verbs A 'doing' word expressing an action, e.g. *He reads* the newspaper every day. Its most important features are:

1. *Tense*. This tells us when the action is/was performed. In Arabic there are only two tenses, present (*I go, am going*) and past (*I went, I have gone*). The future (*I shall go*) is the same as the present with a special prefix.

2. *Inflections*. This means that the prefix and/or suffix of the verb changes according to who is doing the action. For instance, in English most verbs in the present tense change, e.g. *I go, they go*, but *he/she/it goes*. In Arabic there is a different verb part for each person, singular and plural. The part of the verb which remains constant in the middle of all the prefixes and suffixes is called the **stem**. This is an important concept in learning Arabic, and may be compared to the *go-* part of *goes* in the example above.

Note a) that the verb *is/are* is omitted in Arabic, and b) the English verb *to have* is not a real verb in Arabic, but a combination of a preposition and a pronoun.

Vowels The sounds equivalent to *a, e, i, o, u* or combinations of them in English. Arabic has *a, i, u* and their long equivalents *aa, ii, uu*. See also consonants.

Word order In Arabic adjectives usually follow their nouns, e.g. *good man* becomes *man good*. Possessive pronouns are also suffixed to their nouns: *my book* becomes *book-my*.

VERB TABLES

The Arabic Verb

The Arabic verb is best considered from three distinct points of view: grammatical, phonetic and stem-modification.

1 Grammatical

The grammatical variations of the verb are there for two main reasons:
a) to tell us who is carrying or has carried out the action. This is important as, unlike English, Arabic commonly omits the subject pronouns *I, you, he,* etc. so the verb itself has to carry this information;
b) to tell us the timing of the action, i.e. when it takes (has taken/will take etc.) place.

Subject markers
The grammatical term for who is responsible for the action of a verb is called *person.*

Like English, Arabic verbs have three persons:
- the person(s) speaking (*I, we*), called the first person;
- the person(s) spoken to (*you*), called the second person;
- the person(s) spoken about (*he, she, it, they*) called the third person.

However, Arabic makes finer distinctions in some cases:
- The second person has to indicate the sex of the person spoken to. This is called *gender.*
- The Arabic verb has a set of parts referring to *two* people known as the *dual.* English only distinguishes between *one* and *more than one.*

Note: Traditionally the Arabic verb is tabled in the reverse order of persons, i.e. starting with the third. This is because the third person *he*-part is regarded as the simplest, most basic form of the verb. This convention has been employed throughout this book.

	Singular	**Dual**	**Plural**
third person	he she*	they two (m.) they two (f.)	they (m.) they (f.)
second person	you (m.) you (f.)	you two (m. & f.)	you (m.) you (f.)
first person	I (m. & f.)	—	we (m. & f.)

* Since Arabic has no neuter gender, English *it* must be rendered *he* or *she* according to the grammatical gender of the Arabic noun.

Tense

The tense of a verb refers to when the action takes/took/will take place. Arabic has only two true tenses, *present* and *past*.

Other grammatical characteristics

The present tense – but not the past – of the Arabic verb has three variants called *moods*. The normal form of the present tense is called the *indicative*, and the other two forms are the *subjunctive* and the *jussive*. These are not so important in Modern Arabic, as often all three look identical. However, in some types of verb the jussive especially shows changes in spelling, and so all three have been included in the tables. The subjunctive and the jussive are mainly used with certain conjunctions. These are dealt with in the main body of the book.

The *imperative* is a special form of the jussive, used in issuing commands. This is not included in the tables, as its formation from the jussive is explained in Unit 14.

Another distinction is that technically known as *voice*. Normal verbs where the subject is responsible for the action are called *active*: *He ate the cake.* So-called *passive* verbs are those where the grammatical subject has the action of the verb performed on it: *The cake was eaten.*

For technical reasons, passives are much less important in Arabic than in English, but they have been included for the sake of completeness.

2 Phonetic

The Arabic verb is relatively regular. Virtually all verbs take the same prefixes and suffixes, and those that vary do so in a minor way. There are, for example, no so-called irregular or strong verbs as proliferate in European languages, such as English *go, went, has gone/is, was, has been,* and so on.

However, there are several phonetic factors which affect verbs:

a) The presence of one of the letters و or ي as a root letter in any position. These letters tend to be elided or smoothed out into vowels.

b) Verb roots where the third consonant is the same as the second, e.g. **d-l-l**, **m-r-r**, etc. This causes contracted verb forms.

c) The letter ء **hamzah** causes some spelling difficulties when it occurs in a root. However, these are learned by experience and observation and no tables have been given.

Note: Verbs which do not have any of the above features have been termed *sound* (abbreviation **S**) in this book.

3 Stem modification

The tenses of the Arabic verb are formed by attaching prefixes and suffixes to the 'heart' or 'nucleus' of the verb, called the *stem*. An approximate English parallel would be to take *talk* as the stem of that verb. In language instruction we can then say that, for instance, you add the suffix *-s* for the *he*-form – *he talks* – and *-ed* to form the past tense – *talked*.

A significant feature of the Arabic verb is *stem modification*, which means that the stems themselves are modified in a finite number of ways to give different meanings. The nearest we get to this in English is *to fall* and *to fell* (a tree) i.e. *cause it to fall*, but in Arabic the phenomenon is very widespread.

Every Arabic verb has the potential to modify its stem in nine different ways, which, by Western (but not Arab) convention are referred to as *derived forms* and indicated using the Roman numerals I–X, Form I being the base form. It is doubtful if any verb possesses the total of ten derived forms, but it is essential to learn them all, as many basic everyday verbs are up in the high numbers.

Table 1: Prefixes and Suffixes of the Verb

This table gives all the prefixes and suffixes which, when applied to the relevant present or past stem, give all the parts of the Arabic verb. It should be studied in conjunction with the following notes.

The table in transliteration follows English order, from left to right.

Hyphen + letter = suffix (e.g. **-at**)

Letter + hyphen = prefix (e.g. **ya-**)

	Past	**Present**	**Subjunctive/ Jussive**
Singular			
he	STEM-**a**	**ya**-STEM	no written change in sound verbs except for parts given
she	STEM-**at**	**ta**-STEM	
you (m.)	STEM-**ta**	**ta**-STEM	
you (f.)	STEM-**ti**	**ta**-STEM-**iina**	**ta**-STEM-**ii**
I	STEM-**tu**	**a**-STEM	
Dual			
they two (m.)	STEM-**aa**	**ya**-STEM-**aani**	**ya**-STEM-**aa**
they two (f.)	STEM-**ataa**	**ta**-STEM-**aani**	**ta**-STEM-**aa**
you two (m & f)	STEM-**tumaa**	**ta**-STEM-**aani**	**ta**-STEM-**aa**
Plural			
they (m.)	STEM-**uu**	**ya**-STEM-**uuna**	**ya**-STEM-**uu**
they (f.)	STEM-**na**	**ya**-STEM-**na**	
you (m.)	STEM-**tum**	**ta**-STEM-**uuna**	**ta**-STEM-**uu**
you (f.)	STEM-**tunna**	**ta**-STEM-**na**	
we	STEM-**naa**	**na**-STEM	

Tip: Make a habit while learning these verb parts of noting which suffixes begin with a vowel, and which with a consonant.

Here is an Arabic example, using the verb *to write*. In order to highlight the prefixes and suffixes, lengthened ligatures (lines joining the letters) have been used, and the vowelling of the past and present stems (كَتَب and كْتُب respectively) has been omitted.

	Past	Present	Subjunctive/ Jussive
Singular			
he	كتبَ	يَكتب	no written change in sound verbs except for parts given
she	كتبَتْ	تَكتب	
you (m.)	كتبْتَ	تَكتب	
you (f.)	كتبْتِ	تَكتبِـينَ	تَكتبِـي
I	كتبْتُ	أكتب	
Dual			
they two (m.)	كتبَا	يَكتبَـانِ	يَكتبَـا
they two (f.)	كتبَتَا	تَكتبَـانِ	تَكتبَـا
you two (m. & f.)	كتبْتُمَا	تَكتبَـانِ	تَكتبَـا
Plural			
they (m.)	كتبُوا	يَكتبُـونَ	يَكتبُـوا
they (f.)	كتبْنَ	يَكتبْنَ	
you (m.)	كتبْتُمْ	تَكتبُـونَ	تَكتبُـوا
you (f.)	كتبْتُنَّ	تَكتبْنَ	
we	كتبْنَا	نَكتب	

Tip: The Arabic version of the tip given above is to note which stems end with a **sukuun** (no vowel sign) on the last consonant of the root and which do not.

Notes

a) The above tables give all the prefixes and suffixes which, when applied to the appropriate stems, give all the parts of any Arabic verb, with the following minor exceptions:

■ with derived stems II, III and IV (see Table **S**) and *all* passive stems (Table **S**) the prefixes of the present tense are vowelled with **u**, i.e. يَ، تَ، أَ، نَ.

■ in certain stems whose final radical is و or ي certain of the endings are slightly modified in pronunciation, but not in writing. These changes are of little importance in practice, but are dealt with in the appropriate tables.

b) Certain short final short vowels are habitually omitted in speech:

■ Past tense: final vowel of *he*, *you* masculine (but not feminine), and *I* in the singular. Any resulting ambiguity is usually cleared up by context.

■ Present tense: **-i** of the dual forms ending in **-aani**, and **-a** of the second person singular feminine and the plural forms ending in **-uuna** (but not the **-a** of the feminine plural **-na** ending).

c) Note carefully the (unpronounced) **alif** written after plural forms ending in **-uu** in both tenses. This is a spelling convention which applies only to this verb suffix.

d) The moods. Where no written changes are indicated in the table, the unsuffixed parts of the indicative originally ended in **-u**, those of the subjunctive in **-a**, and the jussive with no vowel. These are unmarked in Modern Arabic, and have thus been ignored in this book, only parts which differ in spelling having been noted. You will note that verb parts ending in **-uuna** and **-aani** lose their ن in the subjunctive and jussive – see also note c) above. The feminine plural **-na** ending is not affected.

Verb Tables

Introduction

So that you can identify each verb and cross-reference it with the Verb Tables, we have devised the following system, and tagged all the verbs in the vocabularies and glossaries accordingly.

The verb entries are given as in the following example:

كتب **kataba [S-1 u]** *to write*

Reading from left to right these represent:

1 كَتَبَ The *he*-form of the past tense in the Arabic script (see note page . This also in most cases constitutes the past stem.

2 kataba This is the transliteration of the Arabic in **1** above, and provides the vowel of the middle radical (especially relevant to Form I verbs).

3 [S-1 u] This identifies the verb type so that you can look it up in the tables. This example is an S type, Form I [S-I]. The following lower case letter (here **u**) is the vowel to be used in the present stem. It is only necessary to give this vowel for Form I verbs as other types show no variation.

4 *to write* The meaning.

Reminder: In virtually all Arabic verbs, it is only the stem that changes. Once you have learned the prefixes and suffixes given in the table above, you can apply them to all verbs. So, although there appear to be a lot of tables, you only have to learn between two and four stem-parts for each verb. Your task will therefore be much lighter if you spend some time now mastering the prefixes and suffixes thoroughly.

Table S, Sound Verbs [S-I to S-X]

'Sound' in this context means 'without weakness'. The definition in relation to the Arabic verb is simple: a sound verb is one which:

■ does NOT have و or ى as any of its radicals (root consonants)
■ does NOT have the same letter for its middle and last radical (such as ر-د-د, for example).

If a root does not display either of the above two features, it is sound (**S**).

Important note: Since it is impossible to find a verb which occurs in all the derived forms (II–X), we have followed the convention of using the root ف-ع-ل f-:-l in the following table. Although not particularly user-friendly because of the difficult middle consonant, this has the advantage of being the system which the Arabs use. You will therefore be able to seek advice from native speakers.

Verbs in these categories are marked in the glossaries S-I to S-X (but see special notes on Forms I and IX below).

The following table gives the past and present stems. To construct the required verb part, simply add the suffixes and/or suffixes given in Table 1 above to the appropriate stem, observing the Form I vowellings where necessary.

Active	Past Stem	Present Stem
S-I	فَعَل	فْعَل
S-II	فَعَّل	فَعِّل
S-III	فَاعَل	فَاعِل
S-IV	أَفْعَل	فْعِل
S-V	تَفَعَّل	تَفَعَّل
S-VI	تَفَاعَل	تَفَاعَل
S-VII	اِنْفَعَل	نْفَعِل
S-VIII	اِفْتَعَل	فْتَعِل
S-IX	see notes below	
S-X	اِسْتَفْعَل	سْتَفْعِل

Passive	Past Stem	Present Stem
S-I	فُعِل	فْعَل
S-II	فُعِّل	فَعَّل
S-III	فُوعِل	فَاعَل
S-IV	أُفْعِل	فْعَل
S-V	تُفُعِّل	تَفَعَّل
S-VI	تُفُوعِل	تَفَاعَل
S-VII	none	
S-VIII	اُفْتُعِل	فْتَعَل
S-IX	see notes below	
S-X	اُسْتُفْعِل	سْتَفْعَل

General notes

■ The passive is given in full for the sake of completeness, but it is not worth devoting a lot of time to learning it as it is much more restricted in use than its English equivalent. Form VII does not have a passive, and in some other forms it is rare.

■ Form IX. For technical reasons, this comparatively rare form is given below along with the Doubled Verb (Table D).

Form S-I

This is the only form which has more than one vowel pattern. In the glossaries, the past stem vowelling can be obtained from the transliteration (e.g. **kataba**), while the present stem vowelling is given after the verb type (e.g. **S-I u**). So the verb فَعَل given in the table would be marked **S-I a**. As there is no reliable way to predict these vowellings, they have to be learned along with their verbs. The vowels in the passive of Form I, however, do not change.

Form S-II

This is formed by doubling the middle radical and vowelling according to the table. It often has a causative meaning, e.g. **fahima (I)** *to understand*, **fahhama (II)** *to make someone understand, explain*. The present tense prefixes take a **u**-vowel (see above).

Form S-III

Formed by interposing an **alif** between the first and middle radicals. Again the present tense prefixes take a **u**-vowel.

Form S-IV

Formed by prefixing أ to the root in the perfect. This disappears in the present. Like Form II, this often has a causative meaning.

Form S-V

Formed by prefixing **ta-** and doubling the middle radical. (Note: the past and present stems of Forms V and VI are identical. All the other derived forms above Form I alternate a middle radical vowel of **a** in the past with **i** in the present.)

Form S-VI

Formed by prefixing **ta-** and introducing an **alif** after the first radical. Again both stems are identical.

Form S-VII

Formed by prefixing اِنـ **in-** to the stem and following the vowel pattern given. Like all other forms beginning with **alif** this disappears in the present.

Form S-VIII

Formed by prefixing **alif** and introducing ت after the first radical. Some assimilations occur in this form when certain letters occur as the first radical. These will be pointed out as they occur.

Form S-IX

Because its formation involves the reduplication of the last raditcal, this behaves like a doubled verb, and is therefore given in Table D.

Form S-X

Formed by prefixing اِستـ **ist-** to the root. The **alif** disappears in the present.

Summary

Study this table carefully, as it comprises the bones of the Arabic verb system. Pay attention in particular to the vowel on the middle radical. Remember that you have only two things to learn:

- ▓ the prefixes and suffixes given in Table 1;
- ▓ the variations in the stem vowel of Form I, i.e. that on the middle radical.

Table Q, Quadriliteral Verbs [Q-I and Q-II]

These are verbs which have four consonant roots instead of the usual three consonants. They normally only exist in two derived forms, called I and II although they differ from the normal patterns for those categories (see below).

We use the root **z-l-z-l** which means *to shake something* in Form I, and *to be shaken* in Form II.

Active	Past Stem	Present Stem
Q-I	زَلْزَل	زَلْزِل
Q-II	تَزَلْزَل	تَزَلْزَل

Although conventionally known as Forms Q-I and Q-II, these actually work like S-II and S-V verbs respectively. If you remember that the **shaddah** (doubling sign) used on these represents a letter without a vowel followed by one with a vowel (in this case its twin, e.g. **bb**, **kk**, and so on) you will see that the verbs above show the same sequence of unvowelled letter followed by vowelled letter (in the case of our example, **lz**). Q-I and Q-II therefore form exact parallels to SII and SV. QI, uniquely among Form I verbs, shows no variations in vowelling.

Table D, Doubled Verbs [D-I to D-X]

Introduction

Doubled verbs are those whose middle and last root letters are the same (**d-l-l**, **m-r-r** and the like). Because Form IX involves the doubling of this radical, it is included here rather than in Table S.

All doubled verbs (including Form IX) have two stems for each tense (past and present). It will help you to to understand this if you think along the lines of suffixes which begin with a vowel as opposed to those which begin with a consonant (prefixes don't matter). These two factors determine the stems used.

To put it another way:

- ▓ Past tense. All parts except *he, she, they* (masc.) in the past tense use the normal stem (i.e. like the Sound verb, Table S)

■ Present tense. All parts except the (comparatively rare) second and third person feminine plural use the normal stem.

Apart from those verb parts mentioned above, a contracted stem is used, contracted in this context meaning that the middle and final radicals are reduced to one letter and written with the doubling sign **shaddah**. To illustrate this type of verb, we use the root م–د–ـد **m-d-d**. Form I means *to extend, stretch*. Not all the derived forms given here exist, but the same root is used throughout the table for the sake of uniformity.

Note: Forms D-II and D-V behave like sound verbs as the middle radical is doubled and therefore cannot contract.

NS = normal stem (i.e. as in Table S)		
CS = contracted stem		
Active	**Past Stem**	**Present Stem**
I NS	مدَد	مدُد
I CS	مدّ	مدّ
II	مدَّد	مدِّد
III NS	مادَد	مادِد
III CS	مادّ	مادّ
IV NS	أمدَد	مدِد
IV CS	أمدّ	مدّ
V	تمدَّد	تمدَّد
VI NS	تمادَد	تمادَد
VI CS	تمادّ	تمادّ
VII NS	انمدَد	نمدِد
VII CS	انمدّ	نمدّ
VIII NS	امتدَد	متدِد
VIII CS	امتدّ	متدّ
X NS	استمدَد	ستمدِد
X CS	استمدّ	ستمدّ

The passives are given only for forms that occur reasonably frequently.

Passive	Past Stem	Present Stem
I NS	مُدِد	مْدَد
I CS	مُدّ	مَدّ
IV NS	أُمْدِد	مْدَد
IV CS	أُمِدّ	مَدّ
VIII NS	اُمْتُدِد	مْتَدَد
VIII CS	اُمْتُدّ	مْتَدّ
X NS	اُسْتُمْدِد	سْتَمْدَد
X CS	اُسْتُمِدّ	سْتَمَدّ

Form S-IX

The comparatively rare Form S-IX is not a true doubled verb in terms of root. However, as its construction involves doubling the last radical, it behaves like a doubled verb and has been included here. In Modern Arabic, it is only used with the special adjective roots given in Unit 16, and has no passive. We shall use here **iHmarra** *to become red, to blush.*

Active	Past Stem	Present Stem
IX NS	اِحْمَرِر	حْمَرِر
CS	اِحْمَرّ	حْمَرّ

Form D-I

Like nearly all Form I verbs, the doubled roots admit various vowellings. These are given in the usual way, e.g. **D-I u** (the vowelling of the example in Table D). However, in the past tense, the contracted stem always takes an a-vowel, and the 'true' vowel only appears in the normal stem. In the present, the vowel given goes on the second radical in the normal stem and the first radical in the contracted stem. Here, for example, are the stems of the **D-I a** verb from the root **DH-l-l**:

Active	Past Stem	Present Stem
I NS	ظَلَل	ظْلَل
CS	ظَلّ	ظَلّ

Forms II and V

These behave like S verbs, as the doubling of the middle radical inhibits any contraction.

Table Fw, Verbs with First Radical w [Fw-I to Fw-X]

We use the root w-S-l *to arrive* in Form I as the model for this type of verb.

Active	Past Stem	Present Stem
I	وَصِل	صِل
IV	أَوْصَل	وصِل
VIII	اتَّصَل	تَّصِل
Passive	Past Stem	Present Stem
I	وُصِل	وصَل
IV	أُوصَل	وصَل
VIII	اُتُّصِل	تَّصَل

Forms not given are regular (Table S), or do not occur.

Form I

The main feature of this is that the present stem loses its و altogether. Also, the middle radical of Form I has varying vowels, indicated in the vocabularies by the usual convention. The example verb in the table is **Fw i**.

Form IV

The only slightly unusual feature here is that, in the present, the و combines with the u-vowel of the prefix to form a long vowel **uu**. So, for instance, **yu- + wSil** is pronounced **yuuSil**.

Form VIII

The و becomes assimilated to the following ت, giving **ittaSala, yattaSil**

Tip: This is because Arabic will not allow the sequence **iw**. The same goes for **ui**, so if you concoct a verb form – or any word for that matter – containing such a sequence, it is going to be wrong (see also Table Fy).

Passive

Again, when the و is preceded by **u**-vowel, the two combine into a long **uu**. **Note:** Doubled verbs beginning with و do not drop the letter, but behave like normal doubled verbs (see Table D).

Table Fy, Verbs with First Radical y [Fy-I to Fy-X]

Such verbs are not common. We use the example **yabisa** *to be or become dry*.

Active	Past Stem	Present Stem
I	يَبِس	يْبَس
IV	أَيْبَس	وبِس

Passive	Past Stem	Present Stem
IV	أُيْبِس	وبِس

Forms not given are regular (Table S), or do not occur.

Form I

The ي does not drop out in the present.

Form IV

In the present of IV active and passive, the theoretical combination **ui** is replaced by **uu** (see Table Fw above).

Table Mw, Verbs with Middle Radical w [Mw-I to Mw-X]

Like the Doubled verb, these have two stems for each tense. In this case it is better to call them Long Stem (LS) and Short Stem (SS). The rules for their use are identical in principle to those applying to the Doubled Verb: LS before a suffix beginning with a vowel, and SS before one beginning with a consonant. Please see under Doubled Verb for a more detailed explanation.

We use the root **q-w-l** *to say* in Form I.

Active	Past Stem	Present Stem
I LS	قَال	قُول
I SS	قُل	قُل
IV LS	أَقَال	قِيل
IV SS	أَقَل	قِل
VII LS	انْقَال	نْقَال
VII SS	انْقَل	نْقَل
VIII LS	اقْتَال	قْتَال
VIII SS	اقْتَل	قْتَل
X LS	إسْتَقَال	سْتَقِيل
X SS	إسْتَقَل	سْتَقِل

Jussive

In this type of verb, the jussive differs from the normal present tense and the subjunctive. The prefixes and suffixes are given in Table 1 and Table S, but note that in Mw verbs the short stem is used in all parts of the jussive which do not have a suffix, e.g. تَقُل، يَقُل yaqul, taqul *he, you,* etc. but تَقُولِي، تَقُولُوا، يَقُولُوا، yaquuluu, taquuluu, taquulii *they, you* pl., *you* fem. sing.

Passive

In the passive, the vowelling of the stems is a follows:

Passive	Past Stem	Present Stem
I LS	قِيل	قَال
I SS	قِل	قَل
IV LS	أُقِيل	قَال
IV SS	أُقِل	قَل
VII	none	
VIII LS	اُقْتِيل	قْتَال
VIII SS	اُقْتِل	قْتَل
X LS	اُستُقِيل	سْتَقَال
X SS	اُستُقِل	سْتَقَل

Derived forms

As usual, the forms not mentioned are regular and behave like sound verbs, the و behaving like a consonant.

Table My, Verbs with Middle Radical *y* [My-I to My-X]

Apart from Form I, these behave in an identical way to Mw verbs in the table above. We use the root **S-y-r** *to become*.

Active	Past Stem	Present Stem
I LS	صَار	صِير
I SS	صِر	صِر

Jussive

See Table Mw above. The same principle applies here.

يَصِيرُوا، تَصِيرُوا، تَصِيرِي **yaSir, taSir** *he, you,* etc. but يَصِر، تَصِر **yaSiiruu, taSiiruu, taSiirii** *they, you* pl., *you* fem. sing.

Passive

Same as Table Mw above.

Derived forms

See Table Mw above. These verbs behave in the same way.

Table Ma

This is a slight misnomer, in that these verbs actually have either **w** or **y** as the middle radical. However, as the present tense takes an **a**-vowel, the code **Ma** has been used.

This is a small group of verbs, but it includes some very common ones. We use the root **n-w-m** *to sleep*.

Active	Past Stem	Present Stem
I LS	نَام	نَام
I SS	نِم	نَم

Jussive

See Table Mw above. The same principle applies here.

يَنَامُوا، تَنَامُوا، تَنَامِي **yanam, tanam** *he, you,* etc. but يَنَم، تَنَم **yanaamuu, tanaamuu, tanaamii** *they, you* pl., *you* fem. sing.

Passive
See Table Mw above.

Derived forms
See Table Mw above. These verbs behave in the same way.

Table Lw-I, Verbs with Last Radical *w*

Notes

■ This type of verb and those in the following tables do not lend themselves easily to a reduction into a convenient number of stems, so their conjugations are given in a fuller form and are best learned by heart.

■ The derived forms are the same for all types, so these are given separately below.

We use the root **n-d-w** *to call, invite.*

Active	Past	Present	Subjunctive as present except parts given	Jussive as subj. except parts given
Singular				
he	نَدَا	يَنْدُو		يَنْدُ
she	نَدَتْ	تَنْدُو		تَنْدُ
you (m.)	نَدَوْتَ	تَنْدُو		تَنْدُ
you (f.)	نَدَوْتِ	تَنْدِينَ	تَنْدِي	
I	نَدَوْتُ	أَنْدُو		أَنْدُ
Plural				
they (m.)	نَدَوْا	يَنْدُونَ	يَنْدُوا	
they (f.)	نَدَوْنَ	يَنْدُونَ		
you (m.)	نَدَوْتُمْ	تَنْدُونَ	تَنْدُوا	
you (f.)	نَدَوْتُنَّ	تَنْدُونَ		
we	نَدَوْنَا	نَنْدُو		نَنْدُ

Summary

There are many phonetic factors at work here which cause different sorts of elisions and changes. To list all these would defeat the purpose so, as has been suggested, it is better to learn these verbs by heart, spending more time on the most commonly occurring parts.

Passive	Past	Present	Subjunctive as present except parts given	Jussive as subj. except parts given
Singular				
he	نُدِيَ	يُنْدَى		يُنْدَ
she	نُدِيَتْ	تُنْدَى		تُنْدَ
you (m.)	نُدِيتَ	تُنْدَى		تُنْدَ
you (f.)	نُدِيتِ	تُنْدَيْنَ	تُنْدَيْ	
I	نُدِيتُ	أُنْدَى		أُنْدَ
Plural				
they (m.)	نُدُوا	يُنْدَوْنَ	يُنْدَوْا	
they (f.)	نُدِينَ	يُنْدَوْنَ		
you (m.)	نُدِيتُمْ	تُنْدَوْنَ	تُنْدَوْا	
you (f.)	نُدِيتُنَّ	تُنْدَيْنَ		
we	نُدِينَا	نُنْدَى		نُنْدَ

Table Ly-I, Verbs with Last Radical y

This by far the most common of this type of verb. We shall use the root **r-m-y** *to throw*, and again give the verb in full.

Active	Past	Present	Subjunctive as present except parts given	Jussive as subj. except parts given
Singular				
he	رَمَى	يَرْمِي		يَرْمِ
she	رَمَتْ	تَرْمِي		تَرْمِ
you (m.)	رَمَيْتَ	تَرْمِي		تَرْمِ
you (f.)	رَمَيْتِ	تَرْمِينَ	تَرْمِي	
I	رَمَيْتُ	أَرْمِي		أَرْمِ
Plural				
they (m.)	رَمَوْا	يَرْمُونَ	يَرْمُوا	
they (f.)	رَمَيْنَ	يَرْمِينَ		
you (m.)	رَمَيْتُمْ	تَرْمُونَ	تَرْمُوا	
you (f.)	رَمَيْتُنَّ	تَرْمِينَ		
we	رَمَيْنَا	نَرْمِي		نَرْمِ

Passive

Identical to Lw type. See table above.

Table La-I

Again a slight misnomer. These verbs actually have third radical **w** or **y**, but the past has an **i**-vowel and the present an **a**-vowel on the middle radical. We use the root **l-q-y** *to meet with, find*.

Active	Past	Present	Subjunctive as present except parts given	Jussive as subj. except parts given
Singular				
he	لَقِيَ	يَلْقَى		يَلْقَ
she	لَقِيَتْ	تَلْقَى		تَلْقَ
you (m.)	لَقِيتَ	تَلْقَى		تَلْقَ
you (f.)	لَقِيتِ	تَلْقَيْنَ	تَلْقَيْ	
I	لَقِيتُ	أَلْقَى		أَلْقَ
Plural				
they (m.)	لَقُوا	يَلْقَوْنَ	يَلْقَوْا	
they (f.)	لَقِينَ	يَلْقَيْنَ		
you (m.)	لَقِيتُمْ	تَلْقَوْنَ	تَلْقَوْا	
you (f.)	لَقِيتُنَّ	تَلْقَيْنَ		
we	لَقِينا	نَلْقَى		نَلْقَ

Passive
Identical to Lw type. See table above.

Table Lh-I

The **h** this time stands for *hybrid*. A few verbs conjugate like **r-m-y** in the past (Table Ly), and **l-q-y** in the present (Table La). We shall give merely a few sample parts, using the root **s-:-y** *to hurry, make an effort at something*.

Active	Past	Present	Subjunctive as present except parts given	Jussive as subj. except parts given
Singular				
he	سَعَى	يَسْعَى		يَسْعَ
she	سَعَتْ	تَسْعَى		تَسْعَ

Passive

As usual, the same as all the L-type verbs (see tables above).

L-type Verbs, Derived Forms [Lw/y/a, etc. II–X]

The derived forms are the same for all three types of verb with و or ي as the last radical.

Although a table is given below, there is a short-cut to learning these

- Forms II, III, IV, VII, VIII and X (there is no Form IX) conjugate like **r-m-y** (Table Ly) in both tenses.
- V and VI conjugate like **r-m-y** (Table Ly) in the past, and **l-q-y** (Table La) in the present.

The following table therefore only gives two parts (the *he*-form of the past and the present). The rest of the parts can be found by referring to the two tables mentioned above.

Again we use the root **l-q-y**, which exists in quite a number – but not all – of the derived forms.

Active	Past Stem	Present Stem
II	لَقَّى	يلقِّي
III	لاقَى	يُلاقِي
IV	ألْقَى	يلْقِي
V	تلقَّى	يتلقَّى
VI	تَلاقَى	يتَلاقَى
VII	انْلَقَى	ينْلَقِي
VIII	الْتَقَى	يلْتَقِي
X	اسْتلْقَى	يستلْقِي

continued...

Passive	Past Stem	Present Stem
II	لُقِّيَ	يُلقَّى
III	لُوقِيَ	يُلاقَى
IV	أُلقِيَ	يُلقَى
V	تُلُقِّيَ	يُتلقَّى
VIII	اُلتُقِيَ	يُلتقَى
X	اُستُلقِيَ	يُستلقَى

The forms not given are either non-existent or extremely rare.

Some irregularities

The only really irregular verb in Arabic is لَيْسَ *not to be*, used for negation. This is given in full in Unit 8. It only exists in one tense, which is past in form, but present in meaning.

The verb رَأَى *to see* conjugates in the past like رَمَى (Table Ly), but has the irregular present form يَرَى where the **hamzah** and its supporting **alif** are dropped. This tense is vowelled like the present of La verbs, e.g. يَرَى، تَرَى **yaraa, taraa**, etc.

The verb رَأَى has no imperative, that of the alternative verb نَظَر *to look, see* being used instead (اُنظُر).

Verbs with **hamzah** as one of their radicals are mainly regular, but are sometimes difficult to spell. The rules for this are too complex to be practically useful, and it is better to learn by experience.

There are a number of 'doubly weak' verbs, showing the characteristics of two different types. These and certain other phonetic variations – especially of Form VIII verbs – have been noted in the text.

ARABIC–ENGLISH VOCABULARY

This glossary relates mainly to the texts in the units and the key vocabulary boxes. It is arranged according to the order of the Arabic alphabet (see pages 10–11) as opposed to the root system used by most dictionaries. This should enable you to find words more easily. The Arabic definite article (*the* الـ) has been included with words which always have it (e.g. الدنيا **ad-dunyaa** *the world*), but left out where you are more likely to be looking for the word in its non-definite form (e.g. Sharjah, Arabic الشارقة **ash-shaariqah**). Words which do not take the accusative marker are marked with an asterisk (*).

ا

آلة حاسبة **aalah Haasibah** *computer*

ابتدائي **ibtidaa'ii** *elementary*

ابتسم **ibtasama [S-VIII]** *smile*

ابن، أبناء **ibn, abnaa'*** *son*

ابنة، بنات **ibnah, banaat** *daughter*

أبو الهول **abuu l-hawl** *the Sphynx*

أبو ظبي **abuu DHabi** *Abu Dhabi*

أبيض، بيضاء **abyaD***, fem. **bayDaa'*** *white*

أثر، آثار **athar, aathaar** sing. *track, trace*, pl. also *archaeological remains*

أثري **atharii** *archaeological*

اتساع **ittisaa:** *extent, compass*

أثناء **athnaa'(a)** *during, while*

أجاب **ajaaba [Mw-IV]** *to answer*

اجتماعي **ijtimaa:ii** *social*

اجتمع **ijtama:a [S-VIII]** *meet, come together*

أجمل **ajmal*** *more/most beautiful*

أجنبي، أجانب **ajnabii, ajaanib** *foreign, foreigner*

أحب، يحب **aHabba, yuHibb [D-IV]** *like, love*

احتسب **iHtasaba [S-VIII]** *to award*

احتفل بـ **iHtafala bi- [S-VIII]** *celebrate*

احتل **iHtalla [D-VIII]** *occupy*

أحدث **aHdath** *newest, latest*

إحصاء، ات **iHSaa', -aat** *count, census*

أحمر **aHmar*** *red*

أخ، إخوان / إخوة **akh, ikhwaan** or **ikhwah** *brother*

أخت، أخوات **ukht, akhawaat** *sister*

اختار **ikhtaara [My-VIII]** *to choose*

اخترق **ikhtaraqa [S-VIII]** *to breach*

أخذ **akhadha [S-I u]** *to take*

أخرى **aakhar*** (fem. آخر **ukhraa**) *other*

آخر **aakhir** *end, last part of something*

أخضر **akhDar*** *green*

أخير **akhiir** *last*

أدب، آداب **adab, aadaab** *literature, arts*

أدرك **adraka [S-IV]** *to attain, achieve*

إذا **idhaa** *if*

إذن **ídhan** *so, therefore*

أذاع **adhaa:a [My-IV]** *to broadcast*

أذن **udh(u)n** (fem.) *ear*

أراد **araada [Mw-IV]** *want, wish for*

أربعة **arba:ah** *four*

أردني **urduni** *Jordanian*

أرز **aruzz** *rice*

إرسال **irsaal** *transmission, sending*

أرسل **arsala [S-IV]** *send*

أرض **al-arD** (fem.) *the ground,*
the earth

اسباني **isbaanii** *Spanish*

أستاذ، أساتذة **ustaadh, asaatidhah**
professor

استأجر **ista'jara** [S-X] *to rent, be*
a tenant of

استخدام **istikhdaam** *use, employment*

استخدم **istakhdama** [S-X] *to use, employ*

استرداد **istirdaad** *demanding back,*
reclaiming

استطاع **istaTaa:a** [Mw-X] *to be able*

استعمال **isti:maal** *use, usage*

استغرق **istaghraqa** [S-X] *take, use up,*
occupy (of time)

استقبال، ات **istiqbaal, -aat** *reception*

استقبل **istaqbala** [S-X] *receive, meet*

أسطورة، أساطير **usTuurah, asaaTiir***
legend

أسلوب، أساليب **usluub, asaaliib*** *style,*
method

أسند ل **asnada** [S-IV] *entrust to, vest in*

أسهم **as-hama** [S-IV] *contribute,*
take part

أسود **aswad***, fem. سوداء **sawdaa'***
black

إشارة، ات **ishaarah, -aat** *(traffic) signal*

اشترك **ishtaraka** [S-VIII] *to*
participate, take part

اشترى **ishtaraa** [Ly-VIII] *buy*

أشهر **ash-har*** *more/most famous*

أصاب **aSaaba** *hit, strike*

أصبح **aSbaHa** [S-IV] *become*

أصدر **aSdara** [S-IV] *to publish*

أصفر **aSfar***, fem. صفراء **Safraa'***
yellow

أصل، أصول **aSl, uSuul** *origin, basis*

أضاف **aDaafa** [My-IV] *to add*

أعاد **a:aada** [Mw-IV] *to repeat, renew*

اعتبر **i:tabara** [S-VIII] *to consider,*
regard

اعداد **i:daad** *preparation*

اعدادي **i:daadii** *preparatory*

أعرب عن **a:raba :an** [S-IV] *to state,*
express

أعزب **a:zab*** *bachelor, single*

أعطى **a:Taa** [Ly-IV] *to give*

أعلن **a:lana** [S-IV] *to announce, state*

اعلى **a:laa** *highest; the highest point,*
top

أفاض ب **afaaDa bi-** [My-IV] *flood,*
overflow with

افتتح **iftataHa** [S-VIII] *to commence,*
open

أقام **aqaama** [Mw-IV] *to reside; to*
hold (an event, etc.)

اقتصادي **iqtiSaadii** *economic*

اكتشف **iktashafa** [S-VIII] *discover*

أكثر **akthar*** *more/most*

أكرم **akrama** [S-IV] *honour, be*
hospitable/generous to

أكل **akl** *things to eat, food*

أكل، يأكل **akala, ya'kul** [S-I u] *eat*

أكيد **akiid** *certain, definite*

الآن **al-'aan** *now*

الاسكندرية **al-iskandariyyah**
Alexandria

الإمارات العربية المتحدة **al-imaaraat**
al-:arabiyyah al-muttaHidah
The United Arab Emirates

الأهرام **al-ahraam** *the pyramids*

الحين **al-Hiin** *now*

الدنيا **ad-dunya(a)** (fem.) *the world*

العالم **al-:aalam** *the world*

العامة **al-:aammah** *the (general) public*

ألف، آلاف **alf, aalaaf** *thousand*

الفصحى **al-fuS-Haa** *literary, classical*
(adj. used only with the Arabic
language)

إلا **illaa** *except*

الله **Al-laah** *God, Allah*

ألماني **almaanii** *German*

المغرب **al-maghrib** *sunset ; Morocco*

أمة، أمم **ummah, umam** *nation*

أمام **amaam** *in front of*

امتحان، ات **imtiHaan, -aat** *exam*

امتياز **imtiyaaz** *distinction, privilege*

امرأة، نساء **imra'ah, nisaa'** (irregular plural) *woman*

أمس **ams** *yesterday*

أمس الأول **ams al-awwal** *the day before yesterday*

أمكن **amkana [S-IV]** *to be possible*

إن **in** *if*

انبعث **inba:atha [S-VII]** *emanate, be sent out*

انتاج **intaaj** *production*

أنتج **antaja [S-IV]** *to produce*

انتشار **intishaar** *spread, currency; here popularity*

انتهج **intahaja [S-VIII]** *follow, pursue (a path, method, etc.)*

انتهى **intahaa [Ly-VIII]** *to come to an end, finish*

إنجلترا **ingiltarra** (with **g** as in *garden*) *England*

إنجليزي **ingliizi** *English*

انسان، ناس **insaan, naas** *human being;* pl. *= people*

إنشاء **inshaa'** *foundation, setting up*

اهتمام **ihtimaam** *attention, concern, interest*

أهلا وسهلا **ahlan wa-sahlan** *welcome*

أهم **ahamm** *more/most important*

أو **aw** *or*

أودع **awda:a [Fw-IV]** *to place*

أوروبي، ون **uruubii** *European*

أول **awwal** *first*

أولا **awwalan** *firstly*

أي **ay** *that is*

أي **ayy** *which*

إيمان **iimaan** *belief, faith*

أين **ayna** *where*

ب

باب، أبواب **baab, abwaab** *gate, door*

بادل **baadala [S-III]** *to swap, exchange with someone*

باع **baa:a [My-I]** *to sell*

بجانب **bi-jaanib** *next to, beside*

بحر، بحار **baHr, biHaar** *sea, large river*

بدأ **bada' [S-I a]** *begin*

بدا **badaa [Lw-I]** *to appear, seem, show*

بداية **bidaayah** *beginning*

برج، أبراج **burj, abraaj** *tower*

برجيل، براجيل **barjiil, baraajiil** *traditional wind tower*

برنامج، برامج **barnaamij, baraamij*** *programme*

بريطاني **briiTaanii** *British*

بسط **bassaTa [S-II]** *to simplify*

بصل **baSal** *onions*

بطاقة، ات **buTaaqah, -aat** *card*

بطاقة التسليف **buTaaqat at-tasliif** *credit card*

بطلاقة **bi-Talaaqah** *fluently*

بطولات **buTuulaat** *leading roles*

بعد **ba:d** *after*

بعد ما **ba:d maa** *after (before a verb)*

بعض **ba:D** *some, part of something*

بعيد **ba:fid** *far away, distant*

بل **bal** *rather; here in fact, indeed*

بلد، بلاد/بلدان **balad, bilaad/buldaan** *country*

بناء **binaa'** *building, construction*

بنت، بنات **bint, banaat** *girl, daughter*

بنزين **banziin** *petrol*

بيت، بيوت **bayt, buyuut** *house*

بيرة **biirah** *beer*

بين **bayna** *between, among*

بينما **baynamaa** *while*

ت

تابل، توابل **taabil, tawaabil** *spice*

تاجر، تجار **taajir, tujjaar** *merchant*

تاريخ **taariikh** history

تاريخي **taariikhii** historical

تام **taamm** complete

تأهل **ta'ahhala [S-V]** qualify (إلى **ilaa** for)

تبريد **tabriid** cooling

تبسيط **tabsiiT** simplification

تبع **tabi:a** follow

تجارة **tijaarah** trade, commerce

تجاري **tijaarii** commercial

تخصص **takhaSSaS [S-V]** specialise

تخطيط **takhTiiT** planning

تدريس **tadriis** teaching

تذكرة، تذاكر **tadhkirah,tadhaakir*** ticket

ترحيب **tarHiib** welcome, welcoming (noun)

ترحيبي **tarHiibii** welcoming (adj.)

ترك **taraka [S-I u]** leave, let be

تزوج **tazawwaja [Mw-V]** to marry

تسجيل **tasjiil** registration, scoring

تسديدة، ات **tasdiidah, -aat** shot (football)

تشكيلة، ات **tashkiilah, -aat** selection

تصميم **taSmiim** design, designing

تعادل **ta:aadul** balance, equality (football: draw, equal score)

تعبان **ta:baan** tired

تعلم **ta:allama [S-V]** learn

تعليم **ta:liim** education

تعليمي **ta:liimii** educational

تفاحة، تفاح **tufaaHah, tufaaH** apple

تفرج على **tafarraja :ala [S-V]** watch, look at

تفضل **tafaDDal** Come in (to a man)

تقديم **taqdiim** presentation

تقرير، تقارير **taqriir, taqaariir*** report

تكلم **takallama [S-V]** speak

تكييف **takyiif** air conditioning

تلفزيوني **tilifizyuunii** television (adj.), televisual

تلميذ، تلامذة/تلاميذ **tilmiidh, talaamidhah/talaamiidh** pupil

تمتع بـ **tamatta:a [S-V]** enjoy

تمنى **tamannaa [Ly-V]** to hope, wish

تنس **tanis** tennis

تنظيف **tanDHiif** cleaning

تنفيذ **tanfiidh** implementation, execution

تنقل **tanaqqala [S-V]** to be carried, transported

تنمية **tanmiyah** development

توزيع **tawzii:** distribution

ث

ثالث **thaalith** third (adj.)

ثالثة عشر **thaalithah :ashar** thirteenth

ثانوي **thaanawii** secondary

ثقافي **thaqaafii** cultural

ثقيل **thaqiil** heavy

ثلاثة **thalaathah** three

ثلج **thalj** ice

ثم **thumma** then

ثمرة **thamrah** fruit

ج

جاء، يجيء **jaa'a, yajii' [My-I]** come

جار، جيران **jaar, jiiraan** neighbour

(الـ)جاري **al-jaarii** the current

جاع **jaa:a [Mw-I]** to become hungry

جالس **jaalis** sitting, seated

جامع، جوامع **jaami:, jawaami:*** large mosque

جامعة، ات **jaami:ah** university

جانب، جوانب **jaanib, jawaanib*** side

جانبا **jaaniban** aside, to one side

جبنة **jubnah** cheese

جدا **jíddan** very

جدد **jaddada [D-II]** renew, restore

جديد **jadiid** new

جرب **jarraba [S-II]** try out, taste

جرى **jaraa [Ly-I]** to run

جريدة، جرائد **jariidah, jaraa'id*** newspaper

جسر، جسور **jisr, jusuur** bridge

جعل **ja:ala [S-I a]** *cause, make do something; place, put*

جغرافي **jughraafii** *geographical*

جلب **jalaba [S-I i]** *attract*

جلس **jalasa [S-I i]** *sit, sit down*

جماعة، ات **jamaa:ah, -aat** *group, gathering*

جمال **jamaal** *beauty*

جمعية، ات **jam:iyyah, -aat** *group, assembly, society*

جمل، جمال **jamal, jimaal** *camel*

جميعا **jamii:an** *all together*

جميل **jamfil** *beautiful*

جنسية، ات **jinsiyyah, -aat** *nationality*

جوعان، جوعى **jaw:aan*, jaw:aa*** *hungry*

جولف **guulf** *golf*

جيب، جيوب **jayb, juyuub** *pocket*

جيد **jayyid** *of good quality*

(الـ)جيزة **al-jiizah** *Geezah, a district of Cairo*

ح

حار **Haarr** *hot*

حارس، حراس **Haaris, Hurraas** *guard* (football: *goalkeeper*)

تاسع **taasi:** *ninth*

حاضر، ون **HaaDir, -uun** *present, here*

حافظ على **HaafaDHa :alaa [S-III]** *keep, preserve*

حبة، ات **Habbah, -aat** *grain, seed; also used for counting units of certain fruits and vegetables*

حتى **Hattaa** *until, even*

(الـ)حج **al-Hajj** *the Pilgrimage*

حجر، أحجار **Hajar, aHjaar** *stone*

حد، حدود **Hadd, Huduud** *limit, border*

حديث **Hadiith** *modern, up-to-date*

حديقة، حدائق **Hadiiqah, Hadaa'iq*** *garden, park*

حرارة **Haraarah** *heat*

حزين **Haziin** *sad*

حسب **Hasb** *according to*

حسم **Hasm** *discount*

حسن **Hasan** *beautiful, handsome, good*

حسنا **Hasanan** *well, right, O.K.*

حصن، حصون **HiSn, HuSuun** *fort, fortress*

حضر **HaDara [S-I u]** *attend*

حكم، حكام **Hakam, Hukkaam** *referee, umpire*

حل، حلول **Hall, Huluul** *solution*

حلاوة **Halaawah** *sweetness, beauty*

حمال، ون **Hammaal, -uun** *porter*

حمر **Hammara [S-II]** *to brown, fry*

حمل، أحمال **Himl, aHmaal** *load, burden*

حمية **Himyah** *diet*

حوالي **Hawaalii** *about, approximately*

خ

خادم، خدام **khaadim, khuddaam** *servant*

خادمة، ات **khaadimah, -aat** *(female) servant*

(الـ)خارج **al-khaarij** *the outside, abroad*

خارج **khaarij** *outside*

خاص **khaaSS** *special; private*

خامس **khaamis** *fifth*

خبر **khabbar [S-II]** *to tell, inform*

خبر، أخبار **khabar, akhbaar** *news* (sing. = *an item of news*)

خبز **khubz** *bread*

خدع **khada:a [S-I a]** *to deceive*

خدمة، ات **khidmah, -aat** *service*

خروف، خرفان **kharuuf, khurfaan** *sheep*

خريطة، خرائط **khariiTah, kharaa'iT*** *map*

خفيف **khafiif** *light* (adj.)

خلال **khilaal** *during*

(الـ)خليج العربي **al-khaliij al-:arabii** *the Arabian Gulf*

خليط **khaliiT** *mixture*

خليفة، خلفاء* **khaliifah, khulafaa'***
Caliph, head of the Islamic state

خير **khayr** *(state of) well-being*

د

دائرة، دوائر* **daa'irah, dawaa'ir***
(government) department

داخل **daakhil** *inside, the inside of something*

دخل **dakhala [S-I u]** *to enter*

دراسة، ات **diraasah, -aat** *study*

درس **darasa [S-I u]** *study*

درهم، دراهم* **dirham, daraahim***
dirham (unit of currency)

دقيقة، دقائق* **daqiiqah, daqaa'iq***
minute

دكان، دكاكين* **dukkaan, dakaakiin***
small shop, stall

دمشق* **dimashq*** *Damascus*

دهش **dahisha [S-1 a]** *be surprised, astonished*

دور، أدوار **dawr, adwaar** *role, turn*

دولة، دول **dawlah, duwal** *country, state*

دولي **duwalii** or **dawlii** *international*

ذ

ذاكرة **dhaakirah** *memory*

ذبح **dhabaHa [S-I a]** *slaughter*

ذبيحة، ذبائح* **dhabiiHah, dhabaa'iH***
sacrificial animal

ذقن، ذقون **dhaqn, dhuquun** (fem.)
beard, chin

ذلك **dhaalik(a)** *that* (masc.)

ذهب **dhahaba, [S-I a]** *go*

الذي **alladhii** *who, which, that*
(fem. التي **allatii**)

ر

رائحة، روائح* **raa'iHah, rawaa'iH***
smell, scent, perfume

رائع **raa'i:** *splendid, brilliant, marvellous*

رأى، يرى **ra'aa, yaraa** *to see* (irregular Type Ly-I verb: see Verb Tables)

راية، ات **raayah, -aat** *flag, banner*

رئيس، رؤساء* **ra'iis, ru'asaa'*** *boss, chief*

ربح **rabaHa [S-I a]** *to win, gain, profit*

ربع **rub:** *quarter*

رجل **rijl** *foot* (fem.)

رجل، رجال **rajul, rijaal** *man*

رحب **raHHaba [S-II]** *to welcome* (requires *bi-*)

رحلة، ات **riHlah, -aat** *journey, voyage*

رد **radda [D-i u]** *return something to someone*

درجة، ات **darajah, -aat** *step, degree*

رش **rashsha [D-I u]** *sprinkle, spray*

رشاقة **rashaaqah** *shapeliness, elegance*

رشيد **rashiid** *Rashid (man's name); also Rosetta, a town in Egypt*

رصد **raSada [S-I u]** *observe, watch*

رعى **ra:aa [Lh-I]** *take care of, look after*

رغبة، ات **raghbah, -aat** *desire, wishl*

رف، رفوف **raff, rufuuf** *shelf*

رفع **rafa:a [S-I a]** *to lift, raise*

ركب **rakiba [S-I a]** *ride, mount, get into* (a vehicle)

ركلة، ات **raklah, -aat** *kick*

ركن، أركان **rukn, arkaan** *corner*

ركني **ruknii** *corner* (adj.)

رمز، رموز **ramz, rumuuz** *code, symbol*

رواية، ات **riwaayah, -aat** *novel, story*

رياضة،ات **riyaaDah, -aat** *sport, exercise*

ز

زائر، زوار **zaa'ir, zuwwaar** *visitor*

زاحم **zaaHama [S-III]** *to compete with*

زار **zaara [Mw-I]** *visit*

زبون، زبائن* **zabuun, zabaa'in***
customer, client

زراعي **ziraa:ii** *agricultural*

زمان، أزمنة **zamaan, azminah** *time*

زوجة، -ات **zawjah, -aat** *wife*

زورق، زوارق **zawraq, zawaariq*** *boat*

زي، أزياء **ziyy, azyaa'*** *clothes, fashion, style*

زيارة، -ات **ziyaarah, -aat** *visit*

زيت **zayt** *(edible) oil*

س

سائح، سواح **saa'iH, suwwaaH** *tourist*

سائق،-ون/ساقة **saa'iq, -uun/saaqah** *driver*

سؤال، أسئلة **su'aal, as'ilah** *question*

سادس **saadis** *sixth*

ساعد **saa:ada [S-III]** *to help*

ساعة، -ات **saa:ah, -aat** *hour, time, watch, clock*

سافر **saafara [S-III]** *to travel*

ساكن **saakin** *living, residing*

ساكن، سكان **saakin, sukkaan** *inhabitant, resident*

سأل **sa'ala [S-I a]** *to ask*

سالم **saalim** *safe, sound*

سباحة **sibaaHah** *swimming*

سباق، ات **sibaaq, -aat** *race*

سبح **sabaHa [S-I a]** *swim*

ستة **sittah** *six*

سجل **sajjala [S-II]** *to register, to score*

سحر **siHr** *magic*

سد، سدود **sadd, suduud** *dam*

سدد **saddada [S-II]** *to aim; (football) shoot*

سرعان ما **sur:aan maa** *quickly, before long*

سرعة **sur:ah** *speed*

سعيد، سعداء **sa:iid, su:adaa'*** *happy*

سفيرة، ات **safiirah, -aat** *(female) ambassador*

سفينة، سفن **safiinah, sufun** *ship*

سكب **sakaba [S-I u]** *to pour out*

سلاح، أسلحة **silaaH, asliHah** *weapon, arm*

سلق **salq** *(the action of) boiling something*

سماح **samaaH** *permission*

سمع **sami:a [S-I a]** *to hear, listen*

سمك **samak** *fish (collective)*

سمن **saman** *ghee, clarified butter*

سنة، سنوات **sanah, sanawaat** *year*

سواء **sawaa'an** *equally, whether*

سور، أسوار **suur, aswaar** *wall*

سوق، أسواق **suuq, aswaaq** *(usually fem.) market*

سياحي **siyaaHii** *tourist (adj.), touristic*

سيطر على **sayTara :alaa [Q-I]** *to dominate*

سيطرة **sayTarah** *domination*

سينما، سينمات **siinamaa, siinamaat** *(fem.) cinema*

ش

شاء **shaa'a [Ma-I]** *to wish, will*

شارع، شوارع **shaari:, shawaari:*** *street, road*

(الـ)الشارقة **ash-shaariqah** *Sharjah*

شاشة **shaashah** *screen*

شاطئ **shaaTi'** *shore, beach*

شاعر، شعراء **shaa:ir, shu:araa'*** *poet*

شامل **shaamil** *comprehensive*

شأن، شؤون **sha'n, shu'uun** *affair, important matter*

شاب، شباب **shaab, shabaab** *young person, youth*

شبكة، شباك **shabaka, shibaak** *net, netting*

شتاء **shitaa'*** *winter*

شتى **shattaa** *various*

شجرة، أشجار **shajarah, ashjaar** *tree*

شخص، أشخاص **shakhS, ashkhaaS** *person*

شديد **shadiid** *strong, mighty*

شرب **shariba [S-I a]** *drink*

شرح **sharaHa [S-I] a** *explain*

شركة، ات **sharikah, -aat** *company, firm*

شريحة، شرائح **shariiHah, sharaa'iH***
slice

شريط، أشرطة **shariiT, ashriTah** *tape,*
cassette

شعبي **sha:bii** *folk, popular*

شعر **sha:r** *hair*

شعر **shi:r** *poetry,*

شقة، شقق **shaqqah, shiqaq** *flat, apartment*

شكل، أشكال **shakl, ashkaal** *type, shape*

شمال **shamaal** *left*

شمس **shams** *sun*

شهير **shahiir** *famous*

شوط، أشواط **shawT, ashwaaT** *heat, race;*
football: *half*

شيء، اشياء **shay', ashyaa'*** *thing,*
something

شيد **shayyada [My-II]** *erect, construct*

ص

صاحب، أصحاب **SaaHib, aS-Haab**
owner, master; also sometimes *friend*

صادق **Saadiq** *truthful, true*

(ال)صافي **aS-Saafii** *pure, clear*

صالح **SaaliH** *doing right*

صالون تجميل **Saaluun tajmiil** *beauty*
salon

صحن، صحون **SaHn, SuHuun** *dish*

صحيح **SaHiiH** *correct, right*

صديق، أصدقاء **Sadiiq, aSdiqaa'*** *friend*

صعوبة، ـات **Su:uubah, -aat** *difficulty*

صغير **Saghiir** *young* (person),
small (thing)

صف، صفوف **Saff, Sufuuf** *class* (school)

صفى **Saffaa [Ly-II]** *drain, strain*

صلصة **SalSah** *sauce*

صلى الله عليه وسلم **Sallaa l-Laaahu**
:alay-hi wa-sallam *Prayers*
and Peace be upon Him (said after
mentioning the name of the Prophet)

صوت، أصوات **Sawt, aSwaat** *voice, sound*

صوم **Sawm** *fast, fasting*

صيدلية، ات **Saydaliyyah, -aat** *pharmacy*

صيف **Sayf** *summer*

ض

ضابط، ضباط **DaabiT, DubbaaT** *officer*

جمرك، جمارك **jumruk, jamaarik***
customs, excise

ضربة، ات **Darbah, Darabaat** *a blow, beat*

ضرورة، ات **Duruurah, -aat** *necessity,*
requirement

ضم **Damma [D-I u]** *include, comprise*

ضيف، ضيوف **Dayf, Duyuuf** *guest*

ضيق **Dayyiq** *narrow*

ط

طائرة، ات **Taa'irah, -aat** *aeroplane*

طالب، طلاب/طلبة **Taalib, Tullaab/**
Talabah *student*

طالبة ، طالبات **Taalibah, -aat** *female*
student

طباعة **Tibaa:ah** *typing*

طبع **Taba:a [S-I a]** *print, type*

طبعا **Tab:an** *naturally, of course*

طبق، أطباق **Tabaq, aTbaaq** *plate, dish*

طبقة، ات **Tabaqah, -aat** *layer*

طبيب، أطباء **Tabiib, aTibbaa'*** *doctor*

طبيخ **Tabiikh** *cooking, cuisine*

طبيعة **Tabii:ah** *nature*

طبيعي **Tabii:ii** *natural*

طرد **Tarada [S-I u]** *to banish, drive*
away (football: *send off*)

طريق، طرق **Tariiq, Turuq** *road, way*

طريقة، طرائق **Tariiqah, Taraa'iq***
method, way

طعام **Ta:aam** *food*

طفل، أطفال **Tifl, aTfaal** *child*

طفولة **Tufuulah** *childhood*

طماطم **TamaaTim*** *tomatoes*

طمح إلى **TamaHa ilaa [S-I a]** *aspire to*

طموح **TumuuH** aspiration, ambition

طنطة **TanTaa** Tanta (town in Egypt)

طويل **Tawiil** tall (person), long (thing)

ظ

ظهر **DHuhr** noon

ع

عادة، ات: **aadah, -aat** custom, habit

عادل: **aadil** just, upright

عارض، ون: **aariD, -uun** (male) model

عارضة، ات: **aariDah, -aat** (female) model

عاش: **aasha [My-I]** live, reside

عاصمة، عواصم: **aaSimah, :awaaSim*** capital (city)

عالمي: **aalamii** worldwide

(الـ)عالي: **al-: aalii** high

عام: **aamm** general

عام، أعوام: **aam, a:waam** year

عامل، عمال: **aamil, :ummaal** workman

عبارة، ات: **abaarah, -aat** phrase, expression

عجلة، ات: **ajalah, -aat** wheel, bicycle

عجيب: **ajiib** wonderful

عجيبة، عجائب: **ajiibah, :ajaa'ib*** (object of) wonder

عدد، أعداد: **adad, a:daad** number

عدس: **ads** lentils

عدن: **adan** Aden

عراقي: **iraaqii** Iraqi

عربي: **arabii** Arabic, Arab

عرض: **arD** showing, displaying

عرض، عروض: **arD, :uruuD** offer, deal

عرف: **arafa [S-I i]** to know

عريض: **ariiD** wide

عسكري، عساكر: **askarii, :asaakir*** soldier

عشاء: **ishaa'** late evening (prayer time)

عشرة: **ashrah** ten

عطشان: **aTshaan** thirsty

عفوا: **afwan** you're welcome, don't mention it (reply to thanks)

عقب: **aqaba [S-I u]** come after, follow

علم، علوم: **ilm, :uluum** knowledge, science

علمي: **ilmii** scientific

عصر: **aSr** mid-afternoon

عمان: **ammaan** Amman (capital of Jordan); **:umaan** Oman (Sultanate of)

عمر: **umr** life, age

عمل، أعمال: **amal, a:maal** work, job, business

عمل: **amila [S-I a]** do, work

عمومي: **umuumii** general

عن: **an** about, concerning

عند: **inda** at, with

عندما: **indamaa** when

عنوان، عناوين: **unwaan, :anaawiin*** address

عيادة، ات: **iyaadah, -aat** clinic

عيد، أعياد: **iid, a:yaad** festival

عيد الأضحى: **iid al-aD-Haa** Festival of the Sacrifice

عيد الميلاد: **iid al-miilaad** Christmas

عين، عيون: **ayn, :uyuun** (fem.) eye; also spring (of water)

غ

غاية **ghaayah** extreme, most

(الـ)غرب **al-gharb** the West

غربي، ون **gharbii, -uun** western

غرض، أغراض **gharaD, aghraaD** purpose, goal, end

غرفة، غرف **ghurfah, ghuraf** room

غسالة، ات **ghassaalah, -aat** washing machine

غسل **ghasala [S-I i]** wash

غلى **ghalaa [Ly-I]** to boil, come to the boil

غنم **ghanam** sheep (collective)

غني، أغنياء **ghanii, aghniyaa'*** rich, rich person

غير **ghayr** other than, apart from

ف

فاضل **faaDil** *favourable, good*

فاكهة، فواكه **faakihah, fawaakih*** *fruit*

فاهم **faahim** *understanding*

فتاة، فتيات **fataah, fatayaat** *girl, young woman*

احتفال، ات **iHtifaal, -aat** *celebration*

فترة، ات **fatrah, -aat** *period, time, spell*

فجر **fajr** *dawn*

فخم **fakhm** *magnificent*

فراغ **faraagh** *leisure*

فرصة، فرص **furSah, furaS** *chance, opportunity*

فرض **faraDa [S-I i]** *impose*

فرع، فروع **far:, furuu:** *branch (of a tree, company, etc.)*

فرعوني **far:uunii** *pharaonic*

فريق، فرق **fariiq, firaq** *team*

فستان، فساتين **fustaan, fasaatiin*** *frock, dress*

فصل، فصول **faSl, fuSuul** *section, season (of the year)*

فضل **faDDala [S-II]** *prefer*

فطر **fiTr** *breaking of a fast*

فظيع **faDHii:** *shocking, awful*

فعل **fa:ala [S-I a]** *to do, make*

فعلا **fi:lan** *really, actually, in fact*

فقط **faqaT** *only*

فقير، فقراء **faqiir, fuqaraa'*** *poor, poor person*

فلفل **fulful/filfil** *pepper*

فن، فنون **fann, funuun** *art, craft, technique*

فندق، فنادق **funduq, fanaadiq*** *hotel*

فهد، فهود **fahd, fuhuud** *leopard*

فهم **fahima [S-I a]** *to understand*

فورا **fawran** *immediately*

فوز **fawz** *victory*

فوق **fawqa** *above, over*

في **fii** *in*

فيروز **fayruuz** *Fairuz (female name); a turquoise (gem)*

فيلم، افلام **fiilm, aflaam** *film*

ق

قائمة، ات **qaa'imah, -aat** *list*

قاد **qaada [Mw-I]** *to lead*

قارب، قوارب **qaarib, qawaarib*** *(small) boat*

قاعدة، قواعد **qaa:idah, qawaa:id*** *rule*

قال **qaala [Mw-I]** *to say*

(ال)قاهرة **al-qaahirah** *Cairo*

قبل **qabila [S-I a]** *to accept*

قبيح **qabiiH** *ugly*

قدم **qaddama [S-II]** *to present, serve*

قديم **qadiim** *old, ancient (of things)*

قرأ، يقرأ **qara'a, yaqra' [S-I a]** *read*

قرار، ات **qaraar, -aat** *decision, resolution*

قرص ثابت **qarS thaabit** *hard disk*

قرفة **qirfah** *cinnamon*

قرن، قرون **qarn, quruun** *century*

قرنفل **qurunful** *cloves*

قريب **qariib** *near*

قسم، أقسام **qism, aqsaam** *section, division*

قصة، قصص **qiSSah, qiSaS** *story, tale*

قصد **qaSd** *aim, goal, intent*

قصر، قصور **qaSr, quSuur** *palace*

قطر، أقطار **quTr, aqTaar** *region, area*

قطعة، قطع **qiT:ah, qiTa** *piece*

قلب، قلوب **qalb, quluub** *heart*

قلعة، قلاع **qal:ah, qilaa:** *fort, fortress, citadel*

قليلا **qaliilan** *slightly, a little*

قميص، قمصان **qamiiS, qumSaan** *shirt*

قهر **qahara [S- a]** *to conquer*

قوة، ات **quwwah, -aat** *force, power, strength*

قوسي **qawsii** *curved, bowed*

قيادي **qiyaadii** *leading*

ك

ka- ك *as, like,*

kaa'in كائن *being, existing, situated*

ka's, ku'uus كأس، كؤوس *cup, trophy*

kaamil كامل *complete, whole*

kabiir كبير *big, old* (of people)

kitaab, kutub كتاب، كتب *book*

kitaabah كتابة *writing*

kutayyib كتيب *booklet, brochure*

kathaafah كثافة *density*

kathiir كثير *much, many*

kurah, -aat كرة، ات *ball; also used as a shortened form of* كرة القدم **kurat al-qadam** *football*

kursii, karaasii كرسي، كراسي *chair*

kariha [S-I a] كره *hate*

kariim كريم *noble, generous*

kasaba [S-I i] كسب *earn, gain, win*

kaslaan كسلان *lazy*

kushari كشري *name of an Egyptian lentil dish*

al-ka:bah (ال)كعبة *The Kaabah* (Holy Shrine in Mecca)

ka:k كعك *cake*

kafaa [Ly-I] كفى *to suffice, be sufficient for*

kull كل *each, every, all*

kalaam كلام *speech*

kulliyyah, -aat كلية، ات *college, faculty*

kam كم *how many, how much*

ka-maa كما *just as, also*

kammiyyah, -aat كمية، ات *amount*

kuub, akwaab كوب، أكواب *glass, cup*

kiis, akyaas كيس، أكياس *bag, sack*

aHaaTa [Mw-IV] أحاط *surround*

kayf(a) كيف *how*

ل

laa لا *not, no*

laazim لازم *necessary*

laa:ib, -uun لاعب، ون *player*

laaqaa [Ly-III] لاقى *to meet with*

li'anna لأن *because*

laHDHah, laHaDHaat لحظة، ات *moment*

laHm, luHuum لحم، لحوم *meat*

li-dhaalik لذلك *because of that, for this reason*

ladhiidh لذيذ *delicious, tasty*

liSS, luSuuS لص، لصوص *thief*

laTiif لطيف *pleasant, nice*

la:b لعب *play, game*

la:b, al:aab لعب، ألعاب *playing, game*

la:iba [S-I a] لعب *play*

li-maadha(a) لماذا *why*

landan لندن *London*

layla, -aat, layaalin ليلة، ات، ليال *night*

م

maa, miyaah ماء، مياه *water*

maa'ida, mawaa'id مائدة، موائد *table*

mu'tamar, -aat مؤتمر، ات *conference*

mu'akhkhiran مؤخرا *recently*

maarasa [S-III] مارس *to practise, carry out, perform*

maarkah ماركة *marque, label*

al-maaDii (ال)ماضي *the past*

maakyaaj ماكياج *make-up*

maali' مالئ *filling, filler*

maalii مالي *financial*

mu'allif, -uun مؤلف، ون *author*

mu'min, -uun مؤمن، ون *believing, a believer* (in something)

mi'awii مئوي *centennial, hundredth*

mubaaraah, mubaarayaat مباراة، مباريات *match* (sport)

mabSuuT مبسوط *contented, happy*

mablagh, mabaaligh* مبلغ، مبالغ
sum of money

matjar, mataajir* متجر، متاجر
trading place, shop, stall

muttaHad متحد *united*

متحف، متاحف **matHaf, mataaHif***
museum

متخصص، ون **mutakhaSSiS, -uun**
specialist

متر، أمتار **mitr, amtaar** *metre*

متزوج **mutazawwaj** *married*

متفرج، ون **mutafarrij, -uun** *spectator*

متميز **mutamayyiz** *distinctive,*
prominent

متى **mataa** *when*

مثقف، ون **muthaqqaf, -uun** *cultured,*
educated person

مثل **mithl** *like*

مجال، ات **majaal, -aat** *field, sphere*
of activity

مجانا **majjaanan** *free, gratis*

مجنون، مجانين **majnuun, majaaniin***
mad

مجوهرات **mujawharaat** *articles of*
jewellery

محطة، ات **maHaTTah, -aat** *station*

محل، محلات **maHall, maHallaat**
shop, store

مختلف **mukhtalif** *different, various,*

مخطط **mukhaTTaT** *striped*

مدافع، ون **mudaafi: , -uun** *defender*

مدة **muddah** (period of) *time*

مدرس، ون **mudarris, -uun** *teacher*

مدير، مدراء **mudiir, mudaraa'** *manager*

مدينة، مدن **madiinah, mudun** *town,*
city

مذاق **madhaaq** *flavour*

مذيعة، ـات **mudhii:ah, -aat** (female)
broadcaster

مربع **murabba:** *square* (adj.)

مرة، ات **marrah, -aat** *time, occasion*

مرحبا **marHaban** *welcome*

مرحلة، مراحل **marHalah, maraaHil***
stage, level

مرض، أمراض **maraD, amraaD**
illness, disease

مرمى **marmaa** *goal, goalmouth*

مسابقة، ات **musaabaqah, -aat**
competition

مسؤول، ون **mas'uul, -uun** *official*

مسبح، مسابح **masbaH, masaabiH***
swimming pool

مستشفى، مستشفيات **mustashfaa,**
mustashfayaat *hospital*

مستهدف **mustahdaf** *aimed for*

مستوى **mustawaa** *level, context*

مسرحية، ات **masraHiyyah, -aat**
play (theatrical)

مسروق **masruuq** *stolen*

مسلسل، ات **musalsil, -aat** *serial, series*

مسلم، ون **muslim, -uun** *Muslim*

مسموح **masmuuH** *permitted*

مسيحي، ون **masiiHii, -uun** *Christian*

موسيقى (fem.) **muusiiqaa** *music*

مشاهدة **mushaahadah** *seeing, viewing*

مشروع، مشاريع **mashruu: , mashaarii:***
project

مشغول **mashghuul** *busy*

مشكلة، مشاكل **mushkilah, mashaakil***
problem

مشهور **mashhuur** *famous*

مصدر، مصادر **maSdar, maSaadir***
source

مصر **miSr*** *Egypt*

مطار، ـات **maTaar, -aat** *airport*

مطحون **maT-Huun** *ground, milled*

مطربة، ات **muTribah, -aat** (female)
singer, musician

مطعم، مطاعم **maT:am, maTaa:im***
restaurant

مع **ma:a** *with, together with*

معجون **ma:juun** *paste*

معرض، معارض **ma:raD, ma:aariD***
exhibition, fair

معكرونة **ma:karuunah** *macaroni*

معنى، المعاني **ma:naa, al-ma:aanii**
meaning

مغربي، مغاربة **maghribii, maghaaribah** *Moroccan*

مغنية، ات **mughanniyah, -aat** *(female) singer*

مفتاح، مفاتيح **miftaaH, mafaatiiH*** *key*

مفترض **muftaraD** *assumed, supposed*

مفروض **mafruuDH** *necessary, obligatory*

مفروم **mafruum** *chopped, ground*

مفضل **mufaDDil** *preferring*

مقبل **muqbil** *coming, next*

مقدار، مقادير **miqdaar, maqaadiir*** *quantity, measure*

مقشر **muqashshar** *peeled, skinned*

مقطع **muqaTTa:** *chopped*

مقيم **muqiim** *residing, resident*

مكان، أمكنة **makaan, amkinah** *place*

مكة المكرمة **makkah l-mukarramah** *Holy (City of) Mecca*

مكتب، مكاتب **maktab, makaatib*** *office*

مكتبة، ات **maktabah, -aat** *library, bookshop*

مكتوب **maktuub** *written*

مكتوم **maktuum** *concealed*

(الـ)مكسيك **al-maksiik** *Mexico*

ملابس **malaabis*** *clothes*

ملامح **malaamiH*** *features*

ملح **milH** *salt*

ملعب، ملاعب **mal:ab, malaa:ib*** *sports ground, pitch*

ملعقة، ملاعق **mil:aqah, malaa:iq*** *spoon, spoonful*

ملك، ملوك **malik, muluuk** *king*

مليونير **malyoonayr** *millionaire*

ممتاز **mumtaaz** *excellent*

ممثل، ون **mumaththil, -uun** *actor, representative*

ممنوع **mamnuu:** *forbidden*

من **man** *who?*

من **min** *from*

مناسبة، ات **munaasabah, -aat** *occasion*

منتج، ون **muntij, -uun** *producer*

منذ **mundhu** *since*

منطقة، مناطق **minTaqah, manaaTiq*** *region, area* (football: penalty area)

منظم، ات **munaDHDHim, -aat** *regulator*

منظمة، ات **munaDHDHamah, -aat** *organisation*

منقط **munaqqaT** *spotted*

منبعث **munba:ith** *emanating*

مهاجر، ون **muhaajir, -uun** *emigrant*

مهرب **muharrab** *smuggled*

مهم **muhimm** *important*

مهنة، مهن **mihnah, mihan** *job, trade, profession*

مهندس، ون **muhandis, -uun** *engineer*

موجود **mawjuud** *found, situated, existing*

موديم **muudiim** *modem*

موقع، مواقع **mawqi:, mawaaqi:*** *site, situation, place*

موقف، مواقف **mawqif, mawaaqif*** *stopping, parking place*

مولد النبي **mawlid an-nabii** *(festival of) The Prophet's Birthday*

مولود **mawluud** *born*

ميناء، الموانئ **miinaa', al-mawaanii** *(sometimes fem.) harbour, port*

ن

نائم **naa'im** *sleeping, asleep*

نار **naar** *(fem.) fire*

ناس **naas** *people*

ناشف **naashif** *dry*

ناظر **naaDHara [S-III]** *to equal, compete with*

نافع **naafi:** *useful*

ناقش **naaqasha [S-III]** *discuss*

نام **naama [Ma-I]** *sleep*

نتيجة، نتائج **natiijah, nataa'ij*** *result, outcome*

نجاح **najaaH** *success*

نجح **najaHa [S-I a]** *succeed*
(في *in* something); *pass* (an exam)

نجمة، ات **najmah, -aat** *star, (female)*
film star

النحو **an-naHw** *grammar*

نزول **nuzuul** *descent, descending*

نساء* **nisaa'*** (pl.) *women*

نسمة **nasamah** *individual*
(used in population counts only)

نشاط **nashaaT** *activity*

نصف، أنصاف **niSf, anSaaf** *half,*

نفس، نفوس **nafs, nufuus** (fem.) *self, soul*

نقد، نقود **naqd, nuquud** *cash, money*

نقع **naqa:a [S-I a]** *to soak, steep*

نقل **naql** *transport, transportation*

نمر، نمور **namir, numuur** *tiger*

نهائي **nihaa'ii** *final* (adj.)

نهار **nahaar** *daytime, hours of daylight*

نهاية **nihaayah** *end*

نوع، أنواع **naw:, anwaa:** *kind, sort, type*

نوى **nawaa [Ly-I]** *to intend*

نيل **nayl** *getting, receiving*

ه

هادئ **haadi'** *quiet, gentle*

هال **haal** *cardamom*

هجين، هجن **hajiin, hujun** *racing
camel*

هدف، أهداف **hadaf, ahdaaf** *target,
aim, goal*

هدية، هدايا* **hadiyah, hadaayaa*** *gift,
present*

هذا/هذه **haadha/haadhihi** *this*
(masc./fem.)

هنا **hunaa** *here*

هناك **hunaaka** *there, there is/are*

(ال)هند **al-hind** *India*

هواء **hawaa'** *air*

هواية، ات **hawaayah, -aat** *hobby*

هي **hiya** *she, it*

و

واسع **waasi:** *roomy, spacious*

واقف **waaqif** *standing, stationary*

والد **waalid** *father*

والدة **waalidah** *mother*

وإن **wa-'in** *though, even though*

وجبة، ات **wajabah, -aat** *meal*

وجه، وجوه **wajh, wujuuh** *face,*
(media) personality

وحيد **waHiid** *sole, only, singular*

ود **wadd** *love, friendship*

وراء(ا) **waraa'(a)** *behind*

وسط **wasT** *middle, centre*
(of town, etc.)

وصل **waSala [Fw-I i]** *to arrive*

وصل **waSSal [S-II]** *connect, transport*

وضع **waD:** *putting*

وضع **waDa:a [Fw-I a]** *to put, place*

وظف **waDHDHaf [S-II]** *to hire,
employ*

وقت، أوقات **waqt, awqaat** *time*

وقع **waqa:a [Fw-I a]** *fall*

وقف **waqafa [Fw-I i]** *stop, stand*

وقف **waqqafa [Fw-II]** *stop,
bring to a halt*

وكالة، ات **wakaalah, -aat** *agency*

ولا **wa-laa** *and not, nor*

ولاية،ات **wilaayah, -aat** *administrative
division of a country; state*

ولد، أولاد **walad, awlaad** *boy*
(pl. also *children*)

ولكن **walaakin, walaakinna** *but*

ى

يد **yad** (fem.) *hand*

(ال)يمن **al-yaman** *Yemen*

يمين **yamiin** *right (hand)*

يوم، أيام **yawm, ayyaam** *day*

ENGLISH–ARABIC VOCABULARY

This is again based on the words in the Vocabulary Boxes which relate directly to the texts.

about, approximately حوالي Hawaalii
about, concerning عن :an
above, over فوق fawqa
Abu Dhabi أبو ظبي abuu DHabi
accept قبل qabila [S-I a]
according to حسب Hasb
activity نشاط nashaaT
actor, representative ممثل، ون
  mumaththil, -uun
add أضاف aDaafa [My-IV]
address عنوان، عناوين :unwaan,
  :anaawiin*
Aden عدن :adan
aeroplane طائرة، ات Taa'irah, -aat
affair, important matter شأن، شؤون
  sha'n, shu'uun
after بعد ba:d (before nouns), بعد ما
  ba:d maa (before verbs)
agency وكالة، ات wakaalah, -aat
agricultural زراعي ziraa:ii
aim, goal, intent قصد qaSd
aim, shoot سدد saddada [S-II]
aimed for مستهدف mustahdaf
air هواء hawaa'
air conditioning تكييف takyiif
airport مطار، ـات maTaar, -aat
Alexandria الاسكندرية
  al-iskandariyyah
all together جميعا jamii:an
ambassador (female) سفيرة، ات
  safiirah, -aat

Amman عمان :ammaan
amount كمية، ات kammiyyah, -aat
announce, state أعلن a:lana [S-IV]
answer أجاب ajaaba [Mw-IV]
appear, seem, show بدا badaa [Lw-I]
apple تفاحة، تفاح tufaaHah, tufaaH
Arabian Gulf, the الخليج العربي
  al-khaliij al-:arabii
Arab, Arabic عربي ، عرب :arabii
archaeological أثري atharii
arrive وصل waSala [Fw-I i]
art, craft, technique فن، فنون fann,
  funuun
as, like كـ ka-
aside, to one side جانبا jaaniban
ask سأل sa'ala [S-I a]
aspiration, ambition طموح TumuuH
aspire , have the ambition طمح إلى
  TamaHa ilaa [S-I a]
assembly, society جمعية، ات
  jam:iyyah, -aat
assumed, supposed مفترض muftaraD
at, with عند :inda
attain, achieve أدرك adraka [S-IV]
attend حضر HaDara [S-I u]
attention, concern, interest اهتمام
  ihtimaam
attract جلب jalaba [S-I i]
author مؤلف، ون mu'allif, -uun
award, grant احتسب iHtasaba [S-VIII]
bachelor, single أعزب a:zab

bag, sack كيس، أكياس **kiis, akyaas**

balance, equality تعادل **ta:aadul**

ball, football كرة، ات **kurah, -aat**

banish, drive away (football: *send off*)
طرد **Tarada [S-I u]**

be able استطاع **istaTaa:a [Mw-X]**

be carried, transported تنقل
tanaqqala [S-V]

be surprised, astonished دهش
dahisha [S-1 a]

beard ذقن، ذقون **dhaqn,
dhuquun** (fem.)

beautiful جميل **jamfil**

beautiful, handsome, good حسن **Hasan**

beauty جمال **jamaal**

beauty salon صالون تجميل **Saaluun
tajmiil**

because of that, for this reason
لذلك **li-dhaalik**

because لأن **li'anna**

become hungry جاع **jaa:a [Mw-I]**

become أصبح **aSbaHa [S-IV]**

beer بيرة **biirah**

begin بدأ **bada' S-I a**

beginning بداية **bidaayah**

behind وراء **waraa'(a)**

being, existing, situated كائن **kaa'in**

belief, faith إيمان **iimaan**

believing, a believer (in something)
مؤمن، ون **mu'min, -uun**

beside, next to بجانب **bi-jaanib**

between, among بين **bayna**

big, old كبير **kabiir**

black أسود، سوداء **aswad***, fem.
sawdaa'*

boat زورق، زوارق **zawraq, zawaariq*,**
قارب، قوارب **qaarib, qawaarib***

boil, come the boil غلى **ghalaa [Ly-I]**

*boiling, the action of boiling
something* سلق **salq**

book كتاب، كتب **kitaab, kutub**

born مولود **mawluud**

boss chief رئيس، رؤساء **ra'iis, ru'asaa'***

boy ولد، أولاد **walad, awlaad**
(pl. also *children*)

branch فرع، فروع **far:, furuu:**

breach اخترق **ikhtaraqa [S-VIII]**

bread خبز **khubz**

breaking of a fast فطر **fiTr**

bridge جسر، جسور **jisr, jusuur**

British بريطاني **briiTaanii**

broadcast أذاع **adhaa:a [My-IV]**

broadcaster (female) مذيعة، ات
mudhii:ah, -aat

brochure كتيب **kutayyib**

brother أخ، إخوان / إخوة **akh, ikhwaan**
or **ikhwah**

brown, fry حمر **Hammara [S-II]**

building, construction بناء **binaa'**

busy مشغول **mashghuul**

but ولكن **walaakin, walaakinna**

buy اشترى **ishtaraa [Ly-VIII]**

Cairo القاهرة **al-qaahirah**

cake كعك **ka:k**

Caliph خليفة، خلفاء **khaliifah,
khulafaa'***

camel جمل، جمال **jamal, jimaal,**

camel (for racing) هجين، هجن **hajiin,
hujun**

capital (city) عاصمة، عواصم **:aaSimah,
:awaaSim***

card بطاقة، ات **buTaaqah, -aat**

cardamom هال **haal**

cash, money نقد، نقود **naqd, nuquud**

cause, make do something جعل **ja:ala
[S-I a]**

celebrate احتفل ب **iHtafala bi- S-VIII**

celebration احتفال، ات **iHtifaal, -aat**

centennial, hundredth مئوي **mi'awii**

centre وسط **wasaT**

century قرن، قرون **qarn, quruun**

certain, definite أكيد **akiid**

chair كرسي، كراسي **kursii, karaasii**

chance, opportunity فرصة، فرص
   furSah, furaS

cheese جبنة **jubnah**

child طفل، أطفال **Tifl, aTfaal**

childhood طفولة **Tufuulah**

choose اختار **ikhtaara [My-VIII]**

chopped مقطع **muqaTTa:**

chopped, ground مفروم **mafruum**

Christian مسيحي، ون **masiiHii, -uun**

Christmas عيد الميلاد **iid al-miilaad**

cinema سينما، سينمات **siinamaa,
   siinamaat (fem.)**

cinnamon قرفة **qirfah**

cleaning تنظيف **tanDHiif**

clinic عيادة، ـات **:iyaadah, -aat**

clothes ملابس **malaabis***

cloves قرنفل **qurunful**

code, symbol رمز، رموز **ramz, rumuuz**

college, faculty كلية، ات **kulliyyah, -aat**

come جاء، يجيء **jaa'a, yajii' [My-I]**

come after, follow عقب **:aqaba [S-I u]**

commence, open افتتح **iftataHa
   [S-VIII]**

commercial تجاري **tijaarii**

company, firm, business شركة، ات
   sharikah, -aat

compete with زاحم **zaaHama [S-III]**

competition مسابقة، ات
   musaabaqah, -aat

complete تام **taamm**

complete, whole كامل **kaamil**

comprehensive شامل **shaamil**

computer آلة حاسبة **aalah Haasibah**

concealed مكتوم **maktuum**

conference مؤتمر، ات **mu'tamar, -aat**

connect, transport وصل، يوصل **waSSala,
   yuwaSSil [S-II]**

conquer قهر **qahara [S- a]**

consider, regard اعتبر **i:tabara
   [S-VIII]**

contented, happy مبسوط **mabSuuT**

contribute, take part أسهم **as-hama
   [S-IV]**

cooking, cuisine طبيخ **Tabiikh**

cooling تبريد **tabriid**

corner (adj.) ركني **ruknii**

corner ركن، أركان **rukn, arkaan**

correct, right صحيح **SaHiiH**

count, census إحصاء، ات **iHSaa', -aat**

country بلد، بلاد/بلدان **balad, bilaad/
   buldaan**

country, state دولة، دول **dawlah, duwal**

credit card بطاقة تسليف **buTaaqat
   tasliif**

cultural ثقافي **thaqaafii,**

cultured, educated person مثقف، ـون
   muthaqqaf, -uun

cup, trophy كأس، كؤوس **ka's, ku'uus**

current (adj.) (الـ)جاري **al-jaarii**

curved, bowed قوسي **qawsii**

custom, habit عادة، ات **:aadah, -aat**

customer, client زبون، زبائن **zabuun,
   zabaa'in***

customs, excise جمرك، جمارك **jumruk,
   jamaarik***

dam سد، سدود **sadd, suduud**

Damascus دمشق **dimashq***

daughter ابنة، بنات **ibnah, banaat**

dawn فجر **fajr**

day يوم، أيام **yawm, ayyaam**

daytime, hours of daylight نهار **nahaar**

deceive خدع **khada:a [S-I a]**

decision, resolution قرار، ات
   qaraar, -aat

defender مدافع، ون **mudaafi: , -uun**

delicious, tasty لذيذ **ladhiidh**

demanding back, reclaiming استرداد
   istirdaad

density كثافة **kathaafah**

department (government) دائرة، دوائر
   daa'irah, dawaa'ir*

descent, descending نزول nuzuul

design, designing تصميم taSmiim

desire, wish رغبة، ات raghbah, -aat

development تنمية tanmiyah

diet حمية Himyah

different, various مختلف mukhtalif

difficulty صعوبة، ات Su:uubah, -aat

dirham درهم، دراهم dirham, daraahim*

discount حسم Hasm

discover اكتشف iktashafa [S-VIII]

discuss ناقش، يناقش naaqasha, yunaaqish [S-III]

dish صحن، صحون SaHn, SuHuun

distinction, privilege امتياز imtiyaaz

distinctive, prominent متميز mutamayyiz

distribution توزيع tawzii:

division of a country; state ولاية،ات wilaayah, -aat

do, make فعل fa:ala [S-I a]

do, work عمل، يعمل :amila, ya:mal [S-I a]

doctor طبيب، أطباء Tabiib, aTibbaa'*

dominate سيطر على sayTara :alaa [Q-I]

domination سيطرة sayTarah

door, gate باب، أبواب baab, abwaab

drain, strain صفى Saffaa [Ly-II]

drink شرب shariba [S-I a]

driver سائق،ون/ساقة saa'iq, -uun/saaqah

dry ناشف naashif

during خلال khalaal, أثناء athnaa'(a)

each, every, all كل kull

ear أذن udh(u)n (fem.)

earn, gain, win كسب kasaba [S-I i]

eat أكل، يأكل akala, ya'kul [S-I u]

economic اقتصادي iqtiSaadii

education تعليم ta:liim

educational تعليمى ta:liimii

Egypt مصر miSr*

elementary ابتدائي ibtidaa'ii

emanate, be sent out انبعث inba:atha [S-VII]

emanating منبعث munba:ith

emigrant مهاجر، ون muhaajir, -uun

end نهاية nihaayah

end, last part of something اخر aakhir

engineer مهندس، ون muhandis, -uun

England إنجلترا ingiltarra

English, Englishman إنجليزي ingliizi

enjoy بـ تمتع tamatta:a bi- [S-V]

enter دخل dakhala [S-I u]

entrust , vest in أسند لـ asnada [S-IV]

equal, compete with ناظر naaDHara [S-III]

equally, whether سواء sawaa'an

erect, construct شيد shayyada [My-II]

European أوروبي، ون uruubii

exam امتحان، ات imtiHaan, -aat

excellent ممتاز mumtaaz

except إلا illaa

exhibition, fair معرض، معارض ma:raD, ma:aariD*

explain شرح sharaHa [S-I a]

extent, compass اتساع ittisaa:

extreme, most غاية ghaayah

eye; also spring (of water) عين، عيون :ayn, :uyuun (fem.)

face, (media) personality وجه، وجوه wajh, wujuuh

fall, happen وقع waqa:a [Fw-I a]

famous مشهور shahiir مشهور mashhuur

far away, distant بعيد ba:iid

fashion, style زي، أزياء ziyy, azyaa'*

fast, fasting صوم Sawm

father والد waalid

favourable, good فاضل faaDil

features ملامح malaamiH*

festival; anniversary عيد، أعياد :iid, a:yaad

field, sphere of activity مجال، ات **majaal, -aat**

fifth خامس **khaamis**

filling, filler مالئ **maali'**

film فيلم، افلام **fiilm, aflaam**

final (adj.) نهائي **nihaa'ii**

financial مالي **maalii**

finish, come to an end انتهى **intahaa [Ly-VIII]**

fire نار **naar (fem.)**

first أول **awwal**

firstly أولا **awwalan**

fish (collective) سمك **samak**

flag, banner راية، ات **raayah, -aat**

flat, apartment شقة، شقق **shaqqah, shiqaq**

flavour مذاق **madhaaq**

flood overflow with ب أفاض **afaaDa bi- [My-IV]**

fluently بطلاقة **bi-Talaaqah**

folk, pertaining to the people شعبي **sha:bii**

follow تبع **tabi:a [S-I a]**

follow, pursue (a path, method, etc.) انتهج **intahaja [S-VIII]**

food طعام **Ta:aam**

food, things to eat أكل **akl**

foot رجل **rijl (f.)**

forbidden ممنوع **mamnuu:**

force, power, strength قوة، ات **quwwah, -aat**

foreign, foreigner أجنبي، أجانب **ajnabii, ajaanib***

fort, fortress حصن، حصون **HiSn, HuSuun**; قلعة، قلاع **qal:ah, qilaa:**

found, situated, existing موجود **mawjuud**

foundation, setting up إنشاء **inshaa'**

four أربعة **arba:ah**

free, gratis مجانا **majjaanan**

friend صديق، أصدقاء **Sadiiq, aSdiqaa'***

frock, dress فستان، فساتين **fustaan, fasaatiin***

from من **min**

fruit فاكهة، فواكه **faakihah, fawaakih***

game, playing لعب، ألعاب **la:b, al:aab**

garden, park حديقة، حدائق **Hadiiqah, Hadaa'iq***

Geezah (district of Cairo) الجيزة **al-jiizah**

general عام :**aamm,** عمومي:**umuumii**

geographical جغرافي **jughraafii**

German ألماني **almaanii**

getting, receiving نيل **nayl**

ghee, clarified butter سمن **saman**

gift, present هدية، هدايا **hadiyah, hadaayaa***

girl, daughter بنت، بنات **bint, banaat**

girl, young woman فتاة، فتيات **fataah, fatayaat**

give أعطى **a:Taa [Ly-IV]**

glass, cup كوب، أكواب **kuub, akwaab**

go ذهب **dhahaba, [S-I a]**

goal, goalmouth مرمى **marmaa**

God, Allah الله **Al-laah**

golf جولف **guulf**

good جيد **jayyid**

grain, seed حبة. ات **Habbah, -aat**

grammar النحو **an-naHw**

green أخضر **akhDar***

ground (sports), pitch ملعب، ملاعب **mal:ab, malaa:ib***

ground أرض **arD (fem.)**

ground, milled مطحون **maT-Huun**

group, gathering جماعة، ات **jamaa:ah, -aat**

guard (football: *goalkeeper*) حارس، حراس **Haaris, Hurraas**

guest ضيف، ضيوف **Dayf, Duyuuf**

hair شعر **sha:r**

half نصف، أنصاف **niSf, anSaaf**

hand يد **yad (fem.)**

happy, joyful سعيد، سعداء **sa:iid, su:adaa'***

harbour, port ميناء، الموانى **miinaa', al-mawaanii** (sometimes fem.)

hard disk قرص ثابت **qarS thaabit**

hate كره **kariha [S-I a]**

hear, listen سمع **sami:a [S-I a]**

heart قلب، قلوب **qalb, quluub**

heat (temperature) حرارة **Haraarah**

heat, race (football: *half*) شوط، أشواط **shawT, ashwaaT**

heavy ثقيل **thaqiil**

help ساعد **saa:ada [S-III]**

here هنا **hunaa**

high العالى **al-: aalii**

hire, employ وظف **waDHDHafa [S-II]**

historical تاريخى **taariikhii**

history تاريخ **taariikh**

hit, strike أصاب **aSaaba [Mw-IV]**

hobby هواية، ات **hawaayah, -aat**

honour, be hospitable/generous أكرم **akrama [S-IV]**

hope, wish تمنى **tamannaa [Ly-V]**

hospital مستشفى، مستشفيات **mustashfaa, mustashfayaat**

hot حار **Haarr**

hotel فندق، فنادق **funduq, fanaadiq***

hour, time, watch, clock ساعة، ات **saa:ah, -aat**

house بيت، بيوت **bayt, buyuut**

how كيف **kayf(a)**

how many, how much كم **kam**

human being; pl. = *people* انسان، ناس **insaan, naas**

hungry جوعان، جوعى **jaw:aan*, jaw:aa***

ice ثلج **thalj**

if إن، إذا **in, idhaa** لو *law*

illness, disease مرض، أمراض **maraD, amraaD**

immediately فورا **fawran**

implementation, execution تنفيذ **tanfiidh**

important مهم **muhimm**

impose فرض **faraDa [S-I i]**

in فى **fii**

in front of أمام **amaam**

include, comprise ضم **Damma [D-I u]**

India الهند **al-hind**

individual (used in population counts only) نسمة **nasamah**

inhabitant, resident ساكن، سكان **saakin, sukkaan**

inside داخل **daakhil**

intend نوى **nawaa [Ly-I]**

international دولى **duwalii** or **dawlii**

Iraqi عراقى **:iraaqii**

jewellery, articles of jewellery مجوهرات **mujawharaat**

Jordanian أردنى **urduni**

journey, voyage رحلة، ات **riHlah, -aat**

just, upright عادل **:aadil**

just as, also كما **ka-maa**

Kaabah, The الكعبة **al-ka:bah**

keep, preserve حافظ على **HaafaDHa :alaa [S-III]**

key مفتاح، مفاتيح **miftaaH, mafaatiiH***

kick ركلة، ات **raklah, -aat**

kind, sort, type نوع، أنواع **naw:, anwaa:**

king ملك، ملوك **malik, muluuk**

know عرف **:arafa [S-I i]**

knowledge, science علم، علوم **:ilm, :uluum**

last اخير **akhiir**

late evening (prayer time) عشاء **:ishaa'**

layer طبقة، ات **Tabaqah, -aat**

lazy كسلان **kaslaan**

lead قاد **qaada [Mw-I]**

leading قيادى **qiyaadii**

leading roles بطولات **buTuulaat**

learn تعلم **ta:allama [S-V]**

leave, let be ترك **taraka [S-I u]**

left شمال **shamaal**

legend اساطير، اسطورة، اساطير **usTuurah, asaaTiir***

leisure فراغ **faraagh**

lentils عدس: **ads**

leopard فهد، فهود **fahd, fuhuud**

level, context مستوى **mustawaa**

library, book shop مكتبة، ات **maktabah, -aat**

life, age عمر: **umr**

lift, raise رفع **rafa:a [S-I a]**

light (adj.) خفيف **khafiif**

like مثل **mithl**

like, love أحب، يحب **aHabba, yuHibb [D-IV]**

limit, border حد، حدود **Hadd, Huduud**

list قائمة، ات **qaa'imah, -aat**

literary, classical (Arabic language) الفصحى **al-fuS-Haa**

literature, arts أدب، آداب **adab, aadaab**

live, reside عاش **:aasha [My-I]**

load, burden حمل، أحمال **Himl, aHmaal**

London لندن **landan**

long, tall طويل **Tawiil**

love, friendship ود **wadd**

macaroni معكرونة **ma:karuunah**

mad مجنون، مجانين **majnuun, majaaniin***

magic سحر **siHr**

magnificent فخم **fakhm**

make-up ماكياج **maakyaaj**

man رجل، رجال **rajul, rijaal**

manager مدير، مدراء **mudiir, mudaraa'**

map خريطة، خرائط **khariiTah, kharaa'iT***

market سوق، أسواق **suuq, aswaaq** (usually fem.)

marque, label ماركة **maarkah**

married متزوج **mutazawwaj**

marry تزوج **tazawwaja [Mw-V]**

match (sport) مباراة، مباريات **mubaaraah, mubaarayaat**

meal وجبة، ات **wajabah, -aat**

meaning معنى، المعاني **ma:naa, al-ma:aanii**

meat لحم، لحوم **laHm, luHuum**

meet, come together اجتمع **ijtama:a [S-VIII]**

meet with لاقى **laaqaa [Ly-III]**

memory ذاكرة **dhaakirah**

merchant تاجر، تجار **taajir, tujjaar**

method, way طريقة، طرائق **Tariiqah, Taraa'iq***

metre متر، أمتار **mitr, amtaar**

Mexico المكسيك **al-maksiik**

mid-afternoon عصر **:aSr**

middle وسط **wasaT**

millionaire مليونير **malyoonayr**

minute دقيقة، دقائق **daqiiqah, daqaa'iq***

mixture خليط **khaliiT**

model (male) عارض، ون **:aariD, -uun**, (female) عارضة، ات **:aariDah, -aat**

modem موديم **muudiim**

modern, up-to-date حديث **Hadiith**

moment لحظة، ات **laHDHah, laHaDHaat**

more, most أكثر **akthar***

Moroccan مغربي، مغاربة **maghribii, maghaaribah**

mosque (large) جامع، جوامع **jaami:, jawaami:***

mother والدة **waalidah**

much, many كثير **kathiir**

museum متحف، متاحف **matHaf, mataaHif***

music موسيقى **muusiiqaa** (fem.)

Muslim مسلم، ون **muslim, -uun**

narrow ضيق **Dayyiq**

nation أمة، أمم **ummah, umam**

nationality جنسية، ات **jinsiyyah, -aat**

natural طبيعي **Tabii:ii**

naturally, of course طبعا **Tab:an**

nature طبيعة **Tabii:ah**

near قريب **qariib**

necessary لازم **laazim**

necessary, obligatory مفروض **mafruuDH**

necessity, requirement ضرورة، ات **Duruurah, -aat**

neighbour جار، جيران **jaar, jiiraan**

net, netting شبكة، شباك **shabaka, shibaak**

new جديد **jadiid**

newest, latest أحدث **aHdath**

news خبر، أخبار **khabar, akhbaar**

newspaper جريدة، جرائد **jariidah, jaraa'id***

next, coming مقبل **muqbil**

night ليلة، ات، ليال **layla, -aat, layaalin**

ninth تاسع **taasi:**

noble, generous كريم **kariim**

noon ظهر **DHuhr**

nor ولا **wa-laa**

no, not لا **laa**

novel, story رواية، ات **riwaayah, -aat**

now الآن، الحين **al-'aan, al-Hiin**

number عدد، أعداد **adad, a:daad**

observe, watch رصد **raSada [S-I u]**

occasion مناسبة، ات **munaasabah, -aat**

occupy احتل **iHtalla [D-VIII]**

offer, deal عرض، عروض **:arD, :uruuD**

office مكتب، مكاتب **maktab, makaatib***

officer ضابط، ضباط **DaabiT, DubbaaT**

official مسؤول، ون **mas'uul, -uun**

oil (edible) زيت **zayt**

old, ancient (of things) قديم **qadiim**

Oman (Sultanate of) عمان **:umaan**

onions بصل **baSal**

only فقط **faqaT**

organisation منظمة، ات **munaDHDHamah, -aat**

origin, basis أصل، أصول **aSl, uSuul**

other آخر **aakhar*** (fem. أخرى **ukhraa**)

other than, apart from غير **ghayr**

outside خارج **khaarij**

owner, master; also sometimes friend صاحب، أصحاب **SaaHib, aS-Haab**

palace قصر، قصور **qaSr, quSuur,**

participate, take part اشترك **ishtaraka [S-VIII]**

past, the الماضي **al-maaDii**

paste معجون **ma:juun**

peeled, skinned مقشر **muqashshar**

people ناس **naas**

pepper فلفل **fulful/filfil**

period, time, spell فترة، ات **fatrah, -aat**

permission سماح **samaaH**

permitted مسموح **masmuuH**

person شخص، أشخاص **shakhS, ashkhaaS**

petrol بنزين **banziin**

pharaonic فرعوني **far:uunii**

pharmacy صيدلية، ات **Saydaliyyah, -aat**

phrase, expression عبارة، ات **:abaarah, -aat**

piece قطعة، قطع **qiT:ah, qiTa:**

Pilgrimage, the الحج **al-Hajj**

place مكان، أمكنة **makaan, amkinah**

place أودع **awda:a [Fw-IV]**

planning تخطيط **takhTiiT**

plate, dish طبق، أطباق **Tabaq, aTbaaq**

play, game لعب **la:b**

play (theatrical) مسرحية، ات **masraHiyyah, -aat**

play لعب **la:iba [S-I a]**

player لاعب، ون **laa:ib, -uun**

pleasant, nice لطيف **laTiif**

pocket جيب، جيوب **jayb, juyuub**

poet شاعر، شعراء **shaa:ir, shu:araa'***

poetry شعر **shi:r**

poor, poor person فقير، فقراء **faqiir, fuqaraa'***

porter حمّال، ون Hammaal, -uun

possible, to be أمكن amkana [S-IV]

pour out سكب sakaba [S-I u]

practise, carry out, perform مارس
   maarasa [S-III]

prefer فضّل faDDala [S-II]

preferring مفضّل mufaDDil

preparation اعداد i:daad

preparatory اعدادي i:daadii

present, here حاضر، وون
   HaaDir, -uun

present, serve قدّم qaddama [S-II]

presentation تقديم taqdiim

print, type طبع Taba:a [S-I a]

problem مشكلة، مشاكل mushkilah,
   mashaakil*

produce أنتج antaja [S-IV]

producer منتج، ون muntij, -uun

production انتاج intaaj

professor استاذ، اساتذة ustaadh,
   asaatidhah

programme برنامج، برامج barnaamij,
   baraamij*

project مشروع، مشاريع mashruu:,
   mashaarii:*

public, the general العامّة al-:aammah

publish أصدر aSdara [S-IV]

pupil تلميذ، تلامذة/تلاميذ tilmiidh,
   talaamidhah/talaamiidh*

pure, clear الصافي aS-Saafii

purpose, goal غرض، أغراض gharaD,
   aghraaD

put, place وضع waDa:a [Fw-I a]

putting وضع waD:

pyramids, the الأهرام al-ahraam

qualify تأهّل ta'ahhala [S-V]
   (إلى ilaa for)

quantity, measure مقدار، مقادير
   miqdaar, maqaadiir*

quarter ربع rub:

question سؤال، أسئلة su'aal, as'ilah

quickly, before long سرعان ما
   sur:aan maa

quiet, gentle هادئ haadi'

race سباق، ات sibaaq, -aat

read قرأ، يقرأ qara'a, yaqra' [S-I a]

really, actually, in fact فعلا fi:lan

receive, meet استقبل istaqbala [S-X]

recently مؤخّرا mu'akhkhiran

reception استقبال، ات istiqbaal, -aat

red أحمر aHmar*

referee, umpire حكم، حكّام Hakam,
   Hukkaam

region, area (football: penalty area)
   منطقة، مناطق minTaqah, manaaTiq*

region, zone, area قطر، أقطار quTr,
   aqTaar

register, score سجّل sajjala [S-II]

registration, scoring تسجيل tasjiil

regulator منظم، ات munaDHDHim, -aat

renew, restore جدّد jaddada [D-II]

rent, be a tenant of استأجر ista'jara
   [S-X]

repeat, renew أعاد a:aada [Mw-IV]

report تقرير، تقارير taqriir, taqaariir*

reside; hold (an event, etc.) أقام
   aqaama [Mw-IV]

residing, living ساكن saakin

residing, resident مقيم muqiim

restaurant مطعم، مطاعم maT:am,
   maTaa:im*

result, outcome نتيجة، نتائج
   natiijah, nataa'ij*

return something to someone ردّ إلى
   radda ilaa [D-i u]

return, reciprocate بادل baadala [S-III]

rice أرز aruzz

rich, rich person غني، أغنياء ghanii,
   aghniyaa'*

ride, mount, get into (a vehicle) ركب
   rakiba [S-I a]

right (hand) يمين yamiin

road, way طريق، طرق **Tariiq, Turuq**

role, turn دور، أدوار **dawr, adwaar**

room غرفة، غرف **ghurfah, ghuraf**

roomy, spacious واسع **waasi:**

row, class (in school) صف، صفوف **Saff, Sufuuf**

rule قاعدة، قواعد **qaa:idah, qawaa:id***

run جرى **jaraa [Ly-I]**

sacrificial animal ذبيحة، ذبائح **dhabiiHah, dhabaa'iH***

sad حزين **Haziin**

safe, sound سالم **saalim**

salt ملح **milH**

sauce صلصة **SalSah**

say قال **qaala [Mw-I]**

scientific علمي **:ilmii**

screen شاشة **shaashah**

sea, large river بحر، بحار **baHr, biHaar**

secondary ثانوي **thaanawii**

section, division قسم، أقسام **qism, aqsaam**

section, season (of the year) فصل، فصول **faSl, fuSuul**

see رأى، يرى **ra'aa, yaraa** (irregular Type Ly-I verb: see Verb Tables)

seeing, viewing مشاهدة **mushaahadah**

selection تشكيلة، ات **tashkiilah, -aat**

self; soul نفس، نفوس **nafs, nufuus** (fem.)

sell باع **baa:a [My-I]**

send أرسل **arsala [S-IV]**

serial, series مسلسل، ات **musalsil, -aat**

servant خادم، خدام **khaadim, khuddaam** (fem. خادمة، ات **khaadimah, -aat**)

service خدمة، ات **khidmah, -aat**

shape, kind, type شكل، أشكال **shakl, ashkaal**

shapeliness, elegance, slim figure رشاقة **rashaaqah**

Sharjah الشارقة **ash-shaariqah**

she, it هي **hiya**

sheep خروف، خرفان **kharuuf, khurfaan**; (collective) غنم **ghanam**

shelf رف، رفوف **raff, rufuuf**

ship سفينة، سفن **safiinah, sufun**

shirt قميص، قمصان **qamiiS, qumSaan**

shocking, amazing فظيع **faDHii:**

shop, stall دكان، دكاكين **dukkaan, dakaakiin***

shop, store محل، محلات **maHall, maHallaat**

shore, beach شاطئ **shaaTi'**

shot (football) تسديدة، ات **tasdiidah, -aat**

showing, displaying عرض **:arD**

side جانب، جوانب **jaanib, jawaanib***

signal إشارة، ات **ishaarah, -aat**

simplification تبسيط **tabsiiT**

simplify بسط **bassaTa [S-II]**

since منذ **mundhu**

singer (female) مغنية، ات **mughanniyah, -aat**

singer, musician (female) مطربة، ات **muTribah, -aat**

sister أخت، اخوات **ukht, akhawaat**

sit, sit down جلس **jalasa [S-I i]**

site, situation, place موقع، مواقع **mawqi:, mawaaqi:***

sitting, seated جالس **jaalis**

six ستة **sittah**

sixth سادس **saadis**

slaughter ذبح **dhabaHa [S-I a]**

sleep نام **naama [Ma-I]**

sleeping, asleep نائم **naa'im**

slice شريحة، شرائح **shariiHah, sharaa'iH***

slightly, a little قليلا **qaliilan**

small, young صغير **Saghiir**

smell, scent, perfume رائحة، روائح **raa'iHah, rawaa'iH***

smile ابتسم **ibtasama [S-VIII]**

smuggled مهرب **muharrab**

so, therefore إذا **ídhan**

soak, steep نقع **naqa:a [S-I a]**

social اجتماعي **ijtimaa:ii**

soldier عسكري، عساكر **:askarii, :asaakir***

sole, only, singular وحيد **waHiid**

solution حل، حلول **Hall, Huluul**

some, part of something بعض **ba:D**

son ابن، أبناء **ibn, abnaa'***

source مصدر، مصادر **maSdar, maSaadir***

Spanish اسباني **isbaanii**

speak تكلم، يتكلم **takallama, yatakallam [S-V]**

special; private خاص **khaaSS**

specialise تخصص **takhaSSaS [S-V]**

specialist متخصص، ون **mutakhaSSiS, -uun**

spectator متفرج، ون **mutafarrij, -uun**

speech كلام **kalaam**

speed سرعة **sur:ah**

Sphynx, the أبو الهول **abuu l-hawl**

spice تابل، توابل **taabil, tawaabil**

splendid, brilliant, marvellous رائع **raa'i:**

spoon, spoonful ملعقة، ملاعق **mil:aqah, malaa:iq***

sport, exercise رياضة، ـات **riyaaDah, -aat**

spotted منقط **munaqqaT**

spread, currency انتشار **intishaar**

sprinkle, spray رش **rashsha [D-I u]**

square (adj.) مربع **murabba:**

stage, level مرحلة، مراحل **marHalah, maraaHil***

standing, stationary واقف **waaqif**

star, (female) film star نجمة، ـات **najmah, -aat**

state, express أعرب عن **a:raba :an [S-IV]**

station محطة، ـات **maHaTTah, -aat**

step, degree درجة، ـات **darajah, -aat**

stolen مسروق **masruuq**

stone حجر، أحجار **Hajar, aHjaar**

stop, bring to a halt وقف **waqqafa [Fw-II]**

stop, stand وقف **waqafa [Fw-I i]**

stopping, parking place موقف، مواقف **mawqif, mawaaqif***

story, tale قصة، قصص **qiSSah, qiSaS**

street, road شارع، شوارع **shaari:, shawaari:***

striped مخطط **mukhaTTaT**

strong, mighty شديد **shadiid**

student طالب، طلاب/طلبة **Taalib, Tullaab/Talabah** (fem. طالبة، طالبات **Taalibah, -aat**)

study, studying (noun) دراسة، ـات **diraasah, -aat**

study درس **darasa [S-I u]**

style, method أسلوب، أساليب **usluub, asaaliib***

succeed in something; pass (an exam) نجح **najaHa [S-I a]**

success نجاح **najaaH**

suffice, be sufficient for كفى **kafaa [Ly-I]**

sum (of money) مبلغ، مبالغ **mablagh, mabaaligh***

summer صيف **Sayf**

sun شمس **shams**

sunset; Morocco المغرب **al-maghrib**

surround أحاط **aHaaTa [Mw-IV]**

sweetness حلاوة **Halaawah**

swim سبح **sabaHa [S-I a]**

swimming سباحة **sibaaHah**

swimming pool مسبح، مسابح **masbaH, masaabiH***

table مائدة، موائد **maa'ida, mawaa'id***

take أخذ **akhadha [S-I u]**

take care of, look after رعى **ra:aa [Lh-I]**

take, use up, occupy (of time) استغرق **istaghraqa [S-X]**

tape, cassette شريط، أشرطة **shariiT, ashriTah**

target, aim, goal هدف، أهداف **hadaf, ahdaaf**

teacher مدرس، ون **mudarris, -uun**

teaching تدريس **tadriis**

team فريق، فرق **fariiq, firaq**

television (adj.), televisual تلفزيوني **tilifizyuunii**

tell, inform خبر **khabbar [S-II]**

ten عشرة: **ashrah**

tennis تنس **tanis**

that is, i.e. أي **ay**

then ثم **thumma**

there, there is/are هناك **hunaaka**

thief لص، لصوص **liSS, luSuuS**

thing, something شيء، اشياء **shay', ashyaa'***

third ثالث **thaalith**

thirsty عطشان: **aTshaan**

thirteenth ثالثة عشر **thaalithah :ashar**

this هذا/هذه **haadha/haadhihi** (masc./fem.)

though, even though وإن **wa-'in**

thousand ألف، آلاف **alf, aalaaf**

three ثلاثة **thalaathah**

ticket تذكرة، تذاكر **tadhkirah, tadhaakir**

tiger نمر، نمور **namir, numuur**

time زمان، أزمنة **zamaan, azminah**

time وقت، أوقات **waqt, awqaat**

time (period of) مدة **muddah**

time, occasion مرة، ات **marrah, -aat**

tired تعبان **ta:baan**

tomatoes طماطم **TamaaTim***

tourist سائح، سواح **saa'iH, suwwaaH**

tourist (adj.), touristic سياحي **siyaaHii**

tower برج، أبراج **burj, abraaj**

town, city مدينة، مدن **madiinah, mudun**

track, trace أثر، آثار **athar, aathaar**

trade, commerce تجارة **tijaarah**

trade, profession مهنة، مهن **mihnah, mihan**

trading place, shop, stall متجر، متاجر **matjar, mataajir***

transmission, sending إرسال **irsaal**

transport, transportation نقل **naql**

travel سافر **saafara [S-III]**

tree شجرة، أشجار **shajarah, ashjaar**

truthful, true صادق **Saadiq**

try out, taste جرب **jarraba [S-II]**

typing, printing طباعة **Tibaa:ah**

ugly قبيح **qabiiH**

understand فهم **fahima [S-I a]**

understanding فاهم **faahim**

united متحد **muttaHad**

United Arab Emirates
الإمارات العربية المتحدة **al-imaaraat al-:arabiyyah al-muttaHidah**

university جامعة **jaami:ah**

until, even حتى **Hattaa**

upright, honest صالح **SaaliH**

use, employ استخدم **istakhdama [S-X]**

use, employment استخدام **istikhdaam**

use, usage استعمال **isti:maal**

useful نافع **naafi:**

various شتى **shattaa**

very جدا **jiddan**

victory فوز **fawz**

visit زار **zaara [Mw-I]**

visit زيارة، ات **ziyaarah, -aat**

visitor زائر، زوار **zaa'ir, zuwwaar**

voice, sound صوت، أصوات **Sawt, aSwaat**

wall سور، أسوار **suur, aswaar**

want, wish for أراد **araada [Mw-IV]**

wash غسل **ghasala [S-I i]**

washing machine غسالة، ات **ghassaalah, -aat**

watch, look at تفرج، يتفرج على **tafarraja :ala [S-V]**

water ماء، مياه **maa, miyaah**

weapon, arm سلاح، أسلحة **silaaH, asliHah**

welcome مرحبا **marHaban;** أهلا وسهلا **ahlan wa-sahlan**

welcome رحب ب **raHHaba bi- [S-II]**

welcome, welcoming (noun) ترحيب **tarHiib**

welcoming (adj.) ترحيبي **tarHiibii**

well, right, O.K. حسنا **Hasanan**

well-being (state of) خير **khayr**

West, the الغرب **al-gharb**

western غربي، ون **gharbii, -uun**

wheel, bicycle عجلة، ات **:ajalah, -aat**

when متى **mataa** (in questions); عندما **:indamaa**

where أين **ayna**

which أيّ **ayy**

while بينما **baynamaa**

white أبيض، بيضاء **abyaD*,** fem. **bayDaa'***

who? من **man**

why لماذا **li-maadha(a)**

wide عريض **:ariiD**

wife زوجة، ـات **zawjah, -aat**

win, gain, profit ربح **rabaHa [S-I a]**

wind tower برجيل، براجيل **barjiil, baraajiil**

winter شتاء **shitaa'***

wish, will شاء **shaa'a [Ma-I]**

with, together with مع **ma:a**

woman امرأة، نساء **imra'ah, nisaa'** (irregular plural)

wonder, wonderful thing عجيبة، عجائب **:ajiibah, :ajaa'ib***

wonderful عجيب **:ajiib**

work, job, business عمل، أعمال **:amal, a:maal**

workman عامل، عمال **:aamil, :ummaal**

world, the الدنيا **ad-dunya(a)** (fem.), العالم **al-:aalam**

worldwide عالمي **:aalamii**

writing كتابة **kitaabah**

written مكتوب **maktuub**

year سنة، سنوات **sanah, sanawaat;** عام، أعوام **:aam, a:waam**

yellow أصفر، صفراء **aSfar*,** fem. **Safraa'***

Yemen اليمن **al-yaman**

yesterday أمس **ams**

young person, youth شاب، شباب **shaab, shabaab**

GRAMMAR INDEX

The numbers refer to the units.

Accusative marker	8
Each, every + all	18
Adjectives from nouns	12
Adjectives	
Colours + irregular adjectives	16, 18
Comparatives	15
Superlatives	15
Adverbial accusative	15
Adverbs	
+ accusative marker	8
formation of	16
Agreement, noun and adjectives	1, 3
Asking the price	4
ba:D, + possessive construction	17
Conditional sentences	17
Conjunctions	15
Days of the week	4
Definite and indefinite *is/are* sentences	2
Definite words and phrases	1
Demonstratives	4, 6, 9
Directions: *left, right*	6
Duals	9
Family	5
Feminine **-ah** ending	3
Gender: masculine and feminine	3
Greetings	1, 11
Hidden **-t**	5, 6
How are you?	5
Indefinite words and phrases	1
inna and **anna** + accusative marker	8
Introducing people	5
Is and *are* sentences	2
kam + sing. noun (+ acc. marker)	11
kull *each, every + all*	18
laysa, aSbaHa + accusative marker	8
Means of transport	7
Months	11
Nationality	3
Nationality adjectives	2
Negatives	7, 10

Nouns	
dual + possessive	14
irregular	18
masculine plural + possessive	14
plural: formation	9
Numbers	
cardinal	2, 4, 5
ordinal	11, 13
Object + accusative marker	8
One of something	3
Places in town	6
Possessives	6
Pseudo	6, 14
Prepositions + pronoun suffixes	10
Pronouns	2, 5, 7
Questions	2, 11
Radical **hamzah**	7
Relative pronouns	13
Sun letters	1
Thematic sentences	11
Time	4, 7
Verbs	
future tense	10
imperative	14
imperative: irregular	14
imperative: negative	14
jussive	10
kaana *was/were*	8
passive	13
past continuous tense	10
past tense, noun subject	7
past tense, pronoun subject	7
pluperfect tense	8
present tense	10
stems	7
subjunctive	10
there is/ there are	2
to have	11
types: present stem	10
Word order	6, 7, 8